Contents

Preface

Although the value of sport and its potential contribution to the maintenance of a physically active lifestyle are readily apparent, some physical education programs fail to incorporate teaching–learning environments that fully immerse students in meaningful sport experiences. All too often, physical education students participate in instructional units that contribute little to their competence, understanding, and enthusiasm for sport. These ineffective teaching–learning environments are frequently characterized by inadequate planning, limited skill instruction and practice, use of developmentally inappropriate teaching progressions and game play, and limited or infrequent assessment.

The Sport Education model has received a considerable amount of empirical and anecdotal support as an alternative approach for teaching sport and physical activity in school-based settings. When using Sport Education, the teacher employs a combination of instructional strategies to provide students with a highly authentic and enjoyable educational experience that captures the unique cultural aspects of the particular sport. The purpose of this book is to assist physical educators who may be using Sport Education for the first time by providing ready-to-use seasons and instructional materials. The book also offers more experienced physical educators a wide range of new ideas and strategies for enhancing their own Sport Education seasons.

The season plans, lesson plans, and associated materials contained in this book were developed according to the Pedagogical Approach to Sport Education (PASE) guidelines. PASE is a conceptual framework for planning, implementing, and assessing Sport Education seasons that has been developed collaboratively by educational researchers, teacher educators, and physical educators. The PASE framework and associated resources have also been rigorously field-tested within multiple instructional contexts including middle school, secondary school, university basic instruction programs, and teacher education programs. Accordingly, we believe that the PASE materials described in this book will prove extremely valuable to physical educators working in various capacities.

In part I, we provide an instructional guide of four chapters that describe the theoretical underpinnings of the PASE framework and associated recommendations for practical application. Chapter 1 includes a brief introduction to the Sport Education model and the potential benefits associated with its use in school-based physical education programs, as well as the PASE planning and instructional guidelines for planning, implementing, and assessing developmentally appropriate sport experiences for school-aged children. Chapter 2 addresses the various curricular and instructional issues associated with PASE including season planning, lesson planning, assessment strategies, and behavior management. Chapter 3 provides specific guidelines for implementing many of the unique contextual aspects of a PASE season, along with samples of various teacher-tested instructional materials. Chapter 4 incorporates practical suggestions for integrating other academic disciplines like math, language arts, science, social studies, and technology into physical education in order to create a truly authentic sporting experience.

In part II, we have included three sample PASE seasons: fitness education, basketball, and soccer. The basketball season (chapter 6) includes a comprehensive season plan, a complete set of lesson plans, and all required teaching resources and assessment materials. The fitness education and soccer seasons are included in their entirety on the bound-in CD-ROM for easy access and use, and a comprehensive overview of each season appears in part II (chapters 5 and 7, respectively). These PASE seasons could easily be adopted as whole instructional units or modified based on your program's specific needs or curricular constraints. Two icons appear repeatedly in the PASE lesson plans included in this book.

⟳	Transition. Notes when students are required to move from one area to another.
💬	Teacher talk. Notes when teacher is verbally engaged and providing instruction.

We hope that the information included in this instructional package sparks your interest in PASE and serves as a catalyst to revitalize sport instruction in physical education. It is our desire that teachers choosing to implement PASE understand that they are about to embark on a process that can serve to rejuvenate the veteran, stimulate the beginner, or whet the appetite of any teacher searching for a renewed teaching spirit. Enjoy!

How to Use the CD-ROM

This CD-ROM expands the wealth of materials found in the book by providing PDF files of the complete soccer and fitness education seasons as well as a repeat of the basketball season from the book with more than 400 reproducibles.

If the CD-ROM does not start automatically when you place it in the CD-ROM drive, use the instructions listed under "User Instructions" on page 354 in the back of this book to start up the CD-ROM. Once the CD-ROM is running, you will be greeted with a launch page that will include an introduction to the CD-ROM and a link to the CD-ROM Contents page. Click on the link to the CD-ROM Contents page, and you will see a list of the files found on the CD-ROM, including the complete fitness education, basketball, and soccer seasons and the appendixes for each season. Use these links to navigate to a detailed Contents page that appears at the beginning of each file in each season. This detailed Contents page will contain links to each separate document that appears in each season. Just print out the document you want, and it's ready to use.

Credits

Push-up illustrations on pages 58, 301 reprinted, by permission, from C. Hinson, 1994, *Fitness for children* (Champaign, IL: Human Kinetics), 38.

Arm and leg extension illustrations on pages 58, 301 adapted, by permission, from T. Bompa, 1999, *Total training for young champions* (Champaign, IL: Human Kinetics), 40.

Hamstring curl illustration on pages 58, 301 reprinted, by permission, from National Association for Sport and Physical Education, 2004, *Physical best activity guide: Middle and high school levels*, 2nd ed. CD-ROM (Champaign, IL: Human Kinetics).

Lateral arm raise illustrations on pages 58, 301 reprinted, by permission, from W. Kraemer and S. Fleck, 1997, *Strength training for young athletes*, (Champaign, IL: Human Kinetics), 57.

Curl-up illustrations on pages 58, 301 reprinted, by permission, from C. Hinson, 1994, *Fitness for children* (Champaign, IL: Human Kinetics), 34.

Calf raise illustrations on pages 58, 301 reprinted, by permission, from C. Hinson, 1994, *Fitness for children* (Champaign, IL: Human Kinetics), 40.

Modified pull-up illustration on pages 58, 301 reprinted, by permission, from C. Hinson, 1994, *Fitness for children* (Champaign, IL: Human Kinetics), 37.

Torso twist illustrations on pages 58, 301 reprinted, by permission, from S. Virgilio, 1997, *Fitness education for children* (Champaign, IL: Human Kinetics), 157.

Squat illustrations on pages 58, 301 reprinted, by permission, from C. Hinson, 1994, *Fitness for children* (Champaign, IL: Human Kinetics), 43.

Biceps curl illustrations on pages 58, 301 reprinted, by permission, from National Association for Sport and Physical Education, 2004, *Physical best activity guide: Middle and high school levels*, 2nd ed. CD-ROM (Champaign, IL: Human Kinetics).

Trunk lift illustrations on pages 58, 301 reprinted, by permission, from Cooper Institute, 1999, *Fitnessgram test administration manual,* 2nd ed. (Champaign, IL: Human Kinetics), 24.

Lunge illustration on pages 58, 301 reprinted, by permission, from National Association for Sport and Physical Education, 2004, *Physical best activity guide: Middle and high school levels,* 2nd ed. CD-ROM (Champaign, IL: Human Kinetics).

Basketball official's signals on pages 61, 68, 73, 118, 135, 145, 154, 170, 179, 189, 199, 205, 214, 222, 230, 242, 306 courtesy of EPIC Software Group, Inc.

Low control dribble illustration on pages 72, 133, 278 reprinted, by permission, from H. Wissel, 2004, *Basketball: Steps to success,* 2nd ed. (Champaign, IL: Human Kinetics), 41.

Offensive footwork illustrations on pages 72, 133 reprinted, by permission, from H. Wissel, 2004, *Basketball: Steps to success,* 2nd ed. (Champaign, IL: Human Kinetics), 131.

Dribble to reposition illustration on pages 72, 134 reprinted, by permission, from H. Wissel, 2004, *Basketball: Steps to success,* 2nd ed. (Champaign, IL: Human Kinetics), 119.

Back-saver sit and reach illustrations on pages 104, 268 reprinted, by permission, from Cooper Institute, 1999, *Fitnessgram test administration manual,* 2nd ed. (Champaign, IL: Human Kinetics), 29.

Shoulder stretch illustrations on pages 104, 269 reprinted, by permission, from Cooper Institute, 1999, *Fitnessgram test administration manual,* 2nd ed. (Champaign, IL: Human Kinetics), 30.

Push-up illustrations on pages 104, 270 reprinted, by permission, from Cooper Institute, 1999, *Fitnessgram test administration manual,* 2nd ed. (Champaign, IL: Human Kinetics), 25-26.

Curl-up illustrations on pages 104, 271 reprinted, by permission, from Cooper Institute, 1999, *Fitnessgram test administration manual,* 2nd ed. (Champaign, IL: Human Kinetics), 22-23.

Modified pull-up illustrations on pages 104, 272 reprinted, by permission, from Cooper Institute, 1999, *Fitnessgram test administration manual,* 2nd ed. (Champaign, IL: Human Kinetics), 26.

Trunk lift illustrations on pages 104, 273 reprinted, by permission, from Cooper Institute, 1999, *Fitnessgram test administration manual,* 2nd ed. (Champaign, IL: Human Kinetics), 24.

T-run slide position illustration on pages 104, 275, 299 reprinted, by permission, from H. Wissel, 2004, *Basketball: Steps to success,* 2nd ed. (Champaign, IL: Human Kinetics), 15.

T-run sprint position illustration on pages 104, 275, 299 reprinted, by permission, from National Association for Sport and Physical Education, 1999, *Physical best activity guide: Secondary level* (Champaign, IL: Human Kinetics), 99.

Sprint, lying back start position illustration on page 104 reprinted, by permission, from J. Harris and J. Elbourn, 2002, *Warming Up and Cooling Down,* 2nd ed. (Champaign, IL: Human Kinetics), 19.

Sprint, lying back sprint position illustration on pages 104, 299 reprinted, by permission, from National Association for Sport and Physical Education, 1999, *Physical best activity guide: Secondary level* (Champaign, IL: Human Kinetics), 99.

Speed dribble illustration on pages 143, 279 reprinted, by permission, from H. Wissel, 2004, *Basketball: Steps to success,* 2nd ed. (Champaign, IL: Human Kinetics), 42.

Bounce pass illustration on pages 143, 285 reprinted, by permission, from H. Wissel, 2004, *Basketball: Steps to success,* 2nd ed. (Champaign, IL: Human Kinetics), 28.

Chest pass illustrations on pages 144, 285 reprinted, by permission, from H. Wissel, 2004, *Basketball: Steps to success,* 2nd ed. (Champaign, IL: Human Kinetics), 25.

Triple threat position illustration on page 144 reprinted, by permission, from H. Wissel, 2004, *Basketball: Steps to success,* 2nd ed. (Champaign, IL: Human Kinetics), 117.

Overhead pass illustrations on page 153 reprinted, by permission, from H. Wissel, 2004, *Basketball: Steps to success,* 2nd ed. (Champaign, IL: Human Kinetics), 29, 43.

Sidearm pass illustrations on page 153 reprinted, by permission, from H. Wissel, 2004, *Basketball: Steps to success,* 2nd ed. (Champaign, IL: Human Kinetics), 30, 43.

Set shot illustrations on pages 167, 281 reprinted, by permission, from H. Wissel, 2004, *Basketball: Steps to success,* 2nd ed. (Champaign, IL: Human Kinetics), 63.

Jump shot illustrations on pages 167, 282, 283 reprinted, by permission, from H. Wissel, 2004, *Basketball: Steps to success,* 2nd ed. (Champaign, IL: Human Kinetics), 68.

Defensive footwork illustrations on pages 168, 302 reprinted, by permission, from H. Wissel, 2004, *Basketball: Steps to success,* 2nd ed. (Champaign, IL: Human Kinetics), 15.

Defensive on the ball illustration on page 168 reprinted, by permission, from H. Wissel, 2004, *Basketball: Steps to success,* 2nd ed. (Champaign, IL: Human Kinetics), 19.

Defensive off the ball illustration on page 169 reprinted, by permission, from H. Wissel, 2004, *Basketball: Steps to success,* 2nd ed. (Champaign, IL: Human Kinetics), 141.

Layup illustrations on pages 177, 280 reprinted, by permission, from H. Wissel, 2004, *Basketball: Steps to success,* 2nd ed. (Champaign, IL: Human Kinetics), 76.

Give and go illustrations on page 178 reprinted, by permission, from H. Wissel, 2004, *Basketball: Steps to success,* 2nd ed. (Champaign, IL: Human Kinetics), 134.

Screening on and off the ball illustrations on page 187 reprinted, by permission, from H. Wissel, 2004, *Basketball: Steps to success,* 2nd ed. (Champaign, IL: Human Kinetics), 139, 144.

Pick-and-roll illustrations on page 188 reprinted, by permission, from H. Wissel, 2004, *Basketball: Steps to success,* 2nd ed. (Champaign, IL: Human Kinetics), 144.

Offensive rebounding illustrations on page 204 reprinted, by permission, from H. Wissel, 2004, *Basketball: Steps to success,* 2nd ed. (Champaign, IL: Human Kinetics), 101.

Defensive rebounding illustrations on page 204 reprinted, by permission, from H. Wissel, 2004, *Basketball: Steps to success,* 2nd ed. (Champaign, IL: Human Kinetics), 98.

Offensive post play illustrations on page 213 reprinted, by permission, from H. Wissel, 2004, *Basketball: Steps to success,* 2nd ed. (Champaign, IL: Human Kinetics), 108.

Defensive post play illustration on page 213 reprinted, by permission, from H. Wissel, 2004, *Basketball: Steps to success,* 2nd ed. (Champaign, IL: Human Kinetics), 131.

Player-to-player defense illustration on page 221 reprinted, by permission, from H. Wissel, 2004, *Basketball: Steps to success,* 2nd ed. (Champaign, IL: Human Kinetics), 201.

Zone defense illustration on page 229 reprinted, by permission, from H. Wissel, 2004, *Basketball: Steps to success,* 2nd ed. (Champaign, IL: Human Kinetics), 216.

PACER illustration and data on pages 104, 264 from PACER 2005.

Vertical jump illustrations on pages 274, 302 reprinted, by permission, from H. Wissel, 2004, *Basketball: Steps to success,* 2nd ed. (Champaign, IL: Human Kinetics), 12.

Shuttle run illustrations on pages 276, 302 reprinted, by permission, from H. Wissel, 2004, *Basketball: Steps to success,* 2nd ed. (Champaign, IL: Human Kinetics), 7.

Line jump illustration on pages 277, 302 adapted, by permission, from C. Hopper, 1996, *Health-related fitness for grades 1 & 2* (Champaign, IL: Human Kinetics), 94.

Rebounding illustration on page 284 reprinted, by permission, from H. Wissel, 2004, *Basketball: Steps to Success,* 2nd ed. (Champaign, IL: Human Kinetics), 109.

Jump rope illustration on page 299 reprinted, by permission, from National Association for Sport and Physical Education, 1999, *Physical best activity guide: Secondary level* (Champaign, IL: Human Kinetics), 187.

Flexibility activity card illustrations on page 300 reprinted, by permission, from M. Alter, 1998, *Sport stretch*, 2nd ed. (Champaign, IL: Human Kinetics), 34, 92, 212, 86, 144, 195, 89, 102, 157, 31, 88, 115, 171, 130, 143, 146. © Michael Richardson.

Soccer official's signals on page 347 courtesy of EPIC Software Group, Inc.

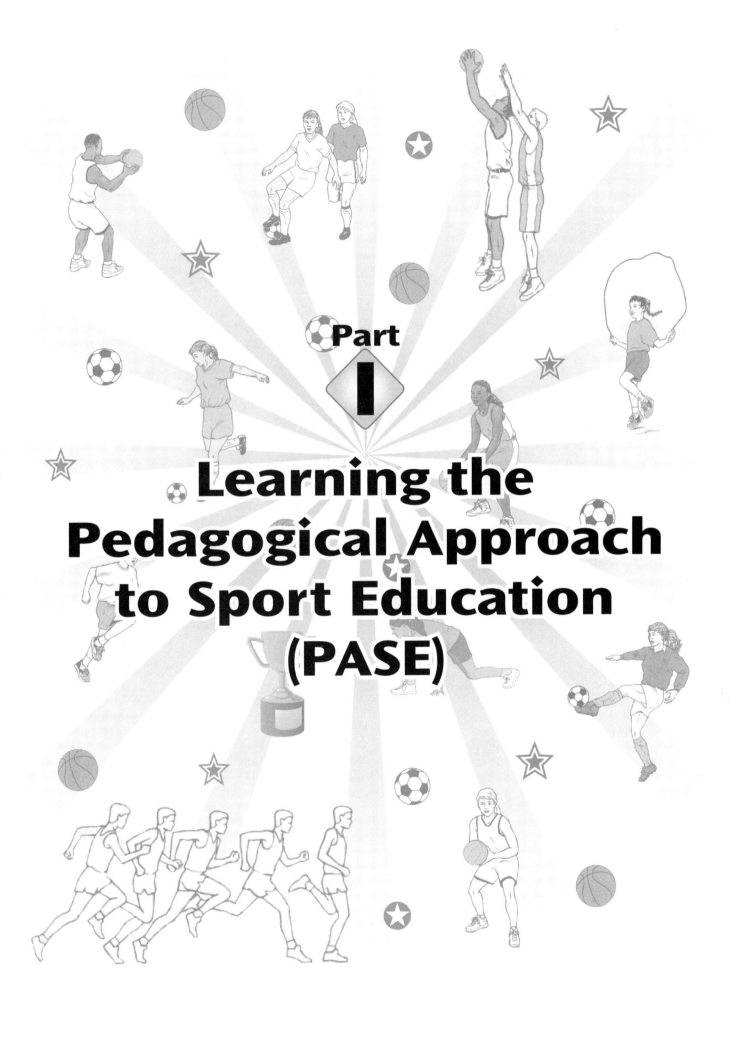

Part I

Learning the Pedagogical Approach to Sport Education (PASE)

Introduction
to PASE

Sport plays an extremely influential role in our society. We play sport in our schools and community recreational leagues, watch it on television, read about it in books, interact with it through Internet fantasy leagues, dramatize it in motion pictures, and simulate it in video games. Many of our sport figures have become household names and cultural icons through their appearances in an endless lineup of television commercials and product endorsements. The personal successes and failures of these highly public figures, both on and off the playing field, frequently dominate current events. On the negative end of the continuum, organized sport has received a great deal of harmful publicity in recent years. Scandals involving youth, collegiate, and professional athletes remain all too common features of the sport landscape. The disturbing images of the remorseful professional athlete engaged in yet another round of legal trouble and the defiant Olympian embroiled in the newest performance-enhancing drug scandal have unfortunately become characteristic of our sporting culture. The list of major sport-related controversies seemingly grows each year in accordance with the corresponding increase in media attention. These types of problems are not unique to sport, however, and will likely be with us for the foreseeable future: sexual assault, college recruiting violations, gambling allegations, drug abuse, fan-on-fan violence, player strikes, and so forth.

Despite the widespread attention given to these negative issues, sport continues to retain an inherent value for many of us and remains an important part of our lives. On a daily basis, we are presented with more positive images of athletes making nearly impossible plays on television's nightly news or game of the week. Their strength, endurance, speed, physical grace, determination, and focus serve as powerful reminders of our remarkable physiological and psychological potential as human beings. The sports pages of the local newspaper represent the first, and sometimes most enjoyable, order of business for some of us on relaxing weekend mornings. To the educated consumer of sport, the reported statistics provide a vivid description of the inner complexity of the game itself. Furthermore, our bookstore and library shelves are full of texts and magazines devoted to the individuals who play the games that make some difference in our lives. At their best, these personalized accounts of victory and defeat have proven to be a source of entertainment, education, and inspiration for interested readers. Collectors invest countless hours and small fortunes accumulating sports trading cards and memorabilia in an attempt to recapture some of their fondest and most meaningful childhood memories. Pilgrimages to local arenas and stadiums are also a routine part of the week for many of us. At some point, we have all been caught up in the wave of excitement and sense of civic pride that spreads throughout a community when the local team earns its way to the league championship game or scores an upset victory over a longtime rival.

Those who truly understand its value, however, know that sport must be experienced, not just watched, listened to, read about, or represented on a collection shelf. Many of us have learned to embrace the sport experience because it affords a potentially limitless opportunity for personal challenge and growth. Beyond the obvious physical and social benefits, advocates endorse sport as an ideal context for developing many of the intangible qualities that contribute to one's success in life. Some of our closest friendships and valuable life lessons, for example, can be traced back to the neighborhood sandlots and gyms where we spent endless hours immersed in sport while simultaneously learning how to communicate, lead, follow, compromise, and compete. The sense of accomplishment that accompanies the completion of a physically demanding preseason conditioning session, the flawless performance of a complex sport skill after hours of practice, the memorization and mastery of the team playbook, or an opponent's handshake at the end of a hard-fought contest is reserved for those who choose to actually play sport.

SPORT EDUCATION

Although the value of sport and its potential contribution to the maintenance of a healthy, physically active lifestyle are readily apparent, some physical education programs fail to incorporate teaching–learning environments that fully immerse students in an authentic sport experience. Many physical educators, for example, continue to use a multiactivity approach to teach team and individual sport skills. This curricular model exposes students to a variety of sports through a series of brief instructional units across the school year. Advocates of the multiactivity approach maintain that this brief but varied exposure is essential because it provides students with a basis for making decisions regarding the types of physical activities they will continue to participate in across the life span. Unfortunately, there are a number of significant limitations associated with this approach to the teaching of sport (Siedentop 1994; Tannehill 1998; Townsend et al. 2003):

1. Limited exposure to rules, strategies, skills, and culture of a sport
2. Inadequate skill and tactical development due to the relatively short length of the instructional unit
3. Isolated sport skill instruction and practice
4. Inauthentic game play and assessment
5. Minimal motivation for students to fully engage in the sport experience

In response to the limitations associated with more traditional approaches to teaching sport and promoting play, Sport Education has been recommended as "a curriculum and instruction model designed to provide authentic, educationally rich sport experiences for girls and boys in the context of school physical education" (Siedentop 2002, p. 409). The Sport Education model has three primary learning outcomes: to educate students to be competent, literate, and enthusiastic sportspersons (Siedentop 1994, 2002). To achieve these meaningful learning outcomes, physical educators who use Sport Education are required to implement a number of alternative curricular and instructional strategies: (a) extend the length of the sport unit; (b) use a combination of teaching styles, such as direct instruction, cooperative learning, and peer teaching; (c) provide authentic opportunities for skill and strategy practice, application, and assessment; and (d) immerse students in the culture of the particular sport by providing them with increased responsibility for their own learning (Siedentop 1994, 1998). Additionally, Sport Education calls for the inclusion of six key features that help to establish the teaching–learning context in which these curricular and instructional modifications are implemented. These critical features include seasons, team affiliation, formal competition, culminating events, record keeping, and festivity (Siedentop 1994).

Anecdotal support from practicing teachers who have used the model and the related scientific research indicate that a number of positive outcomes are associated with student and teacher participation in a well-designed Sport Education season:

Sport education is now teacher-tested throughout the world. There are many variations as teachers add their own unique applications. More than 50 Sport Education articles have been published in the 1990's, an increasing portion of which are research studies, most of which report results that are more similar than different. Teachers and students like Sport Education. Lower-skilled and typically non-participating students seem to gain particularly important benefits. Teachers report that students do become better games players than in traditional approaches. As students become excited about Sport Education, so too do their teachers. Students enjoy the multiple roles and they particularly seem to like learning from their peers. (Siedentop 2002, p. 414)

More specifically, the reported benefits for students include an enhanced personal investment in physical education, improved opportunities for females and lower-skilled students to engage in skill instruction and practice, and increased levels of student achievement. The benefits for teachers relate to a reduced reliance on direct instruction as an exclusive teaching strategy, as well as the provision of more frequent opportunities for the teacher to address the individual needs of each student in the class. The appropriate implementation of a Sport Education season ultimately results in the establishment of a teaching–learning environment that is fun, engaging, stimulating, impartial, demanding, and accommodating. This type of dynamic teaching–learning environment is very likely to produce a renewed interest in physical education among the involved students and teachers (Siedentop 1994).

PEDAGOGICAL APPROACH TO SPORT EDUCATION (PASE)

While the available evidence convincingly supports the use of Sport Education in school-based physical education, a number of curricular variations have been developed, with mixed results (Siedentop 2002). Some of the primary concerns regarding the implementation of the Sport Education model in its various forms relate to the need for (a) guidelines for making the transition from teacher-directed to learner-centered instructional environments, (b) sound practical instructional materials for teachers looking to implement a Sport Education season, (c) effective strategies for incorporating leadership development and teaching tactical game play, (d) better suggestions for helping students to learn about the local sport community and the associated opportunities for lifetime participation, and (e) jointly promoting both fun and competence in physical education (Siedentop 2002).

In response to these important issues and the similar concerns expressed by the numerous physical educators with whom we have collaborated, and to whom we are deeply indebted for their contributions to this book, we have observed the need for a structured set of planning and instructional guidelines that will enable practitioners to effectively design, implement, and assess a Sport Education season or instructional unit. Drawing from our previous experiences and scholarly activity in this area (e.g., Mohr, Townsend, and Bulger 2001, 2002; Townsend et al. 2003), we have developed a conceptual framework for conducting Sport Education seasons in school-based physical education settings. The Pedagogical Approach to Sport Education (PASE) that is described in this book has been developed for physical educators who are looking to establish an instructionally sound sporting experience for their students.

The Sport Education model has its roots in play theory, the cultural aspects of the sport experience, and the classroom management component of the teacher effectiveness literature (Siedentop 2002). As the name suggests, PASE is intended to extend this theoretical basis to more directly account for what we know about effective pedagogy or instruction within a physical education teaching–learning environment. Due to the relatively complex and comprehensive nature of a Sport Education season, it has been our experience that physical educators may have difficulty effectively implementing the model during their initial attempts.

We have developed PASE as a systematic approach for planning, implementing, and assessing a Sport Education season. As depicted in table 1.1 (Season Planning Guidelines), the PASE guidelines for season planning are divided into two distinct components that will be described in greater detail in later chapters. The first planning component addresses six key management issues related to the establishment of an authentic sporting experience, including

Table 1.1 Season Planning Guidelines

Planning component 1: Sport Education model development	Planning component 2: Sport-specific content development
Team selection • Determine method of selection • Develop selection materials Student roles • Determine roles and define responsibilities • Link role completion to grading and accountability system Team identity and affiliation Provide students opportunities to choose: • Team name • Team colors and uniforms • Team cheer • Team mascot Team practice and competition • Develop a season block plan • Determine types of competitions and tournaments • Plan a culminating event • Link practice and competition outcomes to grading and accountability system Class procedures and instruction • Develop rules and daily routines for the season • Determine when, where, and how each lesson component will take place • Link managerial task system to grading and accountability system Student grading and accountability system • Determine student learning outcomes • Develop criteria for each learning outcome • Decide how each criterion will be measured • Integrate team and individual points into the grading system • Produce a record-keeping method (i.e., a grade book)	Sport-specific content development • Select the salient skills for the activity or sport • Identify critical elements and teaching cues for each skill • Design a tactical matrix to determine the salient tactics for the activity or sport • Devise progressive learning activities to develop the skills and associated tactics Activity task cards • Design task cards from activities identified in sport-specific content development step • Provide pictures and written instructional cues • Include criteria for progressing through content • Link task completion to grading and accountability system Sport-specific health-related fitness • Develop a set of fitness task cards (at least three) • Include components of an appropriate warm-up • Account for components of health-related fitness • Sequence activities for safety and injury prevention Student coaching plans • Use age-appropriate language • Provide team skills and tactics practice objectives • Include cues, suggestions, and safety considerations for successful practice • Integrate rules and referee protocols Student assessment of learning outcomes Design the following assessments: • Skill and tactical assessments • Application contest assessments • Behavioral and fair play assessments • Cognitive assessments • Game play and tournament assessments

From "A Pedagogical Approach to Sport Education Season Planning," by D.J. Mohr, J.S. Townsend, and S.M. Bulger, 2001, *Journal of Physical Education, Recreation and Dance,* 73(1), p. 38. Copyright 2001 by the American Alliance for Health, Physical Education, Recreation and Dance. Reprinted with permission.

1. selecting teams,
2. determining student roles,
3. creating team identity and affiliation,
4. designing team practice and competition schedules,
5. adhering to class procedures and instruction, and
6. grading students.

The second planning component focuses on the instructional issues that directly influence student learning. These five planning responsibilities include

1. the development of sport-specific skill and strategy content,
2. the design of activity task cards,
3. the design of fitness task cards,
4. the construction of student coaching plans, and
5. the manufacture of student assessment materials.

SUMMARY

Chapter 1 provided a brief introduction to the Sport Education model and the potential benefits associated with its use within school-based physical education programs. In response to the recommendations and practical concerns expressed by many of the practicing physical educators with whom we have worked, the PASE planning and instructional guidelines outlined in this chapter have been recommended as a conceptual framework for planning, implementing, and assessing developmentally appropriate sport experiences for school-aged children.

Curricular and Instructional Issues in PASE

Sport Education has gained considerable support among a number of educational researchers and practicing teachers as an effective alternative to more traditional approaches for teaching sport within school-based physical education. When used appropriately, the model has been found to provide a highly authentic and engaging sport experience for students across a diverse range of backgrounds and skill levels. In order to accomplish the ambitious curricular goals of producing competent, literate, and enthusiastic sportspersons, the related season and daily lesson plans must be well structured with specific student learning outcomes in mind. The initial planning of a Sport Education season and the accompanying lessons can, however, prove to be a bit overwhelming for practitioners who have not previously used the model. The PASE planning and instructional guidelines highlighted in this chapter are intended to provide guidance for physical education teachers who are interested in applying the model within their program.

PASE SEASON PLANNING

As described in the previous chapter, the PASE season planning guidelines are divided into two component parts, each with its own set of specific responsibilities (see table 1.1 on p. 6). A number of these planning concerns are unique to PASE and should be of primary interest to the physical educator who is looking to put the model into practice effectively. The first planning component addresses the management issues that relate directly to the various cultural aspects of the particular sport. The most critical issues include team selection, student roles, team identity and affiliation, team practice and competition schedules, class procedures and instruction, and student grading and accountability. These planning responsibilities are very important because the decisions made in these areas help to establish the instructional context for the entire season. The number of possible variations in each of these planning areas is virtually limitless, however, and teachers should be encouraged to draw upon their own creativity and positive experiences in sport during the planning process.

The second planning component involves the development of the sport-specific content for the season. This set of planning tasks includes the design of the sport-specific skill and strategy content, the associated skill and strategy task cards, the health-related physical fitness task cards, the student coaching plans, and the student assessment materials. Regardless of the curricular model that is being used, physical educators typically plan and make important instructional decisions in these areas. This planning becomes more complex in a PASE teaching–learning environment, however, because the teacher is trying to address the psychomotor, cognitive, affective, and fitness domains of physical education in an integrated fashion that is highly characteristic of an authentic sport experience. Physical educators must plan to teach skill and tactical development, for example, in a coordinated manner through the provision of a series of progressive learning activities. Skills and tactics taught in isolation are probably of little value to students once they start to engage in the more highly complex application contests that occur during the later phases of a PASE season.

While season planning represents the first and perhaps most critical step in the instructional design process, a great deal of attention must also be afforded to daily lesson planning. As all experienced teachers are well aware, meaningful preclass planning is a prerequisite to effective teaching. This recommendation may be especially important for physical educators who are trying to use PASE for the first time in their classes. The following sections of this chapter will extend the previously described season planning concepts in the areas of daily lesson planning, assessment, behavior management, organizational considerations, and sequencing of a season.

PASE LESSON PLANNING

While there is no one perfect form of Sport Education and while continued innovation is a highly desirable trend (Siedentop 2002), we have found well-structured daily lesson plans to be a critical instructional resource. The PASE lesson planning guidelines have been developed and refined through repeated practice trials and programmatic evaluation efforts. Furthermore, the structure of this lesson plan is highly reflective of our own personal experiences in sport and includes the following lesson segments (see table 2.1 for the daily planning lesson segments).

A number of key factors, including the intended learning outcomes, developmental level of participants, and phase of the season (e.g., early, middle, late), interact to determine the amount of time that students spend engaged in each lesson segment and the exact nature of the planned learning activities (see table 2.2, Daily Responsibility Guidelines). In other words, the time allocated to each lesson segment and the complexity of the involved learning activities change as the season progresses. At the start of the Sport Education season, for example, students may spend most of the lesson time engaged in team practice. As the season advances and competitions become more demanding, students spend a greater amount of time engaging in application contests. Students may also be required to assume more challenging roles and take on greater individual responsibility within each lesson segment as they continue to develop their knowledge and skills across the season. Each segment of the lesson is important, however, and should always be accounted for in some way during a class meeting. It is inappropriate, for instance, to completely eliminate teacher-directed skills and tactics instruction time late in a season.

Check Daily Roles and Responsibilities

As students enter the gymnasium, they should be provided with a protocol for quickly identifying their daily role and the associated managerial or instructional responsibilities. In the interest of making this process as routine and efficient as possible, the teacher must establish the managerial protocol for this lesson component early in the season. We highly recommend that students have access to this important information at the start of each lesson in the form of a team folder, notebook, or poster that is located in a designated home court area. Some physical education teachers have successfully managed this lesson segment by using a role matrix for each team (see Roles and Responsibilities Assignments on p. 52). This type of organizational matrix is helpful because it clearly identifies the students and their corresponding roles for each class meeting. After the students identify their roles for the day, they can refer to the role responsibilities section of the matrix that lists the related tasks. The role descriptors help students fully understand the behavioral requirements associated with each role, so that they can set meaningful personal goals and monitor their own performance.

Table 2.1   Daily Planning Lesson Segments

The PASE Lesson Plan

- Daily roles and responsibilities check
- Team warm-ups and student coaches' meeting
- Team-directed skill and tactics review
- Teacher-directed skill and tactics instruction
- Team practice
- Application contest
- Lesson closure
- Individual and team progress report

Table 2.2 Daily Responsibility Guidelines

Lesson component	Teacher's role	Students' role	Approximate time (min) allocated during season*		
			Early	Mid	Late
Daily roles and responsibilities check	• Provide matrix and list of role responsibilities • Monitor environment	• Identify daily roles • Prepare for warm-up or student coaches' meeting	3	1	1
Team warm-up and student coaches' meeting	• Provide warm-up activities • Provide student coaching plan • Conduct student coaches' meeting	• Fitness trainer leads team warm-up • Student coaches meet with teacher	10	12	14
Team-directed skill and tactics review	• Indirectly facilitate review • Monitor environment • Focus teams when needed	• Student coach directs team review and monitors individuals' and team's progress on goals	10	15	15
Teacher-directed skill and tactics instruction	• Orient learners to new skills and tactics, review previous skills and tactics, or both • Conduct whole-class drills	• Observe teacher • Participate in demonstrations • Engage in intro and review drills	15	10	5
Team practice	• Provide learning activities • Indirectly facilitate practice • Monitor environment • Focus teams when needed	• Student coach directs team practice and monitors team's progress on learning activities	30	20	5
Application contest	• Design contest to apply daily skills and tactics • Provide statistics recording sheet • Advise referees • Manage contest	• Student coach preps team for contest • Scorekeepers record contest statistics • Referees referee contest • Players participate in contest	7	20	40
Lesson closure	• Refocus and review skills and tactics • Question students • Allow for demonstrations • Provide feedback on students' progress • Preview upcoming lesson • Supply out-of-class assignments	• Observe teacher • Answer questions • Engage in demonstrations • Ask questions	5	5	5
Individual and team progress report	• Provide assessment documents • Monitor record-keeping procedures	• Collect, organize, summarize, and record team and individual progress on goals	10	7	5

*Times based on a 90-minute block-scheduled class.

From "Maintaining the PASE: A Day in the Life of Sport Education," by D.J. Mohr, J.S. Townsend, and S.M. Bulger, 2002, *Journal of Physical Education, Recreation and Dance*, 73(1), p. 39. Copyright 2002 by the American Alliance of Health, Physical Education, Recreation and Dance. Reprinted with permission.

Team Warm-Ups and Student Coaches' Meeting

Following the daily role and responsibilities check, the students engage in either a team warm-up or a coaches' meeting. Student coaches meet with the teacher in a common area such as the middle of the gymnasium. During this brief meeting, the teacher informs the student coaches of the daily lesson objectives, provides a brief overview of the lesson, and supplies a coaching plan to facilitate team practice. The student coaching plan (see p. 73) can be viewed as a developmentally appropriate version of a lesson plan, which will be used during team practice. The plan gives the student coach the information needed to provide effective leadership during team practice. Although student coaches are usually selected for this role as a result of their previous sport experience, the physical education teacher maintains the primary responsibility for providing appropriate content and instructionally valid choices for student coaches and their teammates. The student coaching plan represents an effective tool for communicating these instructionally valid choices to students.

While the teacher is conducting the student coaches' meeting, the other students participate in teams in a developmentally appropriate, sport-specific warm-up within their team home court areas. The student who is assuming the role of fitness trainer for the day leads the team through the warm-up. The teacher should develop several fitness activities for the fitness trainer to choose from in order to ensure that the warm-up is of sufficient intensity and duration (see fitness task card for muscular fitness on p. 46).

Team-Directed Skills and Tactics Review

The review segment represents a critical segment of any well-designed physical education lesson. During this portion of the lesson, the teacher provides students with an opportunity to review material that was presented during previous class sessions via previous lessons' student coaching plans (see p. 73) and activity task cards (see p. 74). Working as teams, students can organize and conduct reviews based on individual and team assessments, performances from earlier lessons, or both. Students may decide to organize a team review led by the student coach, for example, or they may decide to practice individual skills in their home court areas. Regardless of the review format, the teacher must circulate throughout the team home court areas to encourage students to use this lesson time appropriately. Teachers can also establish a pattern of daily assessment that serves to further focus student attention during the lesson review. Daily assessment, such as the team goal-setting sheet (see p. 65), ensures that students are monitoring progress toward individual and team goals. It is critical that students can self-identify individual and team strengths and weaknesses through the assessment process if they are to continually improve performance throughout the season.

Teacher-Directed Skills and Tactics Instruction

The teacher's role as a direct transmitter of knowledge is diminished in Sport Education because students are required to actively assume increased responsibility for their own learning. Many teachers, however, implement the model incorrectly by relinquishing too much of their instructional responsibility through their almost exclusive reliance on peer teaching and cooperative learning strategies. While we recognize the value of these learner-centered instructional approaches and make frequent use of them in the accompanying PASE instructional materials, we maintain that the teacher should directly orient the learners to the targeted skills and tactics prior to daily team or individual practice. To assist the teacher with this duty, cards with graphics and cues (see p. 72) are provided. During this lesson segment, the teacher is responsible for stating the daily objectives; providing an anticipatory set; explaining, demonstrating, and questioning students about the involved skills and tactics; providing instructional cues; and conducting a series of brief, guided practice drills with the entire class. As the season progresses, teachers may allocate less time to this segment as the lesson focus shifts from skill and tactical development to game application. If students are to become competent and literate sportspersons, however, teacher-directed skill and tactical instruction should never be completely eliminated from any lesson.

Team Practice

During team practice, peer instruction and cooperative learning become the primary instructional strategies. Student coaches assume responsibility for organizing and monitoring team practice. To facilitate effective peer leadership and aid in responsible decision making, student coaches are provided with student coaching plans at the beginning of the lesson during the previously described student coaches' meeting (see Student Coaching Plan on p. 73). In addition to student coaching plans, each team should have access to a series of progressive learning activities. These learning activities are posted on an activity task card (see p. 74) in each team's home court area. Each team, under the direction of the student coach, can decide if they will move through the learning tasks individually or as a unit. This decision will dictate whether students use the individual or team activity task card recording sheets (see pp. 62 and 63). Team practice is a time when students need to make choices regarding their own learning. These choices help to increase student ownership of their own learning within the classroom. The teacher, however, is ultimately responsible for providing students with appropriate alternatives to choose from for skill and tactical development. By fulfilling this instructional responsibility, the teacher is ensuring individual success within a very student-centered teaching–learning environment.

Application Contest

Students should have the opportunity to apply the skills and tactics that they are practicing in a gamelike contest during each lesson (e.g., application contest description on pp. 76-77). During these application contests, the students and teacher can authentically assess the extent to which the intended skills and tactical knowledge are being developed (e.g., Application Contest Scorecard on p. 78). Careful consideration must be given, however, to the design of developmentally appropriate application contests that afford the students a reasonable opportunity for success. The design should follow a simple-to-complex progression across the season. As the season progresses and students develop a greater mastery of the involved sport skills and tactical awareness, the application contest should become increasingly complex and may account for a significantly greater percentage of lesson time. Early in a season, for example, an application contest may consist of a 30-second individual challenge against the clock. In the middle of the season, the application contest may involve a medium-duration competition that incorporates offensive and defensive tactical implementation in a two-on-two situation. Finally, the end-of-season tournament represents the ultimate application contest. The tournament games may call for the use of small-sided games that last for an extended period of time, and these games may be scored in a more traditional manner. During each daily application contest, students manage the lesson segment by assuming key roles as scorekeepers, and referees. Students identify and prepare for these daily responsibilities at the beginning of the lesson as they enter the gymnasium.

Lesson Closure

The closure represents an important lesson segment in which the teacher brings the lesson full circle. Unfortunately, teachers frequently neglect the lesson closure due to perceived or actual time constraints. An effective closure affords the teacher an opportunity to refocus student attention, review the most relevant skills and concepts, preview the upcoming lesson, and provide relevant out-of-class assignments. In order to refocus student attention and review pertinent information, the teacher can restate the lesson objectives, question students for understanding, and provide opportunities for student demonstrations. These components of the closure should be closely aligned with the teacher-directed instruction provided earlier in the lesson. As a preview for the upcoming lesson, the teacher should also indicate how the concepts and skills from the day's lesson will be applied during future learning experiences.

Individual and Team Progress Report

To conclude the lesson, the teacher should provide students with an opportunity to complete individual or team progress reports or both. These progress reports include a wide variety of possible formats but should focus on the primary goals of Sport Education: to educate students to be competent, literate, and enthusiastic sportspersons. To demonstrate competency, for example, students could do one or more of the following: record individual progress, document the results of peer assessments from the team practice portion of the lesson, compile team statistics from the application contest, or summarize information from a Game Performance Assessment Instrument (GPAI) (Griffin, Mitchell, and Oslin 1997) used during tournament play. Literacy progress could be monitored through the assessment of role requirements; the completion of informal quizzes; the evaluation of personal, team, and class sport practices; or some combination of these. Students can scrutinize the development of enthusiasm through one or more of the following: journal entries; participation logs; personal and social responsibility rubrics; verification of involvement in optional, out-of-class activities.

The completion of regular progress reports affords students a unique opportunity to demonstrate personal responsibility for becoming independent learners. The information gathered from this and other lesson segments enables the students to identify the personal strengths and challenges that are influencing their progress toward becoming competent, literate, and enthusiastic sportspersons. Additionally, the teacher is provided with information relative to student learning on a consistent basis. The information obtained from all lesson segments is crucial to the effectiveness of a PASE season. The consistent evaluation of student progress and the effectiveness of the educational environment can undoubtedly contribute to the establishment of a more dynamic, highly focused teaching–learning environment. For a summary of the most common assessment and instructional materials used during each lesson segment, refer to table 2.3.

PASE Lesson Modifications

The previous sections provided a detailed description of the segments and sequencing that occur in a typical PASE lesson. This PASE lesson format is best suited for 90-minute block-scheduled class periods at the high school level. The recommended lesson format can easily be modified, however, to accommodate a broader range of class schedules. The following list provides physical educators with suggestions for modifying the recommended PASE daily lesson format to better meet their own unique scheduling constraints. These modifications are intended to enable teachers to individualize the recommended lesson plan format to better meet their contextual needs while maintaining a clear instructional focus.

- **First-time users.** Because the initial design and implementation of a PASE season can be overwhelming, we suggest using an experimental-progressive planning approach at first. That is, you should choose a sport that you are comfortable teaching and carefully select a few manageable components of the model to implement in a single class. Then, once you and your students become accustomed to these components, additional components and classes can be added in subsequent seasons. Several

Table 2.3   Lesson Components and Materials Summary

Lesson segment	Common PASE materials per lesson segment
Daily roles and responsibilities check	• Roles and responsibilities assignment matrix • Team score placards
Team warm-up and student coaches' meeting	• Fitness task cards • Personal or team fitness recording sheets • Student coaching plans
Skill and tactics review	• Team goal-setting sheets • Task cards from previous lessons • Student coaching plans from previous lessons
Skill and tactics instruction	• Graphics and cues cards (for teacher use)
Team practice	• Activity task cards • Team or individual activity task card recording sheets • Student coaching plans
Application contest	• Application contest scorecards • Pocket Ref • Application contest descriptions (for teacher use)
Lesson closure	• Out-of-class assignments (e.g., reflective journal, physical activity logs, independent learning activity)
Individual and team progress report	• Individual responsibility level (IRL) rubric and IRL recording sheet • Roles and responsibilities recording sheet • Sports information director sports report • Attendance recording sheets

experimental seasons may pass before "full-scale" Sport Education is in place within every class that you teach. A reflective teacher who carefully selects and systematically implements the components of PASE in an experimental-progressive fashion increases the likelihood of success for everyone involved.

- **Limited time.** Divide the lesson in two. Separate a single lesson into two lessons, preferably between teacher-directed skills and tactics instruction and team practice lesson segments.
- **Limited space or equipment.** Decrease the number of teams while increasing the number of nonsport performer roles (e.g., sport broadcaster, equity officer, sport council member).
- **Developmental level.** Developmental considerations across elementary, middle, and secondary educational levels include choosing an appropriate sport, modifying the rules of the sport, incorporating acceptable competition formats, determining the number of roles and associated responsibilities, and establishing suitable student performance assessments.

ASSESSMENT IN PASE

Prior to any discussion regarding the role of assessment in PASE, it is important to establish clear definitions of the related terminology. *Assessment* is defined as an all-inclusive process that involves the intentional acts of using tests to measure and evaluate student performance relative to set standards or goals. The purpose of assessment is to provide meaningful, performance-related feedback to students, teachers, administrators, and parents. *Tests* are tools, instruments, or protocols designed to measure knowledge, skills, or attitudes. *Measurement* refers to the act of using tests to gather data on students' knowledge, skills, or attitudes. *Evaluation* refers to the practice of determining the worth or value of the data collected during testing and measurement. Collectively tests, measurement, and evaluation represent the assessment process.

Why Assess?

Physical educators typically assess student performance in order to determine class grades. The assessment process can also be used for a number of additional purposes that remain central to the establishment of an effective PASE teaching–learning environment (see table 2.4). The ultimate purpose of assessment in Sport Education, however, is to inform students about their progress toward becoming competent, literate, and enthusiastic sportspersons.

What to Assess?

Educational assessment should focus on specified learning outcomes. In Sport Education, the intended learning outcomes are to "educate students to be players in the fullest sense and to help them develop as competent, literate and enthusiastic sportspeople" (Siedentop 1994, p. 4). A competent sportsperson "has sufficient skills to participate in games satisfactorily, understands and can execute strategies appropriate to the complexity of play, and is a knowledgeable games player" (Siedentop 1994, p. 4). A literate sportsperson "understands and values the rules, rituals, and traditions of sports and distinguishes between good and bad sports practices, whether in children's or professional sport. A literate sports person is both a more able participant and more discerning consumer, whether fan or spectator" (Siedentop 1994, p. 4). An enthusiastic sportsperson "participates and behaves in ways that preserve, protect, and enhance the sports culture, whether it is a local youth sport culture or a national sport culture" (p. 4). Sport Education has 10 additional objectives that students work to achieve on a daily basis (Siedentop 1994):

1. Develop skills and fitness specific to particular sports
2. Appreciate and be able to execute strategic play in sports
3. Participate at a level appropriate to their stage of development
4. Share in the planning and administration of sport experiences
5. Provide responsible leadership
6. Work effectively within a group toward common goals
7. Appreciate the rituals and conventions that give particular sports their unique meanings
8. Develop the capacity to make reasoned decisions about sport issues
9. Develop and apply knowledge about umpiring, refereeing, and training
10. Decide voluntarily to become involved in after-school sport

When to Assess?

In order to accomplish the primary instructional goals associated with a PASE season, assessment needs to be carefully planned and well timed within each lesson. If specific assessment strategies are implemented during the appropriate lesson components, the assessment becomes a more authentic and highly integrated aspect of the instructional

Table 2.4 Assessment in PASE

Purpose	Description of assessment	Sport Education example
Diagnosis	Determining initial capabilities of individuals before a unit of instruction, that is, pretesting. Diagnosis identifies individuals' strengths and weaknesses and affects subsequent planning and instruction.	• Biography sheet • Cognitive test • Skills combine • Game Performance Assessment Instrument (GPAI)
Classification	Separating individuals into like or mixed groups based on a predetermined attribute such as skill level, cognitive ability, gender, age, experience, etc.	• Heterogeneous team selection
Achievement	Identifying a final level of performance, typically determined at the end of an instructional unit, that indicates student obtainment of standards or end-of-unit goals.	• Post-biography sheet • Post-cognitive test • Post-skills combine • Post-GPAI
Improvement	Determining the difference in an individual's level of performance between two points in time.	• Pre- and post-cognitive tests • Pre- and post-skills combine • Pre- and post-GPAI
Motivation	Using varied measurement schedules and multiple tests to monitor student performance, increase accountability, and foster an environment for improvement during an instructional unit.	• Pre- and post-skills combine • Pre- and post-fitness tests • Daily journal • Weekly statistics
Evaluation of instructional units	Determining student achievement in relation to specific objectives for a particular instructional unit. Results are used to modify planning and instruction in subsequent units.	Assessment of • Sport Education goals • Sport Education objectives
Evaluation of the curriculum	Ascertaining overall program effectiveness by comparing the cumulative effects of individual units to program goals. Results are used to modify curricular offerings and instructional processes.	Assessment of • NASPE content standards • NASPE benchmarks • State and local goals
Teacher effectiveness	Verifying the effectiveness of instruction through direct observation of the teaching–learning environment or through student performance.	• Teacher behavior checklist • Student behavior checklist • Student achievement or improvement (or both) related to predetermined standards
Public relations and physical education	Advocating and justifying the physical education program to educational constituents and the community by documenting and publicizing meaningful outcomes that students are obtaining.	• Posting of accomplishments • Awards banquet • Physical education Web page • Local newspaper articles • Physical education newsletters

process (see table 2.3). During each of these lesson components, various assessment strategies can be used to hold students accountable for their learning and for monitoring their own progress.

How to Implement Assessment?

Effective assessment practices in PASE are highly dependent on the physical education teacher's capacity for thoughtful planning. This planning can prove overwhelming, however, when a teacher first attempts to infuse assessment throughout the instructional process. To minimize this potential concern, teachers using PASE for the first time should adopt an experimental-progressive approach to lesson planning and assessment. The following guidelines describe this experimental-progressive approach to assessment in PASE:

1. Choose a sport that you know well and are comfortable teaching and assessing.
2. Start with a single class.
3. Carefully select a few manageable assessment instruments to implement at first.
4. Introduce additional assessment instruments and use more classes as your students become accustomed to the initially selected instruments in the Sport Education seasons that follow.

Throughout the book and CD-ROM a number of assessment examples are provided that require students to assume various levels of responsibility for monitoring their own learning. Teachers should actively prepare their students to use these assessments as a regular part of the instructional process. The following guidelines represent a systematic protocol for training students to take an active role in assessing their own learning:

1. Explain the instrument and its purpose.
2. Through demonstration, clarify how the instrument works.
3. Check for student understanding of how to use the instrument by directly questioning students and allowing for student demonstrations.
4. Provide students with multiple guided and independent opportunities to practice using the instrument.
5. Offer feedback on that practice.
6. Provide more practice in increasingly complex situations that represent how students will ultimately use the instrument.
7. Offer more feedback.
8. Hold the students accountable for accurate data collection.

Teachers who use this systematic training protocol are enhancing the meaningfulness of the information that is collected during the season by accounting for objectivity, reliability, and validity throughout the assessment process.

Assessment of the Teaching–Learning Environment

Within a typical PASE lesson, both the teacher and the student regularly carry out important instructional and managerial functions. The quality with which these basic functions are performed ultimately determines the effectiveness of the teaching–learning environment. To ensure efficient and effective implementation of PASE, a teacher can use the PASE Teacher Observation Instrument (see table 2.5) and the PASE Student Observation Instrument (see table 2.6) to directly monitor the quality of the employed instructional process.

Both observation instruments provide the teacher with a method for directly monitoring the quality of the teaching–learning environment during a lesson. In order to ensure that the PASE planning and instructional guidelines are being properly implemented, it is important for the teacher to evaluate his or her instructional behaviors in combination with the associated student behaviors during each component of the lesson. The process-related data collected through this type of structured observation can then be used to improve the effectiveness of the teaching–learning environment.

These observation instruments should be used on a regular basis in order to provide a clear representation of the overall effectiveness of the teaching–learning environment. Although there is not an established standard, we suggest using each observation instrument at least five times during the season. The more frequently the observation instruments are used to monitor student and teacher behavior, the better. The observation instruments can be used in a variety of ways, including direct observation and videotaped observation of the teaching–learning environment. Irrespective of the manner of implementation, observers should be trained to use the instruments in order to ensure consistent and accurate results. Both the teacher and student observation instruments require the observer to rate the behaviors of the teacher or student depending on which instrument is being used. During each lesson component, the observer determines the quality of the action observed on a scale from 4 to 1, with 4 being exemplary and 1 being unacceptable. Next the observer records the rating and notes strategies for maintaining or improving the ratings associated with each lesson component. As the lesson progresses, the observer continues to watch for, rate, and record the quality of each action.

During a direct observation, a fellow physical education teacher or school administrator can observe the lesson and code the teacher or student actions accordingly. A teacher can also choose to conduct a self-assessment by viewing a videotaped lesson. If a teacher chooses this method for collecting data, he or she needs to take appropriate measures to ensure the quality of the videotaping process. These quality assurance measures include inspecting the video equipment prior to taping the lesson; using the widest camera angle to capture as much of the teaching–learning environment as possible; and placing the video recorder in a secure position so that the safety of the students is not jeopardized. The two methods of observation have proven to be equally effective for providing teachers with important feedback related to maintaining and improving the effectiveness of their teaching–learning environment during a Sport Education season.

Grading in PASE

Assessment is used for many specific purposes in physical education, including the determination of student grades. Most teachers are charged with the responsibility of grading. Grades are intended to quantify student progress and should be derived from sound assessment practices. Unfortunately, many physical education teachers subjectively determine student grades from nonperformance-related variables such as attire, attendance, and attitude. These relatively subjective grading practices represent an area of significant concern for the physical education profession, especially during a time of heightened emphasis on student outcomes and accountability in education. Sound grading practices for physical education should be based primarily on student performance related to predetermined educational goals.

If used appropriately, grades represent the ultimate student accountability system. Siedentop (1994) indicates that "most sport education programs have worked well because teachers have developed clear accountability systems for student performance" (p. 33). If grading systems are to be meaningful for students they must be clear, aligned with program goals, and shared with learners prior to instruction (Siedentop and Tannehill 2000). Physical education teachers can design meaningful grading systems for a Sport Education season by determining appropriate student learning outcomes, establishing criteria for sufficient performance for each outcome, and developing strategies for assessing each outcome.

Because the grading system should be shared with students at the beginning of a season, we suggest using a "season syllabus" like the sample represented on page 40. A season

Table 2.5 PASE Teacher Observation Instrument

Teacher(s) _____

Lesson focus _____

Observer _____

Class/Date _____

Rating scale

4 = exemplary
Action occurred with exceptional quality

3 = acceptable
Action occurred with adequate quality

2 = needs improvement
Action occurred, but with marginal quality

1 = unacceptable
Action did not occur

n/a = not applicable
Action was not necessary to lesson

Instructions: Rate each student action according to the preceding scale and note comments.

Lesson segment	Rating	Teacher actions	Comments
Daily roles and responsibilities check	_____ _____ _____ _____	Provided list of roles and responsibilities Questioned students about role assignments Actively monitored environment Established positive classroom climate via disposition	
Team warm-up and student coaches' meeting	_____ _____ _____ _____ _____	Provided warm-up activities Provided student coaching plan Conducted student coaches' meeting Actively monitored quality and intensity of warm-ups Indirectly facilitated warm-up through fitness trainer	
Team-directed skill and tactics review	_____ _____ _____	Actively monitored quality and intensity of review Indirectly facilitated review through coach Focused teams when necessary	
Teacher-directed skill and tactics instruction	_____ _____ _____ _____ _____ _____ _____ _____	Discussed students' previous performance Stated lesson objectives Provided verbal cues for skills and tactics Demonstrated skills and tactics (whole-part-whole) Linked previous skills and tactics via review Provided explanation of daily rules and official's signals Demonstrated daily rules and official's signals (whole-part-whole) Linked previous rules and official's signals via review	
Team practice	_____ _____ _____ _____	Supplied learning activities Actively monitored quality and intensity of team practice Indirectly facilitated practice through coach Focused teams when necessary	
Application contest	_____ _____ _____ _____ _____ _____	Designed contest to apply daily skills and tactics Provided statistics recording sheet, officials' equipment, and so on Demonstrated contest Used demonstration as practice for scorekeepers and officials Advised officials during contest Managed contest and monitored fair play	
Lesson closure	_____ _____ _____ _____ _____ _____ _____	Refocused on and reviewed skills and tactics, rules. and official's signals Questioned students for comprehension of lesson objectives Allowed for demonstrations Provided feedback on students' progress Previewed upcoming lesson Supplied out-of-class assignments Maintained positive classroom climate throughout lesson	
Individual and team progress report	_____ _____ _____	Provided assessment documents Actively monitored record-keeping procedures Maintained relevance of assessment information through interactions	

Table 2.6 PASE Student Observation Instrument

Team _____

Lesson focus _____

Observer _____

Class/Date _____

Rating scale

4 = exemplary
Action occurred with exceptional quality

3 = acceptable
Action occurred with adequate quality

2 = needs improvement
Action occurred, but with marginal quality

1 = unacceptable
Action should have occurred but did not

n/a = not applicable
Action was not necessary to lesson

Instructions: Rate each student action according to the preceding scale and note comments.

Lesson segment	Rating	Student actions	Comments
Daily roles and responsibilities check	_____ _____ _____ _____	Identified daily roles and responsibilities Prepared for warm-up or student coaches' meeting Managers retrieved necessary materials and equipment All team members wore a team uniform	
Team warm-up and student coaches' meeting	_____ _____ _____	Fitness trainer selected and monitored quality of warm-up Teammates engaged in all components of warm-up Student coaches met with teacher	
Team-directed skill and tactics review		Student coach did the following: _____ Directed team review _____ Monitored individuals' progress on goals _____ Monitored team's progress on goals Teammates did the following: _____ Engaged in review activities (mental, physical, or both)	
Teacher-directed skill and tactics instruction	_____ _____ _____ _____	Observed teacher Asked and answered questions Engaged in demonstrations Participated in intro and review activities	
Team practice		Student coach did the following: _____ Provided guided practice on skill(s) and tactic(s), rules, and official's signals _____ Monitored team's progress on activities _____ Provided positive and specific feedback to teammates _____ Engaged in practice tasks along with teammates Teammates did the following: _____ Engaged in guided practice activities _____ Engaged in skill and tactics practice activities	
Application contest	_____ _____ _____ _____ _____ _____	Student coach prepped team for contest Scorekeepers recorded contest statistics Officials refereed contest Players participated in contest Team members participated fairly Teams respectfully acknowledged one another before and after contest	
Lesson closure	_____ _____ _____	Observed teacher Asked and answered questions Engaged in demonstrations	
Individual and team progress report		Collected, organized, summarized, and recorded the following: _____ Team progress on goals _____ Individual progress on goals _____ Team prepared for next lesson _____ Managers collected and organized materials and equipment	

From *Assessing Student Outcomes in Sport Education: A Pedagogical Approach,* by J.S. Townsend, D.J. Mohr, R.M. Rairigh, and S.M. Bulger, 2003. Copyright 2003 by the American Alliance for Health, Physical Education, Recreation and Dance. Reprinted with permission.

From *Sport Education Seasons* by Sean M. Bulger et al., 2007, Champaign, IL: Human Kinetics.

syllabus clearly communicates the teacher's expectations and provides an overview of the entire season. The following items are commonly included in a Sport Education season syllabus:

- General description of the season
- Learning goals
- Content
- Requirements
- Grading scheme
- Daily calendar

A well-designed season syllabus provides students with a brief summary of the planned learning activities within a season. This description serves as an advance organizer for the season and heightens student awareness and expectations for what lies ahead. Next, the syllabus describes the seasonal goals. Through clear communication of goals at the start of the season, students are more likely to understand, work toward, and achieve the season goals. The season content section of the syllabus specifically identifies the skills and tactics that students can expect to learn as a result of participating in the season. This content outline serves to heighten student motivation in anticipation of learning the skills and tactics for a specific sport or activity. A syllabus also includes the requirements for the season, the point value for each requirement, and the overall grading scale. As this information is provided, students are better able to meet the prescribed season requirements as well as to understand the value of each requirement in relation to the overall grading scale. A season calendar outlines the type and timing of assessment to be used on a day-to-day basis throughout the season. This component of the syllabus supplies students with the information necessary for adequately preparing for each class in advance. In addition, the calendar provides students with a means for monitoring their personal progress throughout the season. Finally, the season requirements are briefly described. This section offers an overview of each requirement and also enables students to prepare for class on a daily basis. As the season progresses, however, additional handouts or instructions will be necessary in order for students to successfully complete many of the season requirements.

BEHAVIOR MANAGEMENT IN PASE

PASE places a great deal of responsibility on students, which can lead to positive increases in student engagement. This is one reason that PASE works so well. This additional student responsibility, however, is sometimes accompanied by concerns regarding behavior and management that are unique to more learner-centered instructional approaches. Accordingly, PASE works best when teachers assume a proactive rather than reactive approach to behavior management. A proactive approach requires the teacher to formulate and implement a well-crafted behavior management plan. On the basis of our experiences with PASE, we have developed a highly effective behavior management plan. This behavior management plan is designed to assist teachers in keeping their students on track to becoming competent, literate, and enthusiastic sportspersons. This section outlines the PASE behavior management plan and provides practical suggestions concerning its implementation.

One of the initial steps in developing a proactive behavior management plan is to establish rules early in a season that clearly outline expectations for appropriate student behavior. Rules should be comprehensive and should be developed with the assistance of your students, but should be limited in number. To supplement existing classroom rules we recommend the use of a PASE Fair Play Agreement (see p. 55) that communicates behavioral expectations for the season. By completing this contract, students are acknowledging that they understand the behavioral criteria associated with fair play and pledge that they will adhere to the criteria or accept the associated consequences.

The next step for developing a behavior management plan is to create and establish classroom routines early in a season. Routines refer to the procedures used to complete commonly occurring classroom events, such as dressing, taking attendance, warming up, transitioning from place to place, handling equipment, and so forth. While a number of these types of routines are included in every physical education lesson, certain routines are unique to PASE (see table 2.2) and may represent novel behavioral challenges for your students. Because students assume greater responsibility for the management of the teaching–learning environment during a PASE lesson, it will be important to establish these routines early in a season. Not only must expectations for all routines be clearly demonstrated and practiced, but also students should be held accountable for successfully completing routines as required.

To assist you in presenting classroom rules and routines in an effective and efficient manner, we have developed a PASE management lesson (see chapter 3 for a more detailed description of this lesson) that can be incorporated at the start of each season. This lesson familiarizes students with the logistical considerations of the PASE lesson format and provides frequent opportunities for engagement with the associated rules and routines. In combination with continual teacher supervision and reinforcement, this introductory lesson will contribute to reduced management time across the rest of the season and more frequent opportunities for students to actively engage in the instructional content.

In previous sections of this text, we addressed the importance of increased student accountability within the PASE framework. As you read the previous passages on rules and routines, you were probably asking "How can I best hold my students accountable for assuming so much responsibility and for following the season rules and routines?" Well, we have the answer to that very question: the PASE accountability system. Over the years, this system has evolved into a highly effective means for holding students accountable. The accountability system is based on the following three basic generalized premises:

1. Grades are powerful motivators.
2. Students like to be acknowledged by the teacher.
3. Students want to be accepted by a peer group.

We have carefully accounted for each of these factors in the PASE accountability system.

Grades represent the ultimate in individual accountability for students. A sound grading scheme, based on individual student performance in relation to predetermined goals, remains a critical component of the PASE accountability system (see requirements, points, and grading scale, pp. 109-111 and p. 40). In this format, grades take on enhanced meaning for both teachers and their students when compared to more traditional forms of grading in physical education. As you might expect, students and teachers have responded favorably to this type of highly structured grading system. Grades alone, however, may not be enough to motivate all students to make the most appropriate decisions possible within your class.

While the PASE grading scheme motivates students to make more responsible choices than traditional grading schemes do, we strongly recommend supplementing the grading with other behavior modification strategies. Unlike most accountability systems, in which students are recognized only for inappropriate behavior, the PASE accountability system positively pinpoints and rewards appropriate behavior as well. The dualistic nature of the PASE accountability system, in which both the positive and negative consequences are applied in recognition of students' individual choices, makes the system unique.

The consequences, both positive and negative, materialize in the form of a team point system. The team point system is based on student performance in each of the following categories: (a) the daily game (application contest), (b) individual role performance, (c) fair play, and (d) rule infractions. Each of the categories corresponds with one of the PASE season goals: competency, literacy, and enthusiasm. The team point system is intended to reinforce student achievement of the overall season goals. Bonus team points can also be awarded for exemplary behaviors at the teacher's discretion (e.g., a show of exceptional sportspersonship).

The points earned in all four categories are calculated at the end of each day's lesson and are added together to determine each team's daily total. Team points are accumulated across each lesson. Team point totals at the end of the season determine the "season champion" as opposed to more typical ways of determining a unit champion, such as the winner of the class tournament. In PASE, the season champions are the most competent, literate, and enthusiastic team. Additionally, team point totals in the form of season-ending team standings are included as an integral part of the grading scheme (see p. 40). It is important to note, however, that final team standings result in the awarding of bonus points to an individual's season grade. In the end, a team's final standing can only benefit an individual student's grade, not detract from it.

To help you keep track of each team's daily points and accumulated totals, we have provided the PASE Daily Team Points Summary sheet on page 43. Furthermore, you should use available wall space for posting daily team point totals so that students know where they stand relative to other teams throughout the entire season. The posting of team points serves as a powerful motivator to the students, perhaps more so than individual grades in some instances.

As students gain a greater understanding of how the team point system works, each point becomes more important to them from a motivational and competitive standpoint. Accordingly, each team member's point-earning potential becomes increasingly valuable to the team. As a result, potentially marginalized students become more accepted by and affiliated with their team because they can contribute in ways that may not have been possible under more traditional team competition formats in physical education (e.g., winner-take-all tournament format).

In conclusion, PASE works best when teachers take a proactive approach to behavior management. A proactive approach requires that the teacher actively work out and successfully implement a well-crafted behavior management plan. The PASE behavior management plan is one such plan that is designed to assist you in keeping your students on track to becoming competent, literate, and enthusiastic sportspersons.

ORGANIZATIONAL CONSIDERATIONS IN PASE

Because PASE is a comprehensive and complex instructional system and may represent a departure from what you and your students have typically used in physical education, it is critical to be well prepared and highly organized before beginning a season. In order to help you in this regard, the next section outlines the following organizational considerations in PASE: organization of instructional materials, organization of the home court or field area, and organization of the eight PASE lesson components.

Many teachers have successfully implemented PASE seasons. Successful implementation was, in part, a result of adequate organization of the instructional materials. Adequate organization of instructional materials assists the teacher and students in acquiring and using the right tools for the right job at the right time. While your options for organizing instructional materials are relatively endless and will depend on your specific teaching context, we have chosen, in part due to space limitations, to restrict our discussion to two strategies that have consistently worked well.

Organizational Strategy 1

Obtain a single vertical file container for each class that you teach and label it accordingly. For example, if you teach four classes, obtain four vertical file containers. Include in this container a vertical file per team and label the files accordingly. For example, if within one class you have six teams, then place six vertical files in the container. Within each file include a team folder to organize that particular team's instructional materials and label it accordingly. Each team folder, for instance, might include the following PASE instructional materials:

- The team membership inventory and fair play agreement (see p. 55)
- The season roles and responsibilities recording sheet (see p. 53)
- The attendance recording sheet (see p. 57)
- The team fitness recording sheet (see p. 60)
- The team activity task card recording sheet (see p. 63)
- The student coaching plans and activity task cards (see pp. 73 and 74, respectively.)

In this organizational strategy the folders are team folders, and as such they contain more team-oriented types of data collection forms. This strategy is easily implemented and may serve as an initial step in the organizational process as you first conduct a PASE season. However, there is a possible limitation of having only team folders. Team folders must house multiple forms for an entire team, and there may not be enough space for many of the individual-oriented type of data collection forms. Accordingly, this strategy may not allow for more individualized, descriptive, and detailed information to be collected.

Organizational Strategy 2

Obtain a single vertical file container for each team within each class that you teach and label it accordingly. For example, if you teach four classes with four teams in each class, then obtain 16 vertical file containers. In each team's container include one vertical file. Within the file include one team folder and an individual folder per team member to organize that particular team's instructional materials, and label them accordingly. For example, if you have four people to a team, you will need a total of five folders: one team folder and four individual folders. Within each team folder you might include any team-oriented type of data collection form. Each of the individual folders, however, should include any individual-oriented type of data collection form. This folder might include, but would not be limited to, the following PASE instructional materials:

- The season syllabus (see p. 40)
- The individual responsibility level recording sheet (see p. 51)
- The personal fitness recording sheet (see p. 59)
- The individual activity task card recording sheet (see p. 62)

In this organizational strategy there are both team and individual folders. Therefore, both team- and individual-oriented types of data can be collected. Accordingly, this strategy allows for more individualized, descriptive, and detailed information to be collected. This strategy is somewhat more complex than strategy 1 and may require additional instruction and practice time for students to master.

Regardless of the strategy you choose to organize the PASE instructional materials, several common strategies have proven beneficial. We suggest that you color-code folders and as many of the instructional materials as possible. For example, the blue team's folders should be blue and should be stored in a blue vertical file container. In addition, you may choose to photocopy data collection forms on blue paper. As you can imagine, color-coding of materials helps to alleviate a host of potential management and organizational problems. Because resources are limited, it is critical that you exercise frugality when copying materials and that you get service from certain instructional materials season after season. When possible, we recommend photocopying materials front to back to limit the use of excess paper. To ensure that materials can withstand the wear and tear of repeated use, you can laminate instructional materials such as the PASE fitness activities, the student coaching plans, and the individual activity task cards. We also advise that you develop protocols for managing the instructional materials. These protocols should then be taught during the management lesson, and students must continually be held accountable for abiding by the established management protocols throughout the remainder of the season.

In addition to developing and implementing a strategy for organizing the PASE instructional materials, it is necessary to contemplate the organization of the teams' home court or field areas. Extremely well-organized team home areas are essential for safe, efficient, and effective use of space. Keeping students safe should be your first order of business, and one way to ensure student safety is to maintain a well-organized team home area. The boundaries for each home area should be clearly marked so that students know exactly where they can and cannot go. Also, a protocol for entering other teams' home areas, to retrieve an errant ball, for example, should be established. Because students are required to use more materials than they may be accustomed to, protocols for storing papers, pencils, folders, balls, and other materials and equipment must also be developed. These and other such safety protocols should be taught and practiced during the management lesson.

If indoors, a team's home area walls should be devoted to affiliation materials such as team posters, flags, pictures, and so forth. In addition, various instructional materials can be posted on the walls, such as role assignments, fitness activities, official's signals, and activity task cards. Materials that are hung should be securely fastened to the wall to ensure the safety of the teams' home areas.

In order to maximize the amount of lesson time devoted to student engagement and minimize the amount of time that students spend disengaged, it is imperative that the teacher organize and use time and space effectively. Students must learn where to go and what to do during each of the eight PASE lesson components. As students enter the playing facility they immediately report to their team's home court or field area. Next students identify their daily role and corresponding responsibilities. In the home area the fitness trainer organizes and leads the team warm-up, while the student coaches report to a common area for the student coaches' meeting with the teacher. Once the warm-up and coaches' meeting conclude, the teams remain in the home area and engage in a team-directed skill and tactics review. Afterward, the students move to a common area and the teacher provides the daily skill and tactics orientation. Following this orientation, students return to their home areas for both team practice and the daily application contest. Students come back to the common area for the lesson closure and progress-reporting phases of the lesson. During a typical PASE lesson, students transition from place to place a number of times. This transition time can add up, thus detracting from time that might be spent in a more productive fashion. To reduce transition time, teachers can use countdowns and award bonus team points to teams that collectively transition to a designated area within a specified time limit.

In conclusion, PASE may be a departure from what you and your students have typically been used to in physical education. This means that the PASE is a change from the ordinary, and change is rarely easy for teachers or students. We believe, however, that you and your students will find the PASE a welcome change. Because of this change, it is important to be well prepared and highly organized before you implement a season. It is equally important to remain well prepared and highly organized throughout the season. Being well prepared and highly organized is time-consuming and labor-intensive at first, but such dedication will pay dividends for both you and your students. You and your students will reap the benefits early in your initial season, and as a result, preparation and organization will become increasingly easy as subsequent seasons are implemented. Eventually, the preparation and organization will become "second nature," and PASE will be regarded as the "typical" way in which physical education is taught within your program.

SEQUENCING OF SEASONS

To increase the likelihood that both you and your students will experience success during the PASE seasons, and to ensure that the model is put into action appropriately, you may choose to use the experimental-progressive approach to implementing the model as discussed earlier in this chapter in the section "PASE Lesson Planning," pages 10-16. Teachers unfamiliar with PASE have used this implementation strategy with great success. The sequence in which the seasons are implemented can have a significant impact on the successful implementation of PASE as well. This section outlines considerations for sequencing PASE seasons.

The design of a PASE season is very comprehensive and systematic. We have designed PASE seasons this way to ensure that within a single season students become competent, literate, and enthusiastic sportspersons. If you choose to teach only one season, there is a good chance that your students will experience success. If you choose to teach one season followed by several others, this degree of success will be exponentially increased. Greater success comes from a transfer of leaning about how PASE works. The transfer of learning is a result of the systematic and streamlined design within and across PASE seasons.

We suggest that you always teach the PASE fitness education season before teaching any other PASE season. We also advocate that this season be taught at the beginning of the school year if possible, although this is not a hard-and-fast requirement. This season should be the initial season because it provides various types of significant foundational information that will be used during subsequent seasons. This foundational information is introduced in the fitness education season and then systematically revisited during subsequent seasons. The foundational information most critical to the efficient implementation of subsequent seasons is as follows: information about fitness testing, information about fitness warm-ups, and general information about the PASE season framework.

The PASE fitness education season has three primary goals that are related to sequencing of seasons. Each of the goals relates to the foundational information just outlined. First, the PASE fitness education season is designed to teach students about health-related fitness. Students learn about each of the components of health-related fitness, how to assess each component, and how to improve each component. This knowledge is critical to the successful implementation of subsequent seasons because it prepares students for engaging in a pretest called the skills and fitness combine. During the combine, student pairs complete various fitness and skills tests. The fitness tests are the same ones that were previously practiced and learned during the PASE fitness education season. After the combine, students set data-based goals and engage in activities throughout the remainder of the season in order to achieve their goals. Near the end of each season, students repeat the combine and determine the degree to which they achieved their goals. If the fitness education season is not taught first, then students are ill prepared to engage in the combine and the associated activities. In this case, time must be taken to teach the fitness test items and corresponding activities within the season during which the combine takes place. Although this is not impossible to do, it is much more efficient to implement the fitness education season before any other season.

Another reason the PASE fitness education season should be taught first is that the season is designed to teach students why an appropriate warm-up is essential and how to warm up properly. In subsequent seasons students engage in a warm-up on a daily basis. The warm-up activities are similar to the ones that were previously practiced and learned during the PASE fitness education season. In addition, the warm-up activities are related to the components of fitness that were previously learned in the fitness education season. Once students complete the fitness education season, they are more capable of engaging in the daily fitness warm-up. This is important because the warm-up is a vital lesson component of the PASE lesson framework. If the fitness education season is not taught first, then students are not prepared to engage in the daily fitness warm-up. In this instance, the teacher must take time to teach the theoretical underpinnings and practical applications associated with the warm-up within the season during which the warm-ups take place. Although this is not impossible, it is more practical to implement the fitness education season before any other season.

Lastly, the PASE fitness education season should be taught first because the season is designed to systematically introduce the student to the logistics of a PASE season. Students learn important general information that will transfer to subsequent seasons and lead to improved teacher and student performance. For example, the teacher and his or her students learn about their responsibilities during each of the eight PASE lesson components. They learn about the rules and routines specific to a PASE season, as well as the PASE behavior management plan. They learn about the PASE instructional materials. They learn about the organization of the home court or field area and other instructional spaces. In general, everything that the teacher and students learn during the PASE fitness education season aids them in being better prepared for subsequent seasons. Throughout the fitness education season the teacher and students become more familiar with the intricacies of the PASE. Enhanced familiarity leads to greater teacher and student performance and increasingly smooth transitions within and across subsequent seasons. While it is not impossible to teach the logistics of a season without first having taught the fitness education season, it is more realistic to implement the fitness education season before any other season.

As you can see, it is important to teach the fitness education season first. If you do not, then you must account for fitness testing, warm-up, and logistical information within the season currently being taught. While it may be possible to account for any one of these informational areas alone, simultaneously accounting for all three represents a daunting task. You can thwart this potential problem, however, by appropriately sequencing the manner in which you introduce PASE seasons. Because the sequence with which the seasons are implemented can have a significant impact on the successful implementation of PASE, we suggest teaching the PASE fitness education season at the beginning of the school year.

Note: From an editorial standpoint, the decision was made to include the basketball season within this book rather than the fitness education season because it represents a more typical application of Sport Education. Furthermore, basketball is widely taught in school physical education, and most teachers are very familiar with the associated content. The fitness education season can be found on the bound-in CD-ROM.

Once the fitness education season is complete, you can choose to teach any PASE season that you desire. You should base this decision on a number of factors, including, but not limited to, seasonality, facilities, equipment, space, characteristics and number of students, student interest in and teacher knowledge of the content, and so forth. We believe that the successes you experience during the first season will only be multiplied in your second season.

SUMMARY

This chapter provided a detailed explanation of the PASE guidelines for season planning, lesson planning, and assessment. Additionally, we presented a number of behavior management and organizational strategies that physical educators have successfully employed to help establish an effective teaching–learning environment when using Sport Education. Given the relative complexity of this instructional approach compared to more traditional methods of teaching physical education, it is important that you fully understand the curricular and instructional issues presented in this chapter before proceeding to season implementation, the topic addressed in the following chapters.

Setting the PASE: Implementing a Season

The first-period bell resonates through the halls. Students enter the gym at a feverish pace, pausing only momentarily to gaze at the current team standings and contemplating their strategy for the day. Student fitness trainers prompt their teammates to warm up well because today is a very important day in physical education class. Student coaches gather their plans and confer with the teacher about the day's events. Students move efficiently into a team review and strategy session, and then on to a bit of instruction from the teacher. Enthusiasm and encouragement bound from home court to home court as each team engages in team practice with little time wasted. Students remain focused and work to prepare for the day's game. Nearing the end of team practice, student officials and scorekeepers meet with the teacher for last-minute preparations before the game. The teacher explains the day's game, and players, officials, and scorekeepers assume their posts. Players shake hands and on the official's signal the game begins. Game performance is rather good, and students are enjoying much success. Cheers and encouragement come from the sidelines. After the game students once again shake hands, coaches sign off on the scorecards, and officials meet with the teacher. The teacher conducts a brief closure. Students then quickly return to their home court and complete their daily postlesson assessments. As the lesson comes to a close the teacher overhears teams strategizing for the following day. Just before the second-period bell, team cheers can be heard coming from all corners of the gymnasium.

PREPARING FOR THE SEASON

Does this sound like a typical lesson in your physical education program? If so, great! If not, do not worry, as the following sections will assist you in preparing to experience this scenario on a daily basis. As you might expect, the ultimate success or failure of a PASE season will largely be determined by the teacher's ability and willingness to plan. This preseason planning is particularly critical in relation to the development of a season syllabus, block plan, grade book, and daily team points scoring summary sheet, all of which are provided for each season in the book/CD-ROM package.

PASE Season Syllabus

In educational settings, the teacher generally assigns grades that are indicative of a student's performance at the culmination of an instructional unit. In the best-case scenario, the measures used to evaluate student performance are objective and formative in nature. In other words, there are specific criteria for measuring performance, and the students have multiple opportunities to demonstrate their attainment of objectives across the instructional period. Unfortunately, these guidelines are not always adhered to, and student evaluation is often based on nonperformance-related variables such as attire, attendance, and attitude. Appropriate grading practices should be based primarily on student performance in relation to predetermined educational goals.

The PASE Season Syllabus on page 40 lets students know what they will be learning and how performance will be evaluated. The syllabus also provides students with a brief summary of the learning activities that are planned for the season. The syllabus serves as an advance organizer for the season and helps to spark students' interest in their learning. The syllabus is divided into the following sections:

1. General description of the season
2. Season learning goals
3. Season content
4. Season requirements
5. Grading scheme
6. Daily calendar

These sections provide a comprehensive overview of the entire PASE season so that students will know what they will be learning and when the learning will occur.

In addition to the description, goals, and content outline, the season syllabus describes the specific learning requirements that students complete during the season. The season requirements briefly summarize the learning activities that the students will eventually engage in. Each requirement is labeled and an associated point value is assigned. Along with these requirements, the students receive a daily calendar that indicates the lesson during which each activity will be completed. This calendar provides students with important information that allows them to prepare in advance for each class session. The calendar also affords the students a systematic method for monitoring their personal progress across the season. As the season progresses, however, additional handouts and explanations may be needed in order for students to successfully complete many of the requirements.

PASE Block Plan

Another important characteristic of PASE is authentic season scheduling. An authentic schedule provides students with complete practice and competition information. This formalized schedule enables teams to maximize their practice time in order to prepare for upcoming competitions. This emphasis on preparation heightens the authentic nature of the PASE season by promoting student interest and excitement regarding upcoming application contests (games) involving other teams. A block plan allows for the students to quickly reference the skills and tactics that will be the focus as well as the type of application contests they will engage in. In addition, the students can refer to the official's signals that will be of importance during that particular lesson's scheduled learning activities. The index numbers in the "Official's signals" column refer to the numbers on the PASE Official's Signals Index (p. 44) and Pocket Reference (p. 61). A block plan also enables the teacher to systematically sequence the skills and tactics for his or her students, thus providing them with an opportunity to see how skills and tactics are interconnected. The PASE Block Plan is designed to replicate a typical sport season and is divided into the following three phases: a preseason, an in-season, and a postseason (see p. 41). The block plan serves to inform both students and teacher of skills and tactics to be learned, practiced, and assessed in future lessons and may be shared with students at the beginning of the season if the teacher chooses to do so.

PASE Grade Book

Assessment in physical education is used for many different purposes, including assigning students grades. Teachers are usually given this responsibility but are rarely shown how to organize, manage, and summarize grading scores collected across a unit of instruction. The PASE Grade Book is provided as a simple method for using individual student scores to determine an overall performance grade (see p. 42; an electronic version of the grade book has been provided on the accompanying CD-ROM). Keep in mind that these grades should be a result of performance-related outcomes that are consistent with the overall goals of the PASE season. The grade book has been designed using a computer-based spreadsheet that allows the teacher to simply enter scores and tabulate grades throughout a season. One benefit of an electronic grade book is that the scores are automatically calculated upon entry and as you complete your final assessment, the season grades are automatically calculated. This easy-to-use format allows the teacher to modify or adjust recorded scores if needed without the inefficiency and potential mess of erasing and re-recording in a traditional grade book. Furthermore, if a teacher needs to modify the number of requirements, an electronic grade book affords the ease of simply deleting a requirement without having to draw lines through it as in a more traditional paper version of record keeping. An additional feature of the PASE Grade Book is the possible use of color coding to indicate special notations. Selected notations could include absences, incomplete assessment or performance, unsportspersonlike conduct, tardiness or lack of preparation, off-task behavior, or excused nonparticipation. Teachers find these types of notations to be invaluable in providing support for the assigning of grades. The grade book includes a column for each requirement (which can be cross-referenced with the PASE Season Syllabus) and is labeled with the lesson and the date during which the lesson takes place. The grade book is an efficient and effective tool for organizing and managing learning data across the season and provides an easy-to-use template for calculating student performance grades both throughout and at the season's end.

PASE Daily Team Points Summary Sheet

As previously discussed, an effective behavioral management system is critical to the successful implementation of a PASE season. The awarding or deducting of team points as a means for motivating students and modifying and maintaining behavior is an important component of this system. The teacher will have to be well organized in order to keep accurate track of which teams are earning and losing points. The PASE Daily Team Points Summary sheet on page 43 is designed to organize and manage this type of information. The three categories in which a team can earn points on a daily basis are role performance, fair play, and application contests. The fourth category is reserved for team point deductions. A team of seven, for example, can earn up to 21 points daily if each team member performs his or her role to criteria and demonstrates the characteristics of fair play throughout the lesson, and if his or her team comes in first during the application contest. Points can be deducted if there is a deficiency in any of these categories. In the event that a student is absent, a teammate can fill the assigned role so that the team can still earn the total points (7 points).

The policy regarding student absences holds true for fair play points as well. If all students present on a team display the required characteristics of fair play across the lesson, the team receives the full fair play points (7 points). The application contest points refer to the place in which each team finishes during the daily competitions. This will vary based upon a team's success each lesson. The final section is labeled "Team point deductions." It is important for students to realize the impact that individual behaviors have on the group as a whole. This is where the saying "There is no 'I' in team" takes on meaning. For each offense that a team commits, such as off-task behavior or breaking of class rules, the associated number of points will be deducted from their team score. The progressive nature of the deductions encourages a team to deal with the offenses in a responsible way or deal with the consequences. In order to maintain student focus and to shape the students' behavior, the offenses should not reset at the end of each lesson. If during lesson 2 a team commits their first offense, reducing their score by 1 point, then the next time an offense occurs they should move to a penalty associated with the second offense (3 points) even if it is several lessons later. This heightens students' awareness of their personal decision making. Likewise they become less inclined to demonstrate off-task behavior again because the consequence is more severe. Resetting the count each lesson essentially gives the team a "freebie" without a penalty. The PASE Daily Team Points Summary allows the teacher to quickly record and tabulate a team's daily and cumulative score across the season.

PASE Official's Signals Index

As part of an effort to develop knowledgeable games players, it is important that students learn to self-regulate their own game play and competitions. A theme that runs throughout PASE is systematic progression. Students should learn to officiate and manage competitions in a progressive fashion as well. It is important that students be provided an opportunity to learn how to manage a contest and to do so using the appropriate official's signals. This additional level of understanding enables them to abide by the rules and self-regulate the games in which they are engaged. The PASE Official's Signals Index on page 44 provides a reference for both the teacher and students regarding which fouls, violations, scoring, and administrative calls are important to a particular sport. The index is not intended as an exhaustive list of officiating signals, but it highlights those that are considered to represent the basic rules and signals needed in order to participate in a given sport. This index can be placed in the home court or field area and can be crossed-referenced with the PASE Pocket Ref on page 61. It is not intended that all of these signals be taught in a single lesson; rather they should be integrated systematically and progressively across the season (see PASE Block Plan on p. 41). When students are allowed and encouraged to self-regulate their own game play, we are moving toward creating more knowledgeable games players.

A CROSS-SECTIONAL REPRESENTATION OF A PASE SEASON

So far you have become familiar with what PASE is and why it has the potential to revolutionize physical education as we know it: the PASE lesson framework, behavior management in the PASE, and organizational and season sequencing considerations in the PASE. We have not yet, however, presented an overview of a typical season. Accordingly, you have probably asked yourself more than once, "What does a PASE season really look like?"

This is a good question because a PASE season will typically consist of 20 or more lessons, with a preseason, an in-season, and a postseason. Because of the scope and complexity of a PASE season, it is important we answer that question by providing you with the "big picture" or an overview of a typical season. In this section we describe a cross section of lessons from a PASE season rather than describing every single lesson. This cross-sectional perspective provides a detailed look at selected parts that you will find in most PASE seasons. It is an efficient means for providing a greater understanding of the interrelationships within and across an entire PASE season without having to explain each lesson. To give you an overview, we have selected the most common sections of a PASE season. These sections consist of

- the PASE skills and fitness pre- and post-combines,
- the PASE management lesson,
- the PASE skill and tactical development lessons,
- the PASE skill and tactical review lessons,
- the PASE postseason tournament lessons, and
- the PASE awards and festival day lesson.

PASE Skills and Fitness Combine

The PASE Skills and Fitness Combine is designed for two purposes. The first is to introduce skills and fitness concepts related to the sport activity being taught. These sport-specific skill and fitness concepts will be important for students who want to experience success during the sport season. In addition, they give students baseline information for setting personal and team goals across the season. The second purpose is to provide information that can be used to objectively select even teams.

The skills and fitness combine is a collection of fitness and skill assessments that provide a baseline of the student's ability prior to instruction. The fitness assessments are aligned with *FITNESSGRAM* 8.0 (Cooper Institute for Aerobics Research 2004) and include health-related fitness activities for cardiovascular endurance, body composition, flexibility, muscular strength, and muscular endurance. With use of the PASE materials, combine stations 1 through 8 always relate to *FITNESSGRAM* 8.0 and the associated components of health-related physical fitness (e.g., PASE Skills and Fitness Combine Station Task Card 5: Push-Up, on p. 46). Measures of skill-related physical fitness, comprising power, agility, speed, balance, etc. are also included. These assessment stations will always be numbers 9 through 12 regardless of the sport content. Finally, the skill assessment stations, which will always be 13 and higher, are specific to the sport season in which your students are currently engaged.

During the combine, students should move in pairs throughout the playing area, collecting their own skill and fitness data and recording the data using the PASE Skills and Fitness Combine Recording Sheet as seen on page 45. The sheet is designed to accommodate all of the student's combine scores. Upon completing a pre-combine station, the student should immediately set a personal goal to be reached during the post-combine assessment. The students will also be able to determine whether they have met the criteria for the healthy fitness zone for each particular health-related fitness activity.

As the students move through the assessment area, each station (assessment) will be labeled with a skills and fitness combine task card. Each assessment card provides a variety of information including instructions, rules, how to score, time limits, a descriptive picture, learning cues, and the *FITNESSGRAM* 8.0 healthy fitness zones for both males and females. Each pair of students should be allowed to move through the combine at their own pace. If time does not allow the completion of the entire combine in one class setting, it is recommended that the combine be split into a fitness assessment lesson and a skill assessment lesson. This should provide ample time to complete the combine. The importance of allowing students time to complete all stations is that this lesson will be repeated later in the season. It is repeated so that the information collected in the pre-combine can be compared to the information collected at the post-combine. Teacher and students alike can then determine improvement and goal attainment. This information is reliable, however, only if the same assessment activities are utilized with the same criteria and setup during both assessment sessions. A space is provided at the end of lesson 1 to document any modifications you make to the combine organization so that the required degree of consistency between pre- and post-combines is achieved.

The second purpose of this skills and fitness combine is to provide information that will aid in team selection. Included in the instructional materials is a PASE Skills and Fitness Combine Draft Composite sheet (see p. 48). The purpose of this worksheet is to allow selected students to create a drafting order for the players they would like to select for their team. The draft composite is designed so that the student coach can list the names of classmates, determine what order he or she would draft them in, and record any notes that may aid in the decision making. This information will allow student coaches or team selectors to make informed decisions about their classmates with regard to skill ability and fitness levels. Students who have been chosen as student coach or team selector should be reminded that their draft order and associated notes are to remain confidential. As such, the draft composites should be collected at the end of the combine lesson and returned to students during the draft. The draft procedures should take place outside of physical education class and should involve only those student coaches or team selectors who completed a draft composite during the skills and fitness pre-combine. This draft may take place before or after school or even during an in-school special time determined by the teacher. To complete the draft each student coach in an alternating method should select one person to be on a team. This process continues until all members of the class have been selected. Once the teams have been determined, the teacher will place each of those teams into a pot for a drawing. This ensures that each coach or selector drafts the most capable team possible since coaches or selectors have no idea which team they will be coaching. Once teams have been drawn, the draft composite sheet should be collected. Again, students should be reminded of the importance of confidentiality and also that they have the opportunity to be truly responsible by maintaining such confidentiality.

PASE Management Lesson

Following the skills and fitness combine and the drafting of teams, students will be introduced to the rules and PASE-specific routines of the sport season. First, students should be placed upon their new team as determined by the draft. Next, the teacher should supply each student with a PASE Season Syllabus (see p. 40) and discuss the expectations for the upcoming season. Once this is complete, students will be ready to engage in a mock lesson. The management lesson is designed to walk students through each of the eight PASE lesson components. The walk-through provides students with information about the routines and individual responsibilities for a particular lesson segment. An entire lesson is dedicated to this so that all of the routines and associated responsibilities can be practiced and learned. While this may take some initial time to teach, dividends will accrue later in the season when more time can be spent on practice and application contests, not on managerial procedures. Furthermore, once this system is taught well one time, the seasons that follow will require fewer explanations and setup time.

During this management day, students, as teams, should be introduced to all assessment and instructional materials that are used in a particular lesson segment. During this management day, students will use the information for the upcoming lesson (lesson 3 in the basketball season). For example, as students are taught about how to check their role (PASE lesson segment 1), they should determine their role for lesson 3. This will prepare them for the following lesson and make the experience more authentic. For each lesson segment the teacher should be addressing the following questions:

- Where do students go?
- What do students do?
- When and how do students fulfill role requirements in that segment?
- What information should be recorded if any?
- How do students record the required information?
- What should students do if they need assistance during a particular lesson segment?

Once each of these questions is answered for all eight lesson segments, the students will engage in their first team competition called an application contest. As described earlier, an application contest is designed to give students an opportunity to apply during a competition the information that has been learned within a lesson. Since the management content is focused on rules and routines, the team competition will spotlight this information. The PASE Application Contest for lesson 2 is cognitive in nature (see form 3.1) and will require students to work as a team to answer specific questions about the mock lesson they just experienced. They will be required to sort through many of the instructional materials to answer questions. This application contest can be likened to a scavenger hunt. With that in mind, it will be paramount that the teacher be prepared for this lesson with all the materials that will be used. This contest will gauge each team's ability to work together and to assess their understanding of the PASE lesson format. Once students are comfortable with what to expect, the teacher should be prepared to provide feedback to students over the next few lessons to gain team adherence to protocols. Use of team points will encourage this task adherence. The management lesson is the foundation of the PASE instructional framework. It is important that the rules and routines be learned so that teacher and students can spend more time focused on learning the sport activity.

Form 3.1   PASE Basketball Cognitive Application Contest 2

Score

_____ / 20

Instructions

- As a team, respond to each of the following statements.
- Your team's goal is to respond to all of the statements correctly.
- Because your team is competing with the other teams during this contest, your chances of winning the contest increase with number of statements answered correctly.
- Best of luck!

1. Shade in your home court area on the basketball floor diagram to the right.

2. List your team members' names and roles for lesson 3 in the space provided.

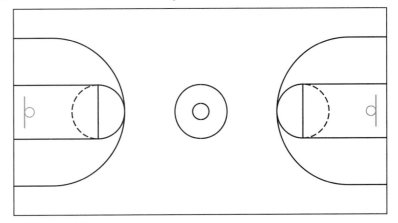

Name	Role	Name	Role

3. On the basketball floor diagram above, place an "X" where the coaches' meeting will be held each day.

4. Identify the muscles stretched if your team chose flexibility workout **Flx 2** during the team warm-up segment of the lesson.

Muscle(s) 1:	Muscle(s) 2:	Muscle(s) 3:	Muscle(s) 4:

5. Identify the following items for the T-run:

Criteria	Scoring	Conditions
•	•	•
•	•	•
•	•	•

6. List one of the "Keys to Success" from the coaching plan for lesson 3:

7. List the three "Official's Signals" to be learned for lesson 3:

Official's signal (4)	Official's signal (8)	Official's signal (1)

8. What takes place after the warm-up and coaches' meeting segment of the daily lesson?

(continued)

9. Shade in the area on the basketball floor diagram where teacher instruction will take place each day. Denote this shaded area with the letters "T.I."

10. Who is responsible for directing team practice?

11. Locate the PASE Activity Task Card for lesson 3. Identify who is responsible for the evaluation of student performance for tasks 3-6, 9-11, 13, 14, and 17-19; for tasks 7 and 15; and for tasks 1, 2, 8, 12, 16, 20, and 21.

Tasks 3-6, 9-11, 13, 14, and 17-19	Tasks 7 and 15	Tasks 1, 2, 8, 12, 16, 20, and 21
•	•	•

12. Locate an Individual Activity Task Card Recording Sheet. Who is responsible for certifying that each team member has successfully completed the tasks for a given lesson? How is the certification noted?

Who certifies?	How certified?
•	•

13. During a typical application contest, what two roles take on a majority of the responsibility to ensure that rules are followed and that scores are accurately recorded?

Role 1?	Role 2?
•	•

14. Identify the skill(s) and tactic(s) to be applied during the PASE Application Contest for lesson 3.

15. Locate the PASE Application Contest Scorecard for lesson 3. List the items that should be filled in on this scorecard.

16. Complete the PASE Individual Responsibility Level (IRL) assessment for lesson 2 (today's lesson).

17. Complete the PASE Team Membership Inventory.

18. Complete the PASE Fair Play Agreement.

19. Complete the PASE Basketball Attendance Recording Sheet.

20. Identify the following codes using the attendance information key on the PASE Basketball Attendance Recording Sheet.

"P"	"L"	"E"	"A"

Skill and Tactics Instruction Lessons

The preseason segment of the PASE season is devoted to improving fitness levels as well as learning the skills and tactics of a sport activity. This is the time when teams prepare for the competitions that occur during the in-season and postseason tournaments. Each lesson follows the same template so that once students have mastered this routine, little instructional time should be wasted. Each skill and tactics instructional lesson is complete with

- a PASE lesson plan (see p. 70),
- graphics and cues (see p. 72),
- student coaching plan (see p. 73),
- activity task card (see p. 74), and
- application contest description and scorecard (see pp. 76 and 78, respectively).

These instructional materials collectively make up the resources needed for this type of lesson.

The materials intended for teacher use are the lesson plan, graphics and cues card, and application contest description. The lesson plan gives the teacher a sequenced list of objectives and activities to take place as well as questions to pose to students to check for their understanding of content. It also provides a list of instructional materials that will be passed out and collected during a particular lesson. The graphics and cues card provides a picture of the skill or tactic to be learned, as well as a description that contextualizes the use of the skill or tactic. In addition, critical features are listed that will aid in teaching the skill or tactic, as well as instructional cues that are meant for communicating with students. The application contest description gives the teacher detailed rules and scoring caveats. Included is a diagram of what the application contest looks like, as well as guidelines for student officials and scorekeepers. The application contest description can also be provided to the student coach of each team prior to the daily application contest.

The materials intended for student use are the student coaching plan, activity task card, and application contest scorecard. The coaching plan is a student version of the teacher's lesson plan. It includes the skills and tactics to be learned and corresponding instructional cues for each. It also provides student coaches with some hints for a successful team practice, as well as the official's signals that will be focused on during the lesson. The coach should refer to this card when providing feedback to teammates during practice and competitions. The activity task card is a progressive, hierarchically sequenced list of learning tasks that systematically teach students the skill or tactics of the lesson. Individual or team activity task card recording sheets (see pp. 62 and 63, respectively) can be used in conjunction with this task card. There are several embedded levels of task accountability built into the activity task card to promote quality task adherence. Finally, the application contest scorecard is provided for students to collect their team information during the daily application contest. This sheet is introduced in a systematically progressive fashion in that only the nonshaded areas of each scorecard should be filled out. The skill and tactics lessons are designed to improve a student's skill ability and tactical awareness and to enhance levels of fitness.

Review Lessons

During the preseason segment of the PASE season, amidst the skill and tactical lessons, will be review lessons. The purpose of these lessons are to allow students an opportunity to practice and improve upon the skills and tactics learned to that point without having to attend to learning new information. It is important during skill and tactics instruction that ample time be provided to practice skills and tactics without the need to worry about adding other skills and tactics to students' repertoires. Review lessons allow students a chance to slow down and take some time to review the information presented over the previous few lessons. During this type of lesson, teams are encouraged to assess their strengths and limitations to this point and to engage in activities that will lead to improvement in the identified areas. In addition, this is an appropriate time to allow students to go back to activity task cards from previous lessons and work on performing each card until it is complete. In order to encourage self- and team assessment behaviors, the application contest used in the previous lesson is used again. It is important to relay this information to the students prior to their team practice so they know what type of skills and tactics to work on specifically. Since they will have already competed in the application contest once, a second and identical competition allows them to set goals based on their initial performance. The primary purpose of these lessons is to afford students an opportunity to practice and improve upon the skills and tactics learned and to provide time for individual and team self-reflection.

Tournament Lessons

The purpose of the tournament lessons (in-season and postseason) is to provide each team with an opportunity to apply the skills and tactics practiced during the preseason segment of the season. This also marks a significant change in the allocation of time during some of the eight PASE lesson segments. During the preseason segment of the season, a significant portion of time was dedicated to team practice in which skills and tactics were being learned and practiced. Upon the arrival of the tournament segment of the season, the allocated time shifts from team practice to team competitions. While time is still spent on team practice, it now takes the form of a skill-based warm-up. For instance, at an organized basketball game, you expect to see a team performing some structured and planned drills to warm up and get a feel for the game. These drills are included in the team practice time and can be found on the PASE Game Preparation Task Card (see p. 81). The majority of the lesson, however, will be dedicated to competitions among the teams. As in the regular-season competitions, each team will supply an official and a scorekeeper for each of their own games. Students will determine who will cover these roles by completing the PASE Tournament Role Assignments sheet (see p. 80) prior to the tournament lessons. This will hold true except for the consolation and championship games held on the final tournament day. On this day, teams not playing in the consolation or championship games will supply the officials and scorekeepers for the teams playing. The teacher may suggest that each of these teams select their best official and scorekeeper to preside over the competitions. The competitions will be managed based on the rules and modifications found on the PASE Tournament Rules page (see p. 83). These rules outline the game parameters including any special modifications, scoring, and tactical stipulations. Because of the systematic implementation of the PASE Application Contest Scorecards (see p. 78) across the season, it is reasonable to think that the students are capable of collecting all the information requested on the scorecard. Thus a PASE Tournament Statistics Summary Sheet (see p. 84) has been designed to collate all the information from the day's competitions and to summarize it for each player on a particular team. The knowledge of results can be used directly to aid teams in goal setting and in determining strategies for their upcoming games. The tournament lessons reflect the segment of the season for which students have prepared during the preseason. The culmination of several weeks of preparation undoubtedly manifests itself in this exciting instructional environment.

Awards Day Lesson

Most sport seasons end with an awards banquet at which important seasonal honors are announced. As the season draws to a close in PASE, it is also important to end on a highly festive note. The awards day provides students with an opportunity to actively reflect on their numerous team and individual accomplishments. Students are presented with awards based on their performance during the season and are given an opportunity to speak to their classmates about these contributions. Prior to the awards day, each student should receive a PASE Season Voting Ballot (see p. 86) with which to vote on various honors. Because each person contributed in some manner to the success of the team, everyone should receive some type of postseason honor. Members of a team will vote for the student who they feel should receive each honor within their own team. These honors will take on heightened importance for students because they are awarded by the individuals who were closest to them throughout the season—their teammates. In order to formalize the awards day for the students, a PASE Awards Day Itinerary (see p. 87) has been developed to inform students of what is to come during the lesson. As shown on the itinerary, the honors are awarded one team at a time following the welcoming address, announcements, and healthy refreshments. Prior to this presentation, each team should be provided with ample time to write an acceptance speech using the PASE Acceptance Speech Criteria found on page 88. According to the acceptance speech criteria, each team will be afforded up to 3 minutes during the awards presentation to deliver their acceptance speech. The lesson will end with the awarding of the season champions, the team that accumulated the most points across the season (see PASE Team Place Finish Awards on p. 90). This festive close will surely serve as a prompt for the next PASE season.

PASE INSTRUCTIONAL MATERIALS

This section contains an explanation of the PASE instructional materials that are used throughout each season. The item descriptions cover the purpose, when to use, suggested use, modifications, and document location. These descriptions should provide you with sufficient information to begin implementing the PASE seasons that are included in later chapters of this book.

PASE Season Syllabus

PASE Basketball Season Syllabus

Instructor(s): _____

Class: _____ Time: _____

BASKETBALL SEASON DESCRIPTION

This basketball season consists of 25 lessons and is divided into three segments: a preseason, an in-season round robin tournament, and a postseason championship tournament. Throughout the season, each student will be responsible for performing various tasks related to playing and managing a basketball season. Good luck!

SEASON GOALS

To become . . .

- a **competent** basketball player: one who is a knowledgeable player and can successfully perform skills and strategies during a game of basketball
- a **literate** basketball player: one who knows the rules and traditions of the sport and can identify appropriate and inappropriate basketball behaviors
- an **enthusiastic** basketball player: one who is involved and behaves in ways that protect, preserve, and enhance the basketball culture
- an **independent learner:** one who demonstrates responsibility for his or her own progress through appropriate goal-setting and goal-monitoring behaviors

SEASON CONTENT

Skills
- Dribbling
- L- and V-cuts
- Passing
- Defensive footwork
- Jump and set shot
- Rebounding
- Layup

Tactics
- Dribble to reposition
- Screen on and off ball
- Triple threat
- Post play
- Defense on and off ball
- Player-to-player defense
- Pick and roll, give and go
- Team zone defense

From *Sport Education Seasons* by Sean M. Bulger et al., 2007, Champaign, IL: Human Kinetics.

SEASON REQUIREMENTS, POINTS, AND GRADING SCALE

Requirement		Point Value					Grading Scale		
	Activity task cards	10	@	2	=	20	A	95 – 100	
	Personal fitness assessment	20	@	1	=	20	A-	93 – 94	Excellent
	Pre- and post-skills and fitness combine	2	@	3	=	6	B+	91 – 92	
	Team goal setting	3	@	2	=	6	B	87 – 90	Above average
	Role performance	20	@	1	=	20	B-	85 – 86	
	Individual responsibility level (IRL)	8	@	1	=	8	C+	83 – 84	
	Written quizzes	2	@	2	=	4	C	79 – 82	Average
	End-of-season awards voting	1	@	1	=	1	C-	77 – 78	
	Reflective journal	2	@	3	=	6	D+	75 – 76	
	Independent learning activity	1	@	4	=	4	D	72 – 74	Below average
	Outside-of-class physical activity log	5	@	1	=	5	D-	70 – 71	
				Total	=	100	F	Below 70	Failing

	Season bonus points	1st place	=	3.0 points	4th place	=	1.5 points
	Added to final point total	2nd place	=	2.5 points	5th place	=	1.0 point
		3rd place	=	2.0 points	6th place	=	0.5 point

From *Sport Education Seasons* by Sean M. Bulger et al., 2007, Champaign, IL: Human Kinetics.

PURPOSE

To provide students with the expectations, requirements, and overall grading system for the season. The syllabus gives the teacher an effective and efficient means for communicating the requirements, as well as giving students a means for assessing their own personal progress.

WHEN TO USE

During the management lesson

SUGGESTED USE

Teachers should provide this syllabus to students as early on in the season as possible, for instance during the management lesson. Provision of the syllabus so early apprises students in advance of the season regarding what content will be covered, which assessments will be used, and which days they will be used on. The teacher should provide each student with his or her own syllabus. If organizing your instructional materials using strategy 2 (p. 24), place a syllabus in each student's folder so students have immediate access to it daily.

MODIFICATIONS

- Modify the number of requirements during your season.
- Adjust the grading scale.

DOCUMENT LOCATION

Chapter 6—pages 110-113 and PASE Basketball CD-ROM–pages 6-9

Instructions: Record your personal progress each day. As you complete a requirement check it off like this "☑."

SEASON CALENDAR AND DAILY ASSESSMENTS

	PRESEASON															IN-SEASON ROUND ROBIN					POSTSEASON			
Lesson	1	2	3	4	5	6	7	8	9	10	11	12	13	14	15	16	17	18	19	20	21	22	23	24	25
Content	Pre-combine	Management	Dribble	Triple threat and pass	Pass	Review I	Set and jump shots	Layups	Pick and roll	Review II	Rebounding	Postplay	Player-to-player defense	Zone defense	Review III	RR tourney	RR tourney	RR tourney	RR tourney	RR tourney	Post-combine	Tourney	Tourney	Tourney	Festival

From *Sport Education Seasons* by Sean M. Bulger et al., 2007, Champaign, IL: Human Kinetics.

PASE Block Plan

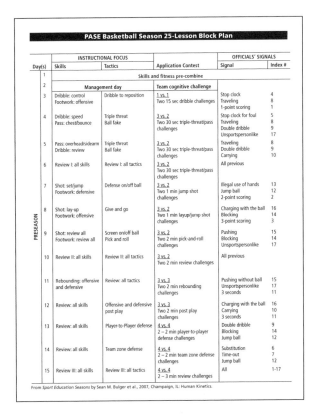

PASE Basketball Season 25-Lesson Block Plan

Day(s)	Skills	Tactics	Application Contest	Signal	Index #
	INSTRUCTIONAL FOCUS			**OFFICIALS' SIGNALS**	
1	Skills and fitness pre-combine				
2	Management day		Team cognitive challenge		
3	Dribble: control Footwork: offensive	Dribble to reposition	1 vs. 1 Two 15 sec dribble challenges	Stop clock Traveling 1-point scoring	4 8 1
4	Dribble: speed Pass: chest/bounce	Triple threat Ball fake	3 vs. 2 Two 30 sec triple-threat/pass challenges	Stop clock for foul Traveling Double dribble Unsportspersonlike	5 8 9 17
5	Pass: overhead/sidearm Dribble: review	Triple threat Ball fake	3 vs. 2 Two 30 sec triple-threat/pass challenges	Traveling Double dribble Carrying	8 9 10
6	Review I: all skills	Review I: all tactics	3 vs. 2 Two 30 sec triple-threat/pass challenges	All previous	
7	Shot: set/jump Footwork: defensive	Defense on/off ball	3 vs. 2 Two 1 min jump shot challenges	Illegal use of hands Jump ball 2-point scoring	13 12 2
8	Shot: lay-up Footwork: offensive	Give and go	3 vs. 2 Two 1 min layup/jump shot challenges	Charging with the ball Blocking 3-point scoring	16 14 3
9	Shot: review all Footwork: review all	Screen on/off ball Pick and roll	3 vs. 2 Two 2 min pick-and-roll challenges	Pushing Blocking Unsportspersonlike	15 14 17
10	Review II: all skills	Review II: all tactics	3 vs. 2 Two 2 min review challenges	All previous	
11	Rebounding: offensive and defensive	Review: all tactics	3 vs. 3 Two 2 min rebounding challenges	Pushing without ball Unsportspersonlike 3 seconds	15 17 11
12	Review: all skills	Offensive and defensive post play	3 vs. 3 Two 2 min post play challenges	Charging with the ball Carrying 3 seconds	16 10 11
13	Review: all skills	Player-to-Player defense	4 vs. 4 2 – 2 min player-to-player defense challenges	Double dribble Blocking Jump ball	9 14 12
14	Review: all skills	Team zone defense	4 vs. 4 2 – 2 min team zone defense challenges	Substitution Time-out Jump ball	6 7 12
15	Review III: all skills	Review III: all tactics	4 vs. 4 2 – 3 min review challenges	All	1-17

(PRESEASON — Days 1–15)

From *Sport Education Seasons* by Sean M. Bulger et al., 2007, Champaign, IL: Human Kinetics.

Day(s)	Skills	Tactics	Application contest	Signal	Index #
	INSTRUCTIONAL FOCUS			**OFFICIALS' SIGNALS**	
16	Review: all skills	Review: all tactics	G1 = 1 vs. 6 G2 = 2 vs. 5 G3 = 3 vs. 4	All	1-17
17	Review: all skills	Review: all tactics	G1 = 6 vs. 4 G2 = 5 vs. 1 G3 = 2 vs. 3	All	1-17
18	Review: all skills	Review: all tactics	G1 = 6 vs. 2 G2 = 5 vs. 3 G3 = 1 vs. 4	All	1-17
19	Review: all skills	Review: all tactics	G1 = 3 vs. 1 G2 = 4 vs. 2 G3 = 5 vs. 6	All	1-17
20	Review: all skills	Review: all tactics	G1 = 3 vs. 6 G2 = 1 vs. 2 G3 = 4 vs. 5	All	1-17
21	Skills and fitness post-combine				
22	Review: all skills	Review: all tactics	G1 = 5th seed vs. 4th seed G2 = 3rd seed vs. 6th seed G3 = 1st seed vs. winner G1	All	1-17
23	Review: all skills	Review: all tactics	G4 = loser G2 vs. loser G3 G5 = 2nd seed vs. winner G2 G6 = loser G1 vs. loser G5	All	1-17
24	Review: all skills	Review: all tactics	Consolation G7 = winner G6 vs. winner G4 Championship G7 = winner G3 vs. winner G5	All	1-17
25	Awards and festival day				

(IN-SEASON ROUND ROBIN TOURNAMENT — Days 16–20; POSTSEASON TOURN. — Days 22–23; FINALS — Days 24–25)

From *Sport Education Seasons* by Sean M. Bulger et al., 2007, Champaign, IL: Human Kinetics.

PURPOSE

To provide the teacher with a day-by-day overview of the PASE season.

WHEN TO USE

Prior to the season

SUGGESTED USE

The block plan provides the teacher with a hierarchically sequenced list of content for the upcoming season. It will enable teachers to see the sequencing of content (skills and tactics) in addition to the types of application tasks being used on a particular day. Also the block plan outlines the systematic integration of official's signals to be focused on during a particular lesson and specifically during the application contest. The block plan is divided into three distinct segments: a preseason, an in-season tournament, and a postseason championship tournament.

MODIFICATIONS

- Modify the content or application contests.
- Adjust the overall days within the season.

DOCUMENT LOCATION

Chapter 6—pages 114-115 and PASE Basketball Season CD-ROM–pages 10-11

PASE Grade Book

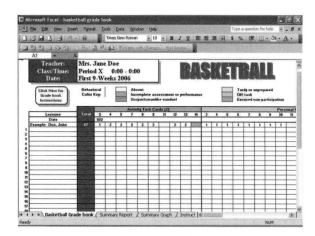

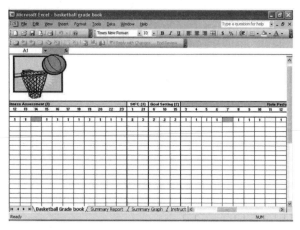

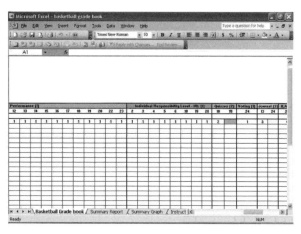

PURPOSE

To supply the teacher with an organizational framework for recording and managing student assessment information.

WHEN TO USE

During the season

SUGGESTED USE

The season grade book is created in a spreadsheet format. The user-friendly template allows the teacher to enter in scores that will automatically tabulate a total. It is suggested that the teacher not necessarily input grades daily but at least once a week. The PASE utilizes formative assessment, which is ongoing and incremental. It is important for the teacher not to let too many assignments pass before inputting the scores. An electronic version of the grade book along with a summary sheet and graph has been provided on the accompanying CD-ROM. Instructions on the grade book can be found by using either the "grade book instructions" link on the first page of each season's grade book or by locating the Instructions worksheet tab on the bottom of the grade book spreadsheet. In addition, a hard copy of this grade book is used in a similar fashion minus the luxury of automatic score aggregation and summary reports.

MODIFICATIONS

- Modify the number of requirements.
- Modify the value of requirements.
- Use paper or electronic version.

DOCUMENT LOCATION

Chapter 6—page 116 and PASE Basketball Season CD-ROM

PASE Daily Team Points Summary

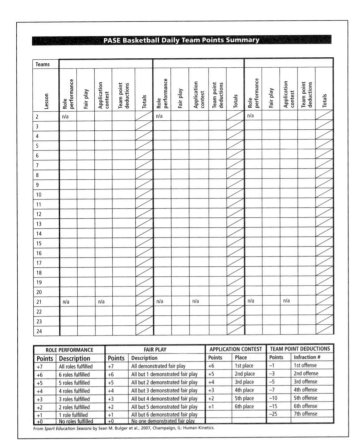

From *Sport Education Seasons* by Sean M. Bulger et al., 2007, Champaign, IL: Human Kinetics.

PURPOSE

To supply the teacher with an efficient method of recording, managing, and tabulating daily team points across the season.

WHEN TO USE

Following each lesson

SUGGESTED USE

The daily team points summary is designed to aid the teacher in managing points accumulated by teams in the areas of role performance, fair play behaviors, application contest place finish, and team deductions. While only one of these categories appears on the syllabus requirements (role performance) and affects a student's own grade, the others affect the team points. These team points are what will determine the overall season champion and place finishes. The teacher should tabulate scores routinely and post these for the students to see, thereby heightening the competitive spirit that surrounds the sport season.

MODIFICATIONS

- Modify the values of points.
- Modify the areas for team point earnings.

DOCUMENT LOCATION

Chapter 6—page 117 and PASE Basketball CD-ROM—page 13

PASE Official's Signals Index

PASE Basketball Official's Signals Index

SCORING

1 — 1 point
2 — 2 points
3 — 3 points

CLOCK RELATED

4, 5 — Stop clock / Stop clock for a foul

ADMINISTRATIVE

6, 7 — Substitution / Time-out (30 second and 60 second)

VIOLATIONS

8 — Traveling
9 — Double dribble
10 — Carrying
11 — 3 seconds
12 — Jump ball

FOULS

13 — Illegal use of hands
14 — Blocking
15 — Pushing without ball
16 — Charging with the ball
17 — Unsportspersonlike

From *Sport Education Seasons* by Sean M. Bulger et al., 2007, Champaign, IL: Human Kinetics.

PURPOSE

The index provides the teacher and students with a complete list of the official's signals that will be utilized during the season.

WHEN TO USE

During the season

SUGGESTED USE

The official's signals index serves as a reference for the teacher as well as a learning tool for the students. Each signal listed has a corresponding number. This number is used as a reference as shown in the block plan. Additionally, this index provides a quick reference for students so they can see a full listing of the signals to be used. The Pocket Ref is a companion to this index and is intended to be more portable.

MODIFICATIONS

Modify the type and number of official's signals used.

DOCUMENT LOCATION

Chapter 6—page 118 and PASE Basketball Season CD-ROM—page 14

PASE Skills and Fitness Combine Recording Sheet

PURPOSE

The combine recording sheet is a concise form on which students can collect, record, and manage their own personal skill and fitness data obtained during the skills and fitness combine.

WHEN TO USE

During the skills and fitness pre- and post-combines

SUGGESTED USE

During the skills and fitness pre- and post-combines, the students will need to be able to collect and manage their own personal data. The recording sheet is designed to allow students to collect information on health-related and skill-related fitness, as well as sport-specific skills. After recording their pretest combine scores, students will immediately goal-set for the posttest. The post-combine will enable students and teacher alike to determine any gains in fitness and skill. Also because *FITNESSGRAM 8.0* is used, students can determine whether or not they have entered the healthy fitness zone for each component of health-related fitness.

MODIFICATIONS

- Modify the number of combine activities.
- Create a sheet to be used by the teacher to record class scores.

DOCUMENT LOCATION

Chapter 6—pages 286-287 and PASE Basketball Season CD-ROM—pages 24-25 in appendix A

PASE Basketball Fitness Combine Recording Sheet

Name: _____   Age: _____   Gender: ☐ Male ☐ Female

INSTRUCTIONS

To record your fitness, combine information for each station:
1. Read the fitness combine activity task card.
2. Perform the activity according to the criteria on the task card.

3. Locate appropriate scoring box for the activity that you completed.
4. Record appropriate measure in the scoring box.
5. Refer to the row showing the example to help you record accurately.

Fitness Components

Activity	HEALTH-RELATED								SKILL-RELATED			
	Aerobic fitness (AF)	Body composition (BC)	Flexibility (Flx)		Muscular fitness (MF)				Power	Agility	Speed	Balance
	PACER	Body mass index	Sit and reach	Shoulder stretch	Push-up	Curl-up	Modified pull-up	Trunk lift	Vertical jump	T-run	Shuttle run	Line jump
Station	1	2	3	4	5	6	7	8	9	10	11	12
Example	Laps #	BMI	Inches:	R: ☐ HFZ L: ☐ HFZ	Reps:	Reps:	Reps:	Inches:	Inches:	Reps:	Reps:	Reps:
	19	19.6	11.5		15	29	7	10	18	3	7	21
	☑ HFZ	☑ HFZ	☑ HFZ		☑ HFZ	☑ HFZ	☑ HFZ	☑ HFZ				
Prescore	Laps #	BMI	Inches:	R: ☐ HFZ L: ☐ HFZ	Reps:	Reps:	Reps:	Inches:	Inches:	Reps:	Reps:	Reps:
	☐ HFZ	☐ HFZ	☐ HFZ		☐ HFZ	☐ HFZ	☐ HFZ	☐ HFZ				
Goals	Laps #	BMI	Inches:	R: ☐ HFZ L: ☐ HFZ	Reps:	Reps:	Reps:	Inches:	Inches:	Reps:	Reps:	Reps:
Postscore	Laps #	BMI	Inches:	R: ☐ HFZ L: ☐ HFZ	Reps:	Reps:	Reps:	Inches:	Inches:	Reps:	Reps:	Reps:
	☐ HFZ	☐ HFZ	☐ HFZ		☐ HFZ	☐ HFZ	☐ HFZ	☐ HFZ				

From *Sport Education Seasons* by Sean M. Bulger et al., 2007, Champaign, IL: Human Kinetics.

PASE Basketball Skills Combine Recording Sheet

Name: _____   Age: _____   Gender: ☐ Male ☐ Female

INSTRUCTIONS

To record your skills, combine information for each station:
1. Read the skills combine activity task card.
2. Perform the activity according to the criteria on the task card.

3. Locate appropriate scoring box for the activity that you completed.
4. Record appropriate measure in the scoring box.
5. Refer to the row showing the example to help you record accurately.

Basketball Skills

Activity	Ball handling		Scoring				Obtaining/Maintaining ball possession		
	Low control dribble	Speed dribble	Layup	Set shot	Jump shot (midrange)	Jump shot (long range)	Rebounding	Passing: chest	Passing: bounce
Station	13	14	15	16	17	18	19	20	
Example	R: 32 L: 17	R: laps 4 L: laps 2	R: 8 L: 5	4 /10	5	2	18	Ticks: IIII IIII IIII III Total #: 18	Ticks: IIII IIII IIII Total #: 14
Prescore	R: ____ L: ____	R: laps____ L: laps____	R: ____ L: ____	____ /10	____	____	____	Ticks: Total #:	Ticks: Total #:
Goals	R: ____ L: ____	R: laps____ L: laps____	R: ____ L: ____	____ /10	____	____	____	Ticks: Total #:	Ticks: Total #:
Postscore	R: ____ L: ____	R: laps____ L: laps____	R: ____ L: ____	____ /10	____	____	____	Ticks: Total #:	Ticks: Total #:

From *Sport Education Seasons* by Sean M. Bulger et al., 2007, Champaign, IL: Human Kinetics.

PASE Skills and Fitness Combine Station Task Cards 1-20

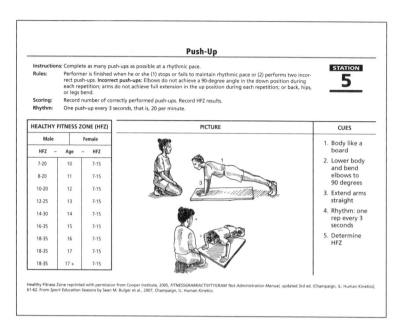

Push-Up

STATION
5

Instructions: Complete as many push-ups as possible at a rhythmic pace.

Rules: Performer is finished when he or she (1) stops or fails to maintain rhythmic pace or (2) performs two incorrect push-ups. **Incorrect push-ups:** Elbows do not achieve a 90-degree angle in the down position during each repetition; arms do not achieve full extension in the up position during each repetition; or back, hips, or legs bend.

Scoring: Record number of correctly performed push-ups. Record HFZ results.

Rhythm: One push-up every 3 seconds, that is, 20 per minute.

HEALTHY FITNESS ZONE (HFZ)			PICTURE	CUES
Male		**Female**		
HFZ –	**Age** –	**HFZ**		1. Body like a board
7-20	10	7-15		2. Lower body and bend elbows to 90 degrees
8-20	11	7-15		3. Extend arms straight
10-20	12	7-15		4. Rhythm: one rep every 3 seconds
12-25	13	7-15		5. Determine HFZ
14-30	14	7-15		
16-35	15	7-15		
18-35	16	7-15		
18-35	17	7-15		
18-35	17 +	7-15		

Healthy Fitness Zone reprinted with permission from Cooper Institute, 2005, *FITNESSGRAM/ACTIVITYGRAM Test Administration Manual*, updated 3rd ed. (Champaign, IL: Human Kinetics), 61-62. From *Sport Education Seasons* by Sean M. Bulger et al., 2007, Champaign, IL: Human Kinetics.

PURPOSE

The station task cards communicate the instructions, rules, and scoring for the skills and fitness combine.

WHEN TO USE

During the skills and fitness pre- and post-combines

SUGGESTED USE

The skills and fitness combine is designed to be self-paced in that students will move to each station in pairs or small groups and complete each activity. In addition to containing information about the instructions and scoring, the station task cards provide a picture or diagram of the station and learning cues.

The health-related fitness activities were designed to be directly aligned with *FITNESSGRAM* 8.0. The healthy fitness zones are also located on each task card (1-8) so students can immediately ascertain if they have met the criteria to be in the zone.

MODIFICATIONS

- Modify the number of combine activities per category.
- Divide the combine lesson across two days: stations 1 through 12 and stations 13 through 20.

DOCUMENT LOCATION

Chapter 6—page 270 and PASE Basketball Season CD-ROM—page 8 in appendix A

PASE Body Mass Index (BMI) Conversion Chart

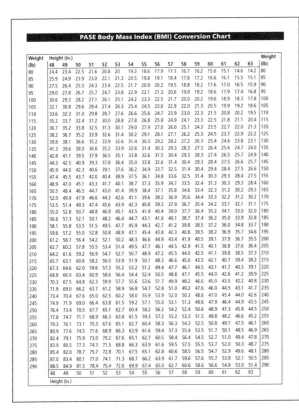

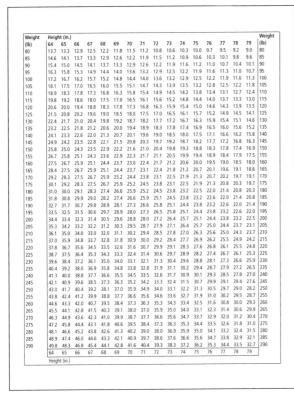

PURPOSE

The BMI chart aids students in determining their personal body mass index. This index provides a measure of the appropriateness of a student's weight relative to height.

WHEN TO USE

During the skills and fitness pre- and post-combines

SUGGESTED USE

As students are completing the skills and fitness combine, one activity is to determine their body mass index. Students should remove their shoes in order to gain a more accurate measure of their height and weight. Once students have measured themselves they should consult the BMI chart to obtain their index number. To find their body mass index, they simply locate their weight in pounds on the vertical axis and their height in inches on the horizontal axis. Where the two intersect is the BMI reading. It is important, when measuring for weight, to place this station in a secluded area of the gym to provide an element of privacy. Students should feel comfortable in the process of determining their height and weight. Once students have identified their index number, they should determine if they fall into the healthy fitness zone (using PASE Skills and Fitness Combine Station Task Cards).

MODIFICATIONS

- For the BMI, substitute a more accurate measure of body composition like a skinfold test.
- Use a standardized formula to determine BMI: weight (kg)/height^2 (m).

DOCUMENT LOCATION

Chapter 6—pages 266-267 and PASE Basketball Season CD-ROM—pages 4-5 in appendix A

PASE Skills and Fitness Combine Draft Composite Sheet

PASE Basketball Skills and Fitness Combine Draft Composite

Instructions: Place each student's name in the name column prior to the combine. Coaches should observe students' performance during the combine and determine a draft order for each student in the class. In addition, coaches should take notes to assist in making decisions during the team selection process.

Note: Coaches must keep all student performance and draft selection information confidential.

Name	Draft order	Notes

From *Sport Education Seasons* by Sean M. Bulger et al., 2007, Champaign, IL: Human Kinetics.

PURPOSE

The draft composite is a tool for team selectors to use during the team draft to record information about their classmates' skills and fitness abilities.

WHEN TO USE

During the skills and fitness pre-combine

SUGGESTED USE

Prior to the pre-combine, the teacher should select students who have demonstrated responsible decision-making capabilities to serve as team selectors for the season. These team selectors at the start of the pre-combine will be provided a draft composite sheet. Throughout the combine, the selectors should move through the learning area, observing and making notes regarding the order in which they would select a particular student in the draft. Following the pre-combine, the composite should be returned to the teacher. This information should be kept confidential and shared only during the team draft.

MODIFICATIONS

Modify the categories on the composite.

DOCUMENT LOCATION

Chapter 6—page 288 and PASE Basketball Season CD-ROM—page 26 in appendix A

PASE Skills and Fitness Combine Draft Selection Form

PASE Basketball Skills and Fitness Combine Draft Selection Form

Instructions: The purpose of this draft is to use the information collected during the skills and fitness combine to create a successful soccer team. Each person will have the opportunity to select first in one of the selection rounds. As a player is selected from the combine sheet, simply draw a line through his or her name. This will aid in avoiding the duplication of selections in later rounds. After the draft is complete, teams will be placed into a pool. Each coach will then randomly select a team from the pool. It is important that you select the most fair and competent team possible during the draft because you may not end up with the team you have drafted. It will be important to keep players' drafting order confidential in order to preserve the integrity of the process. Good luck.

Team: _____

Coach: _____

Round	Player's name
1	
2	
3	
4	
5	
6	
7	
8	

From *Sport Education Seasons* by Sean M. Bulger et al., 2007, Champaign, IL: Human Kinetics.

PURPOSE

The draft selection form is a tool for team selectors to use to record the names of students they select during the draft.

WHEN TO USE

Following the skills and fitness pre-combine

SUGGESTED USE

Following the pre-combine, the teacher should gather the team selectors and provide them with their draft composites. Each team selector then draws a number indicating the order in which he or she will pick during the first round. Each selector then selects one student to be on his or her team and records the student's name in the appropriate box. Once all the players in the class have been selected, teams will be randomly drawn by the selectors. The importance of this is that it will encourage the selectors to select fair teams since they will not know which team they will draw. Once the teams have been drawn, the teacher collects the draft composite sheets and selection forms.

MODIFICATIONS

Modify the number of selection rounds.

DOCUMENT LOCATION

Chapter 6—page 289 and PASE Basketball Season CD-ROM—page 27 in appendix A

PASE Individual Responsibility Level (IRL) Rubric

PASE Basketball Individual Responsibility Level (IRL) Rubric

Instructions: Use the following rubric to determine your individual level of responsibility for each lesson. Record your individual responsibility level on the Individual Responsibility Level Recording Sheet.

4	EXEMPLARY	
	Preparedness	You were on time for class and prepared with appropriate clothes, shoes, and materials.
	Transition	You always stopped, cleaned up, and moved to the next lesson segment as efficiently as possible.
	On task	You were always engaged at a high level during practice and game times and you tried your best.
	Sportspersonship	You maintained a positive attitude throughout all daily activities and displayed good sportspersonship.
	Assessments	You completed all of the team and individual assessments during the lesson fully and honestly.
3	ACCEPTABLE	
	Preparedness	You were late for class but came prepared with appropriate clothes, shoes, and materials.
	Transition	You stopped, cleaned up, and moved to the next lesson segment as efficiently as possible for most of the lesson.
	On task	You engaged at a high level during practice and game times for most of the lesson, but there were times when you did not try your best.
	Sportspersonship	You maintained a positive attitude throughout most daily activities and displayed good sportspersonship.
	Assessments	You completed most of the team and individual assessments during the lesson fully and honestly.
2	NEEDS IMPROVEMENT	
	Preparedness	You were on time for class but did not come prepared with appropriate clothes, shoes, and materials.
	Transition	You rarely stopped, cleaned up, and moved to the next lesson segment as efficiently as possible.
	On task	You rarely engaged at a high level during practice and game times and there were times when you did not try your best.
	Sportspersonship	You maintained a negative attitude throughout most daily activities or displayed poor sportspersonship.
	Assessments	You completed most of the team and individual assessments during the lesson, but the information was not complete or honest.
1	UNACCEPTABLE	
	Preparedness	You were late for class and did not come prepared with appropriate clothes, shoes, and materials.
	Transition	You never stopped, cleaned up, and moved to the next lesson segment as efficiently as possible.
	On task	You were never engaged at a high level during practice and game times and you did not try your best.
	Sportspersonship	You maintained a negative attitude throughout all daily activities and displayed poor sportspersonship.
	Assessments	You did not complete any of the team and individual assessments during the lesson.

From *Sport Education Seasons* by Sean M. Bulger et al., 2007, Champaign, IL: Human Kinetics.

PURPOSE

To provide students with increased awareness of their decision making by giving them a framework for determining the appropriateness of their behavior. The rubric also allows for identification of areas in which more effective decision making is needed.

WHEN TO USE

During individual and team progress reporting

SUGGESTED USE

At the lesson end, students will refer to the rubric to determine their individual level of responsibility for that particular lesson. Students will need to reflect upon their decisions regarding preparedness, efficient transitions, on-task behavior, sportspersonship, and completion of assessments. This rubric should be used as a prompt for student decision making and referred to regularly to shape appropriate behaviors. This rubric is used in combination with the IRL recording sheet.

MODIFICATIONS

- Modify the categories on the IRL.
- Modify the levels on the IRL.

DOCUMENT LOCATION

Chapter 6—page 307 and PASE Basketball Season CD-ROM—page 17 in appendix B

PASE Individual Responsibility Level (IRL) Recording Sheet

PASE Basketball Individual Responsibility Level (IRL) Recording Sheet

Name: _____ Team: _____

Instructions: Determine your individual responsibility level (IRL) for each lesson using the individual responsibility rubric on page 307. Record your score in the "IRL" column and provide a rationale for why you were at that level. Set an IRL goal for the next lesson, and develop a strategy for meeting that goal.

Lesson	IRL	Reason?	IRL goal	Strategy for improvement
Example	1	I forgot my shoes. I got mad and yelled at Sue because she wouldn't pass me the ball.	2	I will leave a pair of shoes in my locker and I'll ask Sue to pass to me.
2				
3				
4				
5				
6				
10				
15				
20				

From *Sport Education Seasons* by Sean M. Bulger et al., 2007, Champaign, IL: Human Kinetics.

PURPOSE

To provide students with increased awareness of their decision making by giving them a tool for recording the appropriateness of their behavior. This form also allows for goal setting and determining strategies for improvement of decision-making abilities.

WHEN TO USE

During individual and team progress reporting

SUGGESTED USE

At the lesson end, students will refer to the PASE Individual Responsibility Level (IRL) Rubric to determine the individual level of responsibility that best represents their performance since the last IRL was completed. They will then record that level with an accompanying rationale. Next, they will goal-set for future lessons and determine a strategy for improvement. This process will take place often during the initial few lessons in order to identify and establish appropriate behavior. In later lessons students will reflect upon a series of lessons as opposed to simply one specific lesson.

MODIFICATIONS

- Modify the number of lessons to be reflected upon.
- Modify the categories of the recording sheet.

DOCUMENT LOCATION

Chapter 6—page 308 and PASE Basketball Season CD-ROM—page 18 in appendix B

PASE Roles and Responsibilities Assignments

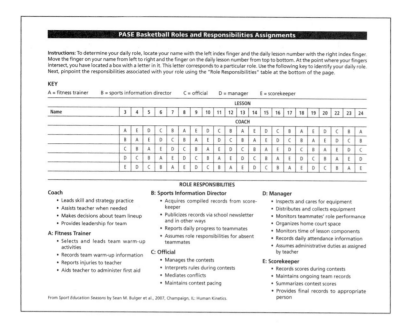

PASE Basketball Roles and Responsibilities Assignments

Instructions: To determine your daily role, locate your name with the left index finger and the daily lesson number with the right index finger. Move the finger on your name from left to right and the finger on the daily lesson number from top to bottom. At the point where your fingers intersect, you have located a box with a letter in it. This letter corresponds to a particular role. Use the following key to identify your daily role. Next, pinpoint the responsibilities associated with your role using the "Role Responsibilities" table at the bottom of the page.

KEY

A = fitness trainer   B = sports information director   C = official   D = manager   E = scorekeeper

Name		LESSON																		
	3	4	5	6	7	8	9	10	11	12	13	14	15	16	17	18	19	20	22	23	24
COACH																					
	A	E	D	C	B	A	E	D	C	B	A	E	D	C	B	A	E	D	C	B	A
	B	A	E	D	C	B	A	E	D	C	B	A	E	D	C	B	A	E	D	C	B
	C	B	A	E	D	C	B	A	E	D	C	B	A	E	D	C	B	A	E	D	C
	D	C	B	A	E	D	C	B	A	E	D	C	B	A	E	D	C	B	A	E	D
	E	D	C	B	A	E	D	C	B	A	E	D	C	B	A	E	D	C	B	A	E

ROLE RESPONSIBILITIES

Coach
- Leads skill and strategy practice
- Assists teacher when needed
- Makes decisions about team lineup
- Provides leadership for team

A: Fitness Trainer
- Selects and leads team warm-up activities
- Records team warm-up information
- Reports injuries to teacher
- Aids teacher to administer first aid

B: Sports Information Director
- Acquires compiled records from score-keeper
- Publicizes records via school newsletter and in other ways
- Reports daily progress to teammates
- Assumes role responsibilities for absent teammates

C: Official
- Manages the contests
- Interprets rules during contests
- Mediates conflicts
- Maintains contest pacing

D: Manager
- Inspects and cares for equipment
- Distributes and collects equipment
- Monitors teammates' role performance
- Organizes home court space
- Monitors time of lesson components
- Records daily attendance information
- Assumes administrative duties as assigned by teacher

E: Scorekeeper
- Records scores during contests
- Maintains ongoing team records
- Summarizes contest scores
- Provides final records to appropriate person

From *Sport Education Seasons* by Sean M. Bulger et al., 2007, Champaign, IL: Human Kinetics.

PURPOSE

To provide students with an efficient means for determining their role for a lesson and the responsibilities associated with completing that role during a PASE lesson.

WHEN TO USE

During the roles and responsibilities check

SUGGESTED USE

Upon entering the classroom, students should immediately locate the roles and responsibilities assignments and determine their role for the day. A key is provided to aid students in interpreting the letter code. Each letter corresponds to one of the roles listed at the bottom of the page. Once students have identified their role, they should take note of the specific responsibilities that the role requires. Because the roles of the students (except for the coach) change daily, it is important that students check the roles and responsibilities assignment sheet on a daily basis.

MODIFICATIONS

- Adjust the number of roles to be performed in a season.
- Modify the order of roles, allowing a student to perform a role multiple times before changing to a new role.

DOCUMENT LOCATION

Chapter 6—page 293 and PASE Basketball Season CD-ROM—page 3 in appendix B

PASE Roles and Responsibilities Recording Sheet

PASE Basketball Roles and Responsibilities Recording Sheet

Name: _____

Instructions: Determine your role and corresponding responsibilities for the day's lesson. At the end of the lesson you will be asked to determine the responsibilities that you successfully completed. For each responsibility successfully completed, place a check [✓] in the box. For each responsibility that you did not successfully complete, place a zero [0] in the box. If an opportunity to complete a responsibility did not occur, place "n/a" (not applicable) in the appropriate box.

Roles and responsibilities	Lesson																					
	3	4	5	6	7	8	9	10	11	12	13	14	15	16	17	18	19	20	21	22	23	24
Coach																						
• Leads skill and strategy practice																						
• Assists teacher when needed																						
• Makes decisions about team lineups																						
• Provides leadership for team																						
A. Fitness trainer																						
• Selects and leads team warm-up activities																						
• Records team warm-up information																						
• Reports injuries to teacher																						
• Aids teacher in administering first aid																						
B. Sports information director																						
• Acquires compiled records from scorekeeper																						
• Publicizes records via school newsletter and other means																						
• Reports progress daily to teammates																						
• Assumes role responsibilities of absent teammates																						
C. Official																						
• Manages contests																						
• Interprets rules during contests																						
• Mediates conflicts																						
• Maintains contest pacing																						
D. Manager																						
• Inspects and cares for equipment																						
• Distributes and collects equipment																						
• Monitors teammates' role performance																						
• Organizes home court space																						
• Monitors time of lesson components																						
• Assumes administrative duties assigned by teacher																						
E. Scorekeeper																						
• Records scores during contests																						
• Maintains ongoing team records																						
• Summarizes contest scores																						
• Provides final records to appropriate person																						

From *Sport Education Seasons* by Sean M. Bulger et al., 2007, Champaign, IL: Human Kinetics.

PURPOSE

To provide students with a means for recording adherence to the assigned role and its responsibilities during a PASE lesson.

WHEN TO USE

During individual and team progress reporting

SUGGESTED USE

At the lesson end, students locate the roles and responsibilities recording sheet and, using the appropriate marks, indicate whether they fulfilled each responsibility for their role during the lesson. Because the roles change on a regular basis, students first locate their role for that particular lesson. They will then record their marks in the appropriate lesson column. A check mark is used to indicate the completion of a responsibility, and a zero is used to indicate a responsibility that was not completed. If during the lesson the student did not have the occasion to perform a particular role responsibility, her or she will simply enter "n/a," indicating that that responsibility is not applicable.

MODIFICATIONS

- Adjust the number of roles that adherence is recorded for across the season.
- Modify the order of roles, allowing students to perform a role multiple times before changing to a new role.

DOCUMENT LOCATION

Chapter 6—page 294 and PASE Basketball Season CD-ROM—page 4 in appendix B

PASE Sports Information Director Sports Report

Basketball Tribune

Author: _____   Team: _____

Date: _____

Article title: _____

_____
_____
_____
_____
_____
_____
_____
_____
_____
_____
_____
_____
_____

Caption: _____

-------------------------(cut here)-------------------------

- Get scores (team and individual) for the day's game from your scorekeeper so that you can include this information in your article (don't take the stats sheet out of class; you may want to jot this info down on the back of the sports page).
- Publicize the day's events and records via a sports page article:
  - Article must be neatly written.
  - Give your sports page article a title. Align article title with your team's color, mascot, name, and so on.
  - Article should cover each team member's contribution to the day's warm-up, review, practice, contest, and so forth.
  - Include your name (author), your team's name, the date, location (i.e., home field nickname), and any other information that you deem important.
- This sports page article is due at the beginning of the next class. It must be returned and must meet the criteria listed in order for you to successfully complete your role.
- You will have the opportunity to share your article with your team and post it in your home field area.

From *Sport Education Seasons* by Sean M. Bulger et al., 2007, Champaign, IL: Human Kinetics.

PURPOSE

To provide the student performing the role of sports information director a method for publicizing the team's progress in an authentic manner.

WHEN TO USE

Outside of class

SUGGESTED USE

The sports information director's role requires that he or she publicize the team's progress via a school newsletter or even a school sports column. The sports report is designed to give students an avenue for reporting this information. The sports information director can use the sports report to depict the team's successes and failures as well as to describe interesting details of game play or practice. Students should complete the sports report and turn it in during the next class to receive credit for performing their role to criteria. It is suggested that the teacher post these sports reports in the team's home playing area. In addition, quality sports reports can be submitted to the school newspaper as part of a regular column on what's happening in physical education.

MODIFICATIONS

- Adjust the type and amount of information required in the sports report.
- Create a place in the gymnasium to post all sports reports.
- Contact local newspaper with reports to advocate the program.

DOCUMENT LOCATION

Chapter 6—page 295 and PASE Basketball Season CD-ROM—page 5 in appendix B

PASE Team Membership Inventory and Fair Play Agreement

PASE Basketball Team Membership Inventory and Fair Play Agreement

Name: _____ Color: _____

Cheer: _____ Mascot: _____

Home court nickname: _____

PASE FAIR PLAY AGREEMENT

We, _____ agree to

- always follow the rules,
- work to achieve our personal and team goals,
- never argue with the officials,
- encourage all of our classmates,
- be gracious in victory and defeat,
- assist teammates at any time,
- show self-control at all times, and
- play hard and fair.

Pledge phrase: As part of this team, I promise to always follow the criteria outlined in the PASE Fair Play Agreement. Should I choose not to follow the agreement, I understand that there are consequences that my team and I must deal with in a responsible fashion.

Signature: _____ Date: _____

Signature: _____ Date: _____

Signature: _____ Date: _____

Signature: _____ Date: _____

Signature: _____ Date: _____

Signature: _____ Date: _____

Signature: _____ Date: _____

Signature: _____ Date: _____

From *Sport Education Seasons* by Sean M. Bulger et al., 2007, Champaign, IL: Human Kinetics.

PURPOSE

To give students an opportunity to establish some team characteristics that will serve to build the affiliation component. This form also provides students with an awareness of fair play expectations related to responsible sport participation.

WHEN TO USE

During the management lesson

SUGGESTED USE

During the initial lessons of the season, it will be important to establish team affiliation. This will serve to heighten student ownership and team camaraderie. The inventory includes selected categories that will develop a team's identity and afford them some unique characteristics that set them apart from the other teams. The areas include a team name, color, cheer, mascot, and so on. Also as part of the inventory, students will sign the PASE Fair Play Agreement. This agreement serves as a behavioral contract between teacher and student and between student and student. The behaviors outlined provide a prompt with which to refocus students' decision making in the event of inappropriate choices. Each team member will sign the pledge, thereby agreeing to abide by the stated rules during the season.

MODIFICATIONS

- Adjust the types of categories used to build affiliation (other suggestions: team country, handshake, logo, corporate sponsor, etc.).
- Modify the behavioral expectations on the fair play agreement.
- Have students copy the pledge phrase from the fair play agreement to heighten the level of personal accountability.

DOCUMENT LOCATION

Chapter 6—page 311 and PASE Basketball Season CD-ROM—page 21 in appendix B

PASE Team Rosters

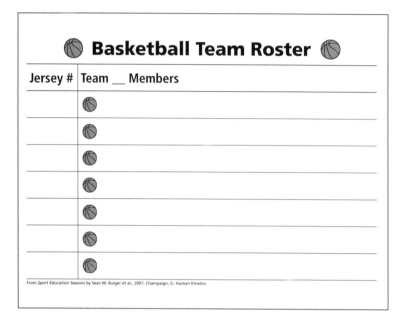

Basketball Team Roster

Jersey #	Team ___ Members

From *Sport Education Seasons* by Sean M. Bulger et al., 2007, Champaign, IL: Human Kinetics.

PURPOSE

To provide teachers and students with a visual aid to identify team members.

WHEN TO USE

During each lesson

SUGGESTED USE

Once teams have been selected, the teacher or students, or teacher and students together, should complete the team rosters. These rosters should include each team member's name in addition to his or her jersey number if numbered pinnies are being used. Even if numbered pinnies are not being used, students can still select their favorite number to increase the feelings of affiliation and authenticity of the season. The team roster should be posted each lesson at the home playing area. In addition, the scorekeeper can use the roster to help identify players from opposing teams that he or she may not be familiar with. This will be important during the posttournament games as scorekeepers will be selected from the teams not playing.

MODIFICATIONS

Modify the type of information being recorded on the roster. You might include a team name, student's hometown, nickname, age, height, and so on.

DOCUMENT LOCATION

Chapter 6—page 292 and PASE Basketball Season CD-ROM—page 2 in appendix B

PASE Attendance Recording Sheet

PASE Basketball Attendance Recording Sheet

Team: _____

Instructions: During the individual and team progress report portion of the lesson, record information about your team's attendance behavior. You will record whether each of your teammates was present, late, dismissed early, or absent. "Present" indicates that a teammate was on time and in class for the entire period. "Late" indicates that a teammate was in class but arrived after the team warm-up had begun. "Early dismissal" indicates that a teammate was unable to complete the entire lesson because he or she left class before the period ended. "Absent" indicates that a teammate was not in class at all.

ATTENDANCE INFORMATION KEY

P = present   L = late   E = early dismissal   A = absent

Lessons	NAMES				
2.					
3.					
4.					
5.					
6.					
7.					
8.					
9.					
10.					
11.					
12.					
13.					
14.					
15.					
16.					
17.					
18.					
19.					
20.					
21.					
22.					
23.					
24.					
25.					

From *Sport Education Seasons* by Sean M. Bulger et al., 2007, Champaign, IL: Human Kinetics.

PURPOSE

To provide students with the responsibility of monitoring their team's attendance on a daily basis. The attendance recording sheet also gives the teacher a record of those present on a given day.

WHEN TO USE

During individual and team progress reporting

SUGGESTED USE

At the lesson's end, the student coach will record his or her team's attendance behavior in the designated columns. The coach indicates the attendance information for each member of the team by using the attendance information key. The coach indicates if a team member was present, late, dismissed early, or absent. This will provide the teacher with an efficient means of determining who was present without taking up valuable instructional time. The added responsibility placed on the coaches heightens their ownership of their team and the importance of their position to the success of the season.

MODIFICATIONS

Modify the information key to add or delete attendance behavior indicators.

DOCUMENT LOCATION

Chapter 6—page 309 and PASE Basketball Season CD-ROM—page 19 in appendix B

PASE Fitness Workouts

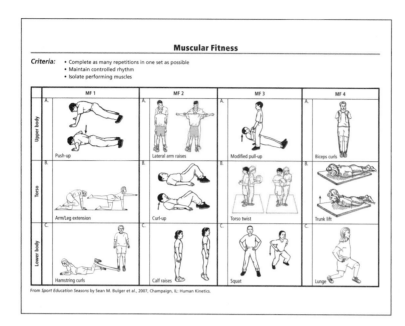

Muscular Fitness

Criteria:
- Complete as many repetitions in one set as possible
- Maintain controlled rhythm
- Isolate performing muscles

From *Sport Education Seasons* by Sean M. Bulger et al., 2007, Champaign, IL: Human Kinetics.

PURPOSE

To develop students' health- and skill-related physical fitness levels and knowledge of appropriate activities that compose a total body warm-up. Additionally, the form affords the teacher a means of communicating a series of developmentally appropriate activities that can be used to prepare for sport-specific activity.

WHEN TO USE

During team warm-ups

SUGGESTED USE

After checking roles and responsibilities, the fitness trainer should select a workout to be completed by the team. The fitness trainer selects a workout number (1, 2, 3, or 4) at the start of the team warm-up. The fitness trainer then supervises the warm-up and monitors the team's progress. It is suggested that each team member move at an individual pace through the fitness activities and record his or her own progress. Students should always follow the same physiologically appropriate sequence in performing activities, which is aerobic fitness, flexibility, muscular fitness, and skill-related fitness. Each card has criteria for completing each type of activity as well as a picture or diagram and options for varying the task. If workout #1 is selected for the day, the students perform workout #1 on each of the cards. They must complete all four workouts before repeating any previously completed workout. These workouts can be used in combination with the personal or team fitness recording sheet.

MODIFICATIONS

- Modify the types of activities that the students perform for each health- and skill-related fitness component.
- Allow the students to select different columns or workout numbers within the same warm-up.
- Preselect the number of workouts that all teams will perform during a given lesson.
- Add some other options to each of the cardiovascular endurance activities.

DOCUMENT LOCATION

Chapter 6—pages 299-302 and PASE Basketball Season CD-ROM—pages 9-12 in appendix B

PASE Personal Fitness Recording Sheet

PASE Basketball Personal Fitness Recording Sheet

Name: _____ Age: _____ Gender: ☐ Male ☐ Female

Instructions: To record your personal fitness information for each lesson:

1. Circle the number of the workout that you completed for each fitness component.
2. If a cell has the symbol "☐," check it off when the workout is correctly completed.
3. If a cell is empty, record a number (e.g., "14") when the workout is successfully completed.

KEY

HFZ = healthy fitness zone

FITNESS COMPONENTS

	Aerobic fitness (AF) and body composition (BC)	Flexibility (Flx)	Muscular fitness (MF)	Skill related (S-R)
Prescore	PACER:____laps ☐ HFZ BMI: ☐ HFZ Height:____in. Weight:____lb	Sit and reach R:____in. ☐ HFZ L:____in. ☐ HFZ Shoulder stretch R ☐ HFZ L ☐ HFZ	Push-up: ☐ HFZ Curl-up: ☐ HFZ Mod. pull-up: ☐ HFZ Trunk lift: ☐ HFZ	1. 2. 3. 4.

Lesson	AF workout no.	Ending heart rate?	Red face?	Sweating?	Breathing heavy?	Flx workout no.	Stretch slowly?	Muscle tension?	No bounce?	Hold 10-30 sec.	MF workout no.	Activity repetitions A.	B.	C.	S-R workout no.	Repetitions
Example	①2 3④	152	☑	☑	☑	①2 3④	☑	☑	☑	☑	①2 3④	12	17	13	①2 3④	6
Practice	1 2 3 4	☐	☐	☐	1 2 3 4	☐	☐	☐	☐	1 2 3 4				1 2 3 4	
3.	1 2 3 4	☐	☐	☐	1 2 3 4	☐	☐	☐	☐	1 2 3 4				1 2 3 4	
4.	1 2 3 4	☐	☐	☐	1 2 3 4	☐	☐	☐	☐	1 2 3 4				1 2 3 4	
5.	1 2 3 4	☐	☐	☐	1 2 3 4	☐	☐	☐	☐	1 2 3 4				1 2 3 4	
6.	1 2 3 4	☐	☐	☐	1 2 3 4	☐	☐	☐	☐	1 2 3 4				1 2 3 4	
7.	1 2 3 4	☐	☐	☐	1 2 3 4	☐	☐	☐	☐	1 2 3 4				1 2 3 4	
8.	1 2 3 4	☐	☐	☐	1 2 3 4	☐	☐	☐	☐	1 2 3 4				1 2 3 4	
9.	1 2 3 4	☐	☐	☐	1 2 3 4	☐	☐	☐	☐	1 2 3 4				1 2 3 4	
10.	1 2 3 4	☐	☐	☐	1 2 3 4	☐	☐	☐	☐	1 2 3 4				1 2 3 4	
11.	1 2 3 4	☐	☐	☐	1 2 3 4	☐	☐	☐	☐	1 2 3 4				1 2 3 4	

From *Sport Education Seasons* by Sean M. Bulger et al., 2007, Champaign, IL: Human Kinetics.

Lesson	AF workout no.	Ending heart rate?	Red face?	Sweating?	Breathing heavy?	Flx workout no.	Stretch slowly?	Muscle tension?	No bounce?	Hold 10-30 sec.	MF workout no.	Activity repetitions A.	B.	C.	S-R workout no.	Repetitions
12.	1 2 3 4	☐	☐	☐	1 2 3 4	☐	☐	☐	☐	1 2 3 4				1 2 3 4	
13.	1 2 3 4	☐	☐	☐	1 2 3 4	☐	☐	☐	☐	1 2 3 4				1 2 3 4	
14.	1 2 3 4	☐	☐	☐	1 2 3 4	☐	☐	☐	☐	1 2 3 4				1 2 3 4	
15.	1 2 3 4	☐	☐	☐	1 2 3 4	☐	☐	☐	☐	1 2 3 4				1 2 3 4	
16.	1 2 3 4	☐	☐	☐	1 2 3 4	☐	☐	☐	☐	1 2 3 4				1 2 3 4	
17.	1 2 3 4	☐	☐	☐	1 2 3 4	☐	☐	☐	☐	1 2 3 4				1 2 3 4	
18.	1 2 3 4	☐	☐	☐	1 2 3 4	☐	☐	☐	☐	1 2 3 4				1 2 3 4	
19.	1 2 3 4	☐	☐	☐	1 2 3 4	☐	☐	☐	☐	1 2 3 4				1 2 3 4	
20.	1 2 3 4	☐	☐	☐	1 2 3 4	☐	☐	☐	☐	1 2 3 4				1 2 3 4	
22.	1 2 3 4	☐	☐	☐	1 2 3 4	☐	☐	☐	☐	1 2 3 4				1 2 3 4	
23.	1 2 3 4	☐	☐	☐	1 2 3 4	☐	☐	☐	☐	1 2 3 4				1 2 3 4	

	Aerobic fitness	Flexibility	Muscular fitness	Skill related
Goals	PACER:____laps ☐ HFZ BMI/%: ☐ HFZ Height:____in. Weight:____lb	Sit and reach R:____in. ☐ HFZ L:____in. ☐ HFZ Shoulder stretch R ☐ HFZ L ☐ HFZ	Push-up: ☐ HFZ Curl-up: ☐ HFZ Mod. pull-up: ☐ HFZ Trunk lift: ☐ HFZ	1. 2. 3. 4.
Postscore	PACER:____laps ☐ HFZ BMI/%: ☐ HFZ Height:____in. Weight:____lb	Sit and reach R:____in. ☐ HFZ L:____in. ☐ HFZ Shoulder stretch R ☐ HFZ L ☐ HFZ	Push-up: ☐ HFZ Curl-up: ☐ HFZ Mod. pull-up: ☐ HFZ Trunk lift: ☐ HFZ	1. 2. 3. 4.

From *Sport Education Seasons* by Sean M. Bulger et al., 2007, Champaign, IL: Human Kinetics.

PURPOSE

To provide students with an effective method of recording and tracking their personal health- and skill-related physical fitness scores over time. Additionally, this form affords the teacher a means of holding students accountable for performing a series of developmentally appropriate activities that can be used to prepare for sport-specific activity.

WHEN TO USE

During team warm-ups

SUGGESTED USE

After performing a selected workout from the fitness activities sheets, each student should record selected information on his or her own personal fitness recording sheet. For each card, students should record which workout number they performed. In addition, for aerobic fitness (AF), they will include their ending heart rate and respond to effort level indicators. For flexibility (Flx), they'll mark whether they met all the criteria for performing the flexibility activities correctly. The muscular fitness (MF) and skill-related (S-R) cards require the students to record the number of repetitions completed during a set. In addition to recording their fitness information during their daily workouts, students have a place to record the fitness scores obtained during the pre-combine. There is also a place for goal setting and post-combine scores.

MODIFICATIONS

- Modify the number of days on which students record fitness information.
- Modify the type of fitness information required.

DOCUMENT LOCATION

Chapter 6—pages 296-297 and PASE Basketball Season CD-ROM—pages 6-7 in appendix B

PASE Team Fitness Recording Sheet

PASE Basketball Team Fitness Recording Sheet

Team: _____

Instructions: To begin each lesson, select a warm-up (1, 2, 3, or 4) and circle your team's choice. Remember that your team cannot repeat a workout that they have previously done until your team has completed all four workouts. Check off each activity as your team completes it. After finishing the warm-up, record the names of your teammates who are absent or late on the Attendance Recording Sheet. Beside each name, use an "A" to indicate absent or an "L" to indicate late. Lastly, sign your name to indicate that the information is correct.

LESSONS																			
	3				4				5				6				7		
Warm-up activities	1	2	3	4	1	2	3	4	1	2	3	4	1	2	3	4	1	2	3	4
Aerobic fitness (AF)	☐				☐				☐				☐				☐		
Flexibility (Flx)	☐				☐				☐				☐				☐		
Muscular fitness (MF)	☐				☐				☐				☐				☐		
Skill-related fitness (S-R)	☐				☐				☐				☐				☐		
Fitness trainer signature																			

	8				9				10				11				12		
Warm-up activities	1	2	3	4	1	2	3	4	1	2	3	4	1	2	3	4	1	2	3	4
AF Aerobic fitness	☐				☐				☐				☐				☐		
Flx Flexibility	☐				☐				☐				☐				☐		
MF Muscular fitness	☐				☐				☐				☐				☐		
S-R Skill-related fitness	☐				☐				☐				☐				☐		
Fitness trainer signature																			

	13				14				15				16				17		
Warm-up activities	1	2	3	4	1	2	3	4	1	2	3	4	1	2	3	4	1	2	3	4
AF Aerobic fitness	☐				☐				☐				☐				☐		
Flx Flexibility	☐				☐				☐				☐				☐		
MF Muscular fitness	☐				☐				☐				☐				☐		
S-R Skill-related fitness	☐				☐				☐				☐				☐		
Fitness trainer signature																			

	18				19				20				22				23		
Warm-up activities	1	2	3	4	1	2	3	4	1	2	3	4	1	2	3	4	1	2	3	4
AF Aerobic fitness	☐				☐				☐				☐				☐		
Flx Flexibility	☐				☐				☐				☐				☐		
MF Muscular fitness	☐				☐				☐				☐				☐		
S-R Skill-related fitness	☐				☐				☐				☐				☐		
Fitness trainer signature																			

From *Sport Education Seasons* by Sean M. Bulger et al., 2007, Champaign, IL: Human Kinetics.

PURPOSE

To provide students with an effective method of recording their team health- and skill-related physical fitness engagement. Additionally, this form gives the teacher a means of holding students accountable as a team for performing a series of developmentally appropriate activities that can be used to prepare for sport-specific activity.

WHEN TO USE

During team warm-ups

SUGGESTED USE

After the fitness trainer selects a workout from the fitness activities sheets, he or she should lead the team through each of the activities. When the workout is completed, the fitness trainer checks off the appropriate box under the lesson in which the workout is taking place. A checked box means that the entire team performed the fitness activities on a particular card to criteria. The signature of the fitness trainer indicates that the information recorded is correct. While this form of assessment provides a much smaller amount of information in relation to personal physical fitness levels, it still provides an adequate measure of accountability for the students.

MODIFICATIONS

- Modify the number of days on which students record fitness information.
- Modify the type of fitness information required.

DOCUMENT LOCATION

Chapter 6—page 298 and PASE Basketball Season CD-ROM—page 8 in appendix B

PASE Official's Pocket Reference—the Pocket Ref

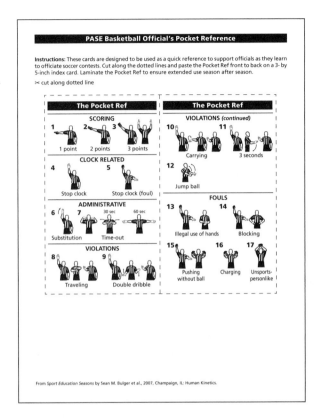

From *Sport Education Seasons* by Sean M. Bulger et al., 2007, Champaign, IL: Human Kinetics.

PURPOSE

To provide students with a complete list of the official's signals in a portable format. This quick reference is designed to be used by the officials during game play to improve the quality of their contest management.

WHEN TO USE

During the application contests

SUGGESTED USE

The official's pocket reference is a consolidated and portable version of the official's signals index. The Pocket Ref was created to provide immediate support to officials during game play. Students are often expected to remember a large quantity of information about contest rules and signals, especially as the season progresses. The pocket reference is an instructional tool that gives the student official a "companion" to aid in the carrying out of his or her responsibilities. All student officials are required to have the Pocket Ref on their person during application contests whether they feel the need to use it or not.

MODIFICATIONS

- Modify the number of signals included in the Pocket Ref.
- Laminate the Pocket Ref for repeated use.
- Punch a hole in the Pocket Ref and attach a type of tether. The students should then attach the Pocket Ref to their wrist, waist, or another area so as to be able to consult the Pocket Ref quickly.

DOCUMENT LOCATION

Chapter 6—page 306 and PASE Soccer Season CD-ROM—page 16 in appendix B

PASE Individual Activity Task Card Recording Sheet

PASE Basketball Individual Activity Task Card Recording Sheet

Name: _____   Team: _____

Instructions: Mark tasks off as you complete them. If a cell has the symbol "□," check it off (like this: "☑") when the task is completed. If a cell has the symbol "#," record a number (e.g., 14) when the task is completed. Leave empty cells blank.

KEY: ✝ = Self-evaluation   ✝✝ = Peer evaluation   ↻ = Coach evaluation

Task	Lesson 3 Dribble to reposition ✝	✝✝	↻	Lesson 4 Speed dribble and chest pass ✝	✝✝	↻	Lesson 5 Dribble review and pass ✝	✝✝	↻	Lesson 7 Shooting and def. mov't. ✝	✝✝	↻	Lesson 8 Layup and give and go ✝	✝✝	↻
1.			□			□			□			□			□
2.			□			□			□			□			□
3.	□			□					□	□					#__
4.	□			□				□		□					□
5.	□			□				□		□					□
6.	□			□			#__					□			□
7.		□			□				□	#__					□
8.	#__			□				□		□					□
9.	□			#__				□				□			□
10.	□			□			#__	□				□			□
11.	□			□				□				□			□
12.	#__			□				□				□			□
13.	□			#__				□				□			□
14.	□				□		#__		□	□			#__		
15.				□			#__			#__			#__		
16.	#__			□			#__					□	#__		
17.	□			#__								□			
18.	□			#__								□			
19.	□											□			
20.			□									□			
21.	#__									#__					
Coach's initials															

(continued)

From *Sport Education Seasons* by Sean M. Bulger et al., 2007, Champaign, IL: Human Kinetics.

PASE Basketball Individual Activity Task Card Recording Sheet *(continued)*

KEY: ✝ = Self-evaluation   ✝✝ = Peer evaluation   ↻ = Coach evaluation

Task	Lesson 9 Shooting, layups, screening ✝	✝✝	↻	Lesson 11 Rebounding ✝	✝✝	↻	Lesson 12 Post play ✝	✝✝	↻	Lesson 13 Player-to-player defense ✝	✝✝	↻	Lesson 14 Team zone defense ✝	✝✝	↻
1.			□			□			□			□			□
2.			□			□			□			□			□
3.	□					□			□			□			□
4.	□					□			□			□			□
5.			□			□			□			□			
6.	□					□			□	#__			□		
7.		□				□			□	#__					
8.		□				□			□			#__			
9.	#__			#__			#__					#__			
10.	#__			#__			#__					#__			
11.	#__						#__								□
12.															
13.															
14.															
15.															
16.															
17.															
18.															
19.															
20.															
21.															
Coach's initials															

From *Sport Education Seasons* by Sean M. Bulger et al., 2007, Champaign, IL: Human Kinetics.

PURPOSE

To afford students the opportunity to record successful completion of learning tasks specified on the activity task cards. This recording sheet also gives the students increased accountability in that they must be able to demonstrate competence in a series of hierarchical, developmentally appropriate instructional activities. Refer to PASE Basketball Activity Task Card 3 on page 136 for an example of how to use this recording sheet and the associated task card.

WHEN TO USE

During team practice

SUGGESTED USE

Under the supervision of the team coach, students should move through the activity task card as a team, or individuals may elect to progress through the tasks at their own rate. Once the student has completed a task and has been assessed by the appropriate individual (self, peer, or coach), he or she should indicate task completion by checking the appropriate box on the individual recording sheet. The recording sheet is labeled with the lesson number, content for the day, and assessment levels. The student should select the appropriate column, indicate tasks completed, and record any quantitative information requested. During review days, students can select activity task cards that they have not completed entirely. When all tasks have been completed for a specific activity task card, the student coach will sign off indicating that the student is indeed done. Refer to PASE Basketball Activity Task Card 3 on page 136 for an example of an individual activity task card.

MODIFICATIONS

- Modify the number of tasks included on the activity task card.
- Modify the number of times students need to record task completion information.

DOCUMENT LOCATION

Chapter 6—pages 303-304 and PASE Basketball Season CD-ROM—pages 13-14 in appendix B

PASE Team Activity Task Card Recording Sheet

PASE Basketball Team Activity Task Card Recording Sheet

Team: _____

Instructions:

- Write each team member's name on the top of the following chart.
- At the end of team practice, record the last task completed.
- During the daily review portion of the lesson or on review days, resume incomplete task cards where you left off. For example, if during lesson 3 team practice you got to task 10, then during lesson 4 review time you can work to complete the lesson 3 task card by resuming practice with task 11.
- Once you have completed all tasks to criteria for a particular lesson, check "Yes."
- If you are unable to complete all tasks for a particular lesson by the end of the season, check "No."
- At the end of the season, certify your record by signing your initials at the bottom of your column.

Names																
Lesson (task card #)	Task number	Completed card by end of season?	Task number	Completed card by end of season?	Task number	Completed card by end of season?	Task number	Completed card by end of season?	Task number	Completed card by end of season?	Task number	Completed card by end of season?	Task number	Completed card by end of season?		
Practice	—	☐ Yes ☐ No	—	☐ Yes ☐ No	—	☐ Yes ☐ No		☐ Yes ☐ No	—	☐ Yes ☐ No		☐ Yes ☐ No	—	☐ Yes ☐ No		
3		☐ Yes ☐ No		☐ Yes ☐ No		☐ Yes ☐ No		☐ Yes ☐ No		☐ Yes ☐ No		☐ Yes ☐ No		☐ Yes ☐ No		
4		☐ Yes ☐ No		☐ Yes ☐ No		☐ Yes ☐ No		☐ Yes ☐ No		☐ Yes ☐ No		☐ Yes ☐ No		☐ Yes ☐ No		
5		☐ Yes ☐ No		☐ Yes ☐ No		☐ Yes ☐ No		☐ Yes ☐ No		☐ Yes ☐ No		☐ Yes ☐ No		☐ Yes ☐ No		
7		☐ Yes ☐ No		☐ Yes ☐ No		☐ Yes ☐ No		☐ Yes ☐ No		☐ Yes ☐ No		☐ Yes ☐ No		☐ Yes ☐ No		
8		☐ Yes ☐ No		☐ Yes ☐ No		☐ Yes ☐ No		☐ Yes ☐ No		☐ Yes ☐ No		☐ Yes ☐ No		☐ Yes ☐ No		
9		☐ Yes ☐ No		☐ Yes ☐ No		☐ Yes ☐ No		☐ Yes ☐ No		☐ Yes ☐ No		☐ Yes ☐ No		☐ Yes ☐ No		
11		☐ Yes ☐ No		☐ Yes ☐ No		☐ Yes ☐ No		☐ Yes ☐ No		☐ Yes ☐ No		☐ Yes ☐ No		☐ Yes ☐ No		
12		☐ Yes ☐ No		☐ Yes ☐ No		☐ Yes ☐ No		☐ Yes ☐ No		☐ Yes ☐ No		☐ Yes ☐ No		☐ Yes ☐ No		
13		☐ Yes ☐ No		☐ Yes ☐ No		☐ Yes ☐ No		☐ Yes ☐ No		☐ Yes ☐ No		☐ Yes ☐ No		☐ Yes ☐ No		
14		☐ Yes ☐ No		☐ Yes ☐ No		☐ Yes ☐ No		☐ Yes ☐ No		☐ Yes ☐ No		☐ Yes ☐ No		☐ Yes ☐ No		
Team's signatures																

From *Sport Education Seasons* by Sean M. Bulger et al., 2007, Champaign, IL: Human Kinetics.

PURPOSE

To afford students the opportunity to record successful completion of learning tasks specified on the activity task cards. Furthermore, the sheet gives students increased accountability in that they must be able to demonstrate competence in a series of hierarchical, developmentally appropriate instructional activities.

WHEN TO USE

During team practice

SUGGESTED USE

Under the supervision of the team coach, students should move through the activity task card as a team, or individuals may elect to progress through the tasks at their own rate. Following team practice, students should remember the task last completed. They will then inform the coach, who will record the information on a team recording sheet. This sheet is an overview of which task team members most recently finished. It is important to note that while students do not check off task completion after each task, they should still be assessed by the appropriate individual—self, peer, or coach—before moving to subsequent tasks. The recording sheet has two main columns: the task number column and the completed-card column. During review days, students can select activity task cards that they have not completed entirely. When all tasks have been completed for a specific activity task card, the student will check off the appropriate box in the completed-card column and sign his or her name at the bottom of the recording sheet.

MODIFICATIONS

- Modify the number of tasks included on the activity task card.
- Modify the number of times students need to record task completion information.

DOCUMENT LOCATION

Chapter 6— page 305 and PASE Basketball Season CD-ROM—page 15 in appendix B

PASE Outside-of-Class Physical Activity Participation Log

PASE Basketball Outside-of-Class Physical Activity Participation Log

Name: _____ Team: _____

Instructions: Select at least four days this week on which you will participate in physical activity outside of class. Plan to do activities that will help increase your skill and fitness levels for the current sport season. Be realistic in setting your goals and planning these activities. Choose activities that you enjoy and can do with a friend or family member. Try to participate in a total of 30 to 60 minutes of physical activity on most, if not all, days of the week.

SCORING CRITERIA

☐ Planned for at least four days of activity by filling in the "Planned" columns for each day.
☐ Performed and completed required information in the "Actual" columns for each day planned.
☐ The activity engaged in aided in increasing levels of fitness or skill related to the season being taught.
☐ Signed by parent or guardian and student.

In order to improve my sport skills and health, this week I plan to do the following:

| Day and date | Physical activity | | How long? | | With whom? | | RPE | |
	Planned	Actual	Planned	Actual	Planned	Actual	Planned	Actual
☐ Monday 05/05/06	In-line skating	In-line skating	1/2 hour	45 min	Alone	With brother	3	4
☐ __/__/__								
☐ __/__/__								
☐ __/__/__								
☐ __/__/__								
☐ __/__/__								
☐ __/__/__								
☐ __/__/__								

RATING OF PERCEIVED ENJOYMENT SCALE

The activity I engage(d) in will be/was:

4—extremely enjoyable   2—somewhat enjoyable
3—mostly enjoyable   1—not enjoyable at all

Student signature _____
Parent/Guardian signature _____
Teacher signature _____

From *Sport Education Seasons* by Sean M. Bulger et al., 2007, Champaign, IL: Human Kinetics.

PURPOSE

To provide students with the opportunity to document, monitor, and increase the amount of time spent engaging in personally meaningful, health-enhancing physical activity. The log serves to encourage regular participation in physical activity during students' leisure time on all days of the week.

WHEN TO USE

Outside of the physical education class

SUGGESTED USE

The log should be provided to students early in the season, usually during the management lesson. Students are then directed to plan for physical activity on at least four days during the upcoming week and to schedule this activity on their log. The teacher should encourage the students to engage in activities related to the content being covered during the current season, but should not limit student choice. After students complete each bout of physical activity they should record the required information in the space provided. At the end of each week the teacher should collect the logs and hand out new logs for the upcoming week.

MODIFICATIONS

- Alter the requirements for outside-of-class physical activity.
- Use team points as an additional incentive for students to engage in outside-of-class physical activity.
- Use team points as an additional incentive for students to accurately complete and hand in the outside-of-class physical activity log.
- Designate time during the school day, after the school day, or on weekends when the gymnasium or field areas can be used for outside-of-class physical activity.

DOCUMENT LOCATION

Chapter 6—page 310 and PASE Basketball Season CD-ROM—page 20 in appendix B

PASE Team Goal-Setting Sheet

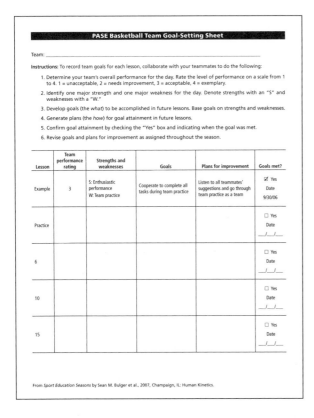

PURPOSE

To provide students with the opportunity to document, monitor, and enhance team performance across a PASE season. The goal-setting sheet prompts students to interact by diagnosing team strengths and weaknesses and developing plans for maintaining strengths and improving upon weaknesses. This instrument facilitates cooperative problem solving and team goal attainment throughout a PASE season.

WHEN TO USE

Completed during the team progress reporting lesson segment; referred to during the team review lesson segment to direct team review efforts

SUGGESTED USE

The goal-setting sheet should be provided to student teams after two or three skill and tactical lessons have been completed so that they will have experiences to diagnose. Once the sheets are distributed, each team is challenged to determine their strengths and weaknesses and subsequently develop goals and strategies for improving performance. The teacher should monitor each team's interactions and encourage individuals to contribute to both the diagnosis and goal and strategy development processes. Once an assigned section of the goal-setting sheet is completed, students can regularly refer back to the sheet during subsequent lessons in order to determine if they have achieved their goal(s). Diagnosis, goal setting, and the evaluation of goals should be viewed as an ongoing, never-ending process as teams strive to improve over the course of a season.

MODIFICATIONS

- Alter the requirements for the goal-setting sheet by adding or reducing the number of days during the season when the goal-setting sheet is filled out.
- Use team points as an additional incentive for students to accurately complete the goal-setting sheet.
- Award team points for the attainment of team goals.

DOCUMENT LOCATION

Chapter 6—page 314 and PASE Basketball Season CD-ROM—page 2 in appendix C

PASE Reflective Journal

PASE Basketball Reflective Journal

Instructions: Answer the following questions completely. Your responses should be related specifically to the lessons that have occurred since your last journal entry. To receive full credit for your journal entry, be sure to address each area of the scoring criteria. Journal writings will be due at the beginning of lessons 13 and 24. For lesson 13, answer questions 1 and 2; for lesson 24, answer questions 3, 4, and 5.

SCORING CRITERIA

☐ Answered assigned questions completely and honestly
☐ Provided specific, personal examples from physical education class to support answers
☐ Used proper grammar and punctuation

Questions

1. During the past lessons you have participated in a variety of different roles. You were required to plan for and organize certain aspects of the PASE basketball season.
   • Describe the parts of the season you planned for and organized. In what ways did your plans work or not work?
   • With what level of responsibility do you feel you completed your planning and organizational duties? Why?
   • How would you plan differently in the future?
   • What role did you enjoy most? Why?

2. In the various roles that you have engaged in as part of the PASE basketball season, you have provided leadership.
   • Describe one way in which you have displayed leadership to your team, to another team, or to the whole class.
   • How did this experience make you feel?
   • What can you do to become a better leader?

3. Throughout the PASE basketball season, your team has developed many goals.
   • List one goal that your team has set and achieved.
   • Provide an explanation as to how you and your teammates accomplished this goal.
   • Describe how meeting this goal made you feel.
   • List a goal that your team has set and has not yet achieved.
   • Provide an explanation of what is preventing your team from meeting that goal.
   • Describe how not yet meeting this goal has made you feel.

4. Your team has developed many rituals during this PASE basketball season.
   • Describe a unique ritual that you and your teammates have created during this PASE basketball season.
   • Why is this an appropriate ritual for this particular sport season?
   • Compare and contrast the ritual your team created with those of other teams.

5. Think back to a situation during the PASE basketball season when you feel you may have been treated unfairly.
   • List who was involved in the situation and describe why you believe the incident occurred.
   • How did you handle this incident?
   • How did this incident make you feel?
   • How could this issue have been handled to create a more positive outcome?

From *Sport Education Seasons* by Sean M. Bulger et al., 2007, Champaign, IL: Human Kinetics.

PURPOSE

To provide students with the opportunity to critically analyze their experiences in physical activity settings.

WHEN TO USE

Outside of the physical education class

SUGGESTED USE

The journal assignment should be provided to students early in the season to increase students' awareness of what they will eventually reflect upon. Student reflections should be due at specific points throughout the season, such as near the end of weeks 3 and 5 or lessons 13 and 24. It is important to schedule journaling assignments carefully so that students have enough experience to reflect upon, but not so much to reflect on that important information is lost. Keep in mind that responses to questions represent students' perceptions and therefore are neither right nor wrong. However, the criteria should be used to promote critical reflection and ensure complete responses.

MODIFICATIONS

- Alter the requirements for the reflective journal.
- Increase or reduce the number of questions used.
- Increase or reduce the number of days during the season when journal entries are handed in.
- Use team points as an additional incentive for students to accurately complete and hand in the journal entries.
- Designate time during a lesson for journaling to take place.

DOCUMENT LOCATION

Chapter 6—page 315 and PASE Basketball Season CD-ROM—page 3 in appendix C

PASE Independent Learning Activity

PASE Basketball Independent Learning Activity

Instructions: Select one of the following roles that you would like to perform within the local community (e.g., the recreation center, the YMCA, for an afternoon). As you determine your choice, note that the criteria for each role are similar to responsibilities that you performed for these roles in physical education class. As you complete the optional role, check off each criterion. Once you have completed the optional role, summarize your experiences. This assignment is due at the beginning of lesson 25.

OPTIONAL ROLE CHOICES AND CRITERIA

Basketball Manager
☐ Inspected and cared for equipment
☐ Assumed administrative duties assigned
☐ Distributed and collected equipment
☐ Monitored time of activities
☐ Monitored participants' performance
☐ Organized practice/game space

Basketball Trainer
☐ Selected appropriate warm-up activities
☐ Reported injuries to appropriate personnel
☐ Led/monitored warm-up activities
☐ Aided in administering first aid if needed

Basketball Reporter
☐ Selected one player from each team to interview following the sporting event
☐ Selected one coach to interview following the sporting event
☐ Acquired statistics
☐ Wrote a 1/2-page sports column

SUMMARY OF EXPERIENCE

Instructions: Write a summary of your optional role experience. Use the following scoring rubric to help you write the summary. Provide an explanation of how you chose your role, how you prepared to complete your role to criteria, and how you met each criterion associated with your role.

SCORING RUBRIC

4 = exemplary
• Fully explained role choice and plan for completing role
• Completed all responsibilities associated with the selected role
• Explained each role responsibility, provided specific examples

3 = acceptable
• Mostly explained role choice and plan for completing role
• Completed most of the responsibilities associated with the selected role
• Explained most of the responsibilities, provided examples

2 = needs improvement
• Vaguely explained role choice and plan for completing role
• Completed few of the responsibilities associated with the selected role
• Explained a few of the responsibilities, used few examples

1 = unacceptable
• Did not explain role choice or plan for completing role
• Did not complete any of the responsibilities associated with the selected role
• Did not explain any of the responsibilities or provide any examples

From *Sport Education Seasons* by Sean M. Bulger et al., 2007, Champaign, IL: Human Kinetics.

PURPOSE

To provide students with the opportunity to further their involvement in physical activity settings in an outside-of-class environment. Additionally, the learning activity may encourage voluntary student involvement within community-based venues.

WHEN TO USE

Outside of the physical education class

SUGGESTED USE

The independent learning activity should be given to students late in the season after they have demonstrated competent role performance. Students should be given a variety of role choices so they can select a role that closely matches their interests and abilities. The teacher should assist students in finding appropriate placements within the community where they will be adequately supervised and their role responsibilities can be carried out to criteria. Because of the variable nature of both the role responsibilities and the contexts under which these roles are performed, the associated scoring rubric should be used to standardize assessment of students' role performance.

MODIFICATIONS

- Alter the number of roles students can select from.
- Alter the responsibilities associated with each role.
- Use team points as an additional incentive for students to engage in outside-of-class roles.
- Use team points as an additional incentive for students to accurately complete and hand in the summary of their outside-of-class physical activity role experience.
- Develop awards to recognize individuals' exemplary role performance.

DOCUMENT LOCATION

Chapter 6—page 316 and PASE Basketball Season CD-ROM—page 4 in appendix C

PASE Knowledge Quiz

PASE Basketball Knowledge Quiz 1

Name_____ Date_____

Instructions: Please answer the following multiple-choice questions by placing your answers in the blank to the left of the question.

____ 1. Which movement would be most efficient when shooting a layup from the right side of the basket?
a. stand on both feet, shoot with right hand
b. take off from the right foot, shoot with left hand
c. take off from left foot, shoot with both hands
d. take off from the left foot, shoot with right hand

____ 2. Which body part is essential to keep in line with the basket when shooting a jump shot?
a. legs
b. shoulders
c. hips
d. arms

____ 3. How many steps can a player take without traveling?
a. 1
b. 2
c. 3
d. 0

____ 4. What is the most significant factor to stress when performing a pass?
a. stepping into the pass
b. keeping the elbows in
c. handling the ball with the fingers
d. using a wrist snap upon release

____ 5. Where should a player's eyes be focused during dribbling?
a. downward in order to control the ball
b. downward in order to see the feet of a defensive player
c. forward in order to pass to a teammate
d. forward in order to alternate hands quickly

____ 6. Player A is cutting for the basket and runs into player B, who had an established guarding position. What is the official's decision?
a. blocking on player A
b. charging on player A
c. blocking on player B
d. charging on player B

____ 7. What is the action of the player without the ball who moves into an open area to receive a pass?
a. cutting
b. feinting
c. driving
d. faking

From *Sport Education Seasons* by Sean M. Bulger et al., 2007, Champaign, IL: Human Kinetics.   *(continued)*

____ 8. What should you do after you set a pick?
a. keep the defensive player from moving
b. wait to receive the pass
c. roll toward the goal, keeping the defensive player at your back
d. roll away from the goal, keeping the defensive player at your back

____ 9. Which statement best describes a give and go?
a. setting a screen against a teammate's guard and roll
b. moving into an open space hoping to receive the ball
c. passing to a teammate followed by a cut and return pass
d. moving in one direction followed by a quick move in another direction

____ 10. The following official's signal represents what?
a. charging
b. illegal use of hands
c. blocking
d. double dribble

PASE BASKETBALL KNOWLEDGE QUIZ 1 KEY

1. d	6. b
2. b	7. a
3. b	8. c
4. d	9. c
5. c	10. d

From *Sport Education Seasons* by Sean M. Bulger et al., 2007, Champaign, IL: Human Kinetics.

PURPOSE

To provide students with the opportunity to demonstrate the knowledge they possess about the skills, tactics, and rules related to the activity being taught.

WHEN TO USE

During the team review, team practice, or team and progress reporting lesson segments

SUGGESTED USE

Quizzes should be administered at specific points across the season once the material of interest has been taught. We have opted for the use of two quizzes to be administered during lessons 10 and 15. Students should be given a reasonable amount of time to complete a quiz. The time allotment should be based on the amount and type of quiz questions and on students' developmental levels and test-taking ability. Be sure to cover the answer key before making copies for the students.

MODIFICATIONS

- Change the number of questions, type of questions, or both.
- Give the quiz to individuals or use as a team quiz.
- Average team quiz scores and assign team points based on the team averages.
- Establish a criterion score such as 80% and assign team points as individuals within a team meet or exceed the criterion score.
- Assign the quiz as an outside-of-class activity.

DOCUMENT LOCATION

Chapter 6—pages 198-199 and PASE Basketball Season CD-ROM—pages 94-95

PASE Event Tasks

PASE Soccer Event Tasks

Instructions: Your team must complete the event task as described. Use the scoring rubric shown after the event task descriptions to help your team plan for and monitor your progress while completing the event task. While there are a variety of ways to plan for and perform the event tasks, each team will be evaluated using the same scoring rubric.

EVENT TASK 1: GRADE 12

Your team has been asked to organize a soccer station as part of a soccer clinic for upper elementary and middle school-aged children in your community. The soccer clinic will require your team to teach one skill or strategy that you learned during the PASE soccer season. Identify the skill or strategy that you will teach and develop a plan for teaching this information to 10 children at a time. Develop and assign individual roles to each member of your team for the soccer clinic. Make sure the responsibilities for each role are clearly defined so that each team member understands his or her specific job for the soccer clinic. The soccer clinic will last for 40 minutes, and your team will teach the station to four groups of 10 children within this time limit.

EVENT TASK 2: GRADE 10

Your team's assignment is to create a script for a play about social acceptance within a soccer event. Create a play that demonstrates your team's understanding of and respect for others during a game of soccer. Identify each of the roles that will be included in your play. Within your play, develop examples of appropriate and inappropriate interactions that might possibly take place during a game of soccer. Examples of sporting issues that your play can include are (a) acceptance of persons from different cultures, (b) the inclusion of students with special needs, (c) playing with students who have differing levels of skill, and (d) spectator behavior. Each team member should have some part in the planning and acting out of your play. The play will last for 7 to 10 minutes.

EVENT TASK 3: GRADE 8

Your soccer team has been chosen to develop an awards banquet to bring the end of the soccer season to a festive close. In planning for the soccer banquet your team must determine the awards to be given and the criteria for each award. As you plan for the soccer awards banquet, remember that each person from every team should receive an award of some kind. Your team must also create an itinerary for the soccer banquet, plan for and invite a guest speaker (preferably a current or former soccer player), and develop a healthy refreshments menu. The awards banquet will last 30 minutes.

SCORING RUBRIC FOR EVENT TASKS

4 = exemplary
- Provided complete and comprehensive rationale for decisions the team made when planning.
- All team members were included and each had a defined role.
- All social interactions were positive; there were no conflicts during planning.
- All ideas from team members were accepted or given equal consideration.

3 = acceptable
- Provided complete and comprehensive rationale for most decisions the team made when planning.
- Most team members were included and most had a defined role.
- Most social interactions were positive; any minor conflicts were resolved during planning.
- Most ideas from team members were accepted or given equal consideration.

2 = needs improvement
- Provided incomplete rationales for decisions the team made when planning.
- Several people on the team were not included and several roles were not clearly defined.
- Most social interactions were negative; some conflicts remained unresolved.
- Most ideas from team members were not accepted or given equal consideration.

1 = unacceptable
- Provided no rationales for the decisions the team made when planning.
- Most team members were not included and no roles were clearly defined.
- All social interactions were negative; most conflicts remained unresolved.
- All ideas from team members were not accepted or given equal consideration.

PURPOSE

To provide students with the opportunity to perform tasks allowing them to utilize their developing skills, knowledge, and dispositions in authentic environments. Event tasks promote critical thinking, teamwork, and personal and social responsibility.

WHEN TO USE

During team practice

SUGGESTED USE

The event task scenarios should be provided to students as early as possible during the season. However, the teacher must carefully match the complexity of the scenario with the students' skills, knowledge, and dispositions. Teams work to complete the event task as a group and should be allotted a reasonable amount of time to complete the task. The time allotment should be based on the complexity of the task, students' developmental readiness, and time constraints within the setting. Since the task is designed to engage students in a cooperative, problem-solving process, the associated scoring rubric should be discussed with students prior to their engagement with the task. It is important to note that task solutions are neither right nor wrong. Solutions, however, should be scored using the criteria from the scoring rubric.

MODIFICATIONS

- Change the number or type of scenarios.
- Alter the requirements of the scenarios.
- Use team points as an additional incentive for students to appropriately engage in event tasks.
- Provide additional time or resources for students to complete the event tasks.

DOCUMENT LOCATION

PASE Soccer Season CD-ROM—page 4 in appendix C

PASE Lesson Plan

PASE BASKETBALL LESSON PLAN 3

Resources: Lesson Focus
- Numbered colored pinnies—six per team (also used during application contest)
- Basketballs—three to six per team (also used during application contest)
- Hula hoops—one per team (used to organize team materials)
- Stopwatches—one per team
- Pencils

Resources: Application Contest
- PASE Application Contest 3
- PASE Application Contest Scorecard 3
- PASE Official's Pocket Reference
- Two to four cones
- Boundary markers
- One clipboard
- Pencils
- Whistles
- Officials' pinnies

Instructional Materials
- PASE IRL Rubric and Recording Sheet (appendix B)
- PASE Attendance Recording Sheet (appendix B)
- PASE Roles and Responsibilities Assignments and Recording Sheet (appendix B)
- PASE Student Coaching Plan 3
- PASE Activity Task Card 3
- PASE Fitness Activities Sheets (appendix B)
- PASE Personal or Team Fitness Recording Sheet (appendix B)
- PASE Individual or Team Activity Task Card Recording Sheet (appendix B)
- PASE Basketball Lesson Plan 4

Instructional Focus
Skills
- Low control dribble
- Offensive footwork

Tactic
- Dribbling to reposition

Objectives
- Develop low control dribble and offensive footwork by progression through learning activities during team practice
- Utilize low control dribble and offensive footwork and demonstrate dribbling to reposition in an application contest
- Demonstrate personal and social responsibility

Team Role Check
- Students enter gymnasium and immediately report to home court area.
- Check daily roles and associated duties from materials provided.

🕐 *Begin team warm-up.*

Team Warm-Up
- Conduct the team warm-up simultaneously to coaches' meeting.
- Fitness trainer monitors team warm-up using the PASE Fitness Activities Sheets.
- Fitness trainer or individuals record performance on team warm-up using either the **Personal** or **Team Fitness Recording Sheet.**

🕐 *Teams transition to daily review.*

Coaches' Meeting
- Conduct the coaches' meeting simultaneously to team warm-up.
- All team coaches report to designated meeting area.
- Teacher provides coaches with **Student Coaching Plan 3** and **Activity Task Card 3.**
- Teacher outlines the day's events.

🕐 *Coaches transition to home court area and join warm-up.*

Team Review
- Review progress of team goals from **lesson 2.** Refer to the activity task cards and application contest results to date.
- Identify areas of need from **lesson 2.**
- Practice to improve in areas of need.

🕐 *Teams transition to designated instructional area for teacher instructions.*

Teacher Instruction
- Introduce daily lesson focus and review **lesson 2.**
- Provide anticipatory set:

💬 The reason we are learning to use the low control dribble and offensive footwork is to create passing lanes by dribbling to reposition. After learning how to move with and without the ball, you will be better at using space to attack the basket.

- Provide information about skills and strategies.
- **Introduce** the following new skills and tactics for the day.
- Complete teacher or student demonstrations (or both) of these skills and tactics:

LOW CONTROL DRIBBLE

Critical features	Instructional cues
Relaxed hand control	Gentle push
Push ball with finger pads	Use of finger pads
Dribble knee to midthigh	Keep ball low
Head up and eyes scanning	Eyes up
Body between ball and defender	Protect ball

PURPOSE

To provide the teacher with an organizational and instructional tool for appropriately implementing PASE lessons. Collectively, the PASE Lesson Plan helps teachers accomplish the goals of PASE and maintain a pedagogical focus throughout a season.

WHEN TO USE

Before and during each lesson

SUGGESTED USE

The lesson plan includes the following:

- Resources
- Instructional materials
- Instructional focus
- Objectives
- Team role check
- Team warm-up and coaches' meeting
- Team review
- Teacher instruction
- Team practice
- Application contest
- Closure
- Individual and team assessment

The teacher should strive to memorize the plan before each lesson. Both the teacher and students are required to carry out specific functions during each lesson component (see table 2.2, Daily Responsibility Guidelines, on p. 11). Accordingly, each lesson component is important and when possible should be accounted for on a daily basis. The time allotted to each lesson segment changes as the season progresses. For example, early in a season more lesson time may be devoted to team practice, while later in the season a majority of lesson time may be devoted to application contests (see table 2.2). While the PASE Lesson Plans are designed for 90-minute block-scheduled classes, you may be required to make modifications to the lessons based on a variety of factors specific to your particular teaching context, such as time, type and number of students, facilities, and equipment.

OFFENSIVE FOOTWORK (L-CUT AND V-CUT)

Critical features	Instructional cues
Keep moving to create passing lanes	Move away from passer
Feint, plant foot to change direction quickly	Quick cut (V or L)
Move toward ball to receive pass	Move toward passer
Assume position with hands set to catch pass	Provide target with hands

DRIBBLING TO REPOSITION

Critical features	Instructional cues
Use critical features of low control dribble	Use proper dribble
Continue to dribble to create passing lanes	Move to open spaces
Players without ball cut to create passing lanes	Teammates use V- or L-cuts to get open
Dribbler anticipates and executes pass	Look to make pass

- **Introduce** today's signals and rules. Demonstrate and explain the following signals and rules:
  - ✦ Stop clock (4)
  - ✦ Traveling (8)
  - ✦ 1-point scoring (1)
- Check for student understanding using questions, student demonstrations, or both.
  - ✦ Q1: "Who can name/demonstrate the critical features for low control dribble?"
  - ✦ Q2: "Who can name/demonstrate the critical features for offensive footwork?"
  - ✦ Q3: "What is the purpose of learning the low control dribble and offensive footwork?"

() Teams transition to home court area for daily team practice.

Team Practice (Refer to Activity Task Card 3 and Individual or Team Activity Task Card Recording Sheet)

Team-directed practice begins. Teacher moves through home court area to facilitate team practice.

- ✦ Manage learning environment.
- ✦ Observe and assess individual and team performance.
- ✦ Provide encouragement and instructional feedback.

() Teams transition back to designated instructional area for application contest.

Application Contest

Teacher explains and demonstrates daily contest (refer to **Application Contest 3**). Identify tactical focus and related skills (refer to **Application Contest Scorecard 3**).

- ✦ Identify contest goals.
- ✦ Discuss procedures for scoring and refereeing.
  - **Scoring:** Use nonshaded areas on **Application Contest Scorecard 3.**

Refereeing: Refer to and use designated referee signals located on the Official's Pocket Reference.

() Teams transition to designated contest areas to perform assigned duties.

- ✦ Teacher actively monitors individual and team performance.

() Teams transition to designated instructional area for closure.

Closure

- ✦ Teacher reviews lesson focus.
- ✦ Teacher discusses assessment of individual and team performance.
- ✦ Check for student understanding using questions and demonstrations (refer back to questions and demonstrations from the introduction, if needed).
- ✦ Allow for student questions and preview **lesson 4.**

() Teams transition to home court areas for individual and team assessment.

Individual and Team Assessment

Assessment summary

- ✦ Complete **PASE IRL Recording Sheet** (each person).
- ✦ Summarize/Complete **Application Contest Scorecard 3** (scorekeeper).
- ✦ Complete **PASE Attendance Recording Sheet** (coach).
- ✦ Complete **PASE Roles and Responsibilities Recording Sheet** (each person).
- ✦ Supervise assessment completion (coach).

() Teams organize materials and exit class from home court areas.

MODIFICATIONS

- First-time users should utilize the "experimental-progressive approach" for implementing lesson components and the associated requirements.
- Alter student requirements within given lesson components.
- Change the number of lesson components addressed within particular lessons.
- Adjust the time allocated to specific lesson components.
- Divide a single lesson in half and teach it across two class meetings.
- Change the number of nonsport-related performer roles.
- Use team points as an additional incentive for students to appropriately engage in each lesson component, transition from one component to the next, or both.

DOCUMENT LOCATION

Chapter 6—pages 129-132 and PASE Basketball Season CD-ROM—pages 25-28

PASE Graphics and Cues

Low Control Dribble

Critical Features
1. Relaxed hand control
2. Push ball with finger pads
3. Dribble knee to midthigh
4. Head up and eyes scanning
5. Body between ball and defender

Instructional Cues
1. Gentle push
2. Use of finger pads
3. Keep ball low
4. Eyes up
5. Protect ball

Description
The low control dribble is used to move the ball up the court. Its purpose is to establish increased control when the dribbler is closely guarded by a defender. Typical use is when the dribbler is transitioning after a shot has been gathered and is moving into defensive position.

Offensive Footwork (V-Cut and L-Cut)

Critical Features
1. Keep moving to create passing lanes
2. Feint, plant foot to change direction quickly
3. Move toward ball to receive pass
4. Assume position with hands set

Instructional Cues
1. Move away from passer
2. Quick cut (V or L)
3. Move toward passer
4. Provide target with hands

Description
This skill consists of cutting movements, stopping quickly, and changing directions. These movements are most typically used without the ball when an offensive player is attempting to get open and create passing lanes. However, they can be combined with skills such as dribbling to enhance their effectiveness.

Dribble to Reposition

Critical Features
1. Use critical features of the low control dribble
2. Continue to dribble to create passing lanes
3. Players without ball cut to create passing lanes
4. Dribbler anticipates and executes pass

Instructional Cues
1. Use proper dribble
2. Move to open spaces
3. Teammates use V- or L-cuts to get open
4. Look to make pass

Description
The purpose of repositioning when you are the ball handler is to force the defense to continually move and also to allow your own teammates an opportunity to move to open areas. By continually moving to an open area you are forcing the defense to make changes, enabling the offense to create spaces to pass to.

PURPOSE

To provide the teacher with an instructional tool for understanding and effectively communicating the daily content. Adequate understanding of the daily content will enhance the teacher's ability to instruct, demonstrate, observe, and provide feedback on the daily skills and tactics taught.

WHEN TO USE

Before or during each lesson or both

SUGGESTED USE

The graphics and cues card includes the following components:

- Critical features
- Instructional cues
- A picture of the daily skill(s), tactic(s), or both
- A brief written description of the daily skill(s), tactic(s), or both

The teacher should strive to memorize the daily graphics and cues card prior to each lesson. While the card can be referred to during the lesson to refresh the teacher's memory, overreliance on the card during a lesson may inhibit efficient instruction. The critical features are provided so that the teacher can develop a greater understanding of the skill or tactic. One should use critical features sparingly when communicating with students. Alternatively, the instructional cues are provided to enhance communication with students during instructions, demonstrations, and feedback. The cues are brief and easy for students to comprehend. The picture is supplied to supplement the written description so that the teacher can give students an adequate demonstration and verbal explanation of the daily content. While the card is designed for the teacher, there is no reason students should not have access to the card if the teacher sees fit.

MODIFICATIONS

- Alter the number and type of instructional cues.
- Photocopy, laminate, and make cards available to student teams.

DOCUMENT LOCATION

Chapter 6—pages 133-134 and PASE Basketball Season CD-ROM—pages 29-30

PASE Student Coaching Plan

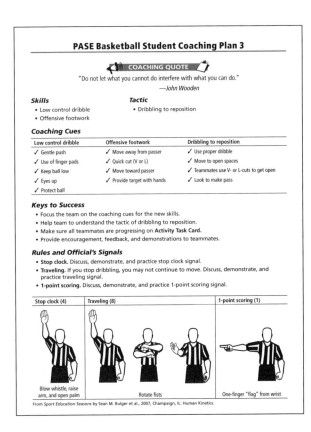

PASE Basketball Student Coaching Plan 3

🔊 COACHING QUOTE

"Do not let what you cannot do interfere with what you can do."
—*John Wooden*

Skills
- Low control dribble
- Offensive footwork

Tactic
- Dribbling to reposition

Coaching Cues

Low control dribble	Offensive footwork	Dribbling to reposition
✓ Gentle push	✓ Move away from passer	✓ Use proper dribble
✓ Use of finger pads	✓ Quick cut (V or L)	✓ Move to open spaces
✓ Keep ball low	✓ Move toward passer	✓ Teammates use V- or L-cuts to get open
✓ Eyes up	✓ Provide target with hands	✓ Look to make pass
✓ Protect ball		

Keys to Success
- Focus the team on the coaching cues for the new skills.
- Help team to understand the tactic of dribbling to reposition.
- Make sure all teammates are progressing on **Activity Task Card.**
- Provide encouragement, feedback, and demonstrations to teammates.

Rules and Official's Signals
- **Stop clock.** Discuss, demonstrate, and practice stop clock signal.
- **Traveling.** If you stop dribbling, you may not continue to move. Discuss, demonstrate, and practice traveling signal.
- **1-point scoring.** Discuss, demonstrate, and practice 1-point scoring signal.

Stop clock (4)	Traveling (8)	1-point scoring (1)
Blow whistle, raise arm, and open palm	Rotate fists	One-finger "flag" from wrist

From *Sport Education Seasons* by Sean M. Bulger et al., 2007, Champaign, IL: Human Kinetics.

PURPOSE

To provide the student coach with an organizational and instructional tool designed to optimize team practice.

WHEN TO USE

- Distributed during student coaches' meeting
- Used during team practice
- Referred to during team review or on days when team practice is dedicated solely to reviewing skills and tactics previously taught

SUGGESTED USE

The student coaching plan includes the following:
- An inspirational quote
- A list of the day's skill(s), tactic(s), or both
- Coaching cues for each of the day's skill(s), tactic(s), or both
- A list of key ideas related to successful team practice
- A list of the day's rules
- A picture of each of the official's signals associated with each rule

The student coaching plan can be thought of as a developmentally appropriate version of a lesson plan. The plan should be distributed and briefly discussed during the student coaches' meeting. The coach must have access to the coaching plan during team practice in order to more successfully motivate, supervise, instruct, and coordinate. The teacher must establish a safety protocol for where to place the plan when the coach is unable to safely secure it, as when he or she is performing skills. Once team practice is over, the coach should file the coaching plan in a folder. In subsequent lessons, either during the team review time or during team practice time on review days, the coach should have access to the folder containing previously used plans in order to optimize team performance and utilize time wisely.

MODIFICATIONS

- Alter the number or content (or both) of the components of the coaching plan.
- Change the time when the coaching plan is distributed or discussed.
- Modify how the coaching plan is filed away during and after use.
- Photocopy and laminate the coaching plan for repeated use from season to season.

After photocopying and laminating, punch holes near the bottom-middle portion of the plan. Next attach a carabiner through the hole and clip the carabiner to a retractable key chain. Student coaches can then attach the "hip clip" on a pocket or to their waistband. This modification reduces the safety hazard associated with loose papers lying on the floor or ground and gives the coaches greater freedom to practice and coach.

DOCUMENT LOCATION

Chapter 6—page 135 and PASE Basketball Season CD-ROM—page 31

PASE Activity Task Card

PASE Basketball Activity Task Card 3

Skills
- Low control dribble
- Offensive footwork

Tactic
- Dribbling to reposition

Learning tasks	Self	Peer	Coach
1. Under the direction of the coach, perform the cues for today's skills five times each.			☐
2. Under the direction of the coach, perform the official's signals for today's lesson five times each.			☐
3. Dribble with preferred hand, without moving, while staying in control for 30 sec.	☐		
4. Dribble with nonpreferred hand, without moving, while staying in control for 30 sec.	☐		
5. Dribble with preferred hand, while moving, in general space in control for 30 sec.	☐		
6. Dribble with nonpreferred hand, while moving, in general space in control for 30 sec.	☐		
7. Dribble alternating between hands, while moving, in general space for 30 sec.		☐	
8. Repeat #7, but this time, count and remember the number of times you switch hands in 30 sec. (Record score only if using **Individual Activity Task Card Recording Sheet**.)	#___		☐
9. Dribble with preferred hand, moving backward, in a straight line for 30 sec.	☐		
10. Dribble with nonpreferred hand, moving backward, in a straight line for 30 sec.	☐		
11. Dribble in a straight line, moving backward, alternating between hands for 30 sec.	☐		
12. Repeat #11, but this time, count and remember the number of times you switch hands in 30 sec. (Record score only if using **Individual Activity Task Card Recording Sheet**.)	#___		☐
13. Dribble with preferred hand, moving sideways, in a zigzag pattern for 30 sec.	☐		
14. Dribble with nonpreferred hand, moving sideways, in a zigzag pattern for 30 sec.	☐		
15. Dribble in a zigzag pattern, moving sideways, alternating between hands for 30 sec.		☐	
16. Repeat #15, but this time, count and remember the number of times you switch hands in 30 sec. (Record score only if using **Individual Activity Task Card Recording Sheet**.)	#___		☐
17. Dribble with preferred hand, allowing a partner to play passive defense for 30 sec.	☐		
18. Dribble with nonpreferred hand, allowing a partner to play passive defense for 30 sec.	☐		
19. Dribble while alternating between hands, allowing a partner to play passive defense for 30 sec.	☐		
20. 1-on-1: In partners, moving through general space, partner A will dribble with either hand while partner B attempts to steal the ball. Partner A should dribble close to or far from body, at medium/low levels, in straight/curved/zigzag pathways, while moving at medium/slow speeds. Partners should not make contact with one another. Switch roles after 30 sec. Answer the following questions and discuss what you discovered about maintaining ball possession and control with a teammate. • Is it easier to dribble with control while the ball is at a high or low level? Why? • Is it harder for the defense to take the ball if it is close to you or far away? Why? • How can you use your body to help maintain possession of the ball?			☐
21. Repeat #20. This time defense earns a point for every steal or knock-away. The partner dribbling will receive 1 point if he or she can maintain control for 30 sec. Remember scores. Repeat again. (Record score only if using **Individual Activity Task Card Recording Sheet**.)	#___		☐

From *Sport Education Seasons* by Sean M. Bulger et al., 2007, Champaign, IL: Human Kinetics.

PURPOSE

An instructional tool designed to provide a series of hierarchically sequenced, developmentally appropriate activities that students engage in to develop skill proficiency and tactical awareness. Additionally, the task card provides a system for efficiently communicating tasks, effectively differentiating instruction, and assisting students to make appropriate choices.

WHEN TO USE

- During team practice
- Referred to during team review or on days when team practice is dedicated solely to reviewing skills and tactics previously taught

SUGGESTED USE

The activity task card includes the following:
- A list of the day's skill(s), tactic(s), or both
- A set of tasks that increase in complexity
- One of three levels of assessment for each task: self, peer, coach
- In some cases, a figure to describe the more complex tasks

The teacher can choose to post the task card in each team's home area, distribute the task card to each individual, provide the card to student coaches only, or use a combination of any of these ideas. Students on a particular team can progress through the task as a team or as individuals at their own rate. Regardless of the method chosen, students progress under the supervision of the coach and must be assessed by the person indicated for each task: self, peer, or coach. Information for each task can be recorded directly on the task card, provided that each individual has a task card, on a team activity task card recording sheet, or on an individual activity task card recording sheet. As with the coaching plan, the teacher must establish a safety protocol for where to place the task cards when not in use. A system needs to be in place for filing away task cards once team practice is over. In subsequent lessons, either during the team review time or during team practice time on review days, the teams should have access to the filing system containing previously used task cards. Students need access to the cards in order to finish completing the tasks or to repeat tasks associated with content related to specific skill or tactical deficiencies identified by the team or the teacher.

MODIFICATIONS

- Alter the number of tasks.
- Change the criteria for each task.
- Modify requirements for assessing each task.
- Adapt the form or requirements (or both) for recording information related to the task card.
- Modify how the task card is filed away during and after use.
- Photocopy and laminate the task card for repeated use from season to season.
- For efficiency, photocopy the coaching plan and the task card from a single lesson back-to-back.

After back-to-back photocopying, hole punch near the bottom-middle portion of the plan. Next attach a carabiner through the hole and clip the carabiner to a retractable key chain. Student coaches can then attach the "hip clip" on a pocket or to their waistband. This modification reduces the safety hazard associated with loose papers lying on the floor or ground and gives the coaches greater freedom to practice and coach.

DOCUMENT LOCATION

Chapter 6—page 136 and PASE Basketball Season CD-ROM—page 32

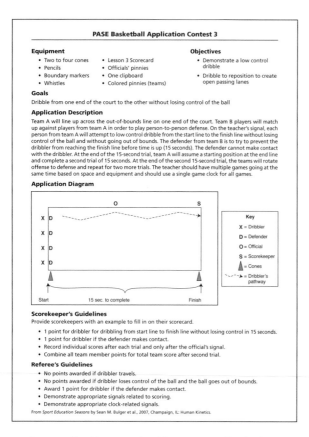

PASE Application Contest Description

PASE Basketball Application Contest 3

Equipment
- Two to four cones
- Pencils
- Boundary markers
- Whistles
- Lesson 3 Scorecard
- Officials' pinnies
- One clipboard
- Colored pinnies (teams)

Objectives
- Demonstrate a low control dribble
- Dribble to reposition to create open passing lanes

Goals
Dribble from one end of the court to the other without losing control of the ball

Application Description
Team A will line up across the out-of-bounds line on one end of the court. Team B players will match up against players from team A in order to play person-to-person defense. On the teacher's signal, each person from team A will attempt to low control dribble from the start line to the finish line without losing control of the ball and without going out of bounds. The defender from team B is to try to prevent the dribbler from reaching the finish line before time is up (15 seconds). The defender cannot make contact with the dribbler. At the end of the 15-second trial, team A will assume a starting position at the end line and complete a second trial of 15 seconds. At the end of the second 15-second trial, the teams will rotate offense to defense and repeat for two more trials. The teacher should have multiple games going at the same time based on space and equipment and should use a single game clock for all games.

Application Diagram

Scorekeeper's Guidelines
Provide scorekeepers with an example to fill in on their scorecard.
- 1 point for dribbler for dribbling from start line to finish line without losing control in 15 seconds.
- 1 point for dribbler if the defender makes contact.
- Record individual scores after each trial and only after the official's signal.
- Combine all team member points for total team score after second trial.

Referee's Guidelines
- No points awarded if dribbler travels.
- No points awarded if dribbler loses control of the ball and the ball goes out of bounds.
- Award 1 point for dribbler if the defender makes contact.
- Demonstrate appropriate signals related to scoring.
- Demonstrate appropriate clock-related signals.

From *Sport Education Seasons* by Sean M. Bulger et al., 2007, Champaign, IL: Human Kinetics.

PURPOSE

An activity designed to provide students with an opportunity to demonstrate, develop, and assess skills and tactical awareness in an authentic, game-like context.

WHEN TO USE

During the application contest

SUGGESTED USE

The application contest description includes the following:

- An equipment list
- Objectives for the contest aligned with the daily lesson objectives
- Goals specific to the contest
- A written description of the contest
- A diagram of the contest to supplement the written description
- A list of guidelines for scorekeepers
- A list of guidelines for officials

An application contest is a game. Each day across the season, students will play a game by engaging in the application contest. The teacher should use the application contest description prior to the lesson in order to prepare for the contest. The equipment list outlines the type and amount of equipment needed for one contest. The teacher should plan for multiple contests to take place simultaneously. While there is no requirement for the number of contests that should take place at one time, there should be as many contests taking place at one time as space and student numbers will allow. Prior to having students engage in the contests, the teacher should explain the contest verbally and via student demonstration. During the application, students who are seated and observing can practice scoring, officiating, or both. The instruction and demonstration period should be performed until students adequately understand the contest. Following the explanation, students engage in the contest as either a player, scorekeeper, or official. The procedures for the contest are outlined in the written description, diagram, and guidelines for scorekeepers and officials. During the contest the teacher is ultimately responsible for overseeing all contests.

At first, it will take time to teach students where to go and what to do during the contests. However, as the lessons progress, students will become increasingly familiar with the contest structure. This increased familiarity will result in more efficient use of the time allocated to the contest. Learning the structure of the contest is not left to chance, however. The contests across a season are designed in a progressive fashion, with subsequent contests building upon previous ones. This progressive design helps teachers and students become more familiar with the structure of the contests as the season advances. Typically, only one or two requirements or rules change from one contest to the next. Such minimal but progressive changes allow students not only to learn the structure of the contests, but also to become more skilled and tactically aware as the season progresses. Another important design feature of the contests is that they call for maximal student engagement. The contest represents a daily culminating event for students. Therefore, the appropriate use of practice time prior to the contests is imperative.

MODIFICATIONS

- Alter the type or number of pieces of equipment or both.
- Change the objectives or goals of the contest or both.
- Modify the rules of the contest.
- Adjust the number of people playing, size of the field, or type of nonperformer roles.
- Make changes to the explanation of the contest.

DOCUMENT LOCATION

Chapter 6—page 137 and PASE Basketball Season CD-ROM—page 33

PASE Application Contest Scorecard

PURPOSE

A tool designed to provide students with the opportunity to perform an essential nonplayer role associated with managing the sport season. Additionally, the scorecard provides data that represent an authentic assessment of students' skill, tactical awareness, or both. This is important in that the scorecard embodies information about student performance related to the objectives and goals of the contest during game play.

WHEN TO USE

- Distributed prior to the application contest
- Used during the application contest
- Referred to during team review or on days when the team is completing the PASE Team Goal-Setting Sheet (see p. 314) or PASE Tournament Statistics Summary Sheet (see p. 319)

SUGGESTED USE

The application contest scorecard includes the following:

- Areas for demographic data such as team, opponent, and date
- Areas for player data such as jersey number, name, and game statistics
- Areas for coach's and scorekeeper's signatures
- Shading that represents areas to be left blank

The scorecard should be distributed to the scorekeepers at the end of team practice or at the beginning of the time allocated to the application contest. Providing the scorecard early will give the scorekeeper time to complete the demographic data. Once the scorecard is distributed, the scorekeeper should practice completing scoring information for a mock student during the teacher instruction and demonstration phase of the application contest. The scorekeeper should complete only the nonshaded areas of the scorecard. The nonshaded areas focus the scorekeeper's attention on the relevant parts of the scorecard for that particular day. The nonshaded areas change in a systematic and progressive fashion from one lesson to the next. As the season progresses and scorekeepers become increasingly competent, the information collected becomes increasingly complex as well. By season's end, the scorekeepers should be able to complete all areas of the scorecard during a single contest. Across the season, however, it is important that the teacher and coaches carefully check the scorecards in order to ensure the accuracy of the collected data. Once completed, the scorecards should be filed in such a way that the teams have access to their data in future lessons. In addition, a system needs to be developed so that the sports information director has access to the scorecards so that he or she can fulfill the assigned role.

MODIFICATIONS

- Alter the type of data to be collected.

PASE Basketball Application Contest Scorecard 3

From Sport Education Seasons by Sean M. Bulger et al., 2007, Champaign, IL: Human Kinetics.

- Change the amount of data to be collected.
- Modify the nonshaded areas of the scorecard.
- Adjust the scorekeeper requirements for using the scorecard.
- Change the time when the scorecard is distributed or discussed.
- Modify how the scorecard is filed away and accessed after the contests.

DOCUMENT LOCATION

Chapter 6—page 138 and PASE Basketball Season CD-ROM—page 34

PASE Tournament Role Assignments

PASE Basketball Tournament Role Assignments

Team: _____

Instructions: Determine individual roles for your team for each of the in-season round robin and championship tournament games. Every team member should perform each of the following roles at least once throughout lessons 16-24: scorekeeper, official, player. No team member is allowed to repeat the scorekeeper's or official's role until everyone else on the team has been either the scorekeeper or official. Once a team member has completed the role of scorekeeper or official, he or she must fulfill the role of player in the next game. If your team cannot decide on a role rotation, scratch out the role column and enter a teammate's name across a single row, thus you will be using the predetermined rotation system denoted by the letters A through F.

TOURNAMENT GAMES

Role	Round robin game 1	Round robin game 2	Round robin game 3	Round robin game 4	Round robin game 5	Tourney game 1	Tourney game 2
Official	A	B	C	D	E	F	A
Player	B	C	D	E	F	A	B
Player	C	D	E	F	A	B	C
Player	D	E	F	A	B	C	D
Scorekeeper	E	F	A	B	C	D	E
Player	F	A	B	C	D	E	F

ROLE RESPONSIBILITIES

Official (A)
- Manages the contests
- Interprets rules during contests
- Mediates conflicts
- Maintains contest pacing

Players (B, C, D, F)
- Participate in contests
- Maintain appropriate sportspersonship
- Utilize the skills learned
- Support teammates during contests

Scorekeeper (E)
- Records scores during contests
- Maintains ongoing team records
- Summarizes contest scores
- Provides final records to appropriate person

From *Sport Education Seasons* by Sean M. Bulger et al., 2007, Champaign, IL: Human Kinetics.

PURPOSE

To provide students with a systematic way to choose role assignments for the in- and postseason tournaments. The role assignment sheet helps the teacher and students organize the tournaments in advance.

WHEN TO USE

- Distributed prior to in-season tournament
- Referred to during in- and postseason tournaments

SUGGESTED USE

The tournament role assignment sheet includes the following:

- Instructions
- List of roles including player, official, and scorekeeper
- List of tournament days and games
- Area for students to write their names, indicating role assignments
- An alternative built-in role assignment system indicated with the letters A through F
- A list of responsibilities associated with each role

The role assignment sheet is distributed to students prior to the onset of the in-season tournament. Once it is distributed, students should be given time to select their role assignments cooperatively with their teammates. The students should be careful to follow the instructions so that no individual performs a nonplayer (scorekeeper or official) role during two consecutive games. If individuals within a team are having difficulty developing an equitable role rotation schedule, there is an embedded system to assist in the assignment process. The letters A through F are located in the top left-hand corner of each cell. Once students place their names in the cells for game 1, each student finds the letter that corresponds with his or her name. Then each student adds his or her name to each cell with the corresponding letter for each of the remaining games. For example, if John is an "A" in game 1, he is the official. In games 2, 3, and 4 John would be a player; in game 5 he would be scorekeeper, and so forth. The embedded role assignment system ensures an equitable role rotation schedule.

MODIFICATIONS

- Alter the number of tournament days.
- Change the number of roles, the responsibilities associated with each role, or both.
- Modify how the students determine role assignments.
- Assign a duty team for each game to fulfill the roles.

DOCUMENT LOCATION

Chapter 6—page 318 and PASE Basketball Season CD-ROM—page 2 in appendix D

PASE Game Preparation Task Card

PASE Basketball Game Preparation Task Card 16-20

Skills

- Passing
- Dribbling
- Shooting
- Offensive/defensive footwork
- Offensive/defensive tactics

Learning tasks	Self	Peer	Coach
1. During the in-season round robin tournament, each team member will be required to perform the roles of official and scorekeeper at least once. Refer to the the **Tournament Role Assignment Sheet** to determine your role responsibility line-up. This will help determine wo will be the official and scorekeeper for today's games. Once roles are identified, get the scorecards, whistles, and so on, and prepare to score or officiate your assigned game.	□		
2. In partners, a dribbler should move from the baseline to the midcourt line while a partner plays defense on the ball. Rotate roles and repeat.		□	
3. In team lines, perform V- and L-cuts while receiving chest, bounce, overhead, and sidearm passes. Players rotate from passer to receiver/cutter following each trial. Repeat until each player has attempted each type of pass once.			□
4. In team lines, with one line shooting and one line rebounding, perform three right-handed and three left-handed layups.			□
5. In team lines, with one line shooting and one line rebounding, perform three jump shots from the right side of the key and three jump shots from the left side of the key.			□
6. Determine defensive assignments according to the Tournament Schedule. If your team will use player-to-player defense, determine matchups. If your team will play zone, then determine player area (zone) assignments.			□
7. Practice game scenarios of your choice. Base your choice on what you think your team needs the most practice on or what you think your upcoming opponent's game plan will be.			□
8. In a team huddle, on the count of three, shout out your team cheer loud enough to show your team's spirit.			□

From *Sport Education Seasons* by Sean M. Bulger et al., 2007, Champaign, IL: Human Kinetics.

In-Season Round Robin Tournament Schedule

Day 16	Visitors		Home
Game 1	1	vs.	6
Game 2	2	vs.	5
Game 3	3	vs.	4

Day 17			
Game 1	6	vs.	4
Game 2	5	vs.	1
Game 3	2	vs.	3

Day 18			
Game 1	6	vs.	2
Game 2	5	vs.	3
Game 3	1	vs.	4

Day 19	Visitors		Home
Game 1	3	vs.	1
Game 2	4	vs.	2
Game 3	5	vs.	6

Day 20			
Game 1	3	vs.	6
Game 2	1	vs.	2
Game 3	4	vs.	5

From *Sport Education Seasons* by Sean M. Bulger et al., 2007, Champaign, IL: Human Kinetics.

PURPOSE

To provide the student coach with an authentic, developmentally appropriate, sport-specific organizational and instructional tool designed to prepare his or her team for engaging in game play. Additionally, the schedule gives students the opportunity to better prepare for specific opponents.

WHEN TO USE

- During in-season and postseason tournaments
- Distributed during student coaches' meeting
- Used during team practice

SUGGESTED USE

The game preparation task card includes the following:

- A list of the skill(s) and tactic(s) covered across the season
- A set of tasks that increase in complexity
- One of three levels of assessment for each task: self, peer, coach
- A tournament schedule

The game preparation task card should be distributed and briefly discussed during the student coaches' meeting. As with the coaching plan and the individual activity task card, the coach must have access to the game preparation task card during team practice in order to more successfully motivate, supervise, instruct, and coordinate practice for tournament games. The teacher must establish a safety protocol for where to place the plan when the coach is unable to safely secure the card, such as when the coach is performing skills. Once team practice is over, the coach should file the game preparation task card in a folder. In subsequent tournament lessons, during the team practice time the coach should have access to the folder containing the game preparation task cards so as to be able to adequately prepare the team for the games.

MODIFICATIONS

- Change the criteria for each task.
- Modify requirements for assessing each task.
- Amend how the game preparation task card is filed away during and after use.

- Adjust the tournament schedule.
- Photocopy and laminate the task card for repeated use from season to season.
- After photocopying, punch holes near the bottom-middle portion of the plan. Next attach a carabiner through the holes, and clip the carabiner to a retractable key chain. Student coaches can then attach the "hip clip" on a pocket or to their waistband. This modification reduces the safety hazard associated with loose papers lying on the floor or ground and gives the coaches greater freedom to move about.

DOCUMENT LOCATION

Chapter 6—pages 246-247 and PASE Basketball Season CD-ROM—pages 142-143

PASE Tournament Rules

PASE Basketball Round Robin Tournament Rules Lessons 16-20

- 3-on-3, half-court
- Four 3-minute quarters with a 3-minute half-time
- Subs at the beginning of each new quarter
- Each person can sub out only once per game
- All baskets made = 2 points
- All fouls = –1 point
- All plays restart at midcourt cone
- After each change of possession, ball must be cleared beyond 3-point arc
- Defense: person-to-person or zone
- Wins = 3 team points
- Fair play = 5 team points
  - Follows rules, never argues
  - Obeys official's calls, never influences officials
  - Cooperative, encouraging
  - Caring, under control
  - Gracious in victory or defeat

From *Sport Education Seasons* by Sean M. Bulger et al., 2007, Champaign, IL: Human Kinetics.

PURPOSE

To provide students with an overview of the tournament rules prior to the start of the tournament games. The tournament rules handout is meant to supplement the teacher's description for the corresponding tournament lessons.

WHEN TO USE

- Used during explanation of the application contest (tournament)
- Referred to throughout the tournament

SUGGESTED USE

The tournament rules sheet is a tool distributed to student teams and briefly discussed so that students develop an understanding of the tournament game regulations before playing. Prior to student engagement in the tournament games, the teacher should clarify the contest rules through verbal explanation and student demonstration.

MODIFICATIONS

- Alter the type or number of pieces of equipment or both.
- Change the objectives or goals of the contest or both.
- Modify the rules of the contest.
- Adjust the number of people playing, size of the field, or type of nonperformer roles.
- Make changes to the explanation of the contest.
- Photocopy and laminate the coaching plan for repeated use from season to season.

DOCUMENT LOCATION

Chapter 6—page 321 and PASE Basketball Season CD-ROM—page 5 in appendix D

PASE Tournament Statistics Summary Sheet

PURPOSE

A tool designed to give students the opportunity to summarize data that represent an authentic assessment of students' skills, tactical awareness, or both. This summary is critical in that it descriptively encapsulates information about student performance during actual tournament game play.

WHEN TO USE

Following each tournament game

SUGGESTED USE

The tournament statistics summary sheet includes the following:

- Areas for student names
- Areas for player data to be transferred from the application contest scorecards for each tournament game

The scorecard should be distributed to the scorekeepers at the end of the first tournament game. Once it has been distributed, the scorekeeper should transfer each student's game data from the application contest scorecard. The

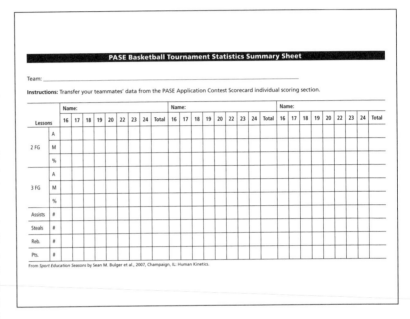

scorekeeper should be careful to transfer the data accurately. Once completed, the summary sheet should be filed in such a way that the upcoming scorekeepers can access the sheet during future lessons. In addition, a system needs to be developed so that the sports information director has access to the scorecards so that he or she can fulfill the assigned role.

MODIFICATIONS

- Alter the type of data to be collected.
- Change the amount of data to be collected.
- Adjust the scorekeeper requirements for using the summary sheet.
- Change the time when the scorecard is distributed or discussed.
- Modify how the scorecard is filed away and accessed after the contests.

DOCUMENT LOCATION

Chapter 6—page 319 and PASE Basketball Season CD-ROM—page 3 in appendix D

PASE Tournament Team Introductions Sheet

PASE Basketball Tournament Team Introductions

Team: _____

Instructions: During the team review and practice, fill out the information on this sheet. This information will be used to introduce each individual from your team during the postseason championship tournament. These introductions will serve to heighten the festivity surrounding the event as well as provide the scorekeeper with a record of each team member. This sheet will be collected following your team warm-ups and game preparation. Prior to the consolation and championship games, players will be introduced one at a time.

Introduction example: Coming in at [height] with an impressive [statistic category] of [statistic], hailing from [hometown], the [team name]'s own [player name].

Height	Statistics showcase: assists, rebounds, steals, points per game	Hometown or city and state	Player name (first, nickname, last)
Example: 5 ft 3 in.	Assists per game: 2.3	Baltimore, Maryland	Sophia "Da Dish" Smith

TEAM SEASON DEMOGRAPHICS

Team round robin season record	Wins		Losses
Team final tournament seeding	Tournament seeding		
Record against today's opponent	Wins		Losses

From *Sport Education Seasons* by Sean M. Bulger et al., 2007, Champaign, IL: Human Kinetics.

PURPOSE

A tool designed to give the teacher, students, or both an opportunity to heighten the festive nature of the postseason tournament. This information allows students to be identified as part of a team and recognizes selected achievements made during the in-season round robin tournament.

WHEN TO USE

Following the first day of postseason tournament game play

SUGGESTED USE

The tournament team introduction sheet includes the following:

- Areas for student names
- Areas for player demographic information such as hometown, nickname, and height; also an area specifically for recognizing a player's contribution to the team
- Areas for team statistics

The team's introduction sheet should be distributed to the team scorekeeper at the end of the first postseason tournament day. Once the sheet is distributed, the scorekeeper, with input from the team, begins to fill in the appropriate information. Once this is done, the information should be presented to the sports information director, who will provide the introductions on the final tournament day.

MODIFICATIONS

- Alter the type of data to be collected.
- Change the amount of data to be collected.
- Adjust the scorekeeper requirements for using the summary sheet.
- Change the time when the scorecard is distributed or discussed.

DOCUMENT LOCATION

Chapter 6—page 320 and PASE Basketball Season CD-ROM—page 4 in appendix D

PASE Voting Ballot

PASE Basketball Voting Ballot

Instructions: For each award, vote for one person from your team. You cannot vote for a person more than once, and be sure to vote for yourself.

Award	Description	Name
MVP	Recognizes distinguished, consistent, and highly skilled performance across the season	
Hustle	Recognizes persistent energy and a vivacious spirit in the face of victory and defeat	
Most Improved	Recognizes an awareness of one's self and an enduring ability to monitor personal progress and obtain personal goals in any situation	
Fair Play	Recognizes an individual's sincere concern for others' rights during all facets of game play	
Best Official	Recognizes outstanding ability to interpret rules and regulate game play without bias	
Leadership	Recognizes unparalleled and potent aptitude to provide direction, overcome obstacles, and model appropriate behaviors in the face of adversity	

From *Sport Education Seasons* by Sean M. Bulger et al., 2007, Champaign, IL: Human Kinetics.

PASE Basketball Voting Ballot—Teacher-Developed Awards

Instructions: Use the space below to create your own awards. For each award, vote for one person from your team. You cannot vote for a person more than once, and be sure to vote for yourself.

Award	Description	Name

From *Sport Education Seasons* by Sean M. Bulger et al., 2007, Champaign, IL: Human Kinetics.

PURPOSE

To provide individual students with an opportunity to recognize their teammates' contributions to a successful season.

WHEN TO USE

Distributed and collected in the lesson prior to the awards day

SUGGESTED USE

The student season voting ballot includes the following:

- Instructions
- A list of the awards
- A description for each award
- An area to record individuals' votes

The season voting ballot should be photocopied and distributed to each student. Each student should be directed to vote for one teammate for each of the awards. Students are allowed to vote for any one teammate only once. Students should be encouraged to vote for themselves. The students should use the description of the award to determine which teammate demonstrated characteristics that most closely match the award description. The voting process should be done independently, and students should not discuss their choices with one another. Once completed, the voting ballots should be collected and the results tabulated by the teacher. Afterward the teacher has the responsibility of creating and completing the actual awards to be presented during the award day ceremonies (see p. 328-333).

MODIFICATIONS

- Alter the number of awards, descriptions of the awards, or both.
- Modify the instructions for completing the awards voting process.

DOCUMENT LOCATION

Chapter 6—pages 324-325 and PASE Basketball Season CD-ROM—pages 2-3 in appendix E

PASE Awards Day Itinerary

PURPOSE

An organization and instructional tool designed to assist the teacher in preparing to bring the season to an authentic and festive close.

WHEN TO USE

- Distributed at the beginning of the awards day banquet
- Referred to throughout the awards day ban-quet

SUGGESTED USE

The awards day itinerary includes the following:

- An outline of the day's events

The awards day itinerary is an out-line of the awards day banquet. The

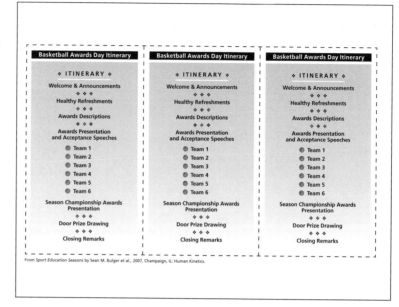

itinerary is intended to supplement the awards day lesson plan and to be used as a student hand-out. The itinerary should be photocopied and cut out prior to the awards day. The itinerary should be distributed to each student in the class at the beginning of the awards day. Students should be encouraged to sit with their teammates during the banquet. Students should be reminded of the fair play agreement and encouraged to be respectful of their teammates and opponents throughout the banquet. The banquet is intended to bring the season to an authentic and festive close.

MODIFICATIONS

- Alter the order, number, or type of activities planned.
- Change the size or color of the itinerary.
- Modify the refreshments.
- Laminate the itineraries so students can save them as an artifact from the season.
- Invite a distinguished guest to present the awards or provide a motivational speech.

DOCUMENT LOCATION

Chapter 6—page 326 and PASE Basketball Season CD-ROM—page 4 in appendix E

PASE Awards Day Acceptance Speech Criteria

PASE Basketball Awards Day Acceptance Speech Criteria

Instructions:

- Following the presentation of individual awards, your team will have the opportunity to deliver an acceptance speech.
- You may elect one or more spokespersons, or each individual can speak.
- Your team will have no longer than 3 minutes to deliver the acceptance speech, regardless of how many people choose to speak.
- Possible topics to discuss during acceptance speech:
  - Team cohesion or "gelling"
  - Spectacular efforts or contributions of individual team members
  - Team's development as it relates to the goals of the season
  - Obstacles that the team faced and overcame during the season
  - Any other important and relevant season highlights

OUR SPEECH OUTLINE

From *Sport Education Seasons* by Sean M. Bulger et al., 2007, Champaign, IL: Human Kinetics.

PURPOSE

To provide students with the expectations for speeches as teams accept their season place finish awards.

WHEN TO USE

- Distributed in the lesson prior to the awards day
- Used during the awards day as students give acceptance speeches

SUGGESTED USE

The acceptance speech criteria outline the expectations for the speeches that each team will be required to deliver when accepting their team season place finish awards. The criteria should be photocopied, cut out, and distributed to teams prior to the awards banquet day. Students should be directed to use the criteria as they plan and write their speeches. Speeches should be turned in prior to the awards day banquet so that the teacher has time to ensure that the speeches meet the criteria and that the content is appropriate. As students deliver their speeches, the teacher can use the criteria as a way to evaluate the speeches.

MODIFICATIONS

- Alter the time requirements for the speech.
- Change the requirements regarding who delivers the speech.
- Modify the topics that students discuss during the speech.
- Adjust the process for developing the speeches.
- Amend the process for evaluating the speeches.

DOCUMENT LOCATION

Chapter 6—page 327 and PASE Basketball Season CD-ROM—page 5 in appendix E

PASE Season Individual Awards

PURPOSE

To provide the students with peer-voted awards that reflect their strongest contribution to their team during the season.

WHEN TO USE

Distributed on the awards day

SUGGESTED USE

The season individual awards reflect the contributions of each individual team member to his or her team throughout the season. Once students have completed the PASE Season Voting Ballot, the teacher should collate that information to determine which students will receive which awards. The importance of this process lies in the notion that all team members provided a valuable contribution to their team during the season and as such should be recognized. Each student on a team should receive an award during the awards day ceremony. It is important that the teacher not attribute more importance to one award than others in the delivery or recognition. Each person's contribution is as important as another in the success of a team.

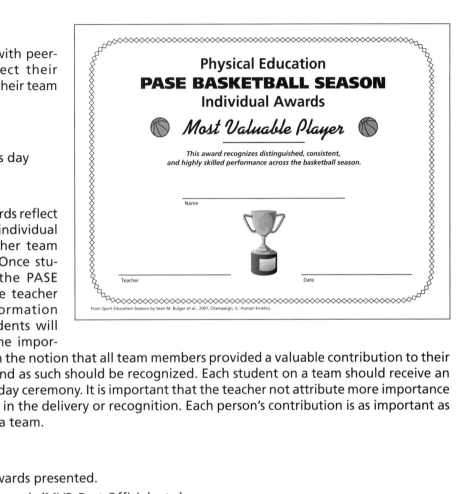

Physical Education
PASE BASKETBALL SEASON
Individual Awards
Most Valuable Player

This award recognizes distinguished, consistent, and highly skilled performance across the basketball season.

Name

Teacher

Date

From *Sport Education Seasons* by Sean M. Bulger et al., 2007, Champaign, IL: Human Kinetics.

MODIFICATIONS

- Alter the type of awards presented.
- Change the list of awards (MVP, Best Official, etc.).
- Modify the descriptions of the awards.

DOCUMENT LOCATION

Chapter 6—pages 328-333 and PASE Basketball Season CD-ROM—pages 6-11 in appendix E

PASE Team Place Finish Awards

PURPOSE

To provide the students with awards indicating their team place finish for the season.

WHEN TO USE

Distributed on the awards day

SUGGESTED USE

The team place finish awards reflect each team's progress toward becoming competent, literate, and enthusiastic sportspersons across the season. These awards are based on the accumulation of points derived from (a) the daily game (application contest), (b) individual role performance, (c) fair play, (d) rule infractions, and (e) bonus team points.

MODIFICATIONS

- Alter the type of awards.
- Modify the means by which awards are earned.

Physical Education
PASE BASKETBALL SEASON
Place Finish Awards

Champions

This award documents the consistent development and execution of excellent performance across the basketball season.

Team

Teacher   Date

From *Sport Education Seasons* by Sean M. Bulger et al., 2007, Champaign, IL: Human Kinetics.

DOCUMENT LOCATION

Chapter 6—pages 334-337 and PASE Basketball Season CD-ROM—page 12-15 in appendix E

SUMMARY

As described in this chapter, the PASE guidelines incorporate a wide variety of instructional strategies and resources that can be integrated into any season. These materials are intended to enhance the quality of the educational experience for students by appealing to multiple learning styles, fostering cooperation among peers, contextualizing sport, and providing frequent opportunities for assessment. While these materials are presented as comprehensive instructional seasons in the chapters that follow, you can easily adapt various components of the PASE framework to your particular instructional context.

Keeping the PASE: Crossing Curricular Boundaries

The teaching of sport in a highly contextualized manner represents the ideal opportunity to integrate concepts from a variety of other academic subjects including math, science, technology, and language arts. The key is to integrate that content in a manner that does not detract from the central mission of physical education: facilitating the development of the knowledge, skills, attitudes, and fitness levels that will enable a person to remain physically active across the life span. This chapter offers practical suggestions for providing interdisciplinary instruction during the implementation of a PASE season.

CROSS-CURRICULAR INTEGRATION

To this point, the intent of this book has been to illustrate how you can use the PASE to revolutionize the teaching of sport within your physical education program. This particular chapter has that same intent and will extend the revolution of teaching sport in your physical education program beyond the borders of your gymnasium or chalk-lined fields. The specific focus of this chapter is cross-curricular integration.

In recent decades, accountability for student achievement has become an increasingly central and important educational issue. Local, state, and national legislation has led to an increased emphasis on accountability for student achievement in the core content areas such as math, reading, and writing. Such heightened accountability has forced school administrators to reevaluate how time during the school day is allocated across content areas. Since the accountability for schools has focused mainly on the core curriculum, more time during the school day has been devoted to those areas. Unfortunately, the fallout of such accountability legislation has manifested in a decrease of time allocated to the so-called peripheral content areas such as art, music, and physical education.

We are sure that many of you who are reading this have witnessed this inverse relationship; as accountability increases in core content areas, contact time with students in physical education dwindles. If this trend continues, we in physical education are destined to lose more and more curricular time to the core content areas and become a less and less valued component of the overall school curriculum. Eventually physical education as we know it will cease to exist.

However, this does not have to happen. With careful planning, physical education can contribute to the core curriculum and assist in advancing student achievement in these areas through cross-curricular integration. As physical education plays this complementary role, individuals outside the physical education profession such as administrators, teachers, parents, and the community at large begin to value physical education more and eventually may see it as equal in importance to the other content areas. Society will value any component of the curriculum that enhances student achievement. Therefore, we should take advantage of this present opportunity.

This is not to say that the only reason to value physical education is for its utilization as a tool for cross-curricular integration. We as physical education professionals have to first be able to justify our programs based on their own merit; but supplementing our justification through cross-curricular integration can only help to solidify our position as an integral part of the total school curriculum.

Most physical educators are responsible for knowing and implementing curricula for multiple grades. Because this is such a demanding task, it is likely that with cross-curricular integration you will be charting territory that may be beyond your area of content expertise. Few would argue that the physical education teacher should also be a content expert in math, language arts, science, and so on. Therefore, to be successful at cross-curricular integration, you will need to seek out these content experts within your school. Next, pose your ideas in an attempt to garner their support and assistance. Lastly, cross-curricular integration is a cutting-edge concept and is one that may require you to think "outside of the box."

The following sections on integrating math, language arts, science, social studies, and technology are provided for the aforementioned reasons. Use the experimental-progressive approach outlined in chapter 2 (pp. 14-16), in the section "PASE Lesson Modifications," to assist you in charting this new territory, enhancing student achievement in content areas in addition to physical education, and renewing society's perspective on the value of physical education. By using the following PASE cross-curricular integration concepts you are on the road to revolutionizing the teaching of sport within your physical education program.

Suggestions for Integrating Math

- The scorekeeper summarizes team statistics on a daily, weekly, or season-long basis.
- Each team can select a publicly traded corporation that would hypothetically endorse them (e.g., Gatorade). The students could follow the stock rating of that company and receive bonus points based upon the performance of their stock. The purpose of this type of assignment is to teach students to select quality companies, track stock performance, and understand the basic nature of financial investment.
- Students can track the statistics of a professional, college, or high school sport team that is engaged in the same sport season. Students could track either an entire team or a player of their choice. The students could then attempt to predict a team's or single player's future performance based on those statistics.

Suggestions for Integrating Language Arts

- Have sports information directors complete the sports report as part of their role requirement.
- Encourage students to write a story detailing the team's successes for either the school or a local paper. It may be possible to encourage the school newspaper to devote a section of the publication to the standings of each class for a particular season. Students may even use some of the statistics collected as part of the story.
- Engage students in the creation of a physical education PASE yearbook. Each team could have a page that would include team picture, member names, affiliation information, and selected photographs documenting their season. The yearbook could be sold to students as a physical education fund-raiser.

- With assistance from the students, publish a monthly or seasonal brochure or newsletter summarizing the sport season and opportunities for engagement in the sport within the local community.

- Arrange for students to develop a promotional advertisement (written, spoken, or both) for their team to hypothetically increase the attendance at their home games.

- Have students collect a story on the same sport event from at least three different periodicals and compare the three stories for factual knowledge and accuracy.

Suggestions for Integrating Science

- Teams can develop their own projects using the scientific method to answer a question of their choosing. The research question should provide them some insight into their team performance or behavior or both. As examples, students might investigate the difference in team performance using one offensive or defensive strategy over another, or examine the relationship between the amounts of practice time and team performance.

- Encourage students to collect weather pattern data and determine if certain weather conditions affect team performance.

- Compare data collected by different teams during the sport competitions to scout other teams and make informed decisions about team strategies.

- Students can analyze skill performance and determine how the quality of a skill affects the outcome. For example, students may be required to throw using variations in form. Distance or accuracy data are recorded for each variation and students determine which throw is better.

- Students can predict distance, velocity, or flight paths of implements based on Newton's laws of motion.

- Students can determine the effects of physical activity or inactivity on the systems of the body.

- Students can develop an individualized physical activity plan based on physiological principles to maintain or enhance fitness levels.

Suggestions for Integrating Social Studies

- Promote the sponsoring of teams by the various departments in the school. The math, language arts, science, art, and social studies areas in your school could sponsor a team from each class. Such departmental competition would ensure advocacy of physical education outside of the gymnasium walls.

- Sport teams can be affiliated with countries from around the world. Each team could then make a class presentation detailing the physical activity opportunities that exist within that country.

- Identify organizations that train and certify sport support personnel. Have teams select two roles (e.g., official's and scorekeeper's) and investigate the requirements for a career in this field.

- Have students create a topographical map outlining the different physical activity outlets that exist across your state.

- Create, with students, a case study about sporting etiquette to prompt discussion of appropriate behaviors in sporting venues.

- Devise and implement an action plan to solve an authentic sport issue. This event task should focus on the environment or society (or both). As an example, you could have students create a script for a play about social acceptance within a sporting context.

Suggestions for Integrating Technology

- Produce a team or class yearbook or bulletin board using digital photographs modified and printed in a software application.

- Have the class or each team create a sport season mix CD of songs that can be played during practice or during the tournament game play warm-ups. For a class mix CD, teams can select a theme song as well as a general song that they would like to see as part of the overall season mix.

- Utilize *FITNESSGRAM/ACTIVITYGRAM* 8.0 by having students record, input, and track their fitness levels and physical activity behaviors. These computer software programs can be used to help students better understand their current levels of health-related fitness and develop a personalized plan for physical activity.

- Teams can design and develop a how-to video for a selected skill that is part of their sport season. They should show the skill form in isolation and then used in context. As one of the requirements, students may be asked to design one or more activities that could be used to practice and learn this skill.

- Teams can create a PowerPoint® presentation on an important topic related to the current sport season.

- Allow teams time to develop electronic playbooks that detail team strategies and designed plays. This could include cover information, a table of contents, and the plays with a description of each.

- Each team could create a home page that could be linked to the physical education department's main page. This page could include current team standings in the league they play in, statistics of players on the team, and sports information director reports.

SUMMARY

Physical education represents an ideal setting for students to apply the knowledge, skills, and abilities they are developing in a wide range of other subject areas. Each PASE lesson provides a number of opportunities for teachers to effectively enhance the teaching–learning environment through cross-curricular integration. The sample learning strategies described in this chapter represent a small fraction of the possible applications, however, and we challenge you to exercise your own creativity in extending PASE beyond the gymnasium or playing field.

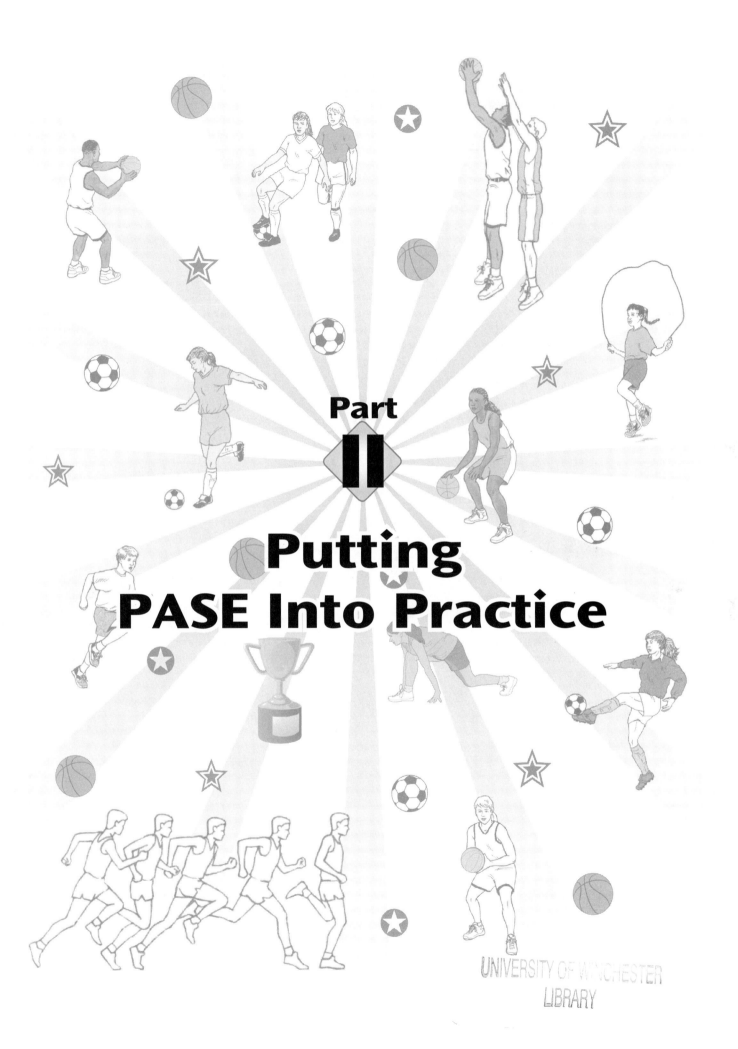

Part II

Putting PASE Into Practice

PASE
Fitness Education
Season Overview

All physical education programs share the overarching purpose of promoting lifetime physical activity and health-enhancing levels of fitness in students. In keeping with this important goal, the areas of health-related fitness and physical activity promotion remain a focus of all PASE seasons and lessons. This chapter presents an overview of an 18-lesson PASE fitness education season that is recommended to be taught as the initial instructional unit of the school year. This season is shorter than others because the learning outcomes, instructional strategies, and assessment techniques employed are reinforced repeatedly throughout the remaining PASE seasons described in the chapters that follow. This chapter includes a sample season syllabus for fitness education, an 18-lesson block plan, a daily club points summary, and a technician's performance index (similar in concept and purpose to the previously described PASE Official's Index). The related lesson plans and instructional resources are included on the accompanying CD-ROM.

FITNESS EDUCATION SEASON
OVERVIEW CONTENTS

Instructor(s): _____

Class: _____

Time: _____

FITNESS EDUCATION SEASON DESCRIPTION

This fitness education season consists of 18 lessons and is divided into three segments: a preseason, in-season, and postseason. Throughout the season, each student will be responsible for performing various tasks related to fitness education. Good luck!

SEASON GOALS

To become…

- **competent:** one who is knowledgeable about physical fitness and can successfully manage his or her own physical activity program.
- **literate:** one who knows the components of physical fitness, basic training principles, and fitness guidelines.
- **enthusiastic:** one who is involved and behaves in ways that protect, preserve, and enhance the fitness education learning environment.
- an **independent learner:** one who demonstrates responsibility for his or her own progress through appropriate goal-setting and goal-monitoring behaviors.

SEASON CONTENT

Fitness Components and Guidelines

- Aerobic Fitness
- Agility
- Muscular Fitness
- FITT Principle
- Flexibility
- *FITNESSGRAM*
- Speed
- Warm-up and cool-down

Training Methods

- Circuit training
- Partner resisted
- Static stretching
- Interval training

SEASON REQUIREMENTS, POINTS, AND GRADING SCALE

Requirement		Point Value					Grading Scale		
	Fitness biography	1	@	5	=	5	A	95 – 100	Excellent
	Pre- and post-fitness combine	2	@	5	=	10	A-	93 – 94	
	Personal fitness assessments	13	@	1	=	13	B+	91 – 92	Above average
	Role performance	12	@	2	=	24	B	87 – 90	
	Individual responsibility level (IRL)	6	@	1	=	6	B-	85 – 86	
	Individual activity tasks	5	@	3	=	15	C+	83 – 84	Average
	Fitness specialist exam	1	@	15	=	15	C	79 – 82	
	Outside-of-class participation log	2	@	3	=	6	C-	77 – 78	
	Fitness challenge design-event task	1	@	4	=	4	D+	75 – 76	Below average
	End-of-season awards voting	1	@	2	=	2	D	72 – 74	
			Total		=	100	D-	70 – 71	
							F	Below 70	Failing

✚	Club season bonus points	1st place	=	3.0 points	4th place	=	1.5 points
	Added to final point total	2nd place	=	2.5 points	5th place	=	1.0 point
		3rd place	=	2.0 points	6th place	=	0.5 point

From *Sport Education Seasons* by Sean M. Bulger et al., 2007, Champaign, IL: Human Kinetics.

Instructions: Record your personal progress each day. As you complete a requirement, check it off like this "☑".

SEASON CALENDAR AND DAILY ASSESSMENTS

Lesson	WORKSHOPS					PRESEASON						IN-SEASON				POSTSEASON		
	1	2	3	4	5	6	7	8	9	10	11	12	13	14	15	16	17	18
Content	Assessment protocol	Pre-fitness combine	Training guidelines	Warm-up & cool-down	Management	Aerobic fitness	Muscular fitness	Flexibility	Speed	Agility	Review	Cross-training circuit	Club fitness challenge design	Fitness Olympics	Fitness Olympics	Fitness specialist exam	Post-fitness combine	Awards day
Date																		

Season requirement icons

Icon	1	2	3	4	5	6	7	8	9	10	11	12	13	14	15	16	17	18
(icon 1)	☐																	
(icon 2)		☐															☐	
(icon 3)				☐	☐	☐	☐	☐	☐	☐	☐	☐	☐	☐	☐	☐	☐	
(icon 4)						☐	☐	☐	☐	☐	☐	☐	☐	☐	☐	☐	☐	
(icon 5)						☐	☐	☐				☐		☐	☐			
(icon 6)						☐	☐	☐	☐	☐								
(icon 7)																☐	☐	
(icon 8)											☐							
(icon 9)													☐					
(icon 10)																☐		
(icon 11)																		

DESCRIPTION OF REQUIREMENTS

	Fitness biography	A personal fitness biography, detailing student's physical activity history, that must be completed by individuals during lesson 1.
	Pre- and post-fitness combine	A variety of stations designed to provide pre- and postseason information for goal setting and monitoring of personal progress between lessons 2 and 17.
	Personal fitness assessments	A set of fitness preparation activities that are completed and whose results are recorded during the club warm-up portion of lessons 4-16.
	Role performance	A performance of roles designed to help manage the fitness education season. Daily roles and responsibilities are identified at the beginning of lessons 6-17.
	Individual responsibility level (IRL)	A reflective activity used for identifying and monitoring one's personal behaviors throughout the fitness education season. To be completed at the end of lessons 6-8, 12, 14, and 15.
	Individual activity tasks	A series of fitness development activities that must be completed by individual club members during club practice in lessons 6-10.
	Fitness specialist exam	A written exam that covers all season content and is used to determine certification levels. Exam is to be completed in lesson 16.
	Outside-of-class participation log	An activity designed to provide additional opportunities for students to engage in meaningful physical activity outside of the physical education class throughout the fitness education season. To be completed and turned in at lessons 11 and 17.
	Fitness challenge design-event task	A written exercise requiring the practical application of the season content to be completed during lesson 13.
	End-of-season awards voting	A voting activity used to identify individuals for awards related to successful physical activity performance during the season. Voting to be completed in lesson 16.
	Club season bonus points	Throughout the season, individuals will earn points for their club. Club points will be acquired from role performance, fair play, and application contest scores.

From *Sport Education Seasons* by Sean M. Bulger et al., 2007, Champaign, IL: Human Kinetics.

Day(s)		INSTRUCTIONAL FOCUS		Application contest	TECHNICIAN'S PERFORMANCE INDEX	
		Fitness component	Fitness guidelines and training methods		Fitness assessment activity	Index #
PRESEASON	1	Fitness assessment activities protocol Use of activities scores for goal setting and assessment of fitness program				
	2	Pre-fitness combine				
	3	Basic training goals Training principles of FITT		Club cognitive challenge		
	4	Rationale for warm-up/cool-down Design of a proper warm-up/cool-down		Club cognitive challenge		
	5	Management day		Club cognitive challenge		
IN-SEASON	6	Aerobic fitness	FITT guidelines Circuit training	Club cognitive challenge Club fitness challenge	PACER	1
	7	Muscular fitness	FITT guidelines Partner-resisted strength training	Club cognitive challenge Club fitness challenge	Push-up Curl-up	5 6
	8	Flexibility	FITT guidelines Static stretching	Club cognitive challenge Club fitness challenge	Sit and reach Shoulder stretch	3 4
	9	Speed	FITT guidelines Interval training	Club cognitive challenge Club fitness challenge	Sprint, lying back start	11
	10	Agility	FITT guidelines Interval training	Club cognitive challenge Club fitness challenge	T-run	10
	11	Review all components	Review all FITT guidelines	Club fitness challenge	Modified pull-up Trunk lift	7 8
POSTSEASON FITNESS CHALLENGES	12	All	Cross-training circuit	Fitness challenge	All	1-11
	13	All	All	Club fitness challenge design	All	1-11
	14	All	All	Fitness Olympics	All	1-11
	15	All	All	Fitness Olympics	All	1-11
FINALS	16	Fitness specialist certification exam				
	17	Post-fitness combine				
	18	Awards and festival day				

Clubs

Lesson	Role performance	Fair play	Application contest	Club point deductions	Totals	Role performance	Fair play	Application contest	Club point deductions	Totals	Role performance	Fair play	Application contest	Club point deductions	Totals
5	n/a					n/a					n/a				
6															
7															
8															
9															
10															
11															
12															
13															
14															
15															
16		n/a					n/a					n/a			
17		n/a					n/a					n/a			

Role performance		Fair play		Application contest		Club point deductions	
Points	Description	Points	Description	Points	Place	Points	Infraction #
+6	All roles fulfilled	+6	All demonstrated fair play	+6	1st place	-1	1st offense
+5	5 roles fulfilled	+5	All but 1 demonstrated fair play	+5	2nd place	-3	2nd offense
+4	4 roles fulfilled	+4	All but 2 demonstrated fair play	+4	3rd place	-5	3rd offense
+3	3 roles fulfilled	+3	All but 3 demonstrated fair play	+3	4th place	-7	4th offense
+2	2 roles fulfilled	+2	All but 4 demonstrated fair play	+2	5th place	-10	5th offense
+1	1 roles fulfilled	+1	All but 5 demonstrated fair play	+1	6th place	-15	6th offense
+0	No roles fulfilled	+0	No one demonstrated fair play			-25	7th offense

AEROBIC FITNESS

1

PACER—Progressive Aerobic Cardiovascular Endurance Run

FLEXIBILITY

3

BACK-SAVER
SIT AND REACH

4

SHOULDER
STRETCH

UPPER BODY MUSCULAR FITNESS

5

PUSH-UP

7

MODIFIED
PULL-UP

ABDOMINAL MUSCULAR FITNESS

6

CURL-UPS

TRUNK EXTENSOR STRENGTH & FLEXIBILITY

8

TRUNK LIFT

AGILITY

10

Slide

Sprint

T-RUN

Slide

Sprint

SPEED

11

SPRINT, LYING BACK START

Start lying down on back
with heels on start line

* Numbers 2, 9, and 12 are intentionally left out of the sequence. The numbers correspond to the fitness combine; 2 is the BMI, 9 is the vertical jump, and 12 is the long jump. None is needed on a regular basis.

From *Sport Education Seasons* by Sean M. Bulger et al., 2007, Champaign, IL: Human Kinetics.

Chapter

6

PASE
Basketball Season

CONTENTS

SEASON OVERVIEW

- PASE Basketball Season Syllabus
- PASE Basketball Season 25-Lesson Block Plan
- PASE Basketball Grade Book sample
- PASE Basketball Daily Team Points Summary
- PASE Basketball Official's Signals Index

Instructor(s): _____

Class: _____ Time: _____

BASKETBALL SEASON DESCRIPTION

This basketball season consists of 25 lessons and is divided into three segments: a preseason, an in-season round robin tournament, and a postseason championship tournament. Throughout the season, each student will be responsible for performing various tasks related to playing and managing a basketball season. Good luck!

SEASON GOALS

To become . . .

- a **competent** basketball player: one who is a knowledgeable player and can successfully perform skills and strategies during a game of basketball
- a **literate** basketball player: one who knows the rules and traditions of the sport and can identify appropriate and inappropriate basketball behaviors
- an **enthusiastic** basketball player: one who is involved and behaves in ways that protect, preserve, and enhance the basketball culture
- an **independent learner:** one who demonstrates responsibility for his or her own progress through appropriate goal-setting and goal-monitoring behaviors

SEASON CONTENT

Skills

- Dribbling
- L- and V-cuts
- Passing
- Defensive footwork
- Jump and set shot
- Rebounding
- Layup

Tactics

- Dribble to reposition
- Screen on and off ball
- Triple threat
- Post play
- Defense on and off ball
- Player-to-player defense
- Pick and roll, give and go
- Team zone defense

From *Sport Education Seasons* by Sean M. Bulger et al., 2007, Champaign, IL: Human Kinetics.

SEASON REQUIREMENTS, POINTS, AND GRADING SCALE

Requirement		Point Value				
	Activity task cards	10	@	2	=	20
	Personal fitness assessment	20	@	1	=	20
	Pre- and post-skills and fitness combine	2	@	3	=	6
	Team goal setting	3	@	2	=	6
	Role performance	20	@	1	=	20
	Individual responsibility level (IRL)	8	@	1	=	8
	Written quizzes	2	@	2	=	4
	End-of-season awards voting	1	@	1	=	1
	Reflective journal	2	@	3	=	6
	Independent learning activity	1	@	4	=	4
	Outside-of-class physical activity log	5	@	1	=	5
				Total	=	100

Grading Scale		
A	95 – 100	
A-	93 – 94	Excellent
B+	91 – 92	
B	87 – 90	Above average
B-	85 – 86	
C+	83 – 84	
C	79 – 82	Average
C-	77 – 78	
D+	75 – 76	
D	72 – 74	Below average
D-	70 – 71	
F	Below 70	Failing

	Season bonus points	1st place	=	3.0 points	4th place	=	1.5 points
	Added to final point total	2nd place	=	2.5 points	5th place	=	1.0 point
		3rd place	=	2.0 points	6th place	=	0.5 point

From *Sport Education Seasons* by Sean M. Bulger et al., 2007, Champaign, IL: Human Kinetics.

Instructions: Record your personal progress each day. As you complete a requirement check it off like this "☑."

SEASON CALENDAR AND DAILY ASSESSMENTS

	PRESEASON															IN-SEASON ROUND ROBIN						POSTSEASON			
Lesson	1	2	3	4	5	6	7	8	9	10	11	12	13	14	15	16	17	18	19	20	21	22	23	24	25
Content	Pre-combine	Management	Dribble	Triple threat and pass	Pass	Review I	Set and jump shots	Layups	Pick and roll	Review II	Rebounding	Postplay	Player-to-player defense	Zone defense	Review III	RR tourney	RR tourney	RR tourney	RR tourney	RR tourney	Post-combine	Tourney	Tourney	Tourney	Festival
Date																									
(icon)			☐	☐	☐		☐	☐	☐		☐	☐	☐	☐											
(icon)			☐	☐	☐	☐	☐	☐	☐	☐	☐	☐	☐	☐	☐	☐	☐	☐	☐	☐		☐	☐		
(icon)	☐					☐				☐					☐						☐				
(icon)						☐				☐					☐					☐					
(icon)		☐	☐	☐	☐	☐	☐	☐	☐	☐	☐	☐	☐	☐	☐	☐	☐	☐	☐	☐		☐	☐	☐	☐
(icon)			☐	☐	☐	☐				☐					☐					☐					
(icon)													☐												
(icon)																								☐	
(icon)																								☐	☐
(icon)																									
(icon)					☐					☐					☐					☐					☐
(icon)																									Pts.

Season Requirement Icons

From Sport Education Seasons by Sean M. Bulger et al., 2007, Champaign, IL: Human Kinetics.

112

	Activity task cards	A series of skill and strategy development activities that must be completed by individual team members during team practice in lessons 3-5, 7-9, and 11-14.
	Personal fitness assessment	A set of fitness development activities that are completed and whose results are recorded during the team warm-up portion of lessons 3-20, 22, and 23.
	Pre- and post-skills and fitness combine	A variety of stations designed to provide pre- and postseason information for goal setting and monitoring of personal progress between lessons 1 and 21.
	Team goal setting	A reflective activity used to identify team strengths and areas needing improvement. To be completed at the end of lessons 6, 10, and 15.
	Role performance	A performance of roles designed to help manage the basketball season. Daily roles and responsibilities are identified at the beginning of lessons 3-20, 22, and 23.
	Individual responsibility level (IRL)	A reflective activity used for identifying and monitoring one's personal behaviors throughout the basketball season. To be completed at the end of lessons 2-6, 10, 15, and 20.
	Written quizzes	A series of written activities used to determine one's knowledge of basketball. In-class or take-home quizzes will be given at lessons 10 and 15.
	End-of-season awards voting	A voting activity used to identify individuals for awards related to successful basketball performance during the season. Voting to be completed in lesson 24.
	Reflective journal	An activity used to promote critical thinking by exploring issues related to participation in the basketball season. Completed in lessons 13 and 24.
	Independent learning activity	Students may choose from one of the following written activities: a personal behavior journal, a fitness/physical activity journal, or a skill and strategy development journal. To be completed by lesson 25.
	Outside-of-class physical activity log	An activity designed to provide additional opportunities for students to engage in meaningful physical activity outside of the physical education class throughout the basketball season. To be completed and turned in at lessons 5, 10, 15, 20, and 25.
	Season bonus points	Throughout the season individuals will earn points for their team. Team points will be acquired from role performance, enthusiastic performance, and application contest scores.

From *Sport Education Seasons* by Sean M. Bulger et al., 2007, Champaign, IL: Human Kinetics.

Day(s)	INSTRUCTIONAL FOCUS		Application Contest	OFFICIALS' SIGNALS	
	Skills	Tactics		Signal	Index #
1	Skills and fitness pre-combine				
2	Management day		Team cognitive challenge		
3	Dribble: control Footwork: offensive	Dribble to reposition	1 vs. 1 Two 15 sec dribble challenges	Stop clock Traveling 1-point scoring	4 8 1
4	Dribble: speed Pass: chest/bounce	Triple threat Ball fake	3 vs. 2 Two 30 sec triple-threat/pass challenges	Stop clock for foul Traveling Double dribble Unsportspersonlike	5 8 9 17
5	Pass: overhead/sidearm Dribble: review	Triple threat Ball fake	3 vs. 2 Two 30 sec triple-threat/pass challenges	Traveling Double dribble Carrying	8 9 10
6	Review I: all skills	Review I: all tactics	3 vs. 2 Two 30 sec triple-threat/pass challenges	All previous	
7	Shot: set/jump Footwork: defensive	Defense on/off ball	3 vs. 2 Two 1 min jump shot challenges	Illegal use of hands Jump ball 2-point scoring	13 12 2
8	Shot: lay-up Footwork: offensive	Give and go	3 vs. 2 Two 1 min layup/jump shot challenges	Charging with the ball Blocking 3-point scoring	16 14 3
9	Shot: review all Footwork: review all	Screen on/off ball Pick and roll	3 vs. 2 Two 2 min pick-and-roll challenges	Pushing Blocking Unsportspersonlike	15 14 17
10	Review II: all skills	Review II: all tactics	3 vs. 2 Two 2 min review challenges	All previous	
11	Rebounding: offensive and defensive	Review: all tactics	3 vs. 3 Two 2 min rebounding challenges	Pushing without ball Unsportspersonlike 3 seconds	15 17 11
12	Review: all skills	Offensive and defensive post play	3 vs. 3 Two 2 min post play challenges	Charging with the ball Carrying 3 seconds	16 10 11
13	Review: all skills	Player-to-Player defense	4 vs. 4 2 – 2 min player-to-player defense challenges	Double dribble Blocking Jump ball	9 14 12
14	Review: all skills	Team zone defense	4 vs. 4 2 – 2 min team zone defense challenges	Substitution Time-out Jump ball	6 7 12
15	Review III: all skills	Review III: all tactics	4 vs. 4 2 – 3 min review challenges	All	1-17

PRESEASON (Days 8–15)

From *Sport Education Seasons* by Sean M. Bulger et al., 2007, Champaign, IL: Human Kinetics.

| Day(s) | INSTRUCTIONAL FOCUS | | Application contest | OFFICIALS' SIGNALS | |
	Skills	Tactics		Signal	Index #
16	Review: all skills	Review: all tactics	G1 = 1 vs. 6 G2 = 2 vs. 5 G3 = 3 vs. 4	All	1-17
17	Review: all skills	Review: all tactics	G1 = 6 vs. 4 G2 = 5 vs. 1 G3 = 2 vs. 3	All	1-17
18	Review: all skills	Review: all tactics	G1 = 6 vs. 2 G2 = 5 vs. 3 G3 = 1 vs. 4	All	1-17
19	Review: all skills	Review: all tactics	G1 = 3 vs. 1 G2 = 4 vs. 2 G3 = 5 vs. 6	All	1-17
20	Review: all skills	Review: all tactics	G1 = 3 vs. 6 G2 = 1 vs. 2 G3 = 4 vs. 5	All	1-17
21	Skills and fitness post-combine				
22	Review: all skills	Review: all tactics	G1 = 5th seed vs. 4th seed G2 = 3rd seed vs. 6th seed G3 = 1st seed vs. winner G1	All	1-17
23	Review: all skills	Review: all tactics	G4 = loser G2 vs. loser G3 G5 = 2nd seed vs. winner G2 G6 = loser G1 vs. loser G5	All	1-17
24	Review: all skills	Review: all tactics	Consolation G7 = winner G6 vs. winner G4 Championship G7 = winner G3 vs. winner G5	All	1-17
25	Awards and festival day				

Left margin labels: IN-SEASON ROUND ROBIN TOURNAMENT (days 16-20), POSTSEASON TOURN. (days 22-23), FINALS (day 24)

From *Sport Education Seasons* by Sean M. Bulger et al., 2007, Champaign, IL: Human Kinetics.

A sample of the grade book program is included in this text (see the following figure). An electronic version of the grade book has been provided on the accompanying CD-ROM.

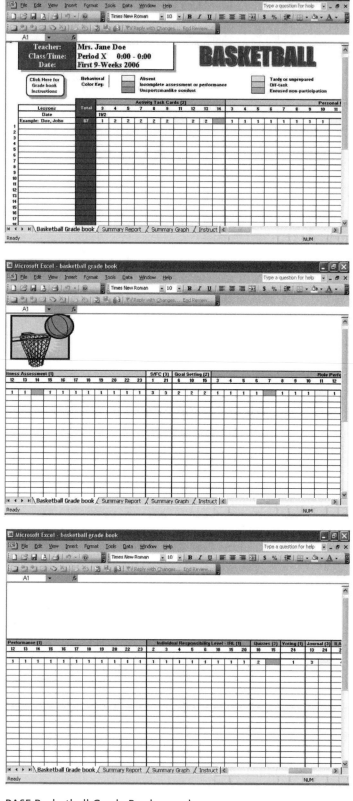

PASE Basketball Grade Book sample.

Teams / Lesson	Role performance	Fair play	Application contest	Team point deductions	Totals	Role performance	Fair play	Application contest	Team point deductions	Totals	Role performance	Fair play	Application contest	Team point deductions	Totals
2	n/a					n/a					n/a				
3															
4															
5															
6															
7															
8															
9															
10															
11															
12															
13															
14															
15															
16															
17															
18															
19															
20															
21	n/a		n/a			n/a		n/a			n/a		n/a		
22															
23															
24															

Role performance		Fair play		Application contest		Team point deductions	
Points	Description	Points	Description	Points	Place	Points	Infraction #
+6	All roles fulfilled	+6	All demonstrated fair play	+6	1st place	-1	1st offense
+5	5 roles fulfilled	+5	5 demonstrated fair play	+5	2nd place	-3	2nd offense
+4	4 roles fulfilled	+4	4 demonstrated fair play	+4	3rd place	-5	3rd offense
+3	3 roles fulfilled	+3	3 demonstrated fair play	+3	4th place	-7	4th offense
+2	2 roles fulfilled	+2	2 demonstrated fair play	+2	5th place	-10	5th offense
+1	1 roles fulfilled	+1	1 demonstrated fair play	+1	6th place	-15	6th offense

From *Sport Education Seasons* by Sean M. Bulger et al., 2007, Champaign, IL: Human Kinetics.

PASE Basketball Official's Signals Index

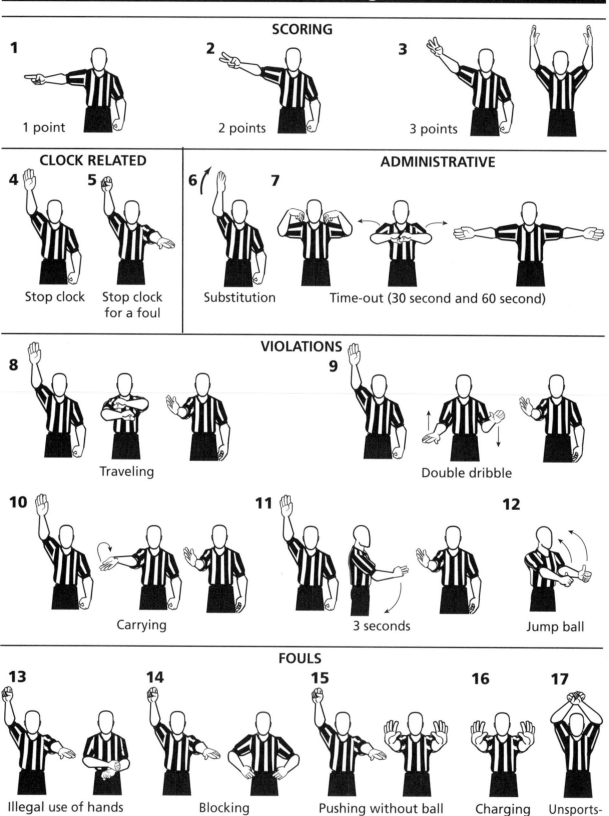

SCORING

1 1 point

2 2 points

3 3 points

CLOCK RELATED

4 Stop clock

5 Stop clock for a foul

ADMINISTRATIVE

6 Substitution

7 Time-out (30 second and 60 second)

VIOLATIONS

8 Traveling

9 Double dribble

10 Carrying

11 3 seconds

12 Jump ball

FOULS

13 Illegal use of hands

14 Blocking

15 Pushing without ball

16 Charging with the ball

17 Unsports-personlike

From *Sport Education Seasons* by Sean M. Bulger et al., 2007, Champaign, IL: Human Kinetics.

LESSON PLANS

PASE BASKETBALL LESSON PLAN 1

Resources: Lesson Focus

- CD player
- *FITNESSGRAM* 8.0 PACER/Cadence CD
- Stopwatches
- Station Task Cards 1-20
- Mats
- Basketballs
- Cones
- 12-inch rulers
- Nine hula hoops (one for each station that uses a ball)
- *FITNESSGRAM* Test Kit

Instructional Materials

- PASE Skills and Fitness Combine Recording Sheets (one per person) (appendix A)
- PASE Draft Composite (one per coach) (appendix A)
- PASE Draft Selection Form (one per coach) (appendix A)
- PASE Fitness and Skills Station Task Cards 1-20 (appendix A)

Instructional Focus

The skills combine is designed to encompass the following:

- A skills and fitness assessment pretest (lesson 1)
- A skills and fitness assessment posttest (lesson 21)
- A data collection process that will enable students to engage in meaningful goal-setting behaviors
- A data collection process that will enable the teacher to monitor student progress throughout the season

Fitness Assessments

- PACER
- BMI
- Sit and reach
- Shoulder stretch
- Push-up
- Curl-up
- Modified pull-up
- Trunk lift
- Vertical jump
- T-run
- Shuttle run
- Line jumps

Skill Assessments

- Low control dribble
- Speed dribble
- Layup
- Set shot
- Jump shot (midrange)
- Jump shot (long range)
- Rebounding
- Pass: chest
- Pass: bounce

See organizational considerations in the "Suggested Modifications" section at the end of lesson plan 1 for a detailed description of how to modify the skills combine to meet your instructional situation.

Objectives

- Obtain data for team selection purposes
- Obtain health-related fitness pretest data
- Obtain skill-related fitness pretest data
- Obtain basketball skill pretest data
- For students to demonstrate personal and social responsibility

Lesson Introduction

- Introduce lesson focus.
- Provide anticipatory set:

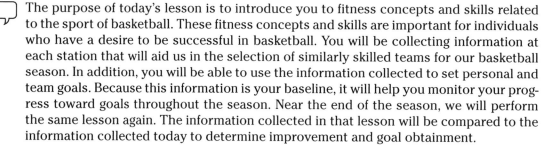

The purpose of today's lesson is to introduce you to fitness concepts and skills related to the sport of basketball. These fitness concepts and skills are important for individuals who have a desire to be successful in basketball. You will be collecting information at each station that will aid us in the selection of similarly skilled teams for our basketball season. In addition, you will be able to use the information collected to set personal and team goals. Because this information is your baseline, it will help you monitor your progress toward goals throughout the season. Near the end of the season, we will perform the same lesson again. The information collected in that lesson will be compared to the information collected today to determine improvement and goal obtainment.

- Provide instructions for completing pre-skills combine:

You will notice that there are 20 stations set up around the gymnasium. You and a partner will be required to visit each station, read the task card, perform the stated activity, and record your scores. Each pair will be assigned a station number, which is where you will begin. When you arrive at any station, read the task card carefully to determine what you are required to do. Pay attention to the floor diagram, picture, and cues to help you to perform the activities correctly. Once you have completed the activity, you will need to record all required information. This information is to be recorded on the **Fitness and Skills Combine Recording Sheet** in the "Prescore" row. Use the row showing the example to ensure accurate scoring. Next, you should immediately set an end-of-season goal for the station just completed and record this information in the "Goals" row. After completing a station, pairs are free to rotate to a new station of their choice. Please look for open stations to rotate to, remembering that your goal is to complete every station today. Note the time criterion at each station and pace yourselves accordingly.

- Complete teacher demonstrations for at least one station and have students practice recording a mock score.
- Check for student understanding using questions, student demonstrations, or both.
  - Q1: "What are the purposes of the fitness and skills combine?"
  - Q2: "What is the first thing that each pair should do when arriving at a new station?"
  - Q3: "After reading the task card and performing the activity, what should you do?"
  - Q4: "Describe what happens after recording the required information at a station."
- Assign pairs to a station and begin pre-skills and fitness combine. (Teacher may elect to run the entire class through the PACER test as a group for the first station.)

Pairs transition to assigned station.

Lesson Body

+ Complete pre-skills and fitness combine.
+ See station task cards for organizational and content information.
+ Teacher manages and monitors learning environment. If the teacher is drafting students to teams, the teacher uses the **Draft Composite** sheet to help make notes on students' performance in fitness and skill as well as using combine information. If student coaches are being used at this point, they may utilize the **Draft Composite** sheet to make notes and begin draft selection but should not be provided combine results such as personal information and scores.

Fitness Component Stations

1. PACER
2. BMI
3. Sit and reach
4. Shoulder stretch
5. Push-up
6. Curl-up
7. Modified pull-up
8. Trunk lift
9. Vertical jump
10. T-run
11. Shuttle run
12. Line jumps

Basketball Skill Stations

13. Low control dribble
14. Speed dribble
15. Layup
16. Set shot
17. Jump shot (midrange)
18. Jump shot (long range)
19. Rebounding
20. Pass: chest and bounce

() *Pairs transition to common area for daily closure.*

Closure

+ Teacher reviews lesson purpose.
+ Check for student understanding using questions and demonstrations. Look for information regarding skills (critical features and cues), tactics, official's signals, rules, and other content- or performance-related questions and demonstrations. You can use questions and demonstrations from the introduction.
+ Teacher discusses individuals' and pairs' daily performance.
+ Allow for student questions and preview **lesson 2.**

() *Pairs organize materials and exit class.*

Suggested Floor Plan

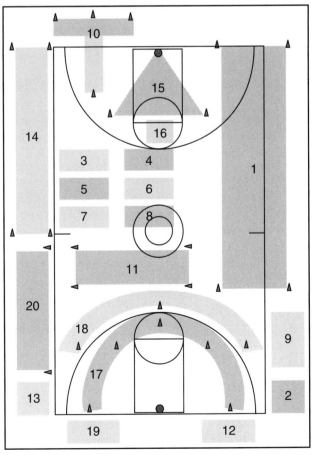

◆ Use the **Draft Selection Form** to create teams based on student performance on the fitness and skills combine. This should be done by the teacher if data from the skills combine are being used. If student coaches are creating the teams, they should use the information they have collected via the **Draft Composite** sheet to select appropriate and fair teams. The teacher should be present for the draft, which is held outside of regular class time.

Suggested Modifications

Note: Pretest and posttest station activities and organizational arrangements should be identical. Identical activities and organizational arrangements will enhance reliability when students compare pre- and posttest information. If stations from pre- to posttests are different in any way, students will be unable to make reliable comparisons when determining individual improvement or goal obtainment. **If you choose to make changes to the pre-skills combine, document changes in the space provided at the end of this lesson.** The following variables represent organizational considerations that the teacher may use to modify the fitness and skills combine to meet his or her instructional situation.

Time Allotment

Decrease or increase the time necessary to complete each station by altering station requirements. **Example:** Increase time requirements for midrange jump shot station from 45 seconds to 1 minute.

Space and Dimensions of Stations

Decrease or increase the area needed by altering station dimensions. **Example:** Use four basketball goals for stations 15 to 18 (shots) instead of two basketball goals.

Activities

Change the overall number of activities included in the fitness and skills combine. **Example:** Limit the number of activities in each fitness component to one; that is, include only one measure for flexibility such as the back-saver sit and reach.

Criteria and Scoring

Change the rules that govern scoring and criteria for correct performance of activities at the basketball skill stations **only.** The *FITNESSGRAM* criteria and scoring should not be altered. If the *FITNESSGRAM* criteria and scoring measures are altered, the healthy fitness zones become void. **Example:** The value of more difficult performances is increased; that is, a made long-range jump shot is worth more than a made midrange jump shot.

Split Fitness and Skills Combine

The fitness and skills combine can be split into more than one lesson depending upon the stations selected, the number of students in a class, facilities, equipment, and class time. **Note:** Because the skills combine is repeated later in the season, any change in the pre-skills and fitness combine should be applied to the post-skills and fitness combine also. **Example:** If the teacher has adequate space and equipment but has insufficient time to complete the fitness and skills combine in a single lesson, he or she can split the combine into a fitness assessment day (stations 1-12) and a basketball skills assessment day (stations 13-20).

Pre-Skills and Fitness Combine Modifications

Station number   Changes

_____

_____

_____

_____

_____

PASE BASKETBALL LESSON PLAN 2

Resources: Lesson Focus

- All instructional materials for **lesson 3,** including roles and responsibilities assignments, fitness activities sheets, student coaching plan, activity task card, application contest and scorecard, team membership inventory and fair play agreement, and team roster as well as all recording sheets (roles and responsibilities, fitness, task card, IRL, attendance)
- Pencils (also used in application contest)

Resources: Application Contest

- PASE Official's Pocket Reference
- PASE Application Contest 2
- PASE Application Contest Scorecard 2

Instructional Materials

- PASE Basketball Season Syllabus
- PASE Roles and Responsibilities Assignments and Recording Sheet (appendix B)
- PASE Fitness Activities Sheets (appendix B)
- PASE Personal or Team Fitness Recording Sheet (appendix B)
- PASE Individual or Team Activity Task Card Recording Sheet (appendix B)
- PASE Sports Information Director Sports Report (appendix B)
- PASE IRL Rubric and Recording Sheet (appendix B)
- PASE Team Roster (appendix B)
- PASE Attendance Recording Sheet (appendix B)
- PASE Team Membership Inventory and Fair Play Agreement (appendix B)
- PASE Outside-of-Class Physical Activity Participation Log (appendix B)

Instructional Focus

To establish the rules, routines, and procedures for the basketball season.

Objectives

- Establish a classroom environment conducive to learning basketball
- Gain the cooperation of students
- Demonstrate lesson components and associated assessments
- For students to demonstrate an understanding of the rules, routines, and procedures by successfully completing the daily application contest

Lesson Introduction

- Introduce lesson focus.
- Provide anticipatory set:

The purpose of today's lesson is to introduce you to the rules, routines, and procedures for our basketball season. By the end of today's lesson you will know the rules, routines, and procedures for each segment of the lesson and you will also be able to perform the requirements for each of these segments. It is important that we learn the rules, routines, and procedures today so that we can focus on basketball for the remainder of the season.

- Provide instructions for completing a mock lesson:

> Today you and your teammates will be completing a mock lesson. Under my direction, we will walk through each segment of a typical lesson for our basketball season. Near the end of today's lesson, each team will complete a challenge and earn team points that will be compiled across the season to determine a season champion. In order for your team to earn as many points as possible, it is important for you to pay close attention to the explanations for each lesson segment. Please feel free to ask questions if you are unsure about the information presented for any lesson segment today. Following the completion of the mock lesson and the team challenge we will discuss the syllabus for the basketball season. Let's get started!

Lesson Body

- Direct students through each lesson segment.
- Discuss the rules, routines, and procedures for each lesson segment.
- Address the following questions when discussing rules, routines, and procedures for lesson segments:
    - Where do students go during each lesson segment?
    - What do students do within each lesson segment?
    - When and how do students fulfill role requirements within each lesson segment?
    - What information should be recorded, if any, during each lesson segment?
    - How do students record the required information?
    - What do students do if they need help during a lesson segment?

Lesson Segment Routines and Procedures

Team Role Check

- Students enter gymnasium and immediately report to home court area.
- Students check daily roles and associated duties on the **PASE Roles and Responsibilities Assignments** provided.

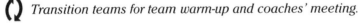 *Transition teams for team warm-up and coaches' meeting.*

Team Warm-Up and Coaches' Meeting

- Fitness trainer monitors team warm-up.
- Individuals or teams progress through fitness activities posted on the **PASE Fitness Activities Sheets.**
- All team coaches report to designated area to meet with teacher.
- Teacher outlines the day's events for the coaches and supplies the **PASE Student Coaching Plan.**
- Coaches transition to home court area and join warm-up.
- Individuals record the required information on their **PASE Personal** or **Team Fitness Recording Sheet.**

 *Transition teams for the daily review segment of the lesson.*

Team Review

- Teams review progress on goals from previous lessons.
- Teams identify areas of need based on progress.
- Teams use this time to practice to improve areas of need.

Transition teams to designated instructional area for teacher instruction lesson segment.

Teacher Instruction

- ◆ Introduce daily lesson focus and review previous lesson's information.
- ◆ Provide anticipatory set about skills and strategies to be learned.
- ◆ Provide information about skills and strategies to be learned.
- ◆ Complete teacher or student demonstrations (or both).
- ◆ Check for student understanding using questions, student demonstrations, or both.
- ◆ Conduct whole-class guided practice drills.

() *Transition teams to home court area for daily team practice.*

Team Practice

- ◆ Student coach organizes and facilitates team practice.
- ◆ Students progress, individually or as teams, through the **PASE Activity Task Card.**
- ◆ Teacher moves through home court area to facilitate team practice and does the following:
    - ◆ Manages learning environment
    - ◆ Observes and assesses individual and team performance
    - ◆ Provides encouragement and instructional feedback
- ◆ Individuals record progress on their PASE Individual or Team Activity Task Card Recording Sheet.

() *Transition teams back to designated instructional area for explanation of application contest.*

Application Contest

- ◆ Teacher explains and demonstrates daily contests described in **PASE Application Contest** and does the following:
    - ◆ Identifies tactical focus and related skills
    - ◆ Identifies contest goals
    - ◆ Discusses procedures for scoring and refereeing

    Scoring: Referees use nonshaded areas on the **PASE Application Contest Scorecard.**

    Refereeing: Refer to and use designated referee signals found on the **PASE Official's Pocket Reference.**

() *Transition teams to designated contest areas to engage in contest and perform assigned duties.*

Closure

- ◆ Review lesson focus.
- ◆ Discuss assessment of individual and team performances.
- ◆ Check for student understanding using questions and demonstrations.
- ◆ Allow for student questions and preview next lesson.

() *Transition teams to home court areas for individual and team assessment lesson segment.*

Individual and Team Assessment

- ◆ Individuals use the **PASE IRL Rubric** for completing the **PASE IRL Recording Sheet** to determine levels of
    - ◆ preparedness, transition, on-task, sportspersonship, and assessment behaviors.
- ◆ Individuals complete the PASE Roles and Responsibilities Recording Sheet to determine
    - ◆ role completion.

- ◆ Coach completes the **PASE Attendance Recording Sheet** to determine
  - ◆ attendance behaviors for the team.

 Teams organize materials and exit class from home court areas.

- ◆ Discuss sports information director's responsibility and refer to the **Sports Information Director Sports Report.**

Closure

- ◆ Complete daily application contest for lesson 2.
- ◆ Distribute and discuss season syllabus.
- ◆ Review lesson 2 purposes.
- ◆ Check for student understanding of lesson 2 information using questions and demonstrations (refer back to questions and demonstrations from the introduction).
- ◆ Teams complete the **PASE Team Membership Inventory and Fair Play Agreement** and **Team Roster** to
  - ◆ establish team affiliation and indicate individual understanding of season expectations.
- ◆ Discuss and hand out **PASE Outside-of-Class Physical Activity Participation Log.** This should be checked or collected from the students on a regular basis as determined by the teacher. Suggested checkpoints are at lessons 5 and 11.
- ◆ Allow for student questions and preview **lesson 3.**

 Teams organize materials and exit class.

Score

_____ / 20

Instructions

- As a team, respond to each of the following items.
- Your team's goal is to respond to all of the items correctly.
- Because your team is competing with the other teams during this contest, your chances of winning the contest increase with number of items answered correctly.
- Best of luck!

1. Shade in your home court area on the basketball floor diagram to the right.

2. List your team members' names and roles for **lesson 3** in the space provided.

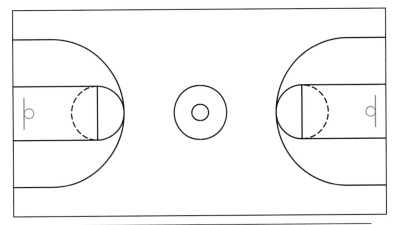

Name	Role	Name	Role

3. On the basketball floor diagram above, place an **"X"** where the coaches' meeting will be held each day.

4. Identify the muscles stretched if your team chose flexibility workout **Flx 2** during the team warm-up segment of the lesson.

5. Identify the following items for the **T-run:**

Criteria	Scoring	Conditions

6. List one of the **"Keys to Success"** from the student coaching plan for **lesson 3:**

7. List the three **"Official's Signals"** to be learned for **lesson 3:**

8. What takes place after the warm-up and coaches' meeting segment of the daily lesson?

(continued)

From *Sport Education Seasons* by Sean M. Bulger et al., 2007, Champaign, IL: Human Kinetics.

9. On the basketball floor diagram, shade in the area where teacher instruction will take place each day. Denote this shaded area with the letters **"T.I."**

10. Who is responsible for directing team practice?

11. Locate the **PASE Activity Task Card** for **lesson 3.** Identify who is responsible for the evaluation of student performance for tasks 3-6, 9-11, 13, 14, and 17-19; for tasks 7 and 15; and for tasks 1, 2, 8, 12, 16, 20, and 21.

Tasks 3-6, 9-11, 13, 14, and 17-19	Tasks 7 and 15	Tasks 1, 2, 8, 12, 16, 20, and 21

12. Locate an **Individual Activity Task Card Recording Sheet.** Who is responsible for certifying that each team member has successfully completed the tasks for a given lesson? How is the certification noted?

13. During a typical application contest, what two roles take on a majority of the responsibility to ensure that rules are followed and that scores are accurately recorded?

14. Identify the skill(s) and tactic(s) to be applied during the **PASE Application Contest** for **lesson 3.**

15. Locate the **PASE Application Contest Scorecard** for **lesson 3.** List the items that should be filled in on this scorecard.

16. Complete the **PASE Individual Responsibility Level (IRL) Recording Sheet** assessment for lesson 2 (today's lesson).

17. Complete the **PASE Team Membership Inventory.**

18. Complete the **PASE Fair Play Agreement.**

19. Complete the **PASE Basketball Attendance Recording Sheet.**

20. Identify the following codes using the attendance information key on the **PASE Basketball Attendance Recording Sheet.**

P	L	E	A

From *Sport Education Seasons* by Sean M. Bulger et al., 2007, Champaign, IL: Human Kinetics.

PASE BASKETBALL LESSON PLAN 3

Resources: Lesson Focus

- Numbered colored pinnies—six per team (also used during application contest)
- Basketballs—three to six per team (also used during application contest)
- Hula hoops—one per team (used to organize team materials)
- Stopwatches—one per team
- Pencils

Resources: Application Contest

- PASE Application Contest 3
- PASE Application Contest Scorecard 3
- PASE Official's Pocket Reference
- Two to four cones
- Boundary markers
- One clipboard
- Pencils
- Whistles
- Officials' pinnies

Instructional Materials

- PASE IRL Rubric and Recording Sheet (appendix B)
- PASE Attendance Recording Sheet (appendix B)
- PASE Roles and Responsibilities Assignments and Recording Sheet (appendix B)
- PASE Student Coaching Plan 3
- PASE Activity Task Card 3
- PASE Fitness Activities Sheets (appendix B)
- PASE Personal or Team Fitness Recording Sheet (appendix B)
- PASE Individual or Team Activity Task Card Recording Sheet (appendix B)
- PASE Basketball Lesson Plan 4

Instructional Focus

Skills
- Low control dribble
- Offensive footwork

Tactic
- Dribbling to reposition

Objectives

- Develop low control dribble and offensive footwork by progression through learning activities during team practice
- Utilize low control dribble and offensive footwork and demonstrate dribbling to reposition in an application contest
- Demonstrate personal and social responsibility

Team Role Check

- ◆ Students enter gymnasium and immediately report to home court area.
- ◆ Check daily roles and associated duties from materials provided.

Begin team warm-up.

Team Warm-Up

- ◆ Conduct the team warm-up simultaneously to coaches' meeting.
- ◆ Fitness trainer monitors team warm-up using the PASE Fitness Activities Sheets.
- ◆ Fitness trainer or individuals record performance on team warm-up using either the **Personal** or **Team Fitness Recording Sheet.**

Teams transition to daily review.

Coaches' Meeting

- ◆ Conduct the coaches' meeting simultaneously to team warm-up.
- ◆ All team coaches report to designated meeting area.
- ◆ Teacher provides coaches with **Student Coaching Plan 3** and **Activity Task Card 3.**
- ◆ Teacher outlines the day's events.

Coaches transition to home court area and join warm-up.

Team Review

- ◆ Review progress of team goals from **lesson 2.** Refer to the activity task cards and application contest results to date.
- ◆ Identify areas of need from **lesson 2.**
- ◆ Practice to improve in areas of need.

Teams transition to designated instructional area for teacher instructions.

Teacher Instruction

- ◆ Introduce daily lesson focus and review **lesson 2.**
- ◆ Provide anticipatory set:

The reason we are learning to use the low control dribble and offensive footwork is to create passing lanes by dribbling to reposition. After learning how to move with and without the ball, you will be better at using space to attack the basket.

- ◆ Provide information about skills and strategies.
- ◆ **Introduce** the following new skills and tactics for the day.
- ◆ Complete teacher or student demonstrations (or both) of these skills and tactics:

LOW CONTROL DRIBBLE

Critical features	Instructional cues
Relaxed hand control	Gentle push
Push ball with finger pads	Use of finger pads
Dribble knee to midthigh	Keep ball low
Head up and eyes scanning	Eyes up
Body between ball and defender	Protect ball

OFFENSIVE FOOTWORK (L-CUT AND V-CUT)

Critical features	Instructional cues
Keep moving to create passing lanes	Move away from passer
Feint, plant foot to change direction quickly	Quick cut (V or L)
Move toward ball to receive pass	Move toward passer
Assume position with hands set to catch pass	Provide target with hands

DRIBBLING TO REPOSITION

Critical features	Instructional cues
Use critical features of low control dribble	Use proper dribble
Continue to dribble to create passing lanes	Move to open spaces
Players without ball cut to create passing lanes	Teammates use V- or L-cuts to get open
Dribbler anticipates and executes pass	Look to make pass

- Provide information about official's signals and rules.
- **Introduce** today's signals and rules. Demonstrate and explain the following signals and rules:
  - Stop clock (4)
  - Traveling (8)
  - 1-point scoring (1)
- Check for student understanding using questions, student demonstrations, or both.
  - Q1: "Who can name/demonstrate the critical features for low control dribble?"
  - Q2: "Who can name/demonstrate the critical features for offensive footwork?"
  - Q3: "What is the purpose of learning the low control dribble and offensive footwork?"

() *Teams transition to home court area for daily team practice.*

Team Practice (Refer to Activity Task Card 3 and Individual or Team Activity Task Card Recording Sheet)

Team-directed practice begins. Teacher moves through home court area to facilitate team practice.

- Manage learning environment.
- Observe and assess individual and team performance.
- Provide encouragement and instructional feedback.

() *Teams transition back to designated instructional area for application contest.*

Application Contest

Teacher explains and demonstrates daily contest (refer to **Application Contest 3**). Identify tactical focus and related skills (refer to **Application Contest Scorecard 3**).

- Identify contest goals.
- Discuss procedures for scoring and refereeing.

    Scoring: Use nonshaded areas on **Application Contest Scorecard 3.**

Refereeing: Refer to and use designated referee signals located on the Official's Pocket Reference.

( ) *Teams transition to designated contest areas to perform assigned duties.*

◆ Teacher actively monitors individual and team performance.

( ) *Teams transition to designated instructional area for closure.*

Closure

◆ Teacher reviews lesson focus.

◆ Teacher discusses assessment of individual and team performance.

◆ Check for student understanding using questions and demonstrations (refer back to questions and demonstrations from the introduction, if needed).

◆ Allow for student questions and preview **lesson 4.**

( ) *Teams transition to home court areas for individual and team assessment.*

Individual and Team Assessment

Assessment summary

◆ Complete **PASE IRL Recording Sheet** (each person).

◆ Summarize/Complete **Application Contest Scorecard 3** (scorekeeper).

◆ Complete **PASE Attendance Recording Sheet** (coach).

◆ Complete **PASE Roles and Responsibilities Recording Sheet** (each person).

◆ Supervise assessment completion (coach).

( ) *Teams organize materials and exit class from home court areas.*

Low Control Dribble

Critical Features

1. Relaxed hand control
2. Push ball with finger pads
3. Dribble knee to midthigh
4. Head up and eyes scanning
5. Body between ball and defender

Instructional Cues

1. Gentle push
2. Use of finger pads
3. Keep ball low
4. Eyes up
5. Protect ball

Description

The low control dribble is used to move the ball up the court. Its purpose is to establish increased control when the dribbler is closely guarded by a defender. Typical use is when the dribbler is transitioning after a shot has been gathered and is moving into defensive position.

Offensive Footwork (V-Cut and L-Cut)

Critical Features

1. Keep moving to create passing lanes
2. Feint, plant foot to change direction quickly
3. Move toward ball to receive pass
4. Assume position with hands set

Instructional Cues

1. Move away from passer
2. Quick cut (V or L)
3. Move toward passer
4. Provide target with hands

Description

This skill consists of cutting movements, stopping quickly, and changing directions. These movements are most typically used without the ball when an offensive player is attempting to get open and create passing lanes. However, they can be combined with skills such as dribbling to enhance their effectiveness.

From *Sport Education Seasons* by Sean M. Bulger et al., 2007, Champaign, IL: Human Kinetics.

Dribble to Reposition

Critical Features

1. Use critical features of the low control dribble
2. Continue to dribble to create passing lanes
3. Players without ball cut to create passing lanes
4. Dribbler anticipates and executes pass

Instructional Cues

1. Use proper dribble
2. Move to open spaces
3. Teammates use V- or L-cuts to get open
4. Look to make pass

Description

The purpose of repositioning when you are the ball handler is to force the defense to continually move and also to allow your own teammates an opportunity to move to open areas. By continually moving to an open area you are forcing the defense to make changes, enabling the offense to create spaces to pass to.

From *Sport Education Seasons* by Sean M. Bulger et al., 2007, Champaign, IL: Human Kinetics.

PASE Basketball Student Coaching Plan 3

"Do not let what you cannot do interfere with what you can do."

—John Wooden

Skills

- Low control dribble
- Offensive footwork

Tactic

- Dribbling to reposition

Coaching Cues

Low control dribble	Offensive footwork	Dribbling to reposition
✓ Gentle push	✓ Move away from passer	✓ Use proper dribble
✓ Use of finger pads	✓ Quick cut (V or L)	✓ Move to open spaces
✓ Keep ball low	✓ Move toward passer	✓ Teammates use V- or L-cuts to get open
✓ Eyes up	✓ Provide target with hands	✓ Look to make pass
✓ Protect ball		

Keys to Success

- Focus the team on the coaching cues for the new skills.
- Help team to understand the tactic of dribbling to reposition.
- Make sure all teammates are progressing on **Activity Task Card.**
- Provide encouragement, feedback, and demonstrations to teammates.

Rules and Official's Signals

- **Stop clock.** Discuss, demonstrate, and practice stop clock signal.
- **Traveling.** If you stop dribbling, you may not continue to move. Discuss, demonstrate, and practice traveling signal.
- **1-point scoring.** Discuss, demonstrate, and practice 1-point scoring signal.

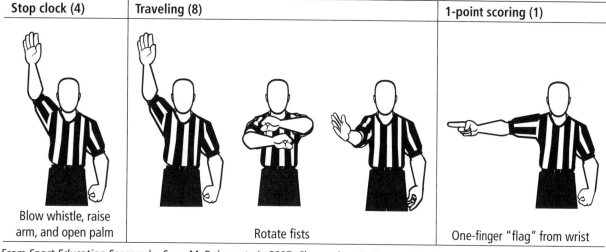

Stop clock (4)	Traveling (8)	1-point scoring (1)
Blow whistle, raise arm, and open palm	Rotate fists	One-finger "flag" from wrist

From *Sport Education Seasons* by Sean M. Bulger et al., 2007, Champaign, IL: Human Kinetics.

PASE Basketball Activity Task Card 3

Skills

- Low control dribble
- Offensive footwork

Tactic

- Dribbling to reposition

Learning tasks	Self	Peer	Coach
1. Under the direction of the coach, perform the cues for today's skills five times each.			☐
2. Under the direction of the coach, perform the official's signals for today's lesson five times each.			☐
3. Dribble with preferred hand, without moving, while staying in control for 30 sec.	☐		
4. Dribble with nonpreferred hand, without moving, while staying in control for 30 sec.	☐		
5. Dribble with preferred hand, while moving, in general space in control for 30 sec.	☐		
6. Dribble with nonpreferred hand, while moving, in general space in control for 30 sec.	☐		
7. Dribble alternating between hands, while moving, in general space for 30 sec.		☐	
8. Repeat #7, but this time, count and remember the number of times you switch hands in 30 sec. (Record score only if using **Individual Activity Task Card Recording Sheet**.)	#___		☐
9. Dribble with preferred hand, moving backward, in a straight line for 30 sec.	☐		
10. Dribble with nonpreferred hand, moving backward, in a straight line for 30 sec.	☐		
11. Dribble in a straight line, moving backward, alternating between hands for 30 sec.	☐		
12. Repeat #11, but this time, count and remember the number of times you switch hands in 30 sec. (Record score only if using **Individual Activity Task Card Recording Sheet**.)	#___		☐
13. Dribble with preferred hand, moving sideways, in a zigzag pattern for 30 sec.	☐		
14. Dribble with nonpreferred hand, moving sideways, in a zigzag pattern for 30 sec.	☐		
15. Dribble in a zigzag pattern, moving sideways, alternating between hands for 30 sec.		☐	
16. Repeat #15, but this time, count and remember the number of times you switch hands in 30 sec. (Record score only if using **Individual Activity Task Card Recording Sheet**.)	#___		☐
17. Dribble with preferred hand, allowing a partner to play passive defense for 30 sec.	☐		
18. Dribble with nonpreferred hand, allowing a partner to play passive defense for 30 sec.	☐		
19. Dribble while alternating between hands, allowing a partner to play passive defense for 30 sec.	☐		
20. 1-on-1: In partners, moving through general space, partner A will dribble with either hand while partner B attempts to steal the ball. Partner A should dribble close to or far from body, at medium/low levels, in straight/curved/zigzag pathways, while moving at medium/slow speeds. Partners should not make contact with one another. Switch roles after 30 sec. Answer the following questions and discuss what you discovered about maintaining ball possession and control with a teammate. • Is it easier to dribble with control while the ball is at a high or low level? Why? • Is it harder for the defense to take the ball if it is close to you or far away? Why? • How can you use your body to help maintain possession of the ball?			☐
21. Repeat #20. This time defense earns a point for every steal or knock-away. The partner dribbling will receive 1 point if he or she can maintain control for 30 sec. Remember scores. Repeat again. (Record score only if using **Individual Activity Task Card Recording Sheet**.)	#___		☐

From *Sport Education Seasons* by Sean M. Bulger et al., 2007, Champaign, IL: Human Kinetics.

Equipment

- Two to four cones
- Pencils
- Boundary markers
- Whistles
- Lesson 3 Scorecard
- Officials' pinnies
- One clipboard
- Colored pinnies (teams)

Objectives

- Demonstrate a low control dribble
- Dribble to reposition to create open passing lanes

Goals

Dribble from one end of the court to the other without losing control of the ball

Application Description

Team A will line up across the out-of-bounds line on one end of the court. Team B players will match up against players from team A in order to play person-to-person defense. On the teacher's signal, each person from team A will attempt to low control dribble from the start line to the finish line without losing control of the ball and without going out of bounds. The defender from team B is to try to prevent the dribbler from reaching the finish line before time is up (15 seconds). The defender cannot make contact with the dribbler. At the end of the 15-second trial, team A will assume a starting position at the end line and complete a second trial of 15 seconds. At the end of the second 15-second trial, the teams will rotate offense to defense and repeat for two more trials. The teacher should have multiple games going at the same time based on space and equipment and should use a single game clock for all games.

Application Diagram

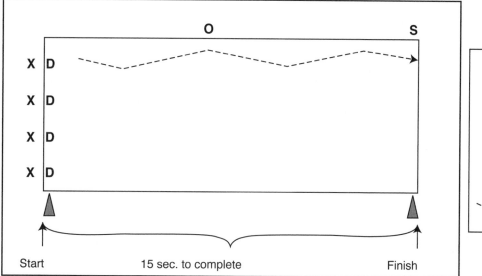

Key

X = Dribbler

D = Defender

O = Official

S = Scorekeeper

▲ = Cones

⌁➤ = Dribbler's pathway

Scorekeeper's Guidelines

Provide scorekeepers with an example to fill in on their scorecard.

- 1 point for dribbler for dribbling from start line to finish line without losing control in 15 seconds.
- 1 point for dribbler if the defender makes contact.
- Record individual scores after each trial and only after the official's signal.
- Combine all team member points for total team score after second trial.

Referee's Guidelines

- No points awarded if dribbler travels.
- No points awarded if dribbler loses control of the ball and the ball goes out of bounds.
- Award 1 point for dribbler if the defender makes contact.
- Demonstrate appropriate signals related to scoring.
- Demonstrate appropriate clock-related signals.

From *Sport Education Seasons* by Sean M. Bulger et al., 2007, Champaign, IL: Human Kinetics.

PASE Basketball Application Contest Scorecard 3

Instructions: Nonshaded areas must be filled in by scorekeeper.

Team		Coach		Date		☐ Home	☐ Away

TEAM FINAL SCORE

Scorekeeper		Opponent	

TEAM SCORING BY HALF

	1st Trial	2nd Trial	OT

SUMMARY / SCORING

Player	1st Trial	2nd Trial	OT	2 FG		3 FG		FT		Steals	Reb.	Pts.
				A	M	A	M	A	M			

Practice row to be filled in by student.

Fouls

	1	2	3	4	5
	1	2	3	4	5
	1	2	3	4	5
	1	2	3	4	5
	1	2	3	4	5
	1	2	3	4	5
	1	2	3	4	5
	1	2	3	4	5

Totals

Team Fouls

1	2	3	4	5	6	7	8	9	10

Alternating Jump Ball Possessions

TEAM TIME-OUTS

Home	Away	Home	Away	Home	Away	Home	Away	Home	Away
1		2		3		4		5	

Running Score

1	2	3	4	5	6	7	8	9	10	11	12	13	14	15	16	17	18	19	20	21	22	23	24	25
26	27	28	29	30	31	32	33	34	35	36	37	38	39	40	41	42	43	44	45	46	47	48	49	50
51	52	53	54	55	56	57	58	59	60	61	62	63	64	65	66	67	68	69	70	71	72	73	74	75
76	77	78	79	80	81	82	83	84	85	86	87	88	89	90	91	92	93	94	95	96	97	98	99	100

Coach's Signature _____

Scorekeeper's Signature _____

From *Sport Education Seasons* by Sean M. Bulger et al., 2007, Champaign, IL: Human Kinetics.

PASE BASKETBALL LESSON PLAN 4

Resources: Lesson Focus

- Numbered colored pinnies—six per team (also used during application contest)
- Basketballs—three to six per team (also used during application contest)
- Hula hoops—one per team (used to organize team materials)
- Stopwatches—one per team
- Pencils

Resources: Application Contest

- PASE Application Contest 4
- PASE Application Contest Scorecard 4
- PASE Official's Pocket Reference
- Two to four cones
- Boundary markers
- One clipboard
- Pencils
- Whistles
- Officials' pinnies

Instructional Materials

- PASE IRL Rubric and Recording Sheet (appendix B)
- PASE Attendance Recording Sheet (appendix B)
- PASE Roles and Responsibilities Assignments and Recording Sheet (appendix B)
- PASE Student Coaching Plan 4
- PASE Activity Task Card 4
- PASE Fitness Activities Sheets (appendix B)
- PASE Personal or Team Fitness Recording Sheet (appendix B)
- PASE Individual or Team Activity Task Card Recording Sheet (appendix B)
- PASE Basketball Lesson Plan 5

Instructional Focus

Skill

- Speed dribble

Tactics

- Triple threat
- Bounce and chest pass

Objectives

- Develop speed dribble, bounce pass, and chest pass by progression through learning activities during team practice
- Utilize the triple-threat position prior to performing effective bounce pass, chest pass, and speed dribble in an application contest
- Demonstrate personal and social responsibility

Team Role Check

- Students enter gymnasium and immediately report to home court area.
- Check daily roles and associated duties from materials provided.

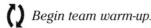 *Begin team warm-up.*

Team Warm-Up

- Conduct the team warm-up simultaneously to coaches' meeting.
- Fitness trainer monitors team warm-up using the PASE Fitness Activities Sheets.
- Fitness trainer or individuals record performance on team warm-up using either the **Personal** or **Team Fitness Recording Sheet.**

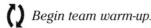 *Teams transition to daily review.*

Coaches' Meeting

- Conduct the coaches' meeting simultaneously to team warm-up.
- All team coaches report to designated meeting area.
- Teacher provides coaches with Student Coaching Plan 4 and Activity Task Card 4.
- Teacher outlines the day's events.

 Coaches transition to home court area and join warm-up.

Team Review

- Review progress of team goals from **lesson 3.** This would be found in the student/team recording sheet which the students have every lesson.
- Identify areas of need from **lesson 3.**
- Practice to improve areas of need.

 Teams transition to designated instructional area for teacher instructions.

Teacher Instruction

- Introduce daily lesson focus and review **lesson 3.**
- Provide anticipatory set:

The purpose of today's lesson is to learn and develop how to effectively use the triple-threat position in performing speed dribbling and passing skills. After developing understanding and basic skill in speed dribbling, bounce pass, and chest pass we will be able to participate in a gamelike situation using the triple-threat position to obtain success.

- Provide information about skills and strategies.
- **Introduce** the following new skills and tactics for the day.
- Complete teacher or student demonstrations (or both) of these skills and tactics:

SPEED DRIBBLE

Critical features	Instructional cues
Relaxed hand control	Gentle push
Push ball with finger pads	Use of finger pads
Dribble midthigh to waist	Ball under control
Head up and eyes scanning	Eyes up
Push ball out in front and chase	Push and chase

BOUNCE PASS

Critical features	Instructional cues
Ball held in two hands at waist level	Use two hands
Step toward receiver	Step
Extend arms down and out, rotate palms outward	Push down and out
Bounce at 2/3 distance between passer and receiver	Bounces close to receiver
	Receive at waist level

CHEST PASS

Critical features	Instructional cues
Ball held in two hands at waist level	Use two hands
Step toward receiver	Step
Extend arms parallel to floor, rotate palms outward	Push out
Receiver moves to receive ball at chest level	Receive at chest

TRIPLE-THREAT POSITION

Critical features	Instructional cues
Square body to basket and defender	Square up
Head up and eyes scanning	Eyes up
Position ball for shooting, passing, and dribbling	Fake shot/pass/dribble
Use drive step to create option to shoot/pass/dribble	Jab step toward defender

- Provide information about official's signals and rules.
- **Introduce** today's signals and rules. Demonstrate and explain the following signals and rules:
    - Stop clock for a foul (5)
    - Traveling (8)
    - Double dribble (9)
    - Unsportspersonlike (17)
- Check for student understanding using questions, student demonstrations, or both.
    - Q1: "Who can tell me the five instructional cues for the speed dribble?"
    - Q2: "Who can demonstrate the critical features of the bounce pass?"
    - Q3: "What is the triple-threat position? Why is it used?"

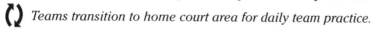 *Teams transition to home court area for daily team practice.*

Team Practice

- Team-directed practice begins (refer to **Activity Task Card 4** and **Individual** or **Team Activity Task Card Recording Sheet**).
- Teacher moves through home court area to facilitate team practice.
    - Manage learning environment.
    - Observe and assess individual and team performance.
    - Provide encouragement and instructional feedback.

Teams transition back to designated instructional area for application contest.

Application Contest

- ◆ Teacher explains and demonstrates daily contest (refer to **Application Contest 4**).
- ◆ Identify tactical focus and related skills (refer to **Application Contest Scorecard 4**).
    - ◆ Identify contest goals.
    - ◆ Discuss procedures for scoring and refereeing:
- ◆ **Scoring:** Use nonshaded areas on **Application Contest Scorecard 4.**
- ◆ **Refereeing:** Refer to and use designated referee signals located on the Official's Pocket Reference.

(♺) *Teams transition to designated contest areas to perform assigned duties.*

- ◆ Teacher actively monitors individual and team performance.

(♺) *Teams transition to designated instructional area for closure.*

Closure

- ◆ Teacher reviews lesson focus.
- ◆ Teacher discusses assessment of individual and team performance.
- ◆ Check for student understanding using questions and demonstrations (refer back to questions and demonstrations from the introduction).
- ◆ Allow for student questions and preview **lesson 5.**

(♺) *Teams transition to home court areas for individual and team assessment.*

Individual and Team Assessment

Assessment summary

- ◆ Complete **PASE IRL Recording Sheet** (each person).
- ◆ Summarize/Complete **Application Contest Scorecard 4** (scorekeeper).
- ◆ Complete **PASE Attendance Recording Sheet** (coach).
- ◆ Complete **PASE Roles and Responsibilities Recording Sheet** (each person).
- ◆ Supervise assessment completion (coach).

(♺) *Teams organize materials and exit class from home court areas.*

Speed Dribble

Critical Features

1. Relaxed hand control
2. Push ball with finger pads
3. Dribble midthigh to waist
4. Head up and eyes scanning
5. Push ball out in front and chase

Instructional Cues

1. Gentle push
2. Use of finger pads
3. Ball under control
4. Eyes up
5. Push and chase

Description

The speed dribble is used to move the ball quickly. The offensive player uses this skill when he or she is not closely guarded and can move at a faster pace. A typical scenario is a fast-break opportunity when the offensive player dribbles the ball quickly down the court with less control than would be the case with a low control dribble.

Bounce Pass

Critical Features

1. Ball held in two hands at waist level
2. Step toward receiver
3. Extend arms down and out, rotate palms outward
4. Bounce at 2/3 distance between passer and receiver

Instructional Cues

1. Use two hands
2. Step
3. Push down and out
4. Bounce close to receiver
5. Receive at waist level

Description

A bounce pass is executed much like a chest pass with the exception that it bounces on its way to the receiver. This pass is used for short distances to go under the defender or into low post players. This pass is slower in delivery, so it should be used near the basket or when the receiver is going to dribble.

From *Sport Education Seasons* by Sean M. Bulger et al., 2007, Champaign, IL: Human Kinetics.

Chest Pass

Critical Features

1. Ball held in two hands at waist level
2. Step toward receiver
3. Extend arms parallel to floor, rotate palms outward
4. Receiver moves to receive ball at chest level

Instructional Cues

1. Use two hands
2. Step
3. Push out
4. Receive at chest

Description

Passing is a method of advancing the ball without having to dribble. Depending on the defensive position and your teammates' proximity, you may use different passes to accomplish your goal of moving the ball. The chest pass should be used whenever possible because it is the quickest way to advance the ball safely. It is most effective for distances of no more than 15 to 20 feet (4.5 to 6 meters).

Triple-Threat Position

Critical Features

1. Square body to basket and defender
2. Head up and eyes scanning
3. Position ball for shooting, passing, and dribbling
4. Use drive step to create option to shoot/pass/dribble

Instructional Cues

1. Square up
2. Eyes up
3. Fake shot/pass/dribble
4. Jab step toward defender

Description

The triple-threat position is used to confuse the defender and to possibly create enough space between you and the defense in efforts to initiate a play. After facing the basket, you have the option to shoot, pass, or dribble. Feinting one of these options and performing another leaves the offensive player with the ability to keep the defense puzzled.

From *Sport Education Seasons* by Sean M. Bulger et al., 2007, Champaign, IL: Human Kinetics.

PASE Basketball Student Coaching Plan 4

COACHING QUOTE

"The will to win is important, but the will to prepare is vital."

—*Joe Paterno*

Skills

- Speed dribble
- Chest pass
- Bounce pass

Tactic

- Triple threat

Coaching Cues

Speed dribble	Bounce pass	Chest pass	Triple threat
✓ Gentle push	✓ Use two hands	✓ Use two hands	✓ Square up
✓ Use finger pads	✓ Step	✓ Step	✓ Eyes up
✓ Ball under control	✓ Push down and out	✓ Push out	✓ Fake shoot/pass/dribble
✓ Eyes up	✓ Bounce close to receiver	✓ Receive at chest	✓ Jab step toward defender
✓ Push and chase			

Keys to Success

- Focus the team on the coaching cues for the new skills.
- Ask teammates to explain the purpose of the triple-threat position.
- Help teammates progress through the **Activity Task Card.**
- Provide encouragement, feedback, and demonstrations to teammates.

Rules and Official's Signals

- **Stop clock for a foul.** Discuss, demonstrate, and practice stop clock for a foul signal.
- **Traveling.** Review traveling violation signal.
- **Double dribble.** Resuming dribbling after stopping dribbling or dribbling with two hands. Discuss, demonstrate, and practice double-dribble violation signal.
- **Unsportspersonlike.** A personal foul in which a player does not directly attempt to play the ball within the spirit and intent of the rules.

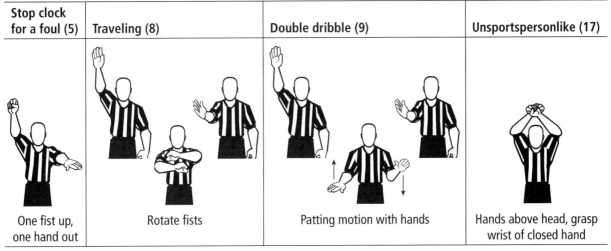

Stop clock for a foul (5)	Traveling (8)	Double dribble (9)	Unsportspersonlike (17)
One fist up, one hand out	Rotate fists	Patting motion with hands	Hands above head, grasp wrist of closed hand

From *Sport Education Seasons* by Sean M. Bulger et al., 2007, Champaign, IL: Human Kinetics.

PASE Basketball Activity Task Card 4

Skills

- Speed dribble
- Chest pass

Tactic

- Triple threat

Learning tasks	Self	Peer	Coach
1. Under the direction of the coach, perform the cues for today's skills five times each.			☐
2. Under the direction of the coach, perform the official's signals for today's lesson five times each.			☐
Prior to doing tasks 3-9, fake a shot or pass from the triple-threat position and then:			
3. Dribble with preferred hand, jogging, while staying in control for 30 sec.	☐		
4. Dribble with nonpreferred hand, jogging, while staying in control for 30 sec.	☐		
5. Dribble alternating hands, jogging, while staying in control for 30 sec.	☐		
6. Dribble with preferred hand, moving fast, while staying in control for 30 sec.	☐		
7. Dribble with nonpreferred hand, moving fast, while staying in control for 30 sec.		☐	
8. Dribble alternating hands, moving fast, while staying in control for 30 sec.	☐		
9. Dribble using single or alternating hands, moving fast for 30 sec. How many times did you lose control? Remember your score. (Record score only if using **Individual Activity Task Card Recording Sheet.**)	#___		☐
Prior to doing tasks 10-17, fake a shot or dribble from the triple-threat position and then:			
10. Successfully bounce pass to a stationary partner 10 times.		☐	
11. Successfully bounce pass to a slow-moving partner who is performing V- or L-cuts eight times.	☐		
12. Successfully bounce pass to a fast-moving partner who is performing V- or L-cuts six times.	☐		
13. How many successful bounce passes can you complete to a partner who is V- or L-cutting in 30 sec? Remember your score. (Record score only if using **Individual Activity Task Card Recording Sheet.**)	#___		☐
14. Successfully chest pass to a stationary partner 10 times.		☐	
15. Successfully chest pass to a slow-moving partner who is performing V- or L-cuts eight times.	☐		
16. Successfully chest pass to a fast-moving partner who is performing V- or L-cuts six times.	☐		
17. How many successful chest passes can you complete to a partner who is V- or L-cutting in 30 sec? Remember your score. (Record score only if using **Individual Activity Task Card Recording Sheet.**)	#___		☐
18. 2-on-1: In groups of three, partners A and B will play a game of keep-away from partner C. To keep the ball away, partners A and B must use chest and bounce passes and the speed dribble. Partners A and B cannot pass without faking from the triple-threat position. How many passes can you complete in 30 sec? Remember your score. (Record score only if using **Individual Activity Task Card Recording Sheet.**) Rotate positions and repeat game. Answer the following questions and discuss what you discovered with a teammate. • Is it easier to dribble with control while moving slow or fast? Why? • Which pass is easier to deliver from a triple-threat position? Why? Which pass is easier to deliver from a speed dribble? Why? • Is it harder for the defense to intercept the ball when you fake or don't fake? Why?	#___		☐

From *Sport Education Seasons* by Sean M. Bulger et al., 2007, Champaign, IL: Human Kinetics.

PASE Basketball Application Contest 4

Equipment
- Two cones
- Pencils
- Boundary markers
- Whistles
- Lesson 4 Scorecard
- Officials' pinnies
- One clipboard
- Colored pinnies (teams)

Objectives
- Demonstrate a speed dribble from the triple-threat position
- Demonstrate a bounce and chest pass from a triple-threat position
- Move without the ball to create an open passing lane
- Demonstrate a clear use of the triple-threat position

Goals

Achieve the maximum number of bounce or chest passes (or both) in two 30-second trials

Application Description

This is a 3 vs. 2 competition, with three offensive players and two defensive players. The offense must begin play from either cone by passing the ball to a teammate. After the ball is in play, the offense must attempt to pass (bounce or chest) the ball as many times as possible to another teammate. Prior to each pass, the offensive player must use a triple-threat fake for the pass to count toward the team score. If the defense intercepts or deflects the ball, the offense retains possession and must restart play at either cone. The competition will last for four 30-second trials, with possession of the ball changing on each new 30-second trial. Substitutions enter the game at the beginning of each new 30-second trial. Each team member must have participated during one of the two 30-second trials. Repeat until each team has been on offense two times. The teacher should have multiple games going at the same time based on space and equipment and use a single game clock for all games.

Application Diagram

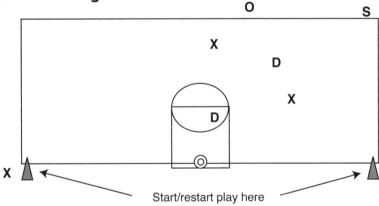

Key

X = Offensive players
D = Defender
O = Official
S = Scorekeeper
▲ = Cones

Start/restart play here

Scorekeeper's Guidelines

Provide scorekeepers with an example to fill in on their scorecard.

- 1 point per successfully completed triple threat and completed pass sequence (passer receives point).
- Record scores for the offensive team after the official's signal indicating a successful fake and pass.
- Combine all team points for both offensive trials for a total team score.

Referee's Guidelines

- No points awarded if a triple-threat fake position is not clearly demonstrated.
- No points awarded if pass is incomplete.
- No points awarded if a pass other than a chest or bounce pass is used.
- Demonstrate appropriate signals for violations.
- Demonstrate appropriate signals related to scoring.
- Demonstrate appropriate clock-related signals.

From *Sport Education Seasons* by Sean M. Bulger et al., 2007, Champaign, IL: Human Kinetics.

PASE Basketball Application Contest Scorecard 4

Instructions: Nonshaded areas must be filled in by scorekeeper.

Team ___ Coach ___ Date ___ ☐ Home ☐ Away

Scorekeeper ___ Opponent ___

TEAM FINAL SCORE

TEAM SCORING BY HALF

	1st Trial	2nd Trial	OT

SCORING

	1st Trial	2nd Trial	OT

SUMMARY

Player	Fouls	2 FG		3 FG		FT		Steals	Reb.	Pts.
		A	M	A	M	A	M			

Practice row to be filled in by student.

Fouls: 1 2 3 4 5 (repeated for each player row)

Team Fouls										Totals
1	2	3	4	5	6	7	8	9	10	

TEAM TIME-OUTS

1		2		3		4		5	
Away	Home	Away	Home	Away	Home	Away	Home	Away	

Alternating Jump Ball Possessions

Home	Away	Home	Away	Home	Away	Home	Away	Home	Away

Running Score

1	2	3	4	5	6	7	8	9	10	11	12	13	14	15	16	17	18	19	20	21	22	23	24	25
26	27	28	29	30	31	32	33	34	35	36	37	38	39	40	41	42	43	44	45	46	47	48	49	50
51	52	53	54	55	56	57	58	59	60	61	62	63	64	65	66	67	68	69	70	71	72	73	74	75
76	77	78	79	80	81	82	83	84	85	86	87	88	89	90	91	92	93	94	95	96	97	98	99	100

Coach's Signature ___

Scorekeeper's Signature ___

PASE BASKETBALL LESSON PLAN 5

Resources: Lesson Focus

- Numbered colored pinnies—six per team (also used during application contest)
- Basketballs—three to six per team (also used during application contest)
- Hula hoops—one per team (used to organize team materials)
- Stopwatches—one per team
- Pencils

Resources: Application Contest

- PASE Application Contest 5
- PASE Application Contest Scorecard 5
- PASE Official's Pocket Reference
- Two to four cones
- Boundary markers
- One clipboard
- Pencils
- Whistles
- Officials' pinnies

Instructional Materials

- PASE IRL Rubric and Recording Sheet (appendix B)
- PASE Attendance Recording Sheet (appendix B)
- PASE Roles and Responsibilities Assignments and Recording Sheet (appendix B)
- PASE Student Coaching Plan 5
- PASE Activity Task Card 5
- PASE Fitness Activities Sheets (appendix B)
- PASE Personal or Team Fitness Recording Sheet (appendix B)
- PASE Individual or Team Activity Task Card Recording Sheet (appendix B)
- PASE Outside-of-Class Physical Activity Participation Log (appendix B)
- PASE Basketball Lesson Plan 6

Instructional Focus

Skills

- Overhand and sidearm pass
- Low control and speed dribble

Tactic

- Triple threat

Objectives

- Develop overhead and sidearm passing by progression through learning activities during team practice
- Review the triple-threat position prior to performing effective overhead pass, sidearm pass, and dribbling skills in an application contest
- Demonstrate personal and social responsibility

Team Role Check

- Students enter gymnasium and immediately report to home court area.
- Check daily roles and associated duties from materials provided.

Begin team warm-up.

Team Warm-Up

- Conduct the team warm-up simultaneously to coaches' meeting.
- Fitness trainer monitors team warm-up using the PASE Fitness Activities Sheets.
- Fitness trainer or individuals record performance on team warm-up using either the **Personal** or **Team Fitness Recording Sheet.**

Teams transition to daily review.

Coaches' Meeting

- Conduct the coaches' meeting simultaneously to team warm-up.
- All team coaches report to designated meeting area.
- Teacher provides coaches with Student Coaching Plan 5 and Activity Task Card 5.
- Teacher outlines the day's events.

Coaches transition to home court area and join warm-up.

Team Review

- Review progress of team goals from **lesson 4.** This would be found in the student/team recording sheet which the students have every lesson.
- Identify areas of need from **lesson 4.**
- Practice to improve areas of need.

Teams transition to designated instructional area for teacher instructions.

Teacher Instruction

- Introduce daily lesson focus and review **lesson 4.**
- Provide anticipatory set:

> The purpose of today's lesson is to introduce two types of passes that are used when you are being closely guarded on offense. Each of these passes is used in specific situations depending on where your teammate is in relationship to you. After learning the two types of passes introduced today, you will be able to better understand which passes and types of dribbling are used in specific game situations.

- Provide information about skills and strategies.
- **Review** these skills and tactics:

LOW CONTROL DRIBBLE

Critical features	Instructional cues
Relaxed hand control	Gentle push
Push ball with finger pads	Use of finger pads
Dribble knee to midthigh	Keep ball low
Head up and eyes scanning	Eyes up
Body between ball and defender	Protect ball

SPEED DRIBBLE

Critical features	Instructional cues
Relaxed hand control	Gentle push
Push ball with finger pads	Use of finger pads
Dribble midthigh to waist	Ball under control
Head up and eyes scanning	Eyes up
Push ball out in front and chase	Push and chase

TRIPLE-THREAT POSITION

Critical features	Instructional cues
Square body to basket and defender	Square up
Head up and eyes scanning	Eyes up
Position ball for shooting, passing, and dribbling	Fake shot/pass/dribble
Use drive step to create option to shoot/pass/dribble	Jab step toward defender

- ◆ **Introduce** the following new skills and tactics for the day.
- ◆ Complete teacher or student demonstrations of these skills and tactics:

OVERHEAD PASS

Critical features	Instructional cues
Ball held in two hands overhead	Use two hands
Move ball from in front of to slightly behind head	Big stretch back
Step toward receiver	Step
Bring ball forward, snap wrists down and out	Chop wood, fingers point to target
Receiver moves toward ball for pass reception	Move to ball (receiver)

SIDEARM PASS

Critical features	Instructional cues
Face opponent, ball held in two hands at waist level	Face defender, secure ball with two hands
Step laterally with nonpivot foot	Step sideways
Extend passing arm backward, parallel to floor with hand placed under ball	Cup ball, swing arm back
Bring ball forward and roll hand across ball to apply spin to ball	Roll hand over ball
Ball travels around defender	Pass around defender
Receiver moves toward ball for pass reception	Move to ball (receiver)

- ◆ Provide information about official's signals and rules.
- ◆ **Introduce** today's signals and rules. Demonstrate and explain the following signals and rules:
  - ◆ Traveling (8)
  - ◆ Double dribbling (9)
  - ◆ Carrying (10)

- Check for student understanding using questions, student demonstrations, or both.
  - Q1: "What are two common critical features between the overhead and the sidearm pass?"
  - Q2: "When would it be most appropriate to use the overhead pass?"
  - Q3: "When would it be most appropriate to use the sidearm pass?"

( ) Teams transition to home court area for daily team practice.

Team Practice

- Team-directed practice begins (refer to **Activity Task Card 5** and **Individual** or **Team Activity Task Card Recording Sheet).**
- Teacher moves through home court area to facilitate team practice.
  - Manage learning environment.
  - Observe and assess individual and team performance.
  - Provide encouragement and instructional feedback.

( ) Teams transition back to designated instructional area for application contest.

Application Contest

- Teacher explains and demonstrates daily contest (refer to **Application Contest 5**).
  - Identify tactical focus and related skills (refer to **Application Contest Scorecard 5**).
  - Identify contest goals.
  - Discuss procedures for scoring and refereeing.
- **Scoring:** Use nonshaded areas on **Application Contest Scorecard 5.**
- **Refereeing:** Refer to and use designated referee signals located on the Official's Pocket Reference.

( ) Teams transition to designated contest areas to perform assigned duties.

- Teacher actively monitors individual and team performance.

( ) Teams transition to designated instructional area for closure.

Closure

- Teacher reviews lesson focus.
- Teacher discusses assessment of individual and team performance.
- Check for student understanding using questions and demonstrations (refer back to questions and demonstrations from the introduction).
- Allow for student questions and preview **lesson 6.**

( ) Teams transition to home court areas for individual and team assessment.

Individual and Team Assessment

- Assessment summary
  - Complete **PASE IRL Recording Sheet** (each person).
  - Summarize/Complete **Application Contest Scorecard 5** (scorekeeper).
  - Complete **PASE Attendance Recording Sheet** (coach).
  - Complete **PASE Roles and Responsibilities Recording Sheet** (each person).
  - Supervise assessment completion (coach).
- Collect the following:
  - Completed PASE Outside-of-Class Physical Activity Participation Log (each person)

( ) Teams organize materials and exit class from home court areas.

Overhead Pass

Critical Features

1. Ball held in two hands overhead
2. Move ball from in front of to slightly behind head
3. Step toward receiver
4. Bring ball forward, snap wrists down and out
5. Receiver moves toward ball for pass reception

Instructional Cues

1. Use two hands
2. Big stretch back
3. Step
4. Chop wood, fingers point to target
5. Move to ball (receiver)

Description

In addition to its use for longer distances, the purpose of the overhead pass is to deliver the ball at a high level over the top of a defender. It can be effective for initiating a set offense, hitting pivot players, passing to cutting teammates, quickly returning a high pass just caught by an offensive player, or initiating a fast break opportunity.

Sidearm Pass

Critical Features

1. Face opponent, ball held in two hands at waist level
2. Step laterally with non-pivot foot
3. Extend passing arm backward, parallel to floor with hand placed under ball
4. Bring ball forward and roll hand across ball to apply spin to ball
5. Ball travels around defender
6. Receiver moves toward ball for pass reception

Instructional Cues

1. Face defender, secure ball with two hands
2. Step sideways
3. Cup ball, swing arm back
4. Roll hand over ball
5. Pass around defender
6. Move to ball (receiver)

Description

The sidearm pass is utilized when the defender is guarding the passer closely and the passer must deliver the ball around the defender's body. The sidearm pass allows the passer to distribute the ball to the side and away from the defender's reach.

From *Sport Education Seasons* by Sean M. Bulger et al., 2007, Champaign, IL: Human Kinetics.

PASE Basketball Student Coaching Plan 5

COACHING QUOTE

"You have to expect things of yourself before you can do them."

—*Michael Jordan*

Skills

- Overhead pass
- Sidearm pass
- Speed dribble

Tactic

- Triple threat

Coaching Cues

Speed dribble	Overhead pass	Sidearm pass	Triple threat
✓ Gentle push	✓ Use two hands	✓ Face defender, secure ball with two hands	✓ Square up
✓ Use finger pads	✓ Big stretch back	✓ Step sideways	✓ Eyes up
✓ Ball thigh high	✓ Step	✓ Cup ball, swing arm back	✓ Fake shot/pass/dribble
✓ Eyes up	✓ Chop wood, fingers point to target	✓ Roll hand over ball	✓ Jab step toward defender
✓ Push and chase	✓ Move to ball (receiver)	✓ Pass around defender	✓ Finish with shot, pass, or dribble
		✓ Move to ball (receiver)	

Keys to Success

- Focus the team on the coaching cues for the new skills.
- Check to see if teammates know when to use each pass (overhead, sidearm, bounce, chest).
- Help teammates progress through the **Activity Task Card.**
- Make sure team moves quickly between different lesson segments.

Rules and Official's Signals

- **Traveling.** Review traveling violation signal.
- **Double dribble.** Review double-dribble violation signal.
- **Carrying.** Improper dribbling technique in which the player is turning the wrist from palm up to palm down with prolonged contact.

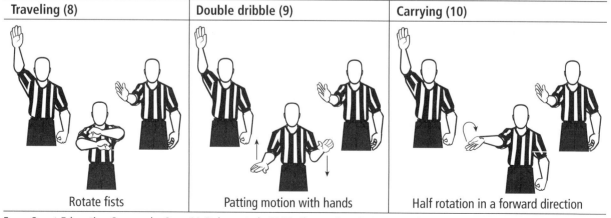

Traveling (8)	Double dribble (9)	Carrying (10)
Rotate fists	Patting motion with hands	Half rotation in a forward direction

From *Sport Education Seasons* by Sean M. Bulger et al., 2007, Champaign, IL: Human Kinetics.

PASE Basketball Activity Task Card 5

Skills
- Overhead and sidearm passes
- Dribble review

Tactic
- Triple-threat review

Learning tasks	Self	Peer	Coach
1. Under the direction of the coach, perform the cues for today's skills two times each.			☐
2. Under the direction of the coach, perform the official's signals for today's lesson three times each.			☐
Prior to doing tasks 3-10, fake a shot or dribble from the triple-threat position and then:			
3. Successfully overhead pass to a stationary partner 10 times.		☐	
4. Successfully overhead pass to a slow-moving partner who is performing V- or L-cuts eight times.	☐		
5. Successfully overhead pass to a fast-moving partner who is performing V- or L-cuts six times.	☐		
6. How many successful overhead passes can you complete to a partner who is V- or L-cutting in 30 sec? Remember your score. (Record score only if using **Individual Activity Task Card Recording Sheet**.)	#____		☐
7. Successfully sidearm pass to a stationary partner 10 times.		☐	.
8. Successfully sidearm pass to a slow-moving partner who is performing V- or L-cuts eight times.	☐		
9. Successfully sidearm pass to a fast-moving partner who is performing V- or L-cuts six times.	☐		
10. How many successful sidearm passes can you complete to a partner who is V- or L-cutting in 30 sec? Remember your score. (Record score only if using **Individual Activity Task Card Recording Sheet**.)	#____		☐
Prior to doing tasks 11-14, fake a shot or pass from the triple-threat position and then:			
11. Dribble with preferred hand, moving fast, while staying in control for 30 sec.	☐		
12. Dribble with nonpreferred hand, moving fast, while staying in control for 30 sec.	☐		
13. Dribble alternating hands, moving fast, while staying in control for 30 sec.		☐	
14. Dribble using single or alternating hands, moving fast for 30 sec. How many times did you lose control? Remember your score. (Record score only if using **Individual Activity Task Card Recording Sheet**.)	#____		☐
15. 2-on-1: In groups of three, partners A and B will play a game of keep-away from partner C, who is playing passive defense. To keep the ball away, partners A and B must use overhead and sidearm passes and the speed dribble. Partners A and B cannot pass without first faking from the triple-threat position. How many passes can you complete in 30 sec? Remember your score. Rotate positions and repeat game. (Record score only if using **Individual Activity Task Card Recording Sheet.**)	#____		☐
16. 2-on-1: In groups of three, partners A and B will play a game of keep-away from partner C, who is playing passive defense. To keep the ball away, partners A and B can use chest, bounce, overhead, or sidearm passes and the dribble. Partners A and B are encouraged to use appropriate fakes from the triple-threat position. How many passes can you complete in 40 sec? Remember your score. Rotate positions and repeat game. (Record score only if using **Individual Activity Task Card Recording Sheet.**) Answer the following questions and discuss what you discovered with a teammate. • What is the triple threat? • Why is it important for offensive ball movement? • Which pass is easier to deliver from a triple-threat position? Why? When should you use each pass? Why? • Which pass do you perform the best? Why?	#____		☐

From *Sport Education Seasons* by Sean M. Bulger et al., 2007, Champaign, IL: Human Kinetics.

Equipment

- Two cones
- Pencils
- Boundary markers
- Whistles
- Lesson 5 Scorecard
- Officials' pinnies
- One clipboard
- Colored pinnies (teams)

Objectives

- Demonstrate a speed dribble from the triple-threat position
- Demonstrate overhead and sidearm passes from a triple-threat position
- Move without the ball to create open passing lanes
- Demonstrate a clear use of the triple-threat position

Goals

Achieve the maximum number of overhead or sidearm passes (or both) in two 30-second trials

Application Description

This is a 3 vs. 2 competition, with three offensive players and two defensive players. The offense must begin play from either cone by passing the ball to a teammate. After the ball is in play, the offense must attempt to pass (overhead or sidearm) the ball as many times as possible to another teammate. Prior to each pass, the offensive player must use a triple-threat fake for the pass to count toward the team score. If the defense intercepts or deflects the ball, the offense retains possession and must restart play at either cone. The competition will last for four 30-second trials, with possession of the ball changing on each new 30-second trial. Substitutions enter the game at the beginning of each new 30-second trial. Each team member must have participated during one of the two 30-second trials. Repeat until each team has been on offense two times. The teacher should have multiple games going at the same time based on space and equipment and use a single game clock for all games.

Application Diagram

Key

X = Offensive players

D = Defender

O = Official

S = Scorekeeper

▲ = Cones

Start/restart play here

Scorekeeper's Guidelines

Provide scorekeepers with an example to fill in on their scorecard.

- 1 point per successfully completed triple threat and completed pass sequence (passer receives point).
- Record scores for the offensive team after the official's signal indicating a successful fake and pass.
- Combine all team points for both offensive trials for a total team score.

Referee's Guidelines

- No points awarded if a triple-threat fake position is not clearly demonstrated.
- No points awarded if pass is incomplete.
- No points awarded if a pass other than an overhead or sidearm pass is used.
- Demonstrate appropriate signals for violations.
- Demonstrate appropriate signals related to scoring.
- Demonstrate appropriate clock-related signals.

From *Sport Education Seasons* by Sean M. Bulger et al., 2007, Champaign, IL: Human Kinetics.

PASE Basketball Application Contest Scorecard 5

Instructions: Nonshaded areas must be filled in by scorekeeper.			☐ Home	☐ Away
Team	Coach	Date	TEAM SCORING BY HALF	TEAM FINAL SCORE
Scorekeeper	Opponent		1st Trial / 2nd Trial / OT	

Fouls					Player	SCORING			SUMMARY								
						1st Trial	2nd Trial	OT	2 FG		3 FG		FT		Steals	Reb.	Pts.
									A	M	A	M	A	M			
1	2	3	4	5	Practice row to be filled in by student.												
1	2	3	4	5													
1	2	3	4	5													
1	2	3	4	5													
1	2	3	4	5													
1	2	3	4	5													
1	2	3	4	5													
1	2	3	4	5													

Team Fouls										Totals				TEAM TIME-OUTS				
1	2	3	4	5	6	7	8	9	10					1	2	3	4	5

Alternating Jump Ball Possessions	Home	Away	Home	Away	Home	Away	Home	Away	Home	Away

Running Score																									
	1	2	3	4	5	6	7	8	9	10	11	12	13	14	15	16	17	18	19	20	21	22	23	24	25
	26	27	28	29	30	31	32	33	34	35	36	37	38	39	40	41	42	43	44	45	46	47	48	49	50
	51	52	53	54	55	56	57	58	59	60	61	62	63	64	65	66	67	68	69	70	71	72	73	74	75
	76	77	78	79	80	81	82	83	84	85	86	87	88	89	90	91	92	93	94	95	96	97	98	99	100

Coach's Signature ____________________ Scorekeeper's Signature ____________________

From *Sport Education Seasons* by Sean M. Bulger et al., 2007, Champaign, IL: Human Kinetics.

PASE BASKETBALL LESSON PLAN 6

Resources: Lesson Focus

- Numbered colored pinnies—six per team (also used during application contest)
- Basketballs—three to six per team (also used during application contest)
- Hula hoops—one per team (used to organize team materials)
- Stopwatches—one per team
- Pencils

Resources: Application Contest

- PASE Application Contest 6
- PASE Application Contest Scorecard 6
- PASE Official's Pocket Reference
- Two to four cones
- Boundary markers
- One clipboard
- Pencils
- Whistles
- Officials' pinnies

Instructional Materials

- PASE IRL Rubric and Recording Sheet (appendix B)
- PASE Attendance Recording Sheet (appendix B)
- PASE Roles and Responsibilities Assignments and Recording Sheet (appendix B)
- PASE Student Coaching Plans 3-5
- PASE Activity Task Cards 3-5
- PASE Fitness Activities Sheets (appendix B)
- PASE Personal or Team Fitness Recording Sheet (appendix B)
- PASE Individual or Team Activity Task Card Recording Sheet (appendix B)
- PASE Outside-of-Class Physical Activity Participation Log (appendix B)
- PASE Independent Learning Activity (appendix C)
- PASE Team Goal-Setting Sheet (appendix C)
- PASE Reflective Journal (appendix C)
- PASE Basketball Lesson Plan 7

Instructional Focus

Skills
- Review skills taught to date.

Tactics
- Review tactics taught to date.

Objectives

- Further develop basketball skills and tactics by progressing through learning activities from previous lessons not yet completed during team practice
- Demonstrate personal and social responsibility

Team Role Check

- Students enter gymnasium and immediately report to home court area.
- Check daily roles and associated duties from materials provided.
- ♺ *Begin team warm-up.*

Team Warm-Up

- Conduct the team warm-up simultaneously to coaches' meeting.
- Fitness trainer leads team through warm-up using the PASE Fitness Activities Sheets.
- Fitness trainer or individuals record performance on team warm-up using either the **Personal** or **Team Fitness Recording Sheet.**

Teams transition to daily review.

Coaches' Meeting

- Conduct the coaches' meeting simultaneously to team warm-up.
- All team coaches report to designated meeting area.
- Teacher provides coaches with choice of Student Coaching Plans 3-5 and Activity Task Cards 3-5.
- Teacher outlines the day's events.

Coaches transition to home court area and join warm-up.

Team Review

- Review progress of team goals from **lessons 3-5.** This would be found in the student/team recording sheet which the students have every lesson.
- Identify areas of need from **lessons 3-5.**
- Record goals on **Team Goal-Setting Sheet.**
- Prepare to practice in identified areas during team practice (utilize task cards and coaching plans from previous lessons).

Teams transition to designated instructional area for teacher instructions.

Teacher Instruction

- Introduce daily lesson focus and review **lessons 3-5.**
- Provide anticipatory set:

Today is the first of three review lessons. The purpose of today's lesson is to review the skills and tactics that we have learned and practiced so far. You will have the opportunity to select and practice skills and tactics that your team needs the most work on. Each of these skills and tactics is important and should be mastered by all of your team members in order to improve your chances of being successful in specific game situations.

- Check for student understanding of previously learned skills and tactics by using questions, student demonstrations, or both.
  - Q1: "What is a common method for moving the ball as an individual?"
  - Q2: "What are the four passes learned so far? When should each be used?"
  - Q3: "What are two ways that you can create space when you don't have the ball?"
  - Q4: "What three moves can you make from the triple-threat position?"
- Provide any additional important information about previously learned skills and tactics.
- Check for student understanding of previously learned official's signals by using questions, student demonstrations, gamelike scenarios, or a combination of these.
  - Unsportspersonlike conduct (17)
  - Carrying (10)
  - 1-point scoring (1)
  - Stop clock (4)
  - Traveling (8)

* Double dribble (9)
* Stop clock for a foul (5)

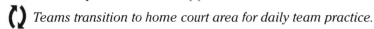 *Teams transition to home court area for daily team practice.*

Team Practice

* Team-directed practice begins (refer to **Activity Task Cards 3-5** and **Individual** or **Team Activity Task Card Recording Sheet**).
* Teacher moves through home court area to facilitate team practice.
    * Manage learning environment.
    * Observe and assess individual and team performance.
    * Provide encouragement and instructional feedback.

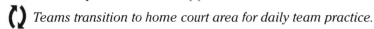 *Teams transition back to designated instructional area for application contest.*

Application Contest

* Teacher explains and demonstrates daily contest (refer to **Application Contest 6**).
    * Identify tactical focus and related skills (refer to **Application Contest Scorecard 6**).
    * Identify contest goals.
    * Discuss procedures for scoring and refereeing.
* **Scoring:** Use nonshaded areas on **Application Contest Scorecard 6.**
* **Refereeing:** Refer to and use designated referee signals located on the Official's Pocket Reference.

 Teams transition to designated contest areas to perform assigned duties.

* Teacher actively monitors individual and team performance.

 Teams transition to designated instructional area for closure.

Closure

* Teacher reviews lesson focus.
* Teacher discusses assessment of individual and team performance.
* Check for student understanding using questions and demonstrations (refer back to questions and demonstrations from the introduction).
* Allow for student questions and preview **lesson 7.**

 Teams transition to home court areas for individual and team assessment.

Individual and Team Assessment

* Assessment summary
    * Complete **PASE IRL Recording Sheet** (each person).
    * Summarize/Complete **Application Contest Scorecard 6** (scorekeeper).
    * Complete **PASE Attendance Recording Sheet** (coach).
    * Complete **PASE Roles and Responsibilities Recording Sheet** (each person).
    * Supervise assessment completion (coach).
* Distribute the following:
    * PASE Outside-of-Class Physical Activity Participation Log (each person)
    * PASE Reflective Journal (each person)
    * PASE Independent Learning Activity (each person)

 Teams organize materials and exit class from home court areas.

Equipment

- Two cones
- Pencils
- Boundary markers
- Whistles
- Lesson 6 Scorecard
- Officials' pinnies
- One clipboard
- Colored pinnies (teams)

Objectives

- Demonstrate a speed dribble from the triple-threat position
- Demonstrate overhead and sidearm passes from a triple-threat position
- Move without the ball to create open passing lanes
- Demonstrate a clear use of the triple-threat position

Goals

Achieve the maximum number of chest, bounce, overhead, and/or sidearm passes in two 30-second trials

Application Description

This is a 3 vs. 2 competition, with three offensive players and two defensive players. The offense must begin play from either cone by passing the ball to a teammate. After the ball is in play, the offense must attempt to pass the ball as many times as possible to another teammate. Prior to each pass, the offensive player must use a triple-threat fake for the pass to count toward the team score. If the defense intercepts or deflects the ball, the offense retains possession and must restart play at either cone. The competition will last for four 30-second trials, with possession of the ball changing on each new 30-second trial. Substitutions enter the game at the beginning of each new 30-second trial. Each team member must have participated during one of the two 30-second trials. Repeat until each team has been on offense two times. The teacher should have multiple games going at the same time based on space and equipment and use a single game clock for all games.

Application Diagram

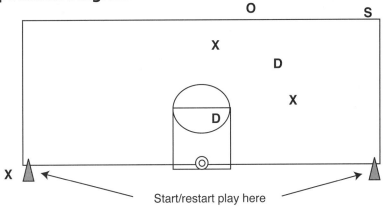

Key	
X	= Offensive players
D	= Defender
O	= Official
S	= Scorekeeper
▲	= Cones

Start/restart play here

Scorekeeper's Guidelines

Provide scorekeepers with an example to fill in on their scorecard.

- 1 point per successfully completed triple threat and completed pass sequence (passer receives point).
- Record scores for the offensive team after the official's signal indicating a successful fake and pass.
- Combine all team points for both offensive trials for a total team score.

Referee's Guidelines

- No points awarded if a triple-threat fake position is not clearly demonstrated.
- No points awarded if pass is incomplete.
- No points awarded if a pass other than a chest, bounce, overhead, or sidearm pass is used.
- Demonstrate appropriate signals for violations.
- Demonstrate appropriate signals related to scoring.
- Demonstrate appropriate clock-related signals.

From *Sport Education Seasons* by Sean M. Bulger et al., 2007, Champaign, IL: Human Kinetics.

PASE Basketball Application Contest Scorecard 6

Instructions: Nonshaded areas must be filled in by scorekeeper.

☐ Home ☐ Away

TEAM FINAL SCORE

Team		Coach		Date
Scorekeeper			Opponent	

TEAM SCORING BY HALF

	1st Trial	2nd Trial	OT

SCORING

	1st Trial	2nd Trial	OT

SUMMARY

Player	2 FG		3 FG		FT		Steals	Reb.	Pts.
	A	M	A	M	A	M			

Fouls

1	2	3	4	5

Practice row to be filled in by student.

1	2	3	4	5
1	2	3	4	5
1	2	3	4	5
1	2	3	4	5
1	2	3	4	5
1	2	3	4	5
1	2	3	4	5

Totals

Team Fouls

1	2	3	4	5	6	7	8	9	10

TEAM TIME-OUTS

	1		2		3		4		5	
	Away	Home	Away	Home	Away	Home	Away	Home	Away	

Alternating Jump Ball Possessions

Home	Away	Home	Away	Home	Away	Home	Away	Home	Away	Home	Away	Home	Away	Home	Away	Home	Away	Home	Away	Home	Away	Home	Away	Home	Away

Running Score

1	2	3	4	5	6	7	8	9	10	11	12	13	14	15	16	17	18	19	20	21	22	23	24	25
26	27	28	29	30	31	32	33	34	35	36	37	38	39	40	41	42	43	44	45	46	47	48	49	50
51	52	53	54	55	56	57	58	59	60	61	62	63	64	65	66	67	68	69	70	71	72	73	74	75
76	77	78	79	80	81	82	83	84	85	86	87	88	89	90	91	92	93	94	95	96	97	98	99	100

Coach's Signature _____

Scorekeeper's Signature _____

PASE BASKETBALL LESSON PLAN 7

Resources: Lesson Focus

- Numbered colored pinnies—six per team (also used during application contest)
- Basketballs—three to six per team (also used during application contest)
- Hula hoops—one per team (used to organize team materials)
- Stopwatches—one per team
- Pencils

Resources: Application Contest

- PASE Application Contest 7
- PASE Application Contest Scorecard 7
- PASE Official's Pocket Reference
- Two to four cones
- Boundary markers
- One clipboard
- Pencils
- Whistles
- Officials' pinnies

Instructional Materials

- PASE Attendance Recording Sheet (appendix B)
- PASE Roles and Responsibilities Assignments and Recording Sheet (appendix B)
- PASE Student Coaching Plan 7
- PASE Activity Task Card 7
- PASE Fitness Activities Sheets (appendix B)
- PASE Personal or Team Fitness Recording Sheet (appendix B)
- PASE Individual or Team Activity Task Card Recording Sheet (appendix B)
- PASE Basketball Lesson Plan 8

Instructional Focus

Skills

- Set shot
- Jump shot
- Defensive footwork

Tactic

- Defense on and off the ball

Objectives

- Develop set and jump shots and defensive footwork by progression through learning activities during team practice
- Utilize set and jump shots and defensive footwork and demonstrate defense on and off the ball in an application contest
- Demonstrate personal and social responsibility

Team Role Check

- ◆ Students enter gymnasium and immediately report to home court area.
- ◆ Check daily roles and associated duties from materials provided.

↻ *Begin team warm-up.*

Team Warm-Up

- ◆ Conduct the team warm-up simultaneously to coaches' meeting.
- ◆ Fitness trainer monitors team warm-up using the PASE Fitness Activities Sheets.
- ◆ Fitness trainer or individuals record performance on team warm-up using either the **Personal** or **Team Fitness Recording Sheet.**

↻ *Teams transition to daily review.*

Coaches' Meeting

- ◆ Conduct the coaches' meeting simultaneously to team warm-up.
- ◆ All team coaches report to designated meeting area.
- ◆ Teacher provides coaches with **Student Coaching Plan 7** and **Activity Task Card 7.**
- ◆ Teacher outlines the day's events.

↻ *Coaches transition to home court area and join warm-up.*

Team Review

- ◆ Review progress of team goals from **lesson 6.** This would be found in the student/team recording sheet which the students have every lesson.
- ◆ Identify areas of need from **lesson 6.**
- ◆ Practice to improve areas of need.

↻ *Teams transition to designated instructional area for teacher instructions.*

Teacher Instruction

- ◆ Introduce daily lesson focus and review **lesson 6.**
- ◆ Provide anticipatory set:

💬 The reason we are learning to use the set and jump shots is that they are the main methods used to score points in the game of basketball. You will also learn to defend against these shots and dribbling by practicing defensive movements against players with and without the ball.

- ◆ Provide information about skills and strategies.
- ◆ **Introduce** the following new skills and tactics for the day.
- ◆ Complete teacher or student demonstrations (or both) of these skills and tactics:

SET SHOT

Critical features	Instructional cues
Wide base, feet at shoulder-width	Balanced position
Move ball upward with two hands	Take up with two hands
Maintain floor-to-feet contact	Feet to floor
Arms extend fully, wrists and fingers snap toward basket	Straighten arm, wave good-bye to ball

JUMP SHOT

Critical features	Instructional cues
Wide base, feet at shoulder-width	Balanced position
Move ball upward with two hands	Take up with two hands
Jump straight up off of two feet	Jump straight up
Arms extend fully, wrists and fingers snap toward basket	Straighten arm, wave good-bye to ball
Ball released at height of jump	High release

DEFENSIVE FOOTWORK

Critical features	Instructional cues
Sitting position, feet at shoulder-width	Defensive position
Hands up and out, arms flexed	Ready hands
Short, quick, choppy steps keeping feet apart	Quick feet, scoot
Maintain low center of gravity while moving	Low hips

DEFENSE ON THE BALL

Critical features	Instructional cues
Sitting position, feet at shoulder-width	Defensive position
Short, quick, choppy steps keeping feet apart	Quick feet, scoot
Focus on dribbler's midsection	Watch waist
Force dribbler to change directions	Force misdirection
Apply pressure when opponent picks up dribble	Chest to chest

DEFENSE OFF THE BALL

Critical features	Instructional cues
Sitting position, feet at shoulder-width	Defensive position
Short, quick, choppy steps keeping feet apart	Quick feet, scoot
Use peripheral vision to view ball and offensive assignment	Split vision
Apply increasing pressure as opponent nears ball or basket	"Close to" equals more pressure
Deny ball and prevent the back-door cut	Front, no overplay

◆ Provide information about official's signals and rules.

◆ **Introduce** today's signals and rules. Demonstrate and explain the following signals and rules:

  ◆ Illegal use of hands (13)

  ◆ Jump ball (12)

  ◆ 2-point scoring (2)

◆ Check for student understanding using questions, student demonstrations, or both.

  ◆ Q1: "Who can name/demonstrate the critical features for set/jump shot?"

  ◆ Q2: "Who can name/demonstrate the critical features for defensive footwork?"

◆ Q3: "What is the purpose of learning these different shots and defensive movements?"

( ) *Teams transition to home court area for daily team practice.*

Team Practice

- ◆ Team-directed practice begins (refer to **Activity Task Card 7** and **Individual** or **Team Activity Task Card Recording Sheet**).
- ◆ Teacher moves through home court area to facilitate team practice.
  - ◆ Manage learning environment.
  - ◆ Observe and assess individual and team performance.
  - ◆ Provide encouragement and instructional feedback.

( ) *Teams transition back to designated instructional area for application contest.*

Application Contest

- ◆ Teacher explains and demonstrates daily contest (refer to **Application Contest 7**).
  - ◆ Identify tactical focus and related skills (refer to **Application Contest Scorecard 7**).
  - ◆ Identify contest goals.
  - ◆ Discuss procedures for scoring and refereeing.
- ◆ **Scoring:** Use nonshaded areas on **Application Contest Scorecard 7.**
- ◆ **Refereeing:** Refer to and use designated referee signals located on the Official's Pocket Reference.

( ) *Teams transition to designated contest areas to perform assigned duties.*

- ◆ Teacher actively monitors individual and team performance.

( ) *Teams transition to designated instructional area for closure.*

Closure

- ◆ Teacher reviews lesson focus.
- ◆ Teacher discusses assessment of individual and team performance.
- ◆ Check for student understanding using questions and demonstrations (refer back to questions and demonstrations from the introduction).
- ◆ Allow for student questions and preview **lesson 8.**

( ) *Teams transition to home court areas for individual and team assessment.*

Individual and Team Assessment

Assessment summary

- ◆ Summarize/Complete **Application Contest Scorecard 7** (scorekeeper).
- ◆ Complete **PASE Attendance Recording Sheet** (coach).
- ◆ Complete **PASE Roles and Responsibilities Recording Sheet** (each person).
- ◆ Supervise assessment completion (coach).

( ) *Teams organize materials and exit class from home court areas.*

Set Shot

Critical Features

1. Wide base, feet at shoulder-width
2. Move ball upward with two hands
3. Maintain floor-to-feet contact
4. Arms extend fully, wrists and fingers snap toward basket

Instructional Cues

1. Balanced position
2. Take up with two hands
3. Feet to floor
4. Straighten arm, wave good-bye to ball

Description

The set shot is a method of scoring that requires the offensive player to be stationary. The typical example of such a shot is the foul shot, in which the player's feet do not leave the ground. A set shot is not usually seen in offensive sets because uncontested shots, with the offensive player not needing to elevate, are uncommon.

Jump Shot

Critical Features

1. Wide base, feet at shoulder-width
2. Move ball upward with two hands
3. Jump straight up off of two feet
4. Arm extends fully, wrists and fingers snap toward basket
5. Ball released at height of jump

Instructional Cues

1. Balanced position
2. Take up with two hands
3. Jump straight up
4. Straighten arm, wave good-bye to ball
5. High release

Description

The purpose of the jump shot is to enable the offensive player to elevate, allowing him or her to shoot over the top of defenders. This skill has become the most common and the primary shot used in a game of basketball. The evolution of the game and abilities of players have led to the fast-paced style that exists. This shot is effective in the open court as well as when a player is closely guarded.

From *Sport Education Seasons* by Sean M. Bulger et al., 2007, Champaign, IL: Human Kinetics.

Defensive Footwork

Critical Features

1. Sitting position, feet at shoulder-width
2. Hands up and out, arms flexed
3. Short, quick, choppy steps keeping feet apart
4. Maintain low center of gravity while moving

Instructional Cues

1. Defensive position
2. Ready hands
3. Quick feet, scoot
4. Low hips

Description

Defensive footwork refers to the skills of moving without the ball when on defense. Efficient movement, whether in a zone or player-to-player defense, is critical to stopping offensive scoring. Movements such as the defensive scoot and position are examples of defensive footwork.

Defense on the Ball

Critical Features

1. Sitting position, feet at shoulder-width
2. Short, quick, choppy steps keeping feet apart
3. Focus on dribbler's midsection
4. Force dribbler to change directions
5. Apply pressure when opponent picks up dribble

Instructional Cues

1. Defensive position
2. Quick feet, scoot
3. Watch waist
4. Force misdirection
5. Chest to chest

Description

This strategy requires the skills of slide stepping, drop stepping, and attack and retreat maneuvers. A player executes the strategy most effectively by remaining between the ball and the basket when the offense has possession.

From *Sport Education Seasons* by Sean M. Bulger et al., 2007, Champaign, IL: Human Kinetics.

Defense off the Ball

Critical Features

1. Sitting position, feet at shoulder-width
2. Short, quick, choppy steps keeping feet apart
3. Use peripheral vision to view ball and offensive assignment
4. Apply increasing pressure as opponent nears ball or basket
5. Deny ball and prevent back-door cut

Instructional Cues

1. Defensive position
2. Quick feet, scoot
3. Split vision
4. "Close to" equals more pressure
5. Front, no overplay

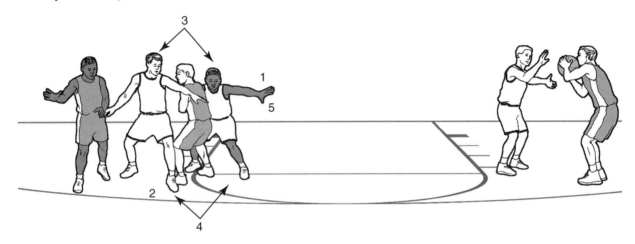

Description

When an offensive player does not have the ball, he or she is usually moving around the court attempting to get into position to receive a pass. Although your offensive assignment does not have the ball, if you are a good defender you will work hard to deny access to a pass. The closer to the basket the offensive person gets, the closer the defender should play the person. The farther from the basket the offensive player is, the more relaxed the defense can become.

From *Sport Education Seasons* by Sean M. Bulger et al., 2007, Champaign, IL: Human Kinetics.

PASE Basketball Student Coaching Plan 7

"If you don't have time to do it right, when will you have time to do it over?"

—*John Wooden*

Skills

- Set and jump shots
- Defensive footwork

Tactics

- Defense on and off the ball

Coaching Cues

Set/Jump shot	Defensive footwork	Defense on the ball	Defense off the ball
✓ Balanced position	✓ Defensive position	✓ Defensive position	✓ Defensive position
✓ Take up with two hands	✓ Ready hands	✓ Quick feet, scoot	✓ Quick feet, scoot
✓ Set: feet to floor	✓ Quick feet, scoot	✓ Watch waist	✓ Split vision
✓ Jump: jump straight up	✓ Low hips	✓ Force misdirection	✓ "Close to" equals more pressure
✓ Straighten arm, wave good-bye to ball		✓ Chest to chest	✓ Front, no overplay
✓ Jump: high release			

Keys to Success

- Focus the team on the coaching cues for the new skills.
- Check to see if teammates know when to use each skill (set and jump shots, defense on and off).
- Help teammates progress through the **Activity Task Card.**
- Make sure team moves quickly between different lesson segments.

Rules and Official's Signals

- **Illegal use of hands.** Using your hands to gain an advantage or restrict freedom of an opponent. Discuss, demonstrate, and practice illegal use of hands signal.
- **Jump ball.** Occurs at the start of the game or overtime, and results when a violation is committed simultaneously by both teams or possession cannot be determined. Discuss, demonstrate, and practice jump ball signal.
- **2-point scoring.** Discuss, demonstrate, and practice the 2-point scoring signal.

Illegal use of hands (13)	Jump ball (12)	2-point scoring (2)

Strike wrist of open hand with wrist of closed hand	Thumbs up	Two-finger "flag" from wrist

From *Sport Education Seasons* by Sean M. Bulger et al., 2007, Champaign, IL: Human Kinetics.

PASE Basketball Activity Task Card 7

Skills

- Set and jump shots
- Defensive footwork

Tactics

- Defense on and off the ball

Learning tasks	Self	Peer	Coach
1. Under the direction of the coach, perform the cues for today's skills five times each.			☐
2. Under the direction of the coach, perform the official's signals for today's lesson five times each.			☐
3. Perform the set shot in the air without a basket 15 times.	☐		
4. Perform the set shot to a mark on the wall about basket height 15 times.	☐		
5. With a partner, 10 feet (3 meters) apart, perform the set shot back and forth 15 times.	☐		
6. Perform the set shot from directly in front of a basket 15 feet (4.5 meters) away seven times.		☐	
7. Repeat #6, but this time count and remember the number of shots you make from a total of 10. (Record score only if using **Individual Activity Task Card Recording Sheet.**)	#___		☐
8. Perform the jump shot into the air without a ball or basket 15 times.	☐		
9. Perform the jump shot into the air with a ball but no basket 15 times.	☐		
10. Perform the jump shot to a mark on the wall about basket height five times.	☐		
11. With a partner, 10 feet apart, perform the jump shot back and forth 15 times.		☐	
12. Perform the jump shot from facing the basket 10 feet away eight times.		☐	
13. Perform the jump shot from the baseline angle to the basket 10 feet away eight times.	☐		
14. Perform the jump shot from a 45-degree angle to the basket 10 feet away eight times.	☐		
15. Repeat #14, but this time count and remember the number of times you make a jump shot in 40 sec. (Record score only if using **Individual Activity Task Card Recording Sheet.**)	#___		☐
16. Repeat #14, but this time dribble and transition to a jump shot 10 times without stopping.		☐	
17. Moving without the ball, make L- and V-cuts while being guarded by a defender for 45 sec.		☐	
18. Using dribbling skills without shooting, move while being guarded by a defender for 45 sec.		☐	
19. Using dribbling skills, move to make a jump shot while being guarded by a defender for 45 sec.		☐	
20. 2-on-2: In partners, moving through general space, partner A will dribble with either hand while partner B attempts to create passing lanes using offensive movements. Partner A should dribble close to/far from basket, at a variety of levels and speeds, while looking to make a jump shot. Partners C and D will play defense, alternating defense on and off the ball depending on the situation. Switch roles after 40 sec. Answer the following questions and discuss what you discovered about maintaining ball possession and control with a teammate. • Is it easier to make a jump shot from near the basket or far from the basket? Why? • Is it harder for the defense to take the ball if you are constantly moving? Why? • How can you use your teammate to help maintain possession of the ball and to score?			☐
21. Repeat #20. This time, defense earns a point for every steal, knock-away, or missed shot. The partners dribbling and shooting will receive 1 point if they can maintain control for 30 sec or make a successful jump shot. Record scores. Repeat.	#___		☐

Equipment

- Two cones
- Pencils
- Boundary markers
- Whistles
- Lesson 7 Scorecard
- Officials' pinnies
- One clipboard
- Colored pinnies (teams)

Objectives

- Demonstrate a jump shot from the triple-threat position
- Demonstrate defensive movements (position, on the ball, and off the ball)
- Move without the ball to create open passing lanes
- Demonstrate a clear use of the triple-threat position

Goals

Achieve the maximum number of successful jump shots in four 1-minute trials

Application Description

This is a 3 vs. 2 competition, with three offensive players and two defensive players. The offense must begin play from either cone by passing the ball to a teammate. After the ball is in play, the offense must attempt to move the ball via dribbling and passing in an attempt to create successful jump shots. If the defense intercepts or deflects the ball, the offense retains possession and must restart play at either cone. Play also restarts at either cone when a shot is made or missed. The competition will last for four 1-minute trials, with possession of the ball changing on each new 1-minute trial. Substitutions enter the game at the beginning of each new 1-minute trial. Each team member must have participated during two of the four 1-minute trials. Repeat until each team has been on offense two times. The teacher should have multiple games going at the same time based on space and equipment and use a single game clock for all games.

Application Diagram

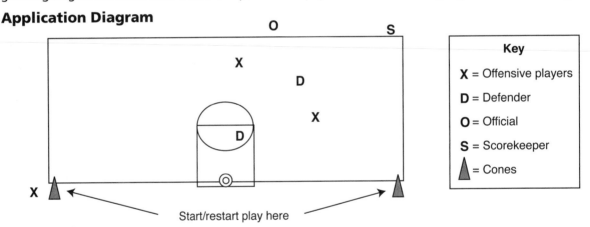

Start/restart play here

Scorekeeper's Guidelines

Provide scorekeepers with an example to fill in on their scorecard.

- 1 point per jump shot that is unsuccessful but contacts the rim.
- 2 points per jump shot that is successful.
- Record scores for the offensive team after the official's signal indicating a successful shot or pass sequence.
- Combine all team points for both offensive trials for a total team score.

Referee's Guidelines

- No points awarded if shot is performed from the lane area.
- No points awarded if a shot is performed from the 3-point area.
- No points if same player shoots two consecutive times.
- Demonstrate appropriate signals for violations.
- Demonstrate appropriate signals related to scoring.
- Demonstrate appropriate clock-related signals.

From *Sport Education Seasons* by Sean M. Bulger et al., 2007, Champaign, IL: Human Kinetics.

PASE Basketball Application Contest Scorecard 7

Instructions: Nonshaded areas must be filled in by scorekeeper.

☐ Home ☐ Away

| Team | | Coach | | Date |
| Scorekeeper | | Opponent | | |

TEAM SCORING BY HALF

TEAM FINAL SCORE

	1st Trial	2nd Trial	OT

SCORING

Player	1st Trial	2nd Trial	OT
Practice row to be filled in by student.			

SUMMARY

	2 FG		3 FG		FT		Steals	Reb.	Pts.
	A	M	A	M	A	M			

Fouls

1	2	3	4	5
1	2	3	4	5
1	2	3	4	5
1	2	3	4	5
1	2	3	4	5
1	2	3	4	5
1	2	3	4	5
1	2	3	4	5

Totals

Team Fouls

1	2	3	4	5	6	7	8	9	10

TEAM TIME-OUTS

1	2	3	4	5
Away	Home	Away	Home	Away

Alternating Jump Ball Possessions

| Home | Away | Home | Away | Home | Away | Home | Away | Home | Away | Home | Away | Home |

Running Score

1	2	3	4	5	6	7	8	9	10	11	12	13	14	15	16	17	18	19	20	21	22	23	24	25
26	27	28	29	30	31	32	33	34	35	36	37	38	39	40	41	42	43	44	45	46	47	48	49	50
51	52	53	54	55	56	57	58	59	60	61	62	63	64	65	66	67	68	69	70	71	72	73	74	75
76	77	78	79	80	81	82	83	84	85	86	87	88	89	90	91	92	93	94	95	96	97	98	99	100

Coach's Signature _____

Scorekeeper's Signature _____

From Sport Education Seasons by Sean M. Bulger et al., 2007, Champaign, IL: Human Kinetics.

PASE BASKETBALL LESSON PLAN 8

Resources: Lesson Focus

+ Numbered colored pinnies—six per team (also used during application contest)
+ Basketballs—three to six per team (also used during application contest)
+ Hula hoops—one per team (used to organize team materials)
+ Stopwatches—one per team
+ Pencils

Resources: Application Contest

+ PASE Application Contest 8
+ PASE Application Contest Scorecard 8
+ PASE Official's Pocket Reference
+ Two to four cones
+ Boundary markers
+ One clipboard
+ Pencils
+ Whistles
+ Officials' pinnies

Instructional Materials

+ PASE Attendance Recording Sheet (appendix B)
+ PASE Roles and Responsibilities Assignments and Recording Sheet (appendix B)
+ PASE Student Coaching Plan 8
+ PASE Activity Task Card 8
+ PASE Fitness Activities Sheets (appendix B)
+ PASE Personal or Team Fitness Recording Sheet (appendix B)
+ PASE Individual or Team Activity Task Card Recording Sheet (appendix B)
+ PASE Basketball Lesson Plan 9

Instructional Focus

Skills

+ Layup
+ Offensive footwork

Tactic

+ Give and go

Objectives

+ Develop layups and offensive footwork by progression through learning activities during team practice
+ Review the triple-threat position prior to performing effective layup, overhead pass, sidearm pass, jump shot, and dribbling skills in an application contest
+ Demonstrate personal and social responsibility

Team Role Check

- Students enter gymnasium and immediately report to home court area.
- Check daily roles and associated duties from materials provided.

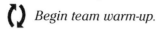 *Begin team warm-up.*

Team Warm-Up

- Conduct the team warm-up simultaneously to coaches' meeting.
- Fitness trainer monitors team warm-up using the PASE Fitness Activities Sheets.
- Fitness trainer or individuals record performance on team warm-up using either the **Personal** or **Team Fitness Recording Sheet.**

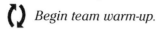 *Teams transition to daily review.*

Coaches' Meeting

- Conduct the coaches' meeting simultaneously to team warm-up.
- All team coaches report to designated meeting area.
- Teacher provides coaches with Student Coaching Plan 8 and Activity Task Card 8.
- Teacher outlines the day's events.

 Coaches transition to home court area and join warm-up.

Team Review

- Review progress of team goals from **lesson 7.** This would be found in the student/team recording sheet which the students have every lesson.
- Identify areas of need from **lesson 7.**
- Practice to improve areas of need.

 Teams transition to designated instructional area for teacher instructions.

Teacher Instruction

- Introduce daily lesson focus and review **lesson 7.**
- Provide anticipatory set:

> The reason we are learning to use the layup shot is that in addition to the jump and set shots, layups are the main methods used to score points in the game of basketball. You will also learn a specific strategy for creating a passing lane and getting a teammate the ball utilizing previously learned offensive footwork.

- Provide information about skills and strategies.
- **Introduce** the following new skills and tactics for the day.
- Complete teacher or student demonstrations (or both) of the following skills and tactics:

LAYUP	
Critical features	**Instructional cues**
Drive powerfully to basket	Power drive
Take ball up with two hands	Up with two hands
Take off on nonshooting foot	Left hand–right foot, right hand–left foot
Release ball at peak of jump with one hand	One-hand gentle release
Use backboard when possible	Bank ball

OFFENSIVE FOOTWORK (L-CUT AND V-CUT)
(REFER TO LESSON 3 MATERIALS FOR GRAPHICS AND CUES CARD)

Critical features	Instructional cues
Keep moving to create passing lanes	Move away from passer
Feint, plant foot to change direction quickly	Quick cut (V or L)
Move toward ball to receive pass	Move toward passer
Assume position with hands set to catch pass	Provide target with hands
Keep moving to create passing lanes	Move away from passer

GIVE AND GO

Critical features	Instructional cues
Assume triple-threat position	Triple threat
Execute drive step	Jab step
Pass ball to teammate	Give
Feint away and cut toward basket	Go
Prepare to receive ball	Ready hands

- Provide information about official's signals and rules.
- **Introduce** today's signals and rules. Demonstrate and explain the following signals and rules:
  - Charging with the ball (16)
  - Blocking (14)
  - 3-point scoring (3)
- Check for student understanding using questions, student demonstrations, or both.
  - Q1: "When would it be most appropriate to use the layup shot?"
  - Q2: "When would it be most appropriate to use the give and go?"
  - Q3: "Why would you want to use the give and go?"

() *Teams transition to home court area for daily team practice.*

Team Practice

- Team-directed practice begins (refer to **Activity Task Card 8** and **Individual** or **Team Activity Task Card Recording Sheet**).
- Teacher moves through home court area to facilitate team practice.
  - Manage learning environment.
  - Observe and assess individual and team performance.
  - Provide encouragement and instructional feedback.

() *Teams transition back to designated instructional area for application contest.*

Application Contest

- Teacher explains and demonstrates daily contest (refer to **Application Contest 8**).
  - Identify tactical focus and related skills (refer to **Application Contest Scorecard 8**).
  - Identify contest goals.
  - Discuss procedures for scoring and refereeing.
- **Scoring:** Use nonshaded areas on **Application Contest Scorecard 8.**
- **Refereeing:** Refer to and use designated referee signals located on the Official's Pocket Reference.

() *Teams transition to designated contest areas to perform assigned duties.*

- Teacher actively monitors individual and team performance.

() *Teams transition to designated instructional area for closure.*

Closure

- Teacher reviews lesson focus.
- Teacher discusses assessment of individual and team performance.
- Check for student understanding using questions and demonstrations (refer back to questions and demonstrations from the introduction).
- Allow for student questions and preview **lesson 9.**

() *Teams transition to home court areas for individual and team assessment.*

Individual and Team Assessment

Assessment summary

- Summarize/Complete **Application Contest Scorecard 8** (scorekeeper).
- Complete **PASE Attendance Recording Sheet** (coach).
- Complete **PASE Roles and Responsibilities Recording Sheet** (each person).
- Supervise assessment completion (coach).

() *Teams organize materials and exit class from home court areas.*

Layup

Critical Features

1. Drive powerfully to basket
2. Take ball up with two hands
3. Take off on nonshooting foot
4. Release ball at peak of jump with one hand
5. Use backboard when possible

Instructional Cues

1. Power drive
2. Up with two hands
3. Left hand–right foot, right hand–left foot
4. One-hand gentle release
5. Bank ball

Description

The layup is intended to be utilized when you are close to the basket in an effort to get an uncontested shot off.

Give and Go

Critical Features

1. Assume triple-threat position
2. Execute drive step
3. Pass ball to teammate
4. Feint away and cut toward basket
5. Prepare to receive ball

Instructional Cues

1. Triple threat
2. Jab step
3. Give
4. Go
5. Ready hands

Description

The give and go is one of the most basic strategies in basketball. Its name is very descriptive of its function. An offensive player gives (passes) the ball to a teammate and simultaneously cuts to the basket looking for a layup or close-quarters shot.

From *Sport Education Seasons* by Sean M. Bulger et al., 2007, Champaign, IL: Human Kinetics.

PASE Basketball Student Coaching Plan 8

"Great teamwork is the only way we create the breakthroughs that define our careers."

—Pat Riley

Skills

- Layup
- Offensive footwork (L-cut and V-cut)

Tactic

- Give and go

Coaching Cues

Layup	Offensive footwork	Give and go
✓ Power drive	✓ Move away from passer	✓ Triple threat
✓ Up with two hands	✓ Quick cut (V or L)	✓ Jab step
✓ Left hand–right foot or right hand–left foot	✓ Move toward passer	✓ Give
✓ One-hand gentle release	✓ Provide target with hands	✓ Go
✓ Bank ball	✓ Move away from passer	✓ Ready hands

Keys to Success

- Focus the team on the coaching cues for the new skills.
- Check to see if teammates know how to use each cut (L-cut and V-cut).
- Help teammates progress through the **Activity Task Card.**
- Make sure team moves quickly between different lesson segments.

Rules and Official's Signals

- **Charging with the ball.** Personal contact with the ball by pushing or moving into an opposing player's torso. Discuss, demonstrate, and practice charging signal.
- **Blocking.** Illegal personal contact that impedes the progress of an opposing player with or without the ball. Discuss, demonstrate, and practice blocking signal.
- **3-point scoring.** Introduce 3-point scoring signal.

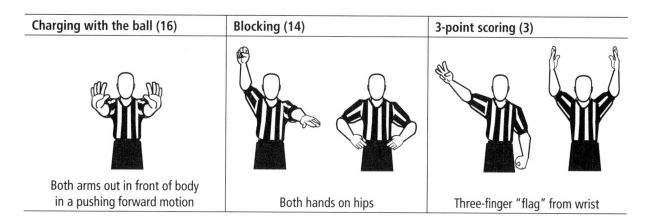

Charging with the ball (16)	Blocking (14)	3-point scoring (3)
Both arms out in front of body in a pushing forward motion	Both hands on hips	Three-finger "flag" from wrist

From *Sport Education Seasons* by Sean M. Bulger et al., 2007, Champaign, IL: Human Kinetics.

PASE Basketball Activity Task Card 8

Skills
- Layup
- Offensive footwork (L-cut and V-cut)

Tactic
- Give and go

Learning tasks	Self	Peer	Coach
1. Under the direction of the coach, perform the cues for today's skills two times each.			☐
2. Under the direction of the coach, perform the official's signals for today's lesson three times each.			☐
3. From a two-step walk, perform the layup shot in the air without a basket or ball 15 times.	☐		
4. Based on critical features, how many successful layups can you complete in the air without a basket or ball in 30 sec? (Record score only if using **Individual Activity Task Card Recording Sheet**.)	#___		☐
5. From a walk, perform the layup shot at the basket without a ball five times from both sides.	☐		
6. From a walk, perform the layup shot at the basket with a ball five times from both sides.		☐	
7. From a jog, perform the layup shot at the basket without a ball eight times from both sides.	☐		
8. From a jog, perform the layup shot at the basket with a ball eight times from both sides.	☐		
9. Without a ball or defenders, perform the give and go five times.		☐	
10. With a ball and no defenders, perform the give and go five times.		☐	
11. With a ball and passive defenders, perform the give and go five times.		☐	
Tasks 12-14 should be initiated with a give-and-go maneuver.			
12. Without a defender, cut toward the basket, finishing with a layup five times from both sides.		☐	
13. Repeat #12 adding in a passive defender.		☐	
14. With a defender, how many successful give and go to layups can you make in 30 sec? (Record score only if using **Individual Activity Task Card Recording Sheet**.)	#___		☐
15. 2-on-1: In groups of three, partners A and B will play a game of give and go with partner C, who is playing passive defense. In order for partners A and B to score, they must use all previously learned skills in combination with the give and go. The only scoring method that can be used is a layup, which must be preceded by a give-and-go maneuver. How many layups can you complete in 40 sec? Record your score. Rotate positions and repeat game. Answer the following questions and discuss what you discovered about the give and go and proximity of shooting. • What is the give and go? Why is it important for offensive ball movement? • Which shot is most likely to result from a give and go? Why? When should you use each shot? Why? • Which shot do you perform the best? Why?	#___		☐
16. Repeat #15. This time the defender earns a point for every steal, knock-away, or missed shot. The partners on offense will receive 1 point if they can maintain control for 30 sec or make a successful give-and-go maneuver finishing in a layup. Record scores. Repeat.	#___		☐

From *Sport Education Seasons* by Sean M. Bulger et al., 2007, Champaign, IL: Human Kinetics.

Equipment

- Two cones
- Pencils
- Boundary markers
- Whistles
- Lesson 8 Scorecard
- Officials' pinnies
- One clipboard
- Colored pinnies (teams)

Objectives

- Demonstrate a layup
- Demonstrate a give and go
- Dribble to reposition and L- and V-cuts to create open passing lanes

Goals

Achieve the maximum number of successful jump shots or layups (or both) in two 1-minute trials

Application Description

This is a 3 vs. 2 competition, with three offensive players and two defensive players. The offense must begin play from either cone by passing the ball to a teammate. After the ball is in play, the offense must attempt to move the ball via dribbling and passing in an attempt to create successful jump shots or layups. If the defense intercepts or deflects the ball, the offense retains possession and must restart play at either cone. Play also restarts at either cone when a shot is made or missed. The competition will last for four 1-minute trials, with possession of the ball changing on each new 1-minute trial. Substitutions enter the game at the beginning of each new 1-minute trial. Each team member must have participated during two of the four 1-minute trials. Repeat until each team has been on offense two times. The teacher should have multiple games going at the same time based on space and equipment and use a single game clock for all games.

Application Diagram

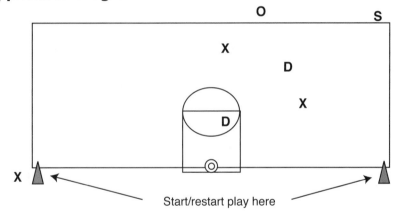

Start/restart play here

Key

X = Offensive players
D = Defender
O = Official
S = Scorekeeper
▲ = Cones

Scorekeeper's Guidelines

Provide scorekeepers with an example to fill in on their scorecard.

- 1 point per jump shot that is successful.
- 3 points per layup that is successful.
- Record scores for the offensive team after the official's signal indicating a successful shot.
- Combine all team points for both offensive trials for a total team score.

Referee's Guidelines

- No points awarded if a jump shot is performed from the lane area.
- No points awarded if a jump shot is performed from the 3-point area.
- No points if same player shoots two consecutive times.
- Demonstrate appropriate signals for violations.
- Demonstrate appropriate signals related to scoring.
- Demonstrate appropriate clock-related signals.

From *Sport Education Seasons* by Sean M. Bulger et al., 2007, Champaign, IL: Human Kinetics.

PASE Basketball Application Contest Scorecard 8

Instructions: Nonshaded areas must be filled in by scorekeeper.

□ Home   □ Away

Team	Coach	Date
Scorekeeper	Opponent	

TEAM FINAL SCORE

TEAM SCORING BY HALF

	1st Trial	2nd Trial	OT

SCORING

	1st Trial	2nd Trial	OT

Fouls						Player
1	2	3	4	5		Practice row to be filled in by student.
1	2	3	4	5		
1	2	3	4	5		
1	2	3	4	5		
1	2	3	4	5		
1	2	3	4	5		
1	2	3	4	5		
1	2	3	4	5		
1	2	3	4	5		

SUMMARY

	2 FG		3 FG		FT		Pts.	Reb.	Steals
	A	M	A	M	A	M			

Team Fouls

1	2	3	4	5	6	7	8	9	10	Totals

TEAM TIME-OUTS

1		2		3		4		5	
Away	Home	Away	Home	Away	Home	Away	Home	Away	Home

Alternating Jump Ball Possessions

Home	Away	Home	Away	Home	Away	Home	Away	Home	Away

Running Score

1	2	3	4	5	6	7	8	9	10	11	12	13	14	15	16	17	18	19	20	21	22	23	24	25
26	27	28	29	30	31	32	33	34	35	36	37	38	39	40	41	42	43	44	45	46	47	48	49	50
51	52	53	54	55	56	57	58	59	60	61	62	63	64	65	66	67	68	69	70	71	72	73	74	75
76	77	78	79	80	81	82	83	84	85	86	87	88	89	90	91	92	93	94	95	96	97	98	99	100

Coach's Signature _____

Scorekeeper's Signature _____

From *Sport Education Seasons* by Sean M. Bulger et al., 2007, Champaign, IL: Human Kinetics.

PASE BASKETBALL LESSON PLAN 9

Resources: Lesson Focus

- Numbered colored pinnies—six per team (also used during application contest)
- Basketballs—three to six per team (also used during application contest)
- Hula hoops—one per team (used to organize team materials)
- Stopwatches—one per team
- Pencils

Resources: Application Contest

- PASE Application Contest 9
- PASE Application Contest Scorecard 9
- PASE Official's Pocket Reference
- Two to four cones
- Boundary markers
- One clipboard
- Pencils
- Whistles
- Officials' pinnies

Instructional Materials

- PASE Attendance Recording Sheet (appendix B)
- PASE Roles and Responsibilities Assignments and Recording Sheet (appendix B)
- PASE Student Coaching Plan 9
- PASE Activity Task Card 9
- PASE Fitness Activities Sheets (appendix B)
- PASE Personal or Team Fitness Recording Sheet (appendix B)
- PASE Individual or Team Activity Task Card Recording Sheet (appendix B)
- PASE Basketball Lesson Plan 10

Instructional Focus

Skills

- Shooting review
- Footwork review

Tactics

- Screening on and off the ball
- Pick and roll

Objectives

- Develop screening and pick-and-roll skills by progression through learning activities during team practice
- Review jump shot, layup, and footwork
- Demonstrate personal and social responsibility

Team Role Check

- Students enter gymnasium and immediately report to home court area.
- Check daily roles and associated duties from materials provided.

♻ *Begin team warm-up.*

Team Warm-Up

- Conduct the team warm-up simultaneously to coaches' meeting.
- Fitness trainer monitors team warm-up using the PASE Fitness Activities Sheets.
- Fitness trainer or individuals record performance on team warm-up using either the **Personal** or **Team Fitness Recording Sheet.**

♻ *Teams transition to daily review.*

Coaches' Meeting

- ◆ Conduct the coaches' meeting simultaneously to team warm-up.
- ◆ All team coaches report to designated meeting area.
- ◆ Teacher provides coaches with Student Coaching Plan 9 and Activity Task Card 9.
- ◆ Teacher outlines the day's events.

↺ *Coaches transition to home court area and join warm-up.*

Team Review

- ◆ Review progress of team goals from **lesson 8.** This would be found in the student/team recording sheet which the students have every lesson.
- ◆ Identify areas of need from **lesson 8.**
- ◆ Practice to improve areas of need (use task cards and coaching plans from previous lessons).

↺ *Teams transition to designated instructional area for teacher instructions.*

Teacher Instruction

- ◆ Introduce daily lesson focus and review **lesson 8.**
- ◆ Provide anticipatory set:

💬 The purpose of today's lesson is to introduce you to two offensive tactics: screening and the pick and roll. The pick and roll is used to create scoring opportunities. Prior to scoring it is important that the offense is using screens on and off the ball to create passing lanes, which set up pick-and-roll opportunities. After learning the two tactics introduced today, you will be able to better understand how and when to perform these tactics during game situations.

- ◆ Provide information about skills and strategies.
- ◆ **Review** these skills and tactics:

SET AND JUMP SHOTS

Critical features	Instructional cues
Wide base, feet at shoulder-width	Balanced position
Move ball upward with two hands	Take up with two hands
Jump: jump straight up off of two feet Set: maintain floor-to-foot contact	Jump: jump straight up Set: feet to floor
Arm extends fully, wrists and fingers snap toward basket	Straighten arm, wave good-bye to ball
Jump: ball released at height of jump	Jump: high release

LAYUP

Critical features	Instructional cues
Drive powerfully to basket	Power drive
Take ball up with two hands	Up with two hands
Take off on nonshooting foot	Opposition
Release ball at peak of jump with one hand	One-hand release
Use backboard when possible	Bank it

OFFENSIVE FOOTWORK (L-CUT AND V-CUT)

Critical features	Instructional cues
Keep moving to create passing lanes	Move away from passer
Feint, plant foot to change direction quickly	Quick cut (V or L)
Move toward ball to receive pass	Move toward passer
Assume position with hands set to catch pass	Provide target with hands

DEFENSIVE FOOTWORK

Critical features	Instructional cues
Sitting position, feet at shoulder-width	Defensive position
Hands up and out, arms flexed	Ready hands
Short, quick, choppy steps keeping feet apart	Quick feet, scoot
Maintain low center of gravity while moving	Low hips

* **Introduce** the following new skills and tactics for the day.
* Complete teacher or student demonstrations (or both) of these skills and tactics:

SCREENING ON AND OFF OF BALL

Critical features	Instructional cues
Set screen on side of defender	Side screen
Defensive position with arms crossed low	Screen ready position
Remain stationary when within one step of defender	Hold position
Prepare for contact	Brace body
Prepare to move toward basket or to the ball	Roll quickly off of screen

PICK AND ROLL

Critical features	Instructional cues
Set screen for dribbler	Pick
Dribbler moves close to and by the screen to elude defender	Dribble by shoulder to shoulder
Screener rolls out of screening position toward basket	Roll
If defenders do not switch, dribbler maintains possession of ball	No switch equals keep
If defenders switch, dribbler passes ball to rolling screener	Switch equals pass

* Provide information about official's signals and rules.
* **Introduce** today's signals and rules. Demonstrate and explain the following signals and rules:
    * Pushing without the ball (15)
    * Blocking (14)
    * Unsportspersonlike (17)
* Check for student understanding using questions, student demonstrations, or both.
    * Q1: "When shooting a right-hand layup, which foot do you take off of and which hand do you use?"

- Q2: "At what angles are the L- and V-cuts made?"
- Q3: "What should you do after setting a screen or pick? Why?"

↻ *Teams transition to home court area for daily team practice.*

Team Practice

- Team-directed practice begins (refer to **Activity Task Card 9**).
- Teacher moves through home court area to facilitate team practice.
  - Manage learning environment.
  - Observe and assess individual and team performance.
  - Provide encouragement and instructional feedback.

↻ *Teams transition back to designated instructional area for application contest.*

Application Contest

- Teacher explains and demonstrates daily contest (refer to **Application Contest 9** and **Individual** or **Team Activity Task Card Recording Sheet**).
  - Identify tactical focus and related skills (refer to **Application Contest Scorecard 9**).
  - Identify contest goals.
  - Discuss procedures for scoring and refereeing.
- **Scoring:** Use nonshaded areas on **Application Contest Scorecard 9.**
- **Refereeing:** Refer to and use designated referee signals located on the Official's Pocket Reference.

↻ *Teams transition to designated contest areas to perform assigned duties.*

- Teacher actively monitors individual and team performance.

↻ *Teams transition to designated instructional area for closure.*

Closure

- Teacher reviews lesson focus.
- Teacher discusses assessment of individual and team performance.
- Check for student understanding using questions and demonstrations (can refer back to questions and demonstrations from the introduction).
- Allow for student questions and preview **lesson 10.**

↻ *Teams transition to home court areas for individual and team assessment.*

Individual and Team Assessment

Assessment summary

- Summarize/Complete **Application Contest Scorecard 9** (scorekeeper).
- Complete **PASE Attendance Recording Sheet** (coach).
- Complete **PASE Roles and Responsibilities Recording Sheet** (each person).
- Supervise assessment completion (coach).

↻ *Teams organize materials and exit class from home court areas.*

Screening on and off the Ball

Critical Features

1. Set screen on side of defender
2. Defensive position with arms crossed low
3. Remain stationary when within one step of defender
4. Prepare for contact
5. Prepare to move toward basket or to the ball

Instructional Cues

1. Side screen
2. Screen ready position
3. Hold position
4. Brace body
5. Roll quickly off of screen

Description

The purpose of screening is to block a defensive player near or away from the ball in order to free up an offensive player to create more scoring opportunities. An offensive player moves toward a defensive player and attempts to set a "pick" or to block his or her movement in a given direction, allowing an offensive player to get open. The offensive player screening or setting the "pick" must be stationary.

From *Sport Education Seasons* by Sean M. Bulger et al., 2007, Champaign, IL: Human Kinetics.

Pick and Roll

Critical Features

1. Set screen for dribbler
2. Dribbler moves close to and by the screen to elude defender
3. Screener rolls out of screening position toward basket
4. If defenders do not switch, dribbler maintains possession of ball
5. If defenders switch, dribbler passes ball to rolling screener

Instructional Cues

1. Pick
2. Dribble by shoulder to shoulder
3. Roll
4. No switch equals keep
5. Switch equals pass

Description

With this skill, an offensive player sets a pick and then rolls away from the defensive player in order to get open and receive a pass. This skill enables the offensive player to set up a scoring opportunity.

From *Sport Education Seasons* by Sean M. Bulger et al., 2007, Champaign, IL: Human Kinetics.

PASE Basketball Student Coaching Plan 9

"Anyone who has never made a mistake has never tried anything new."

—Albert Einstein

Skills

- Set and jump shot and layup review
- Offensive and defensive footwork review

Tactic

- Screening on and off the ball

Coaching Cues

Set/Jump shots	Layup	Screening on/off ball	Pick and roll
✓ Balanced position	✓ Power drive	✓ Side screen	✓ Pick
✓ Take up with two hands	✓ Up with two hands	✓ Screen ready position	✓ Dribble by shoulder to shoulder
✓ Set: feet to floor	✓ Left hand–right foot or right hand–left foot	✓ Hold position	✓ Roll
✓ Jump: jump straight up	✓ One-hand gentle release	✓ Brace body	✓ No switch equals keep
✓ Straighten arm, wave good-bye to ball	✓ Bank ball	✓ Roll quickly off of screen	✓ Switch equals pass
✓ High release			

Keys to Success

- Focus the team on the coaching cues for the new skills.
- Check to see if teammates know when to use a pick and roll.
- Help teammates progress through the **Activity Task Card.**
- Make sure team moves quickly between different lesson segments.

Rules and Official's Signals

- **Pushing without the ball.** Making contact with an opponent using your hands in a horizontal manner that may inhibit opponent's performance. Discuss, demonstrate, and practice pushing signal.
- **Blocking.** Review blocking signal.
- **Unsportspersonlike.** Review unsportspersonlike signal.

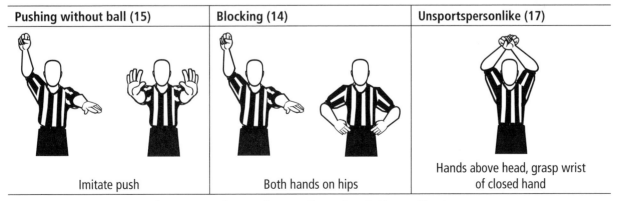

Pushing without ball (15)	Blocking (14)	Unsportspersonlike (17)
Imitate push	Both hands on hips	Hands above head, grasp wrist of closed hand

From *Sport Education Seasons* by Sean M. Bulger et al., 2007, Champaign, IL: Human Kinetics.

PASE Basketball Activity Task Card 9

Skills

- Set and jump shot and layup review
- Offensive footwork review

Tactics

- Screening on and off the ball
- Pick and roll

Learning tasks	Self	Peer	Coach
1. Under the direction of the coach, perform the cues for today's new skills two times each.			☐
2. Under the direction of the coach, perform the official's signals for today's lesson three times each.			☐
3. Set a screen on a defender who is walking five times.	☐		
4. Set a screen on a defender who is jogging five times.	☐		
5. Set a screen on a defender who is walking, and after screening, roll to the basket five times.			☐
6. Set a screen on a defender who is jogging, and after screening, roll to the basket five times.		☐	
7. Set a screen on a defender who is walking, and after screening, roll to the basket and receive a pass from the dribbler five times.		☐	
8. Set a screen on a defender who is jogging, and after screening, roll to the basket and receive a pass from the dribbler five times.		☐	
9. How many pick and rolls can you successfully execute in 30 sec? (Record score only if using **Individual Activity Task Card Recording Sheet**.)	#___		☐
10. 3-on-3: In groups of six, play a game of keep-away from the defense for 30 sec. After the 30 sec is completed, switch offensive and defensive positions. To score, you must create open passing lanes by using screens. Each successful pass is a point for the offense. Repeat this game until each player has had an opportunity to play on offense twice. (Record score only if using **Individual Activity Task Card Recording Sheet**.)	#___		☐
11. Using the following questions, determine the skills and tactics your team needs to review. Locate the appropriate task cards and begin the review. Identify which task you last completed, using the **Individual Activity Task Card Recording Sheet** located in the coach's folder. Answer the following questions and discuss what you discovered with a teammate. • In which application contests so far has your team performed well? • In which application contests so far has your team not performed so well? • Which skills and tactics should you practice to improve your future performance? (Record score only if using **Individual Activity Task Card Recording Sheet**.)	#___		☐

From *Sport Education Seasons* by Sean M. Bulger et al., 2007, Champaign, IL: Human Kinetics.

Equipment

- Two cones
- Pencils
- Boundary markers
- Whistles
- Lesson 9 Scorecard
- Officials' pinnies
- One clipboard
- Colored pinnies (teams)

Objectives

- Demonstrate a screen on and off the ball
- Demonstrate a pick and roll
- Dribble to reposition and L- and V-cuts to create open passing lanes

Goals

Achieve the maximum number of successful jump shots or layups (or both) as a result of a pick and roll in two 2-minute trials

Application Description

This is a 3 vs. 2 competition, with three offensive players and two defensive players. The offense must begin play from either cone by passing the ball to a teammate. After the ball is in play, the offense must attempt to move the ball via dribbling, passing, and screening in an attempt to create successful jump shots and layups. For a basket to be scored, it must be preceded by a pick and roll. If the defense intercepts or deflects the ball, the offense retains possession and must restart play at either cone. Play also restarts at either cone when a shot is made or missed. The competition will last for four 2-minute trials, with possession of the ball changing on each new 2-minute trial. Substitutions enter the game at the beginning of each new 2-minute trial. Each team member must have participated during two of the four 2-minute trials. Repeat until each team has been on offense two times. The teacher should have multiple games going at the same time based on space and equipment and use a single game clock for all games.

Application Diagram

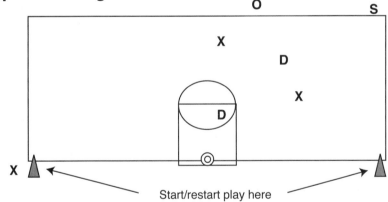

Key

X = Offensive players
D = Defender
O = Official
S = Scorekeeper
▲ = Cones

Start/restart play here

Scorekeeper's Guidelines

Provide scorekeepers with an example to fill in on their scorecard.

- 2 points per jump shot that is successful if preceded by a pick and roll.
- 2 points per layup that is successful if preceded by a pick and roll.
- Record scores for the offensive team after the official's signal indicating a successful shot.
- Combine all team points for both offensive trials for a total team score.

Referee's Guidelines

- No points awarded if a jump shot is performed from the 3-point area.
- No points if same player shoots two consecutive times.
- No points if shot is not initiated with a pick and roll.
- Demonstrate appropriate signals for violations.
- Demonstrate appropriate signals related to scoring.
- Demonstrate appropriate clock-related signals.

From *Sport Education Seasons* by Sean M. Bulger et al., 2007, Champaign, IL: Human Kinetics.

PASE Basketball Application Contest Scorecard 9

Instructions: Nonshaded areas must be filled in by scorekeeper.

☐ Home   ☐ Away

Team	Coach	Date
Scorekeeper	Opponent	

TEAM FINAL SCORE

TEAM SCORING BY HALF

	1st Trial	2nd Trial	OT

SCORING

	1st Trial	2nd Trial	OT

SUMMARY

Player	Fouls					2 FG		3 FG			FT			Steals	Reb.	Pts.
						A	M	A	M		A	M				

Practice row to be filled in by student.

1	2	3	4	5												
1	2	3	4	5												
1	2	3	4	5												
1	2	3	4	5												
1	2	3	4	5												
1	2	3	4	5												
1	2	3	4	5												
1	2	3	4	5												

Totals

Team Fouls

1	2	3	4	5	6	7	8	9	10

TEAM TIME-OUTS

1	2	3	4	5
Away	Home	Away	Home	Away

Alternating Jump Ball Possessions

	Home	Away	Home	Away	Home	Away	Home	Away	Home	Away	Home	Away	Home	Away	Home
Running Score	1	2	3	4	5	6	7	8	9	10	11	12	13	14	15	16
	26	27	28	29	30	31	32	33	34	35	36	37	38	39	40	41
	51	52	53	54	55	56	57	58	59	60	61	62	63	64	65	66
	76	77	78	79	80	81	82	83	84	85	86	87	88	89	90	91

17	18	19	20	21	22	23	24	25
42	43	44	45	46	47	48	49	50
67	68	69	70	71	72	73	74	75
92	93	94	95	96	97	98	99	100

Coach's Signature _____

Scorekeeper's Signature _____

From *Sport Education Seasons* by Sean M. Bulger et al., 2007, Champaign, IL: Human Kinetics.

PASE BASKETBALL LESSON PLAN 10

Resources: Lesson Focus

- Numbered colored pinnies—six per team (also used during application contest)
- Basketballs—three to six per team (also used during application contest)
- Hula hoops—one per team (used to organize team materials)
- Stopwatches—one per team
- Pencils

Resources: Application Contest

- PASE Application Contest 10
- PASE Application Contest Scorecard 10
- PASE Official's Pocket Reference
- Two to four cones
- Boundary markers
- One clipboard
- Pencils
- Whistles
- Officials' pinnies

Instructional Materials

- PASE IRL Rubric and Recording Sheet (appendix B)
- PASE Attendance Recording Sheet (appendix B)
- PASE Roles and Responsibilities Assignments and Recording Sheet (appendix B)
- PASE Student Coaching Plans 3-5, 7-9
- PASE Activity Task Cards 3-5, 7-9
- PASE Fitness Activities Sheets (appendix B)
- PASE Personal or Team Fitness Recording Sheet (appendix B)
- PASE Individual or Team Activity Task Card Recording Sheet (appendix B)
- PASE Basketball Lesson Plan 11
- PASE Knowledge Quiz 1
- PASE Team Goal-Setting Sheet (appendix C)

Instructional Focus

Skills

- Review skills taught to date.

Tactics

- Review tactics taught to date.

Objectives

- Further develop basketball skills and tactics by progressing through learning activities from previous lessons not yet completed during team practice
- Demonstrate personal and social responsibility

Team Role Check

- Students enter gymnasium and immediately report to home court area.
- Check daily roles and associated duties from materials provided.

 Begin team warm-up.

Team Warm-Up

- Conduct the team warm-up simultaneously to coaches' meeting.
- Fitness trainer leads team through warm-up using the PASE Fitness Activities Sheets.
- Fitness trainer or individuals record performance on team warm-up using either the **Personal** or **Team Fitness Recording Sheet.**

 Teams transition to daily review.

Coaches' Meeting

- ◆ Conduct the coaches' meeting simultaneously to team warm-up.
- ◆ All team coaches report to designated meeting area.
- ◆ Teacher provides coaches with choice of Student Coaching Plans 3-5 and 7-9 and Activity Task Cards 3-5 and 7-9.
- ◆ Teacher outlines the day's events.

↻ *Coaches transition to home court area and join warm-up.*

Team Review

- ◆ Review progress of team goals from **lessons 3-9.**
- ◆ Identify areas of need from **lessons 3-9.**
- ◆ Record goals on **Team Goal-Setting Sheet.**
- ◆ Prepare to practice in identified areas during team practice (use task cards and coaching plans from previous lessons).

↻ *Teams transition to designated instructional area for teacher instructions.*

Teacher Instruction

- ◆ Introduce daily lesson focus and review **lessons 3-9.**
- ◆ Provide anticipatory set:

💬 Today is the second of three review lessons. The purpose of today's lesson is to review the skills and tactics that we have learned and practiced so far. You will have the opportunity to select and practice skills and tactics that your team needs the most work on. Each of these skills and tactics is important and should be mastered by all of your team members in order to improve your chances of being successful in specific game situations.

- ◆ Check for student understanding of previously learned skills and tactics by using questions, student demonstrations, or both.
  - ◆ Q1: "What is a common method for moving the ball as an individual?"
  - ◆ Q2: "What are the four passes learned so far? When should each be used?"
  - ◆ Q3: "What are two ways that you can create space when you don't have the ball?"
  - ◆ Q4: "What three moves can you make from the triple-threat position?"
  - ◆ Q5: "What are three types of shots that we have learned?"
  - ◆ Q6: "What is the difference between defense on and off the ball?"
  - ◆ Q7: "What are two offensive tactics used for scoring with a layup?"
- ◆ Provide any additional important information about previously learned skills and tactics.
- ◆ Check for student understanding of previously learned official's signals by using questions, student demonstrations, gamelike scenarios, or a combination of these.
  - ◆ 1-, 2-, and 3-point scoring (1, 2, 3)
  - ◆ Charging with the ball (16)
  - ◆ Stop clock (4)
  - ◆ Blocking (14)
  - ◆ Unsportspersonlike (17)
  - ◆ Traveling (8)
  - ◆ Pushing without the ball (15)
  - ◆ Double dribble (9)
  - ◆ Illegal use of hands (13)
  - ◆ Carrying (10)

 ◆ Stop clock for a foul (5)
 ◆ Jump ball (12)

◯ *Teams transition to home court area for daily team practice.*

Team Practice

 ◆ Complete **Knowledge Quiz 1** (refer to **Knowledge Quiz 1;** be sure to cover the answer key before making copies for students).
 ◆ Team-directed practice begins (refer to **Activity Task Cards 3-5** and **7-9** and **Individual** or **Team Activity Task Card Recording Sheet**).
 ◆ Teacher moves through home court area to facilitate team practice.
    ◆ Manage learning environment.
    ◆ Observe and assess individual and team performance.
    ◆ Provide encouragement and instructional feedback.

◯ *Teams transition back to designated instructional area for application contest.*

Application Contest

 ◆ Teacher explains and demonstrates daily contest (refer to **Application Contest 10**).
    ◆ Identify tactical focus and related skills (refer to **Application Contest Scorecard 10**).
    ◆ Identify contest goals.
    ◆ Discuss procedures for scoring and refereeing:
 ◆ **Scoring:** Use nonshaded areas on **Application Contest Scorecard 10.**
 ◆ **Refereeing:** Refer to and use designated referee signals located on the Official's Pocket Reference.

◯ *Teams transition to designated contest areas to perform assigned duties.*

 ◆ Teacher actively monitors individual and team performance.

◯ *Teams transition to designated instructional area for closure.*

Closure

 ◆ Teacher reviews lesson focus.
 ◆ Teacher discusses assessment of individual and team performance.
 ◆ Check for student understanding using questions and demonstrations (refer back to questions and demonstrations from the introduction).
 ◆ Allow for student questions and preview **lesson 11.**

◯ *Teams transition to home court areas for individual and team assessment.*

Individual and Team Assessment

Assessment summary

 ◆ Complete **PASE IRL Recording Sheet** (each person).
 ◆ Summarize/Complete **Application Contest Scorecard 10** (scorekeeper).
 ◆ Complete **PASE Attendance Recording Sheet** (coach).
 ◆ Complete **PASE Roles and Responsibilities Recording Sheet** (each person).
 ◆ Supervise assessment completion (coach).
 ◆ Collect the following:
    ◆ **PASE Outside-of-Class Physical Activity Participation Log** (each person)

◯ *Teams organize materials and exit class from home court areas.*

PASE Basketball Application Contest 10

Equipment

- Two cones
- Pencils
- Boundary markers
- Whistles
- Lesson 10 Scorecard
- Officials' pinnies
- One clipboard
- Colored pinnies (teams)

Objectives

- Demonstrate a screen on and off the ball
- Demonstrate a pick and roll
- Dribble to reposition and L- and V-cuts to create open passing lanes

Goals

Achieve the maximum number of successful jump shots or layups (or both) in two 2-minute trials

Application Description

This is a 3 vs. 2 competition, with three offensive players and two defensive players. The offense must begin play from either cone by passing the ball to a teammate. After the ball is in play, the offense must attempt to move the ball via dribbling, passing, and screening in an attempt to create successful jump shots and layups. If the defense intercepts or deflects the ball, the offense retains possession and must restart play at either cone. Play also restarts at either cone when a shot is made or missed. The competition will last for four 2-minute trials, with possession of the ball changing on each new 2-minute trial. Substitutions enter the game at the beginning of each new 2-minute trial. Each team member must have participated during two of the four 2-minute trials. Repeat until each team has been on offense two times. The teacher should have multiple games going at the same time based on space and equipment and use a single game clock for all games.

Application Diagram

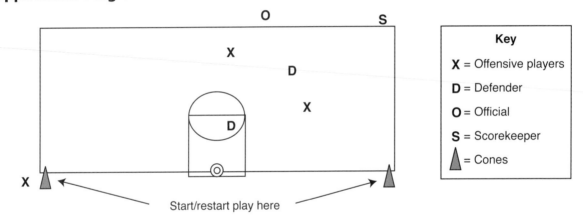

Start/restart play here

Key

X = Offensive players
D = Defender
O = Official
S = Scorekeeper
▲ = Cones

Scorekeeper's Guidelines

Provide scorekeepers with an example to fill in on their scorecard.

- 2 points per jump shot that is successful.
- 2 points per layup that is successful.
- Record scores for the offensive team after the official's signal indicating a successful shot.
- Combine all team points for both offensive trials for a total team score.

Referee's Guidelines

- No points awarded if a jump shot is performed from the 3-point area.
- No points if same player shoots two consecutive times.
- Demonstrate appropriate signals for violations.
- Demonstrate appropriate signals related to scoring.
- Demonstrate appropriate clock-related signals.

From *Sport Education Seasons* by Sean M. Bulger et al., 2007, Champaign, IL: Human Kinetics.

PASE Basketball Application Contest Scorecard 10

Instructions: Nonshaded areas must be filled in by scorekeeper.

Team ☐ Home ☐ Away

Coach

Date

Scorekeeper

Opponent

TEAM FINAL SCORE

TEAM SCORING BY HALF

	1st Trial	2nd Trial	OT

SCORING

	1st Trial	2nd Trial	OT

SUMMARY

Player	2 FG		3 FG		FT		Steals	Reb.	Pts.
	A	M	A	M	A	M			

Practice row to be filled in by student.

Fouls

	1	2	3	4	5

Team Fouls

1	2	3	4	5	6	7	8	9	10	Totals

TEAM TIME-OUTS

1	2	3	4	5
Away	Home	Away	Home	Away	Home	Away	Home

Alternating Jump Ball Possessions

Home	Away	Home	Away	Home	Away	Home	Away	Home	Away

Running Score

1	2	3	4	5	6	7	8	9	10	11	12	13	14	15	16	17	18	19	20	21	22	23	24	25
26	27	28	29	30	31	32	33	34	35	36	37	38	39	40	41	42	43	44	45	46	47	48	49	50
51	52	53	54	55	56	57	58	59	60	61	62	63	64	65	66	67	68	69	70	71	72	73	74	75
76	77	78	79	80	81	82	83	84	85	86	87	88	89	90	91	92	93	94	95	96	97	98	99	100

Coach's Signature

Scorekeeper's Signature

Name_____ Date_____

Instructions: Please answer the following multiple-choice questions by placing your answers in the blank to the left of the question.

___ 1. Which movement would be most efficient when shooting a layup from the right side of the basket?
    a. stand on both feet, shoot with right hand
    b. take off from the right foot, shoot with left hand
    c. take off from left foot, shoot with both hands
    d. take off from the left foot, shoot with right hand

___ 2. Which body part is essential to keep in line with the basket when shooting a jump shot?
    a. legs
    b. shoulders
    c. hips
    d. arms

___ 3. How many steps can a player take without traveling?
    a. 1
    b. 2
    c. 3
    d. 0

___ 4. What is the most significant factor to stress when performing a pass?
    a. stepping into the pass
    b. keeping the elbows in
    c. handling the ball with the fingers
    d. using a wrist snap upon release

___ 5. Where should a player's eyes be focused during dribbling?
    a. downward in order to control the ball
    b. downward in order to see the feet of a defensive player
    c. forward in order to pass to a teammate
    d. forward in order to alternate hands quickly

___ 6. Player A is cutting for the basket and runs into player B, who had an established guarding position. What is the official's decision?
    a. blocking on player A
    b. charging on player A
    c. blocking on player B
    d. charging on player B

___ 7. What is the action of the player without the ball who moves into an open area to receive a pass?
    a. cutting
    b. feinting
    c. driving
    d. faking

From *Sport Education Seasons* by Sean M. Bulger et al., 2007, Champaign, IL: Human Kinetics.

____ 8. What should you do after you set a pick?

    a. keep the defensive player from moving

    b. wait to receive the pass

    c. roll toward the goal, keeping the defensive player at your back

    d. roll away from the goal, keeping the defensive player at your back

____ 9. Which statement best describes a give and go?

    a. setting a screen against a teammate's guard and roll

    b. moving into an open space hoping to receive the ball

    c. passing to a teammate followed by a cut and return pass

    d. moving in one direction followed by a quick move in another direction

____ 10. The following official's signal represents what?

    a. charging

    b. illegal use of hands

    c. blocking

    d. double dribble

PASE BASKETBALL KNOWLEDGE QUIZ 1 KEY

1. d	6. b
2. b	7. a
3. b	8. c
4. d	9. c
5. c	10. d

From *Sport Education Seasons* by Sean M. Bulger et al., 2007, Champaign, IL: Human Kinetics.

PASE BASKETBALL LESSON PLAN 11

Resources: Lesson Focus

- Numbered colored pinnies—six per team (also used during application contest)
- Basketballs—three to six per team (also used during application contest)
- Hula hoops—one per team (used to organize team materials)
- Stopwatches—one per team
- Pencils

Resources: Application Contest

- PASE Application Contest 11
- PASE Application Contest Scorecard 11
- PASE Official's Pocket Reference
- Two to four cones
- Boundary markers
- One clipboard
- Pencils
- Whistles
- Officials' pinnies

Instructional Materials

- PASE Attendance Recording Sheet (appendix B)
- PASE Roles and Responsibilities Assignments and Recording Sheet (appendix B)
- PASE Student Coaching Plan 11
- PASE Activity Task Card 11
- PASE Fitness Activities Sheets (appendix B)
- PASE Personal or Team Fitness Recording Sheet (appendix B)
- PASE Individual or Team Activity Task Card Recording Sheet (appendix B)
- PASE Outside-of-Class Physical Activity Participation Log (appendix B)
- PASE Basketball Lesson Plan 12

Instructional Focus

Skills

- Offensive rebounding
- Defensive rebounding

Tactic

None

Objectives

- Develop rebounding skills by progression through learning activities during team practice
- Utilize previously learned tactics in an application contest
- Demonstrate personal and social responsibility

Team Role Check

- Students enter gymnasium and immediately report to home court area.
- Check daily roles and associated duties from materials provided.

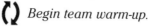 *Begin team warm-up.*

Team Warm-Up

- Conduct the team warm-up simultaneously to coaches' meeting.
- Fitness trainer leads team through warm-up using the PASE Fitness Activities Sheets.
- Fitness trainer or individuals record performance on team warm-up using either the **Personal** or **Team Fitness Recording Sheet.**

Teams transition to daily review.

Coaches' Meeting

- Conduct the coaches' meeting simultaneously to team warm-up.
- All team coaches report to designated meeting area.
- Teacher provides coaches with Student Coaching Plan 11 and Activity Task Card 11.
- Teacher outlines the day's events.

Coaches transition to home court area and join warm-up.

Team Review

- Review progress of team goals from **lesson 10.** This would be found in the student/team recording sheet which the students have every lesson.
- Identify areas of need from **lesson 10.**
- Practice to improve areas of need.

Teams transition to designated instructional area for teacher instructions.

Teacher Instruction

- Introduce daily lesson focus and review **lesson 10.**
- Provide anticipatory set:

The purpose of today's lesson is to introduce two types of rebounding that are used following a shot. Each of these rebounding techniques is used in specific situations depending on whether you're on offense or defense. The importance of these techniques is that they can help you gain or retain possession of the ball. After learning the two types of rebounding techniques introduced today, you will be able to better understand and execute rebounds in game situations.

- Provide information about skills and strategies.
- **Introduce** the following new skills for the day.
- Complete teacher and student demonstrations (or both) of these skills and tactics:

OFFENSIVE REBOUNDING

Critical features	Instructional cues
Anticipate angle of rebounding shot	React to shot
Feint direction to confuse defensive rebounder	Fake direction
Roll off of defensive contact in opposite direction of feint	Roll off
Jump for ball with raised arms	Jump and reach
Bring ball to chest with elbows out	Protect ball

DEFENSIVE REBOUNDING

Critical features	Instructional cues
Anticipate angle of rebounding shot	React to shot
Position body between basket or ball and offensive rebounder	Locate position
Maintain contact with offensive player	Keep contact
Jump for ball with raised arms	Jump and reach
Prepare to make outlet pass to teammate	Look to pass

- Provide information about official's signals and rules.
- **Introduce** today's signals and rules. Demonstrate and explain the following signals and rules:
    - Pushing without the ball (15)
    - Unsportspersonlike (17)
    - 3 seconds (11)
- Check for student understanding using questions, student demonstrations, or both.
    - Q1: "What is the advantage of offensive rebounding?"
    - Q2: "When preparing to rebound the ball, what is the first thing you should do?"
    - Q3: "After rebounding the ball what should you do? Why?"

( ) *Teams transition to home court area for daily team practice.*

Team Practice

- Team-directed practice begins (refer to **Activity Task Card 11** and **Individual** or **Team Activity Task Card Recording Sheet**).
- Teacher moves through home court area to facilitate team practice.
    - Manage learning environment.
    - Observe and assess individual and team performance.
    - Provide encouragement and instructional feedback.

( ) *Teams transition back to designated instructional area for application contest.*

Application Contest

- Teacher explains and demonstrates daily contest (refer to **Application Contest 11**).
    - Identify tactical focus and related skills (refer to **Application Contest Scorecard 11**).
    - Identify contest goals.
    - Discuss procedures for scoring and refereeing.
- **Scoring:** Use nonshaded areas on **Application Contest Scorecard 11.**
- **Refereeing:** Refer to and use designated referee signals located on the Official's Pocket Reference.

( ) *Teams transition to designated contest areas to perform assigned duties.*

- Teacher actively monitors individual and team performance.

( ) *Teams transition to designated instructional area for closure.*

Closure

- Teacher reviews lesson focus.
- Teacher discusses assessment of individual and team performance.

- Check for student understanding using questions and demonstrations (refer back to questions and demonstrations from the introduction).
- Allow for student questions and preview **lesson 12.**

♻ *Teams transition to home court areas for individual and team assessment.*

Individual and Team Assessment

- Assessment summary
    - Summarize/Complete **Application Contest Scorecard 11** (scorekeeper).
    - Complete **PASE Attendance Recording Sheet** (coach).
    - Complete **PASE Roles and Responsibilities Recording Sheet** (each person).
    - Supervise assessment completion (coach).
- Distribute the following:
    - **PASE Outside-of-Class Physical Activity Participation Log** (each person)

♻ *Teams organize materials and exit class from home court areas.*

Offensive Rebounding

Critical Features

1. Anticipate angle of rebounding shot
2. Feint direction to confuse defensive rebounder
3. Roll off of defensive contact in opposite direction of feint
4. Jump for ball with raised arms
5. Bring ball to chest with elbows out

Instructional Cues

1. React to shot
2. Fake direction
3. Roll off
4. Jump and reach
5. Protect ball

Description

The offensive rebounding skill is the act of gaining possession of the ball by the offensive team following a missed field goal attempt by a player on the same team. The offensive player is typically behind the defensive player at the start of the sequence, so constant movement must be a characteristic of an offensive rebounder.

Defensive Rebounding

Critical Features

1. Anticipate angle of rebounding shot
2. Position body between basket or ball and offensive rebounder
3. Maintain contact with offensive player
4. Jump for ball with raised arms
5. Prepare to make outlet pass to teammate

Instructional Cues

1. React to shot
2. Locate position
3. Keep contact
4. Jump and reach
5. Look to pass

Description

Defensive rebounding is the act of gaining possession of the ball by the defensive team after the offensive team has attempted and missed a field goal. Because more shots are missed than made in a basketball game, this skill takes on importance. Gaining possession prevents the opponent from scoring points and often translates into one team's controlling the game tempo.

From *Sport Education Seasons* by Sean M. Bulger et al., 2007, Champaign, IL: Human Kinetics.

PASE Basketball Student Coaching Plan 11

COACHING QUOTE

"Failure to prepare is preparing for failure."

—*John Wooden*

Skills

- Offensive rebounding
- Defensive rebounding

Tactics

- Review all.

Coaching Cues

Offensive rebounding	Defensive rebounding
✓ React to shot	✓ React to shot
✓ Fake direction	✓ Locate position
✓ Roll off	✓ Keep contact
✓ Jump and reach	✓ Jump and reach
✓ Protect ball	✓ Look to pass

Keys to Success

- Focus the team on the coaching cues for the new skills.
- Check to see if teammates know how to rebound without fouling their opponent.
- Help teammates progress through the **Activity Task Card.**
- Make sure team moves quickly between different lesson segments.

Rules and Official's Signals

- **Pushing without ball.** Review pushing signal.
- **Unsportspersonlike.** Review unsportspersonlike signal.
- **3 seconds.** An offensive player remains in the 3-second lane longer than 3 seconds while the ball is in play. Discuss, demonstrate, and practice 3-second signal.

Pushing without ball (15)	Unsportspersonlike (17)	3 seconds (11)
Imitate push	Hands above head, grasp wrist of closed hand	Arm extended, show three fingers

From *Sport Education Seasons* by Sean M. Bulger et al., 2007, Champaign, IL: Human Kinetics.

PASE Basketball Activity Task Card 11

Skills

- Offensive rebounding
- Defensive rebounding

Tactics

- Review all.

Learning tasks	Self	Peer	Coach
1. Under the direction of the coach, perform the cues for today's skills two times each.			☐
2. Under the direction of the coach, perform the official's signals for today's lesson three times each.			☐
3. In pairs, around the basket without a ball, pretend to secure a defensive rebound on the coach's signal five times. Switch roles so each partner attempts the defensive rebound five times. (Offensive player is passive.)		☐	
4. In pairs, around the basket without a ball, pretend to secure an offensive rebound on the coach's signal five times. Switch roles so each partner attempts the offensive rebound five times. (Defensive player is passive.)		☐	
5. In pairs, around the basket with a ball, secure a defensive rebound from a shot taken by the coach from the foul line five times. Switch roles so each partner attempts the defensive rebound five times. (Offensive player is passive.)		☐	
6. In pairs, around the basket with a ball, secure an offensive rebound from a shot taken by the coach from the foul line five times. Switch roles so each partner attempts the offensive rebound five times. (Defensive player is passive.)		☐	
7. In pairs, around the basket with a ball, secure a defensive rebound from a shot taken by the coach from a 45-degree angle to the right five times. Switch roles so each partner attempts the defensive rebound five times. (Offensive player is passive.)		☐	
8. In pairs, around the basket with a ball, secure an offensive rebound from a shot taken by the coach from a 45-degree angle to the left five times. Switch roles so each partner attempts the offensive rebound five times. (Defensive player is passive.)		☐	
9. In pairs, around the basket with a ball, secure a rebound from a shot taken by the coach from either the right, left, or straight ahead five times. Switch roles so each partner is on defense five times. (Both players are active.) Answer the following questions and discuss what you discovered about rebounding against an opponent. (Record score only if using **Individual Activity Task Card Recording Sheet.**) • Is it easier to secure an offensive or defensive rebound? Why? • What should you do to be able to secure an offensive rebound? Why? • How can you use your body to help rebound the ball?	#___		☐
10. Repeat #9. This time, defense earns a point for every rebound and outlet pass sequence. Remember scores. (Record score only if using **Individual Activity Task Card Recording Sheet.**)	#___		☐

From *Sport Education Seasons* by Sean M. Bulger et al., 2007, Champaign, IL: Human Kinetics.

Equipment

- Two cones
- Pencils
- Boundary markers
- Whistles
- Lesson 11 Scorecard
- Officials' pinnies
- One clipboard
- Colored pinnies (teams)

Objectives

Demonstrate offensive and defensive rebounding

Goals

Achieve the maximum number of successful jump shots or layups (or both) and offensive or defensive rebounds in two 2-minute trials

Application Description

This is a 3 vs. 3 competition, with three offensive players and three defensive players. The offense must begin play from either cone by passing the ball to a teammate. After the ball is in play, the offense must attempt to move the ball via dribbling, passing, and screening in an attempt to create successful jump shots and layups. Following a missed shot, players attempt to secure a rebound. Once a rebound has been secured, play restarts at the cones. If the defense intercepts or deflects the ball, the offense retains possession and must restart play at either cone. The competition will last for four 2-minute trials, with possession of the ball changing on each new 2-minute trial. Substitutions enter the game at the beginning of each new 2-minute trial. Each team member must have participated during two of the four 2-minute trials. Repeat until each team has been on offense two times. The teacher should have multiple games going at the same time based on space and equipment and use a single game clock for all games.

Application Diagram

Start/restart play here

Key

X = Offensive players
D = Defender
O = Official
S = Scorekeeper
= Cones

Scorekeeper's Guidelines

Provide scorekeepers with an example to fill in on their scorecard.

- 2 points per jump shot or layup that is successful.
- 2 points per offensive rebound that is successfully secured.
- 2 points per defensive rebound that is successfully secured and followed by a successful outlet pass.
- Record scores for the offensive team after the official's signal indicating a successful shot or rebound.
- Combine all team points for a total team score.

Referee's Guidelines

- No points awarded if a jump shot is performed from the 3-point area.
- No points if same player shoots two consecutive times.
- Demonstrate appropriate signals for violations.
- Demonstrate appropriate signals related to scoring.
- Demonstrate appropriate clock-related signals.

From *Sport Education Seasons* by Sean M. Bulger et al., 2007, Champaign, IL: Human Kinetics.

PASE Basketball Application Contest Scorecard 11

Instructions: Nonshaded areas must be filled in by scorekeeper.

☐ Home ☐ Away

Team		Coach		Site	
Timer		Scorekeeper		Date	

FINAL SCORE

TEAM SCORING BY PERIODS

	1st	2nd	3rd	4th	OT

SCORING

Player	1st trial	2nd trial	3rd trial	4th trial	OT
Practice row to be filled in by student.					

SUMMARY

	2 FG		3 FG		FT		Steals	Reb.	Pts.
	A	M	A	M	A	M			

Fouls

	1	2	3	4	5
	1	2	3	4	5
	1	2	3	4	5
	1	2	3	4	5
	1	2	3	4	5
	1	2	3	4	5
	1	2	3	4	5
	1	2	3	4	5
	1	2	3	4	5

Totals

Team fouls

1	2	3	4	5	6	7	8	9	10

Alternating jump ball possessions

TEAM TIME-OUTS

	1		2		3		4		5
	Away	Home	Away	Home	Away	Home	Away	Home	Home

Running Score	1	2	3	4	5	6	7	8	9	10	11	12	13	14	15	16	17	18	19	20	21	22	23	24	25
	26	27	28	29	30	31	32	33	34	35	36	37	38	39	40	41	42	43	44	45	46	47	48	49	50
	51	52	53	54	55	56	57	58	59	60	61	62	63	64	65	66	67	68	69	70	71	72	73	74	75
	76	77	78	79	80	81	82	83	84	85	86	87	88	89	90	91	92	93	94	95	96	97	98	99	100

Coach's Signature _____

Scorekeeper's Signature _____

From *Sport Education Seasons* by Sean M. Bulger et al., 2007, Champaign, IL: Human Kinetics.

PASE BASKETBALL LESSON PLAN 12

Resources: Lesson Focus

- Numbered colored pinnies—six per team (also used during application contest)
- Basketballs—three to six per team (also used during application contest)
- Hula hoops—one per team (used to organize team materials)
- Stopwatches—one per team
- Pencils

Resources: Application Contest

- PASE Application Contest 12
- PASE Application Contest Scorecard 12
- PASE Official's Pocket Reference
- Two to four cones
- Boundary markers
- One clipboard
- Pencils
- Whistles
- Officials' pinnies

Instructional Materials

- PASE Attendance Recording Sheet (appendix B)
- PASE Roles and Responsibilities Assignments and Recording Sheet (appendix B)
- PASE Student Coaching Plan 12
- PASE Activity Task Card 12
- PASE Fitness Activities Sheets (appendix B)
- PASE Personal or Team Fitness Recording Sheet (appendix B)
- PASE Individual or Team Activity Task Card Recording Sheet (appendix B)
- PASE Basketball Lesson Plan 13

Instructional Focus

Skills	Tactics
• All	• Offensive post play
	• Defensive post play

Objectives

- Develop post play skills by progression through learning activities during team practice
- Utilize previously learned tactics in an application contest
- Demonstrate personal and social responsibility

Team Role Check

- Students enter gymnasium and immediately report to home court area.
- Check daily roles and associated duties from materials provided.
- ↻ *Begin team warm-up.*

Team Warm-Up

- ◆ Conduct the team warm-up simultaneously to coaches' meeting.
- ◆ Fitness trainer leads team through warm-up using the PASE Fitness Activities Sheets.
- ◆ Fitness trainer or individuals record performance on team warm-up using either the **Personal** or **Team Fitness Recording Sheet.**

Teams transition to daily review.

Coaches' Meeting

- ◆ Conduct the coaches' meeting simultaneously to team warm-up.
- ◆ All team coaches report to designated meeting area.
- Teacher provides coaches with Student Coaching Plan 12 and Activity Task Card 12. Teacher outlines the day's events.

Coaches transition to home court area and join warm-up.

Team Review

- ◆ Review progress of team goals from **lesson 11.** This would be found in the student/team recording sheet which the students have every lesson.
- ◆ Identify areas of need from **lesson 11.**
- Practice to improve areas of need.

Teams transition to designated instructional area for teacher instructions.

Teacher Instruction

- ◆ Introduce daily lesson focus and review **lesson 11.**
- Provide anticipatory set:

The purpose of today's lesson is to introduce offensive and defensive post play. The offensive player is considered to be in post play position when located on the edge of the lane with his or her back to the basket. The low post position is on the lane close to the basket, and the high post position is on the lane near the foul line. During effective post play the offensive post players have the responsibility of positioning themselves in front of the defensive player (low or high) in order to receive a pass and make an offensive play. During the offensive post play set, the defense must be able to deny the pass to the post player by either splitting or fronting the offensive post player. Once an offensive post player receives the ball, the defender must be positioned in such a way as to deny a shot or pass.

- ◆ Provide information about skills and strategies.
- ◆ **Introduce** the following new skills and tactics for the day.
- ◆ Complete teacher or student demonstrations (or both) of these skills and tactics:

OFFENSIVE POST PLAY

Critical features	Instructional cues
Keep defender to one side using upper body on that side	Deny front position
Defender fronting: push defender toward foul line and cut back to basket	Push high and cut
Defender splitting: feint away and cut to opposite side of the defender toward ball	Fake and roll
Continually move to maintain position, keeping feet in front of defenders	Move feet
Avoid standing in lane area for more than 3 seconds at a time	3-second rule

DEFENSIVE POST PLAY

Critical features	Instructional cues
Keep hand and foot nearest ball between offense and ball, and place opposite hand and foot between opponent and basket	Split defender
Below foul line: deny the ball by playing behind the opponent between the opponent and basket	Baseline side
Above foul line: deny ball by placing body slightly behind the opponent to ball side	Watch back-door cut
Keep moving to maintain balance and position	Keep moving
If post player goes outside, remain in lane to provide help to teammates	Look to help

- ◆ Provide information about official's signals and rules.
- ◆ **Introduce** today's signals and rules. Demonstrate and explain the following signals and rules:
  - ◆ Charging with the ball (16)
  - ◆ Carrying (10)
  - ◆ 3 seconds (11)
- ◆ Complete teacher or student demonstrations (or both).
- ◆ Check for student understanding using questions, student demonstrations, or both.
  - ◆ Q1: "Where should you be located to be considered a high/low post player?"
  - ◆ Q2: "What type of passes would you use to get the ball to a player in the low/high post?"
  - ◆ Q3: "When should you split/front your opponent?"
  - ◆ Q4: "How can you get your teammates open in the high/low post?"

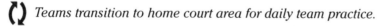 *Teams transition to home court area for daily team practice.*

Team Practice

- ◆ Team-directed practice begins (refer to **Activity Task Card 12** and **Individual** or **Team Activity Task Card Recording Sheet**).
- ◆ Teacher moves through home court area to facilitate team practice.
  - ◆ Manage learning environment.
  - ◆ Observe and assess individual and team performance.
  - ◆ Provide encouragement and instructional feedback.

Teams transition back to designated instructional area for application contest.

Application Contest

- ◆ Teacher explains and demonstrates daily contest (refer to **Application Contest 12**).
  - ◆ Identify tactical focus and related skills (refer to **Application Contest Scorecard 12**).
  - ◆ Identify contest goals.
  - ◆ Discuss procedures for scoring and refereeing.
- ◆ **Scoring:** Use nonshaded areas on **Application Contest Scorecard 12.**
- ◆ **Refereeing:** Refer to and use designated referee signals located on the Official's Pocket Reference.

Teams transition to designated contest areas to perform assigned duties.

- ◆ Teacher actively monitors individual and team performance.

 Teams transition to designated instructional area for closure.

Closure

- ◆ Teacher reviews lesson focus.
- ◆ Teacher discusses assessment of individual and team performance.
- ◆ Check for student understanding using questions and demonstrations (refer back to questions and demonstrations from the introduction).
- ◆ Allow for student questions and preview **lesson 13.**

 Teams transition to home court areas for individual and team assessment.

Individual and Team Assessment

Assessment summary
- ◆ Summarize/Complete **Application Contest Scorecard 12** (scorekeeper).
- ◆ Complete **PASE Attendance Recording Sheet** (coach).
- ◆ Complete **PASE Roles and Responsibilities Recording Sheet** (each person).
- ◆ Supervise assessment completion (coach).

 Teams organize materials and exit class from home court areas.

Offensive Post Play

Critical Features

1. Keep defender to one side using upper body on that side.
2. Defender fronting: push defender high toward foul line and cut back to basket.
3. Defender splitting: feint away and cut to opposite side of the defender toward ball.
4. Continually move to maintain position, keeping feet in front of defenders.
5. Avoid standing in lane area for more than 3 seconds at a time.

Instructional Cues

1. Deny front position
2. Push high and cut
3. Fake and roll
4. Move feet
5. 3-second rule

Description

The offensive player is considered to be in post play position when located on the edge of the lane with his or her back to the basket. The low post position is on the lane close to the basket, and the high post position is on the lane near the foul line. During effective post play the offensive post players have the responsibility of positioning themselves in front of the defensive player (low or high) in order to receive a pass and make an offensive play.

Defensive Post Play

Critical Features

1. Keep hand and foot nearest ball between offense and ball, and place opposite hand and foot between opponent and basket
2. Below foul line: deny the ball by playing behind opponent between the opponent and basket
3. Above foul line: deny ball by placing body slightly behind the opponent to ball side
4. Keep moving to maintain balance and position
5. If post player goes outside, remain in lane to provide help to teammates

Instructional Cues

1. Split defender
2. Baseline side
3. Watch back-door cut
4. Keep moving
5. Look to help

Description

During the offensive post play set, the defense must be able to deny the pass to the post player by either splitting or fronting the offensive post player. Once an offensive post player receives the ball, the defender must position him- or herself in such a way as to deny a shot or pass.

From *Sport Education Seasons* by Sean M. Bulger et al., 2007, Champaign, IL: Human Kinetics.

PASE Basketball Student Coaching Plan 12

COACHING QUOTE

"It's not necessarily the time you put in at practice; it's what you put into practice."

—Eric Lindross

Skills

- Offensive post play
- Defensive post play

Tactic

- Attacking the goal

Coaching Cues

Offensive post play		Defensive post play	
✓ Deny front position	✓ Move feet	✓ Split defender	✓ Keep moving
✓ Push high and cut	✓ 3-second rule	✓ Baseline side	✓ Look to help
✓ Fake and roll		✓ Watch back-door cut	

Keys to Success

- Focus the team on the coaching cues for the new skills.
- Check to see if teammates know when to post at the block or the elbow.
- Help teammates progress through the **Activity Task Card.**
- Make sure team moves quickly between different lesson segments.

Rules and Official's Signals

- **Charging with ball.** Review charging with the ball signal.
- **Carrying.** Review carrying signal.
- **3 seconds.** Review 3-second signal.

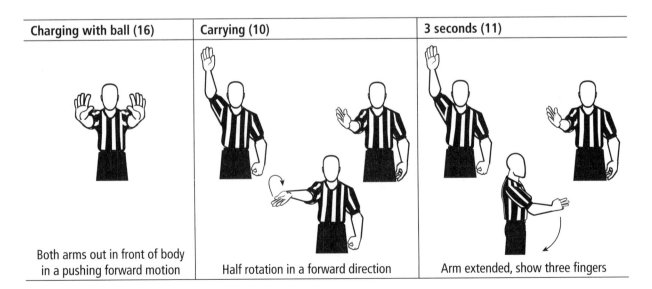

Charging with ball (16)	Carrying (10)	3 seconds (11)
Both arms out in front of body in a pushing forward motion	Half rotation in a forward direction	Arm extended, show three fingers

From *Sport Education Seasons* by Sean M. Bulger et al., 2007, Champaign, IL: Human Kinetics.

PASE Basketball Activity Task Card 12

Skills
- Offensive post play
- Defensive post play

Tactic
- Attacking the basket

Learning tasks	Self	Peer	Coach
1. Under the direction of the coach, perform the cues for today's skills two times each.			☐
2. Under the direction of the coach, perform the official's signals for today's lesson three times each.			☐
3. In pairs, without a ball, attempt to set up in the low post area and pretend to receive a pass, drop step, and shoot a layup on the coach's signal five times. Switch roles so each partner attempts the low post play five times. (Defensive player is passive and in a splitting position.) Repeat from the opposite side of the lane.		☐	
4. In pairs, without a ball, attempt to set up in the low post area and pretend to receive a pass, drop step, and shoot a layup on the coach's signal five times. Switch roles so each partner attempts the low post play five times. (Defensive player is active and in a fronting position.) Repeat from the opposite side of the lane.		☐	
5. In pairs, without a ball, attempt to set up in the high post area and pretend to receive a pass, front turn, and shoot a jump shot on the coach's signal five times. Switch roles so each partner attempts the high post play five times. (Defensive player is passive and in a splitting position.) Repeat from the opposite side of the lane.		☐	
6. In groups of three, with a ball, attempt to set up in the low post area and receive a pass, drop step, and shoot a layup on the coach's signal five times. Switch roles so each partner attempts the low post play five times. (Defensive player is passive and in a splitting position.) Repeat from the opposite side of the lane.		☐	
7. In groups of three, with a ball, attempt to set up in the low post area and receive a pass, drop step, and shoot a layup on the coach's signal five times. Switch roles so each partner attempts the low post play five times. (Defensive player is passive and in a fronting position.) Repeat from the opposite side of the lane.		☐	
8. In groups of three, with a ball, attempt to set up in the high post area and receive a pass, front turn, and shoot a jump shot on the coach's signal five times. Switch roles so each partner attempts the high post play five times. (Defensive player is passive and in a splitting position.) Repeat from the opposite side of the lane.		☐	
9. In groups of three, with a ball, attempt to set up in the high or low post area and receive a pass, drop step or front turn, and shoot a layup or jump shot on the coach's signal five times. Switch roles so each partner attempts the high post play five times. (Defensive player is active and in a splitting or fronting position.) Repeat from the opposite side of the lane. Answer the following questions and discuss what you discovered about offensive and defensive post play. (Record score only if using **Individual Activity Task Card Recording Sheet.**) • When should you play defense in fronting or splitting position? Why? • What should you do after receiving a pass in the low and high posts? Why? • What happens if you are on offense and you stay in the lane for more than 3 sec? • Can you create any plays that use screens/picks in the low and high post to get the offensive post player open to receive a pass?	#___		☐
10. Repeat #9. This time the defense earns a point for every steal. The offense earns a point for every basket scored from the low or high post position. Remember scores. (Record score only if using **Individual Activity Task Card Recording Sheet.**)	#___		☐

From *Sport Education Seasons* by Sean M. Bulger et al., 2007, Champaign, IL: Human Kinetics.

Equipment

- Two cones
- Pencils
- Boundary markers
- Whistles
- Lesson 12 Scorecard
- Officials' pinnies
- One clipboard
- Colored pinnies (teams)

Objectives

Demonstrate low and high post offensive and defensive positioning

Goals

Achieve the maximum number of successful jump shots or layups (or both) from the low or high post area in two 2-minute trials

Application Description

This is a 3 vs. 3 competition, with three offensive players and three defensive players. The offense must begin play from either cone by passing the ball to a teammate. After the ball is in play, the offense must attempt to move the ball via dribbling, passing, and screening in an attempt to create successful jump shots and layups from the low or high post areas. Following a missed shot, players attempt to secure a rebound. Once a rebound has been secured, play restarts at the cones. If the defense intercepts or deflects the ball, the offense retains possession and must restart play at either cone. The competition will last for four 2-minute trials, with possession of the ball changing on each new 2-minute trial. Substitutions enter the game at the beginning of each new 2-minute trial. Each team member must have participated during two of the four 2-minute trials. Repeat until each team has been on offense two times. The teacher should have multiple games going at the same time based on space and equipment and use a single game clock for all games.

Application Diagram

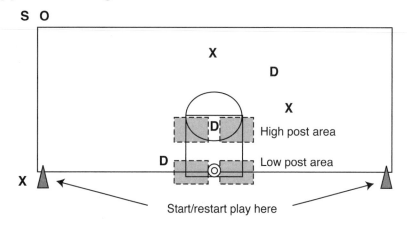

Scorekeeper's Guidelines

Provide scorekeepers with an example to fill in on their scorecard.

- 2 points per layup or jump shot that is successful from the low or high post only.
- Record scores for the offensive team after the official's signal indicating a successful layup or shot.
- Combine all team points for a total team score.

Referee's Guidelines

- No points awarded if a layup or jump shot is performed from an area other than the low or high post.
- No points if same player shoots two consecutive times.
- Demonstrate appropriate signals for violations.
- Demonstrate appropriate signals related to scoring.
- Demonstrate appropriate clock-related signals.

From *Sport Education Seasons* by Sean M. Bulger et al., 2007, Champaign, IL: Human Kinetics.

PASE Basketball Application Contest Scorecard 12

Instructions: Nonshaded areas must be filled in by scorekeeper.

☐ Home ☐ Away

| Team | | Coach | | Site | |
| Timer | | Scorekeeper | | Date | |

TEAM SCORING BY PERIODS

	1st	2nd	3rd	4th	OT

FINAL SCORE

SCORING

Player	1st trial	2nd trial	3rd trial	4th trial	OT
Practice row to be filled in by student.					

Fouls

1	2	3	4	5
1	2	3	4	5
1	2	3	4	5
1	2	3	4	5
1	2	3	4	5
1	2	3	4	5
1	2	3	4	5
1	2	3	4	5

SUMMARY

	2 FG		3 FG		FT		Steals	Reb.	Pts.
	A	M	A	M	A	M			

Totals

Team fouls										
1	2	3	4	5	6	7	8	9	10	

Alternating jump ball possessions

TEAM TIME-OUTS

	1	2	3	4	5
Away					
Home					

Running Score	1	2	3	4	5	6	7	8	9	10	11	12	13	14	15	16	17	18	19	20	21	22	23	24	25
	26	27	28	29	30	31	32	33	34	35	36	37	38	39	40	41	42	43	44	45	46	47	48	49	50
	51	52	53	54	55	56	57	58	59	60	61	62	63	64	65	66	67	68	69	70	71	72	73	74	75
	76	77	78	79	80	81	82	83	84	85	86	87	88	89	90	91	92	93	94	95	96	97	98	99	100

Coach's Signature _____

Scorekeeper's Signature _____

From Sport Education Seasons by Sean M. Bulger et al., 2007, Champaign, IL: Human Kinetics.

PASE BASKETBALL LESSON PLAN 13

Resources: Lesson Focus

- Numbered colored pinnies—six per team (also used during application contest)
- Basketballs—three to six per team (also used during application contest)
- Hula hoops—one per team (used to organize team materials)
- Stopwatches—one per team
- Pencils

Resources: Application Contest

- PASE Application Contest 13
- PASE Application Contest Scorecard 13
- PASE Official's Pocket Reference
- Two to four cones
- Boundary markers
- One clipboard
- Pencils
- Whistles
- Officials' pinnies

Instructional Materials

- PASE Attendance Recording Sheet (appendix B)
- PASE Roles and Responsibilities Assignments and Recording Sheet (appendix B)
- PASE Student Coaching Plan 13
- PASE Activity Task Card 13
- PASE Fitness Activities Sheets (appendix B)
- PASE Personal or Team Fitness Recording Sheet (appendix B)
- PASE Individual or Team Activity Task Card Recording Sheet (appendix B)
- PASE Basketball Lesson Plan 14

Instructional Focus

Skills	Tactic
• All	• Player-to-player defense

Objectives

- Develop player-to-player defense by progression through learning activities during team practice
- Review defensive footwork
- Demonstrate personal and social responsibility

Team Role Check

- Students enter gymnasium and immediately report to home court area.
- Check daily roles and associated duties from materials provided.

() *Begin team warm-up.*

Team Warm-Up

- Conduct the team warm-up simultaneously to coaches' meeting.
- Fitness trainer leads team through warm-up using the PASE Fitness Activities Sheets.
- Fitness trainer or individuals record performance on team warm-up using either the **Personal** or **Team Fitness Recording Sheet.**

Teams transition to daily review.

Coaches' Meeting

- Conduct the coaches' meeting simultaneously to team warm-up.
- All team coaches report to designated meeting area.
- Teacher provides coaches with Student Coaching Plan 13 and Activity Task Card 13.
- Teacher outlines the day's events.

Coaches transition to home court area and join warm-up.

Team Review

- Review progress of team goals from **lesson 12.** This would be found in the student/team recording sheet which the students have every lesson.
- Identify areas of need from **lesson 12.**
- Practice to improve areas of need.
- Review defensive footwork skill utilizing critical features and instructional cues from **lesson 7.**

Teams transition to designated instructional area for teacher instructions.

Teacher Instruction

- Introduce daily lesson focus and review **lesson 12.**
- Provide anticipatory set:

The purpose of today's lesson is to introduce player-to-player defense. Player-to-player defense is used to match players of similar abilities and sizes. This is a team concept, so it will be important for all members to understand their individual roles when performing this type of defensive tactic. You have already learned the main individual components of player-to-player defense, which are defensive footwork and defense on and off the ball. After learning this type of team defense, you will be better able to keep your opponents from scoring in specific game situations.

- Provide information about skills and strategies:
  - **Introduce** the following new skills and tactics for the day.
  - Review defensive footwork skill utilizing critical features and instructional cues from **lesson 7.**
  - Complete teacher or student demonstrations (or both) of this tactic:

PLAYER-TO-PLAYER DEFENSE

Critical features	Instructional cues
Determine matchup assignments	Even matchup
Pick up assignment/Apply defensive pressure according to team strategy	Pick up
Apply pressure to make offensive player uncomfortable	Apply pressure
Defender is positioned between player (ball) and basket	Stay between
Deny passes to post area	Deny entry pass

- ◆ Provide information about official's signals and rules.
- ◆ **Introduce** today's signals and rules. Demonstrate and explain the following signals and rules:
    - ◆ Double dribble (9)
    - ◆ Blocking (14)
    - ◆ Jump ball (12)
- ◆ Check for student understanding using questions, student demonstrations, or both.
    - ◆ Q1: "Why is it important to match yourself with someone with similar ability and size?"
    - ◆ Q2: "What might be the result if you did not stay with your assigned opponent?"
    - ◆ Q3: "What is the difference in defensive pressure when playing defense on and off the ball?"

() *Teams transition to home court area for daily team practice.*

Team Practice

- ◆ Team-directed practice begins (refer to **Activity Task Card 13** and **Individual** or **Team Activity Task Card Recording Sheet**).
- ◆ Teacher moves through home court area to facilitate team practice.
    - ◆ Manage learning environment.
    - ◆ Observe and assess individual and team performance.
    - ◆ Provide encouragement and instructional feedback.

() *Teams transition back to designated instructional area for application contest.*

Application Contest

- ◆ Teacher explains and demonstrates daily contest (refer to **Application Contest 13**).
    - ◆ Identify tactical focus and related skills (refer to **Application Contest Scorecard 13**).
    - ◆ Identify contest goals.
    - ◆ Discuss procedures for scoring and refereeing.
- ◆ **Scoring:** Use nonshaded areas on **Application Contest Scorecard 13.**
- ◆ **Refereeing:** Refer to and use designated referee signals located on the Official's Pocket Reference.

() *Teams transition to designated contest areas to perform assigned duties.*

- ◆ Teacher actively monitors individual and team performance.

() *Teams transition to designated instructional area for closure.*

Closure

- ◆ Teacher reviews lesson focus.
- ◆ Teacher discusses assessment of individual and team performance.
- ◆ Check for student understanding using questions and demonstrations (refer back to questions and demonstrations from the introduction).
- ◆ Allow for student questions and preview **lesson 14.**

() *Teams transition to home court areas for individual and team assessment.*

Individual and Team Assessment

- ◆ Assessment summary
  - ◆ Summarize/Complete **Application Contest Scorecard 13** (scorekeeper).
  - ◆ Complete **PASE Attendance Recording Sheet** (coach).
  - ◆ Complete **PASE Roles and Responsibilities Recording Sheet** (each person).
  - ◆ Supervise assessment completion (coach).
- ◆ Collect the following:
  - ◆ **PASE Reflective Journal** (each person)

 Teams organize materials and exit class from home court areas.

Player-to-Player Defense

Critical Features

1. Determine matchup assignments
2. Pick up assignment/Apply defensive pressure according to team strategy
3. Apply pressure to make offensive player uncomfortable
4. Defender is positioned between player (ball) and basket
5. Deny passes to post area

Instructional Cues

1. Even matchup
2. Pick up
3. Apply pressure
4. Stay between
5. Deny entry pass

Description

Depending on the abilities of a team, a strategy for defending an offense is to match up one of your players with one of the other team's players. It is each defender's responsibility to follow and guard his or her assigned player with and without the ball.

From *Sport Education Seasons* by Sean M. Bulger et al., 2007, Champaign, IL: Human Kinetics.

PASE Basketball Student Coaching Plan 13

Skills

- Review all.

Tactic

- Player-to-player defense

Coaching Cues

Player-to-player defense
✓ Even matchup
✓ Pick up
✓ Apply pressure
✓ Deny entry pass
✓ Stay between

Keys to Success

- Focus the team on the coaching cues for the new skills.
- Check to see if teammates know how much pressure to apply when guarding their opponent.
- Help teammates progress through the **Activity Task Card.**
- Make sure team moves quickly between different lesson segments.

Rules and Official's Signals

- **Double dribble.** Review double-dribble signal.
- **Blocking.** Review blocking signal.
- **Jump ball.** Review jump ball signal.

Double dribble (9)	Blocking (14)	Jump ball (12)
Patting motion with hands	Both hands on hips	Thumbs up

From *Sport Education Seasons* by Sean M. Bulger et al., 2007, Champaign, IL: Human Kinetics.

PASE Basketball Activity Task Card 13

Skill

- Defensive footwork

Tactic

- Player-to-player defense

Learning tasks	Self	Peer	Coach
1. Under the direction of the coach, perform the cues for today's skills five times each.			☐
2. Under the direction of the coach, perform the official's signals for today's lesson five times each.			☐
3. Following the coach's signal, slide, alternating directions to the left, right, forward, and backward for 1 min.			☐
4. Mirror a partner by sliding, alternating directions to the left, right, forward, and backward for 1 min.		☐	
5. 1-on-1: One partner will dribble the ball while the defensive partner plays defense on the ball for 30 sec. Switch roles and repeat.		☐	
6. Repeat #5. This time 1 point is awarded to the offensive player if the defensive player commits an illegal use of hands foul. If the defense steals the ball without fouling, they earn 1 point. (Record score only if using **Individual Activity Task Card Recording Sheet.**)	#___		☐
7. 2-on-2: Two offensive players will play keep-away using all the previously learned passes, cuts, and dribbling skills while the other two players engage in player-to-player defense on and off the ball. Any remaining players will officiate the game and call illegal-use-of-hands fouls. Any foul results in 1 point for the offense, and a steal results in 1 point for the defense. Play for 1 min and rotate roles among offense, defense, and officials. (Record score only if using **Individual Activity Task Card Recording Sheet.**) • What type of pressure should you apply close to the basket? Why? • What type of pressure should you apply far from the basket? Why? • What is the first thing your team should do when preparing to use player-to-player defense?	#___		☐

From *Sport Education Seasons* by Sean M. Bulger et al., 2007, Champaign, IL: Human Kinetics.

Equipment

- Two cones
- Pencils
- Boundary markers
- Whistles
- Lesson 13 Scorecard
- Officials' pinnies
- One clipboard
- Colored pinnies (teams)

Objectives

Demonstrate player-to-player defense

Goals

Achieve the maximum number of successful jump shots or layups (or both) in two 2-minute trials

Application Description

This is a 4 vs. 4 competition, with four offensive players and four defensive players. The defense must play person-to-person defense. The offense must begin play from the cone by either passing the ball to a teammate or dribbling into the playing area. The player inbounding the ball cannot be guarded until he or she has passed the ball to a teammate or dribbled across the safety zone line. After the ball is in play, the offense must attempt to move the ball via dribbling, passing, and screening in an attempt to create successful jump shots and layups. Play is continuous even after missed shots. Play is restarted at the cone for one of the following reasons only: (1) a successful shot, (2) a secured defensive rebound, (3) a defensive steal, (4) ball knocked out of bounds, (5) a defensive foul, or (6) an offensive violation. The competition will last for four 2-minute trials, with possession of the ball changing on each new 2-minute trial. The teacher will stop play once during each 2-minute trial, having the students "freeze" in place on the signal. The teacher stops play to check for appropriate person-to-person defensive positioning. If all defensive players are within one arm's length of their assigned opponent, then the defense earns 2 points. Substitutions enter the game at the beginning of each new 2-minute trial. Each team member must have participated during two of the four 2-minute trials. Repeat until each team has been on offense two times. The teacher should have multiple games going at the same time based on space and equipment and use a single game clock for all games.

Application Diagram

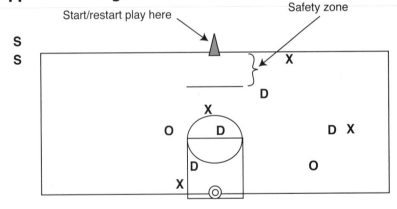

Scorekeeper's Guidelines

Provide scorekeepers with an example to fill in on their scorecard.

- 2 points per jump shot or layup that is successful.
- 1 point per defensive foul (point awarded to offense).
- 2 points per appropriate defensive positioning on the "freeze" signal (points awarded to defense).
- Record scores for the offensive team after the official's signal indicating a successful shot or defensive foul.
- Combine all team points for a total team score.

Referee's Guidelines

- No points awarded if a jump shot is performed from the 3-point area.
- No points if same player shoots two consecutive times.
- Demonstrate appropriate signals for violations and fouls.
- Demonstrate appropriate signals related to scoring.
- Demonstrate appropriate clock-related signals.

From *Sport Education Seasons* by Sean M. Bulger et al., 2007, Champaign, IL: Human Kinetics.

PASE Basketball Application Contest Scorecard 13

Instructions: Nonshaded areas must be filled in by scorekeeper.

☐ Home ☐ Away

| Team | Coach | Site | FINAL SCORE |
| Timer | Scorekeeper | Date | |

TEAM SCORING BY PERIODS

	1st	2nd	3rd	4th	OT

SCORING

	Player	1st trial	2nd trial	3rd trial	4th trial	OT
Fouls 1 2 3 4 5	Practice row to be filled in by student.					
1 2 3 4 5						
1 2 3 4 5						
1 2 3 4 5						
1 2 3 4 5						
1 2 3 4 5						
1 2 3 4 5						
1 2 3 4 5						

SUMMARY

	2 FG		3 FG		FT		Steals	Reb.	Pts.
	A	M	A	M	A	M			

Totals

Team fouls
1	2	3	4	5	6	7	8	9	10

TEAM TIME-OUTS

1		2		3		4	5
Away	Home	Home	Away	Away	Home	Home	Home

Alternating jump ball possessions

| Home | Away | Home | Away | Away | Home | Home | Away | Home | Home | | | | | | |

Running Score

1	2	3	4	5	6	7	8	9	10	11	12	13	14	15	16	17	18	19	20	21	22	23	24	25
26	27	28	29	30	31	32	33	34	35	36	37	38	39	40	41	42	43	44	45	46	47	48	49	50
51	52	53	54	55	56	57	58	59	60	61	62	63	64	65	66	67	68	69	70	71	72	73	74	75
76	77	78	79	80	81	82	83	84	85	86	87	88	89	90	91	92	93	94	95	96	97	98	99	100

Coach's Signature _____

Scorekeeper's Signature _____

From Sport Education Seasons by Sean M. Bulger et al., 2007, Champaign, IL: Human Kinetics.

PASE BASKETBALL LESSON PLAN 14

Resources: Lesson Focus

- Numbered colored pinnies—six per team (also used during application contest)
- Basketballs—three to six per team (also used during application contest)
- Hula hoops—one per team (used to organize team materials)
- Stopwatches—one per team
- Pencils

Resources: Application Contest

- PASE Application Contest 14
- PASE Application Contest Scorecard 14
- PASE Official's Pocket Reference
- Two to four cones
- Boundary markers
- One clipboard
- Pencils
- Whistles
- Officials' pinnies

Instructional Materials

- PASE Attendance Recording Sheet (appendix B)
- PASE Roles and Responsibilities Assignments and Recording Sheet (appendix B)
- PASE Student Coaching Plan 14
- PASE Activity Task Card 14
- PASE Fitness Activities Sheets (appendix B)
- PASE Personal or Team Fitness Recording Sheet (appendix B)
- PASE Individual or Team Activity Task Card Recording Sheet (appendix B)
- PASE Basketball Lesson Plan 15

Instructional Focus

Skills
- Review all

Tactic
- Zone defense

Objectives

- Develop team zone defense by progression through learning activities during team practice
- Utilize previously learned skills and tactics during an application contest
- Demonstrate personal and social responsibility

Team Role Check

- Students enter gymnasium and immediately report to home court area.
- Check daily roles and associated duties from materials provided.

() *Begin team warm-up.*

Team Warm-Up

- Conduct the team warm-up simultaneously to coaches' meeting.
- Fitness trainer leads team through warm-up using the PASE Fitness Activities Sheets.
- Fitness trainer or individuals record performance on team warm-up using either the **Personal** or **Team Fitness Recording Sheet.**

() *Teams transition to daily review.*

Coaches' Meeting

- ◆ Conduct the coaches' meeting simultaneously to team warm-up.
- ◆ All team coaches report to designated meeting area.
- ◆ Teacher provides coaches with Student Coaching Plan 14 and Activity Task Card 14.
- ◆ Teacher outlines the day's events.

 *Coaches transition to home court area and join warm-up.*

Team Review

- ◆ Review progress of team goals from **lesson 13.** This would be found in the student/team recording sheet which the students have every lesson.
- ◆ Identify areas of need from **lesson 13.**
- ◆ Practice to improve areas of need.

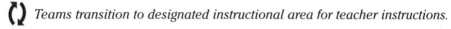 *Teams transition to designated instructional area for teacher instructions.*

Teacher Instruction

- ◆ Introduce daily lesson focus and review **lesson 13.**
- ◆ Provide anticipatory set:

The purpose of today's lesson is to introduce the tactic of team zone defense. In zone defenses you defend a space or area of the court and guard any offensive player who enters that area. The following list represents some of the strengths of good team zone defenses: limits inside shots, protects the basket, creates better rebounding position, and increases opportunities for quick transition from defense to offense. However, zone defense is not easy to master, and lots of practice is required in order to counter the effects of poor zone defense. The offense can gain the following advantages when poor zone defense is played: unchallenged outside shots, easy penetration in the lane, good offensive rebounding position. After learning the team zone defenses introduced today, you will be able to better defend against your opponents in specific game situations.

- ◆ Provide information about skills and strategies.
- ◆ **Introduce** the following new tactic for the day.
- ◆ Complete teacher or student demonstrations (or both) of this tactic:

ZONE DEFENSE

Critical features	Instructional cues
Determine space assignments	Know your zone
Defend an area rather than a player	Defend your space
Defender shifts zone placement to guard passing lanes	Shadow ball, cut off passing lanes
Keep hands up and feet moving at all times	Hands up, move
When zone is empty, move to assist teammate in adjacent zone	Help

- ◆ Provide information about official's signals and rules.
- ◆ **Introduce** today's signals and rules. Demonstrate and explain the following signals and rules:
    - ◆ Substitution (6)
    - ◆ Time-out (7)
    - ◆ Jump ball (12)

- ◆ Check for student understanding using questions, student demonstrations, or both.
  - ◆ Q1: "What are two advantages of team zone defense?"
  - ◆ Q2: "When would it be most appropriate to use team zone defense?"
  - ◆ Q3: "What are the major differences between team zone and player-to-player defenses?"

Teams transition to home court area for daily team practice.

Team Practice

- ◆ Team-directed practice begins (refer to **Activity Task Card 14**).
- ◆ Teacher moves through home court area to facilitate team practice.
  - ◆ Manage learning environment.
  - ◆ Observe and assess individual and team performance.
  - ◆ Provide encouragement and instructional feedback.

Teams transition back to designated instructional area for application contest.

Application Contest

- ◆ Teacher explains and demonstrates daily contest (refer to **Application Contest 14** and **Individual** or **Team Activity Task Card Recording Sheet**).
  - ◆ Identify tactical focus and related skills (refer to **Application Contest Scorecard 14**).
  - ◆ Identify contest goals.
  - ◆ Discuss procedures for scoring and refereeing.
- ◆ **Scoring:** Use nonshaded areas on **Application Contest Scorecard 14.**
- ◆ **Refereeing:** Refer to and use designated referee signals located on the Official's Pocket Reference.

Teams transition to designated contest areas to perform assigned duties.

- ◆ Teacher actively monitors individual and team performance.

Teams transition to designated instructional area for closure.

Closure

- ◆ Teacher reviews lesson focus.
- ◆ Teacher discusses assessment of individual and team performance.
- ◆ Check for student understanding using questions and demonstrations (refer back to questions and demonstrations from the introduction).
- ◆ Allow for student questions and preview **lesson 15.**

Teams transition to home court areas for individual and team assessment.

Individual and Team Assessment

Assessment summary

- ◆ Summarize/Complete **Application Contest Scorecard 14** (scorekeeper).
- ◆ Complete **PASE Attendance Recording Sheet** (coach).
- ◆ Complete **PASE Roles and Responsibilities Recording Sheet** (each person).
- ◆ Supervise assessment completion (coach).

Teams organize materials and exit class from home court areas.

Zone Defense

Critical Features

1. Determine space assignments
2. Defend an area rather than a player
3. Defender shifts zone placement to guard passing lanes
4. Keep hands up and feet moving at all times
5. When zone is empty, move to assist teammate in adjacent zone

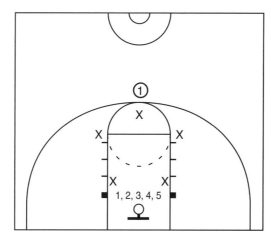

Instructional Cues

1. Know your zone
2. Defend your space
3. Shadow ball, cut off passing lanes
4. Hands up, move
5. Help

Description

The intent of this strategy is to concentrate primarily on the offensive player with the ball. Each defensive player guards an area as opposed to guarding a particular person. The purpose of this defensive set is to force opponents into taking longer, more difficult shots because of the defense's ability to protect the lane and basket. It also provides the defense with better rebounding position and perhaps more opportunity to begin the transition from defense to offense from a fast break. Various zone defenses are the 1-3-1, 1-2-2, 2-3, and 2-1-2.

From *Sport Education Seasons* by Sean M. Bulger et al., 2007, Champaign, IL: Human Kinetics.

PASE Basketball Student Coaching Plan 14

COACHING QUOTE

"The way a team plays as a whole determines its success."

—*Babe Ruth*

Skills
- Review all.

Tactic
- Zone defense

Coaching Cues

Zone defense
✓ Know your zone
✓ Defend your space
✓ Shadow ball, cut off passing lanes
✓ Hands up, move
✓ Help

Keys to Success
- Focus the team on the coaching cues for the new skills.
- Check to see if teammates know when to provide defensive support by repositioning.
- Help teammates progress through the **Activity Task Card.**
- Make sure team moves quickly between different lesson segments.

Rules and Official's Signals
- **Substitution.** Replacing player(s) on the court with players from the bench. May occur during a dead ball or a time-out.
- **Time-out.** A designated time that a coach or player may take to make changes in the game. The clock is stopped during this period of time.
- **Jump ball.** Review jump ball signal.

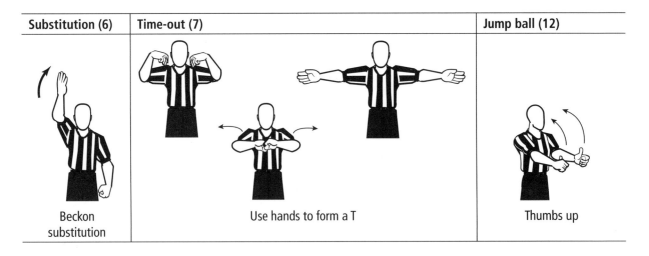

Substitution (6)	Time-out (7)	Jump ball (12)
Beckon substitution	Use hands to form a T	Thumbs up

From *Sport Education Seasons* by Sean M. Bulger et al., 2007, Champaign, IL: Human Kinetics.

PASE Basketball Activity Task Card 14

Skill

- Defensive footwork

Tactic

- Zone defense

Learning tasks	Self	Peer	Coach
1. Under the direction of the coach, perform the cues for today's skills two times each.			☐
2. Under the direction of the coach, perform the official's signals for today's lesson three times each.		.	☐
3. Following the coach's signal, slide, alternating directions to the left, right, forward, and backward for 30 sec.			☐
Complete tasks 4-10 using a 2-2 zone defensive set (see following diagram).			
4. Assign zones (the space that players are responsible for defending) to each member of your team.			☐
5. Locate your zone.	☐		
6. Walk the perimeter of your zone.	☐		
7. Following the coach's signal, slide, alternating directions to the left, right, forward, and backward in your zone for 30 sec.			☐
8. Under the direction of the coach, two offensive players will quickly pass and dribble the ball around the perimeter (3-point line). The defense should shift the zone with each movement of the ball. On every fifth pass, everyone must freeze in order to check for appropriate zone positioning. Rotate players from offense to defense and rotate defensive players to a new zone area after every fifth pass. Continue task until each person has been on offense. (Record score only if using **Individual Activity Task Card Recording Sheet**.)	#___		☐
9. Repeat #8. This time the offense is trying to penetrate the zone off of the dribble or with a pass. Each time the offense penetrates the zone and has control of the ball while in the lane, the offense scores 1 point. If the defense steals the ball without fouling, they earn 1 point. Restart play after each point scored. Rotate players from offense to defense and rotate defensive players to a new zone area after every 3 points. Continue task until each person has been on offense. (Record score only if using **Individual Activity Task Card Recording Sheet**.)	#___		☐
10. Repeat #9. This time the offense can shoot. The defense tries to force the offense to take long shots and limit their short-shot opportunities. After the shot the defense locates the offensive player in his or her zone, blocks him or her out, gets the rebound, and makes an outlet pass. For each successful shot the offense earns 1 point. For each successful rebound and outlet pass sequence the defense earns 1 point. Rotate players from offense to defense and rotate defensive players to a new zone area after every 3 points. Continue task until each person has been on offense. (Record score only if using **Individual Activity Task Card Recording Sheet**.)	#___		☐

(continued)

From *Sport Education Seasons* by Sean M. Bulger et al., 2007, Champaign, IL: Human Kinetics.

Learning tasks	Self	Peer	Coach
Repeat tasks 4-10 using a 1-2-1 zone defensive set (see following diagram).			
11. Answer the following questions as you prepare for today's application contest. • Which zone defensive set will you use in today's application contest? Why? • What are the advantages of a zone defense as opposed to a person-to-person defense? • How do you reduce the chance that the offense will make an entry pass or dribble into the lane when you are playing a zone defense?			☐

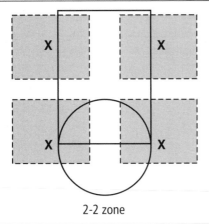

2-2 zone

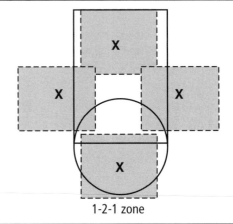

1-2-1 zone

Equipment

- Two cones
- Pencils
- Boundary markers
- Whistles
- Lesson 14 Scorecard
- Officials' pinnies
- One clipboard
- Colored pinnies (teams)

Objectives

Demonstrate zone defense

Goals

Achieve the maximum number of successful jump shots or layups (or both) in two 2-minute trials

Application Description

This is a 4 vs. 4 competition, with four offensive players and four defensive players. The defense must play either a 2-2 or a 1-2-1 zone defensive set. The offense must begin play from the cone by either passing the ball to a teammate or dribbling into the playing area. The player inbounding the ball cannot be guarded until he or she has passed the ball to a teammate or dribbled across the safety zone line. After the ball is in play, the offense must attempt to move the ball via dribbling, passing, and screening in an attempt to create successful jump shots and layups. Play is continuous even after missed shots. Play is restarted at the cone for one of the following reasons only: (1) a successful shot attempt, (2) a secured defensive rebound, (3) a defensive steal, (4) ball knocked out of bounds, (5) a defensive foul, or (6) an offensive violation. The competition will last for four 2-minute trials, with possession of the ball changing on each new 2-minute trial. The teacher will stop play once during each 2-minute trial, having the students "freeze" in place on the signal. The teacher stops play to check for appropriate zone defensive positioning. If all defensive players are within their assigned zones, then the defense earns 2 points. Substitutions enter the game at the beginning of each new 2-minute trial. Each team member must have participated during two of the four 2-minute trials. Repeat until each team has been on offense two times. The teacher should have multiple games going at the same time based on space and equipment and use a single game clock for all games.

Application Diagram

Start/restart play here

Key

X = Offensive players

D = Defender

O = Official

S = Scorekeeper

▲ = Cones

Scorekeeper's Guidelines

Provide scorekeepers with an example to fill in on their scorecard.

- 2 points per jump shot or layup that is successful.
- 1 point per defensive foul (point awarded to offense).
- 2 points per appropriate zone defensive positioning (points awarded to defense).
- Record scores for the offensive team after the official's signal indicating a successful shot or defensive foul.
- Combine all team points for a total team score.

Referee's Guidelines

- No points awarded if a jump shot is performed from the 3-point area.
- No points if same player shoots two consecutive times.
- Demonstrate appropriate signals for violations and fouls.
- Demonstrate appropriate signals related to scoring.
- Demonstrate appropriate clock-related signals.

From *Sport Education Seasons* by Sean M. Bulger et al., 2007, Champaign, IL: Human Kinetics.

PASE Basketball Application Contest Scorecard 14

Instructions: Nonshaded areas must be filled in by scorekeeper.

☐ Home ☐ Away

| Team | Coach | Site | FINAL SCORE |
| Timer | Scorekeeper | Date | |

TEAM SCORING BY PERIODS

	1st	2nd	3rd	4th	OT
Home					

SCORING

Player	1st trial	2nd trial	3rd trial	4th trial	OT
Practice row to be filled in by student.					

SUMMARY

Player	2 FG A	2 FG M	3 FG A	3 FG M	FT A	FT M	Steals	Reb.	Pts.

Fouls

1	2	3	4	5
1	2	3	4	5
1	2	3	4	5
1	2	3	4	5
1	2	3	4	5
1	2	3	4	5
1	2	3	4	5
1	2	3	4	5

Totals

Team fouls

1	2	3	4	5	6	7	8	9	10

Alternating jump ball possessions

TEAM TIME-OUTS

1	2	3	4	5
Away	Home	Away	Home	Away	Home	Away	Home	Home

Running Score

1	2	3	4	5	6	7	8	9	10	11	12	13	14	15	16	17	18	19	20	21	22	23	24	25
26	27	28	29	30	31	32	33	34	35	36	37	38	39	40	41	42	43	44	45	46	47	48	49	50
51	52	53	54	55	56	57	58	59	60	61	62	63	64	65	66	67	68	69	70	71	72	73	74	75
76	77	78	79	80	81	82	83	84	85	86	87	88	89	90	91	92	93	94	95	96	97	98	99	100

Coach's Signature _____

Scorekeeper's Signature _____

From *Sport Education Seasons* by Sean M. Bulger et al., 2007, Champaign, IL: Human Kinetics.

PASE BASKETBALL LESSON PLAN 15

Resources: Lesson Focus

- Numbered colored pinnies—six per team (also used during application contest)
- Basketballs—three to six per team (also used during application contest)
- Hula hoops—one per team (used to organize team materials)
- Stopwatches—one per team
- Pencils

Resources: Application Contest

- PASE Application Contest 15
- PASE Application Contest Scorecard 15
- PASE Official's Pocket Reference
- Two to four cones
- Boundary markers
- One clipboard
- Pencils
- Whistles
- Officials' pinnies

Instructional Materials

- PASE IRL Rubric and Recording Sheet (appendix B)
- PASE Attendance Recording Sheet (appendix B)
- PASE Roles and Responsibilities Assignments and Recording Sheet (appendix B)
- PASE Student Coaching Plans 3-5, 7-9, and 11-14
- PASE Activity Task Cards 3-5, 7-9, and 11-14
- PASE Fitness Activities Sheets (appendix B)
- PASE Personal or Team Fitness Recording Sheet (appendix B)
- Team Goal-Setting Sheet (appendix C)
- PASE Basketball Lesson Plan 16
- Knowledge Quiz 2
- PASE Basketball Season Tournament Role Assignments (appendix D)
- PASE Outside-of-Class Physical Activity Participation Log (appendix B)
- Students should have access to task cards and coaching plans for all previous lessons.

Instructional Focus

Skills
- Review skills taught to date.

Tactics
- Review tactics taught to date.

Objectives

- Further develop basketball skills and tactics by progressing through learning activities from previous lessons not yet completed during team practice
- Demonstrate personal and social responsibility

Team Role Check

- Students enter gymnasium and immediately report to home court area.
- Check daily roles and associated duties from materials provided.

↻ *Begin team warm-up.*

Team Warm-Up

- ◆ Conduct the team warm-up simultaneously to coaches' meeting.
- ◆ Fitness trainer leads team through warm-up using the PASE Fitness Activities Sheets.
- ◆ Fitness trainer or individuals record performance on team warm-up using either the **Personal** or **Team Fitness Recording Sheet.**

( ) *Teams transition to daily review.*

Coaches' Meeting

- ◆ Conduct the coaches' meeting simultaneously to team warm-up.
- ◆ All team coaches report to designated meeting area.
- ◆ Teacher provides coaches with choice of Student Coaching Plans 3-5, 7-9, and 11-14 and Activity Task Cards 3-5, 7-9, and 11-14.
- ◆ Teacher outlines the day's events.

( ) *Coaches transition to home court area and join warm-up.*

Team Review

- ◆ Review progress of team goals from **lessons 3-14.** This would be found in the student/team recording sheet which the students have every lesson.
- ◆ Identify areas of need from **lessons 3-14.**
- ◆ Record goals on **Team Goal-Setting Sheet.**
- ◆ Prepare to practice in identified areas during team practice (utilize task cards and coaching plans from previous lessons).

( ) *Teams transition to designated instructional area for teacher instructions.*

Teacher Instruction

- ◆ Introduce daily lesson focus and review **lessons 3-14.**
- ◆ Provide anticipatory set:

Today is the third of three review lessons. The purpose of today's lesson is to review the skills and tactics that we have learned and practiced so far. You will have the opportunity to select and practice skills and tactics that your team needs the most work on. Each of these skills and tactics is important and should be mastered by all of your team members in order to improve your chances of being successful in the upcoming round robin and the postseason double elimination tournaments.

- ◆ Check for student understanding of previously learned skills and tactics by using questions, student demonstrations, or both.
  - ◆ Q1: "What is a common method for moving the ball as an individual?"
  - ◆ Q2: "What are the four passes learned so far? When should each be used?"
  - ◆ Q3: "What are two ways that you can create space when you don't have the ball?"
  - ◆ Q4: "What three moves can you make from the triple-threat position?"
  - ◆ Q5: "What are three types of shots that we have learned?"
  - ◆ Q6: "What are two offensive tactics used for scoring with a layup?"
  - ◆ Q7: "What is the difference between defense on and off the ball?"
  - ◆ Q8: "What is the difference between offensive and defensive rebounding?"
  - ◆ Q9: "What is the difference between offensive and defensive post play?"
  - ◆ Q10: "What is the difference between player-to-player and zone defenses?"
- ◆ Provide any additional important information about previously learned skills and tactics.

◆ Check for student understanding of previously learned official's signals by using questions, student demonstrations, gamelike scenarios, or some combination of these.

  ◆ 1-, 2-, and 3-point scoring (1, 2, 3)
  ◆ Charging with the ball (16)
  ◆ 3 seconds in the lane (11)
  ◆ Blocking (14)
  ◆ Substitution (6)
  ◆ Traveling (8)
  ◆ Pushing without the ball (15)
  ◆ Time-out (7)
  ◆ Double dribble (9)
  ◆ Illegal use of hands (13)
  ◆ Stop clock (4)
  ◆ Carrying (10)
  ◆ Jump ball (12)
  ◆ Unsportspersonlike (17)
  ◆ Stop clock for a foul (5)

↻ *Teams transition to home court area for daily team practice.*

Team Practice

◆ Complete **Knowledge Quiz 2** (refer to **Knowledge Quiz 2;** be sure to cover the answer key before making copies for students).

◆ Team-directed practice begins (refer to **Activity Task Cards 3-5, 7-9,** and **11-14**).

◆ Teacher moves through home court area to facilitate team practice.

  ◆ Manage learning environment.
  ◆ Observe and assess individual and team performance.
  ◆ Provide encouragement and instructional feedback.

↻ *Teams transition back to designated instructional area for application contest.*

Application Contest

◆ Teacher explains and demonstrates daily contest (refer to **Application Contest 15**).

  ◆ Identify tactical focus and related skills (refer to **Application Contest Scorecard 15**).
  ◆ Identify contest goals.
  ◆ Discuss procedures for scoring and refereeing.

◆ **Scoring:** Use nonshaded areas on **Application Contest Scorecard 15.**

◆ **Refereeing:** Refer to and use designated referee signals located on the Official's Pocket Reference.

↻ *Teams transition to designated contest areas to perform assigned duties.*

◆ Teacher actively monitors individual and team performance.

↻ *Teams transition to designated instructional area for closure.*

Closure

◆ Teacher reviews lesson focus.

◆ Teacher discusses assessment of individual and team performance.

- ◆ Check for student understanding using questions and demonstrations (refer back to questions and demonstrations from the introduction).
- ◆ Allow for student questions and preview **lesson 16.**

Teams transition to home court areas for individual and team assessment.

Individual and Team Assessment

- ◆ Assessment summary
    - ◆ Complete **PASE IRL Recording Sheet** (each person).
    - ◆ Summarize/Complete **Application Contest Scorecard 15** (scorekeeper).
    - ◆ Complete **PASE Attendance Recording Sheet** (coach).
    - ◆ Complete **PASE Roles and Responsibilities Recording Sheet** (each person).
    - ◆ Complete **PASE Basketball Season Tournament Role Assignments.**
    - ◆ Supervise assessment completion (coach).
- ◆ Collect the following:
    - ◆ **PASE Outside-of-Class Physical Activity Participation Log** (each person)

Teams organize materials and exit class from home court areas.

Equipment

- Two cones
- Pencils
- Boundary markers
- Whistles
- Lesson 15 Scorecard
- Officials' pinnies
- One clipboard
- Colored pinnies (teams)

Objectives

Demonstrate offensive and defensive skills and tactics

Goals

Achieve the maximum number of successful jump shots or layups (or both) in two 3-minute trials

Application Description

This is a 4 vs. 4 competition, with four offensive players and four defensive players. The defense must play a 2-2 zone, a 1-2-1 zone, or person-to-person defense. The offense must begin play from the cone by either passing the ball to a teammate or dribbling into the playing area. The player inbounding the ball cannot be guarded until he or she has passed the ball to a teammate or dribbled across the safety zone line. After the ball is in play, the offense must attempt to move the ball via dribbling, passing, and screening in an attempt to create successful jump shots and layups. Play is continuous even after missed shots. Play is restarted at the cone for one of the following reasons only: (1) a successful shot attempt, (2) a secured defensive rebound, (3) a defensive steal, (4) ball knocked out of bounds, (5) a defensive foul, or (6) an offensive violation. The competition will last for four 3-minute trials with possession of the ball changing on each new 3-minute trial. Substitutions enter the game at the beginning of each new 3-minute trial. Each team member must have participated during two of the four 3-minute trials. Repeat until each team has been on offense two times. The teacher should have multiple games going at the same time based on space and equipment and use a single game clock for all games.

Application Diagram

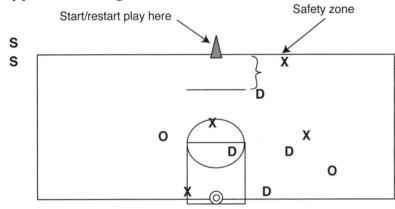

Example: 1–2–1 zone defense

Scorekeeper's Guidelines

Provide scorekeepers with an example to fill in on their scorecard.

- 2 points per jump shot or layup that is successful.
- 1 point per defensive foul (point awarded to offense).
- Record scores for the offensive team after the official's signal indicating a successful shot or defensive foul.
- Combine all team points for a total team score.

Referee's Guidelines

- No points awarded if a jump shot is performed from the 3-point area.
- No points if same player shoots two consecutive times.
- Demonstrate appropriate signals for violations and fouls.
- Demonstrate appropriate signals related to scoring.
- Demonstrate appropriate clock-related signals.

From *Sport Education Seasons* by Sean M. Bulger et al., 2007, Champaign, IL: Human Kinetics.

PASE Basketball Application Contest Scorecard 15

Instructions: Nonshaded areas must be filled in by scorekeeper.

☐ Home ☐ Away

Team		Coach		Site	
Timer		Scorekeeper		Date	

FINAL SCORE

TEAM SCORING BY PERIODS

	1st	2nd	3rd	4th	OT

SCORING

Player	1st trial	2nd trial	3rd trial	4th trial	OT
Practice row to be filled in by student.					

Fouls: 1 2 3 4 5 (per player row)

SUMMARY

	2 FG		3 FG		FT		Steals	Reb.	Pts.
	A	M	A	M	A	M			

Totals

Team fouls

1	2	3	4	5	6	7	8	9	10

TEAM TIME-OUTS

	1	2	3	4	5
	Away	Home	Away	Home	Home

Alternating jump ball possessions

Home	Away	Home	Away	Home	Home	Away	Home	Away	Home

Running Score

1	2	3	4	5	6	7	8	9	10	11	12	13	14	15	16	17	18	19	20	21	22	23	24	25
26	27	28	29	30	31	32	33	34	35	36	37	38	39	40	41	42	43	44	45	46	47	48	49	50
51	52	53	54	55	56	57	58	59	60	61	62	63	64	65	66	67	68	69	70	71	72	73	74	75
76	77	78	79	80	81	82	83	84	85	86	87	88	89	90	91	92	93	94	95	96	97	98	99	100

Coach's Signature _____   Scorekeeper's Signature _____

From Sport Education Seasons by Sean M. Bulger et al., 2007, Champaign, IL: Human Kinetics.

Name _____ Date _____

Instructions: Please answer the following multiple-choice questions by placing your answers in the blank to the left of the question.

___ 1. What is the major strength of a player-to-player defense?

    a. It increases fast breaks.

    b. It is effective against screens.

    c. It tires out opponents by spreading their offense.

    d. It matches opponents as to ability, speed, or size or a combination of these.

___ 2. What is the main point that distinguishes a zone defense from a player-to-player defense?

    a. The zone defense is more effective against slow players.

    b. The zone defense requires a player to guard an area.

    c. The player-to-player defense requires running with an opponent.

    d. The player-to-player defense is more difficult to learn.

___ 3. What is the best pass to move the ball around a zone defense?

    a. sidearm pass

    b. overhead pass

    c. baseball pass

    d. bounce pass

___ 4. What is a 3-second violation?

    a. An offensive player is guarded closely for 3 seconds.

    b. A team is 3 seconds late coming from the huddle after a time-out.

    c. An offensive player stays inside the free throw lane more than 3 seconds without the ball.

    d. A defensive player stays inside the free throw lane for 3 seconds.

___ 5. When is a back-door cutting action generally used?

    a. when you are being overplayed in a player-to-player defense

    b. against a 2-3 zone defense

    c. when facing a sagging player-to-player defense

    d. against any defense

___ 6. What is the key to successful rebounding?

    a. jumping

    b. arms and hand position

    c. not fouling

    d. positioning

___ 7. What play by the offensive team would move them rapidly from the back court to the front court in an attempt to gain an offensive advantage?

    a. fast break

    b. bounce pass

    c. full-court press

    d. give and go

(continued)

From *Sport Education Seasons* by Sean M. Bulger et al., 2007, Champaign, IL: Human Kinetics.

___ 8. A foul is committed against a player who is in the act of shooting. In spite of the foul the player makes the basket. Does the shot count and are any free throws awarded?

    a. No, one free throw is awarded.

    b. Yes, no free throw is awarded.

    c. Yes, one free throw is awarded.

    d. No, two free throws are awarded.

___ 9. The following official's signal represents what?

    a. unsportspersonlike

    b. pushing

    c. carrying

    d. 3 seconds

___10. Which diagram shows a 2-1-2 zone defense?

a. 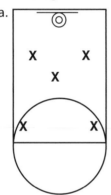 b. 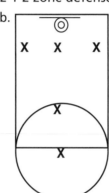 c. 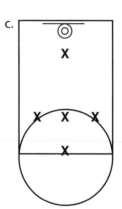 d.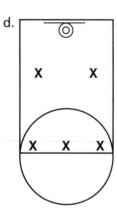

PASE BASKETBALL KNOWLEDGE QUIZ 2 KEY

1. d	6. d
2. b	7. a
3. b	8. c
4. c	9. a
5. a	10. a

From *Sport Education Seasons* by Sean M. Bulger et al., 2007, Champaign, IL: Human Kinetics.

PASE BASKETBALL LESSON PLAN 16-20

Resources: Lesson Focus

- Numbered colored pinnies—six per team (also used during application contest)
- Basketballs—three to six per team (also used during application contest)
- Hula hoops—one per team (used to organize team materials)
- Stopwatches—one per team
- Pencils

Resources: Application Contest

- PASE Application Contest 16-20
- PASE Application Contest Scorecard 16-20
- PASE Official's Pocket Reference
- Two to four cones
- Boundary markers
- One clipboard
- Pencils
- Whistles
- Officials' pinnies

Instructional Materials

- PASE IRL Rubric and Recording Sheet (only for lesson 20) (appendix B)
- PASE Attendance Recording Sheet (appendix B)
- PASE Roles and Responsibilities Assignments and Recording Sheet (appendix B)
- PASE Game Preparation Task Card 16-20
- PASE Fitness Activities Sheets (appendix B)
- PASE Personal or Team Fitness Recording Sheet (appendix B)
- Tournament Statistics Summary Sheet (appendix D)
- Round Robin Tourney Rules (appendix D)
- PASE Outside-of-Class Physical Activity Participation Log (appendix B)
- PASE Tournament Role Assignments Sheet (appendix D)
- PASE Basketball Lesson Plan 21

Instructional Focus

Skills

- Review all

Tactics

- Review all

Objectives

- Further develop basketball skills and tactics by engaging in round robin tournament game play
- Demonstrate personal and social responsibility

Team Role Check

- Students enter gymnasium and immediately report to home court area.
- Check daily roles and associated duties from materials provided.

↻ *Begin team warm-up.*

Team Warm-Up

- ◆ Conduct the team warm-up simultaneously to coaches' meeting.
- ◆ Fitness trainer leads team through warm-up using the PASE Fitness Activities Sheets.
- ◆ Fitness trainer or individuals record performance on team warm-up using either the **Personal** or **Team Fitness Recording Sheet.**

⟳ *Teams transition to daily review.*

Coaches' Meeting

- ◆ Conduct the coaches' meeting simultaneously to team warm-up.
- ◆ All team coaches report to designated meeting area.
- ◆ Teacher informs coaches of round robin tournament schedule and provides coaches with **PASE Game Preparation Task Card 16-20** (in-season round robin tournament) and **Round Robin Tournament Rules.**
- ◆ Teacher outlines the day's events.

⟳ *Coaches transition to the home court area and join warm-up.*

Team Review

- ◆ Review progress of team goals from **lessons 3-15.** This would be found in the student/team recording sheet which the students have every lesson.
- ◆ Identify areas of need from **lessons 3-15.**
- ◆ Prepare to practice in identified areas during team practice.

⟳ *Teams transition to designated instructional area for teacher instructions.*

Teacher Instruction

- ◆ Introduce daily lesson focus.
- ◆ Provide anticipatory set:

💬 Today you will be involved in the in-season round robin tournament. The purpose of today's lesson is to give your team an opportunity to apply the skills and tactics we have practiced during the preseason phase of our basketball season. In addition, the results of the round robin tournament will be used in part to determine the seeding for the postseason championship tournament. Your team will have the opportunity to engage in a basketball warm-up and determine the officials and scorekeepers prior to each game. It is important that you keep in mind that each person has to fulfill the role of either scorekeeper or official at least once during the in-season round robin tournament. You are not allowed to perform the role of scorekeeper or official during two consecutive games (you must alternate player roles with that of scorekeeper or official).

- ◆ Advise students that after completing the **PASE Game Preparation Task Card** they should be able to answer the following questions:
    - ◆ Q1: "What will your team do to be successful during the in-season round robin tournament?"
    - ◆ Q2: "What type of defense will you use?"
    - ◆ Q3: "Who are your official and scorekeeper for the day's game(s)?"
- ◆ Advise student officials that they will be responsible for all official's signals during the scrimmage.

⟳ *Teams transition to home court area for daily team practice.*

Team Practice

- Team-directed practice begins (refer to **PASE Game Preparation Task Card 16-20**—in-season round robin tournament).
- Teacher moves through home court area to facilitate team practice.
    - Manage learning environment.
    - Observe and assess individual and team performance.
    - Provide encouragement and instructional feedback.

Teams transition back to designated instructional area for application contest.

Application Contest

- Teacher explains and demonstrates daily contest (refer to **Application Contest 16-20**).
    - Identify tactical focus and related skills (refer to **Application Contest Scorecard 16-20**).
    - Identify contest goals.
    - Discuss procedures for scoring and refereeing.
- **Scoring:** Use nonshaded areas on **Application Contest Scorecard 16-20.**
- **Refereeing:** Refer to and use designated referee signals located on the Official's Pocket Reference.

Teams transition to designated contest areas to perform assigned duties.

- Teacher actively monitors individual and team performance.

Teams transition to designated instructional area for closure.

Closure

- Teacher reviews lesson focus.
- Teacher discusses assessment of individual and team performance.
- Check for student understanding using questions and demonstrations (refer back to questions and demonstrations from the introduction).
- Allow for student questions and preview **lessons 17-21.**

Teams transition to home court areas for individual and team assessment.

Individual and Team Assessment

- Assessment summary
    - Complete **PASE IRL Recording Sheet** (lesson 20—each person).
    - Summarize/Complete **Application Contest Scorecard 16-20** (scorekeeper).
    - Complete **PASE Attendance Recording Sheet** (coach).
    - Complete **PASE Roles and Responsibilities Recording Sheet** (each person).
    - Supervise assessment completion (coach).
- Distribute the following in lesson 16:
    - **PASE Tournament Statistics Summary Sheet** (each person)
    - **PASE Outside-of-Class Physical Activity Participation Log** (each person)
- Collect the following in lesson 20:
    - **PASE Outside-of-Class Physical Activity Participation Log** (each person)

Teams organize materials and exit class from home court areas.

PASE Basketball Game Preparation Task Card 16-20

Skills

- Passing
- Dribbling
- Shooting
- Offensive/defensive footwork
- Offensive/defensive tactics

Learning tasks	Self	Peer	Coach
1. During the in-season round robin tournament, each team member will be required to perform the roles of official and scorekeeper at least once. Refer to the **Tournament Role Assignment Sheet** to determine your role responsibility line-up. This will help determine who will be the official and scorekeeper for today's games. Once roles are identified, get the scorecards, whistles, and so on, and prepare to score or officiate your assigned game.	☐		
2. In partners, a dribbler should move from the baseline to the midcourt line while a partner plays defense on the ball. Rotate roles and repeat.		☐	
3. In team lines, perform V- and L-cuts while receiving chest, bounce, overhead, and sidearm passes. Players rotate from passer to receiver/cutter following each trial. Repeat until each player has attempted each type of pass once.			☐
4. In team lines, with one line shooting and one line rebounding, perform three right-handed and three left-handed layups.			☐
5. In team lines, with one line shooting and one line rebounding, perform three jump shots from the right side of the key and three jump shots from the left side of the key.			☐
6. Determine defensive assignments according to the Tournament Schedule. If your team will use player-to-player defense, determine matchups. If your team will play zone, then determine player area (zone) assignments.			☐
7. Practice game scenarios of your choice. Base your choice on what you think your team needs the most practice on or what you think your upcoming opponent's game plan will be.			☐
8. In a team huddle, on the count of three, shout out your team cheer loud enough to show your team's spirit.			☐

From *Sport Education Seasons* by Sean M. Bulger et al., 2007, Champaign, IL: Human Kinetics.

Day 16	Visitors		Home
Game 1	1	vs.	6
Game 2	2	vs.	5
Game 3	3	vs.	4

Day 17			
Game 1	6	vs.	4
Game 2	5	vs.	1
Game 3	2	vs.	3

Day 18			
Game 1	6	vs.	2
Game 2	5	vs.	3
Game 3	1	vs.	4

Day 19	Visitors		Home
Game 1	3	vs.	1
Game 2	4	vs.	2
Game 3	5	vs.	6

Day 20			
Game 1	3	vs.	6
Game 2	1	vs.	2
Game 3	4	vs.	5

From *Sport Education Seasons* by Sean M. Bulger et al., 2007, Champaign, IL: Human Kinetics.

PASE Basketball Application Contest 16-20

Equipment

- Two cones
- Pencils
- Boundary markers
- Whistles

- Lesson 16-20 Scorecard
- Officials' pinnies
- One clipboard
- Colored pinnies (teams)

Objectives

Demonstrate skills and tactics learned to date

Goals

Achieve the maximum number of successful jump shots or layups (or both) in two 3-minute trials

Application Description

This is a 3 vs. 3 competition, with three offensive players and three defensive players. The offense must begin play from the cone located at the top of the key via either passing the ball to a teammate or dribbling into the playing area. The same player cannot inbound the ball on two consecutive restarts. After the ball is in play, the offense must attempt to move the ball via dribbling, passing, and screening in an attempt to create successful jump shots and layups. Play is continuous even after missed shots. On every change of possession the ball must be cleared beyond the 3-point line. Play is restarted at the cone for one of the following reasons only: (1) a successful shot attempt, (2) ball knocked out of bounds, (3) a defensive foul, or (4) an offensive violation. The competition will last for four 3-minute trials, with possession of the ball changing on each new 3-minute trial. A 3-minute half-time will be instituted between the second and third periods. Substitutions enter the game at the beginning of each new 3-minute trial. Each team member must have participated during two of the four 3-minute trials. Repeat until each team has been on offense two times. The teacher should have multiple games going at the same time based on space and equipment and use a single game clock for all games.

Application Diagram

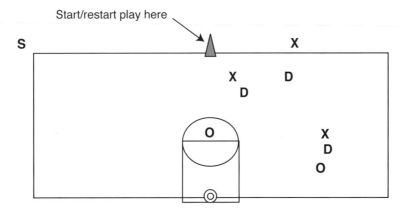

Scorekeeper's Guidelines

- 2 points per jump shot or layup that is successful.
- 1 point per defensive foul (point awarded to offense).
- Record scores for the offensive team after the official's signal indicating a successful shot or defensive foul.
- Combine all team points for a total team score.

Referee's Guidelines

- No points awarded if a jump shot is performed from the 3-point area.
- No points if same player shoots two consecutive times.
- Demonstrate appropriate signals for violations and fouls.
- Demonstrate appropriate signals related to scoring.
- Demonstrate appropriate clock-related signals.

From *Sport Education Seasons* by Sean M. Bulger et al., 2007, Champaign, IL: Human Kinetics.

PASE Basketball Application Contest Scorecard 16-20

Instructions: Nonshaded areas must be filled in by scorekeeper.

☐ Home ☐ Away

Team		Coach		Site	
Timer		Scorekeeper		Date	

FINAL SCORE

TEAM SCORING BY PERIODS

	1st	2nd	3rd	4th	OT

SCORING

Player	1st trial	2nd trial	3rd trial	4th trial	OT
Practice row to be filled in by student.					

Fouls

	1	2	3	4	5
	1	2	3	4	5
	1	2	3	4	5
	1	2	3	4	5
	1	2	3	4	5
	1	2	3	4	5
	1	2	3	4	5
	1	2	3	4	5

SUMMARY

	2 FG		3 FG		FT		Steals	Reb.	Pts.
	A	M	A	M	A	M			

Totals

Team fouls

1	2	3	4	5	6	7	8	9	10

Alternating jump ball possessions

TEAM TIME-OUTS

	1	2	3	4	5
	Away	Home	Away	Home	Away
	Home	Away	Home	Away	Home

Running Score

1	2	3	4	5	6	7	8	9	10	11	12	13	14	15	16	17	18	19	20	21	22	23	24	25
26	27	28	29	30	31	32	33	34	35	36	37	38	39	40	41	42	43	44	45	46	47	48	49	50
51	52	53	54	55	56	57	58	59	60	61	62	63	64	65	66	67	68	69	70	71	72	73	74	75
76	77	78	79	80	81	82	83	84	85	86	87	88	89	90	91	92	93	94	95	96	97	98	99	100

Coach's Signature _____

Scorekeeper's Signature _____

From *Sport Education Seasons* by Sean M. Bulger et al., 2007, Champaign, IL: Human Kinetics.

249

PASE BASKETBALL LESSON PLAN 21

Resources: Lesson Focus

- CD player
- *FITNESSGRAM* 8.0 PACER/Cadence CD
- Stopwatches
- Mats
- *FITNESSGRAM* Test Kit
- Nine hula hoops (one per station that uses a ball)
- Basketballs
- Cones
- 12-inch rulers
- Nine hula hoops (one for each station that uses a ball)

Instructional Materials

- PASE Skills and Fitness Combine Recording Sheets (one per person) (appendix A)
- PASE Fitness and Skills Station Task Cards 1-20 (appendix A)
- PASE Outside-of-Class Physical Activity Participation Log (appendix B)
- PASE Basketball Lesson Plan 22

Instructional Focus

The skills combine is designed to encompass the following:

- A skills and fitness assessment pretest (lesson 1)
- A skills and fitness assessment posttest (lesson 21)
- A data collection process that will enable students to engage in meaningful goal-setting behaviors
- A data collection process that will enable the teacher to monitor student progress throughout the season

Fitness Assessments

- PACER
- Modified pull-up
- BMI
- Trunk lift
- Sit and reach
- Vertical jump
- Shoulder stretch
- T-run
- Push-up
- Shuttle run
- Curl-up
- Line jump

Skill Assessments

- Low control dribble
- Rebounding
- Speed dribble
- Pass: chest
- Layup
- Pass: bounce
- Set shot
- Jump shot (midrange)
- Jump shot (long range)

Objectives

- Obtain data for team selection purposes
- Obtain health-related fitness posttest data
- Obtain skill-related fitness posttest data
- Obtain basketball skill posttest data
- For students to demonstrate personal and social responsibility

Lesson Introduction

- Introduce lesson focus.
- Provide anticipatory set:

The purpose of today's lesson is to assess your improvement and goal obtainment in fitness concepts and skills related to the sport of basketball. These fitness concepts and skills have been important during the season in preparing you to be a successful and knowledgeable basketball player. As in the first skills combine, you will be collecting information at each station that will allow you to document your personal growth throughout the season. This information will also help you set new goals as you engage in basketball-related activities outside of the physical education classroom.

- Provide instructions for completing the post-skills and fitness combine:

You will notice that there are 20 stations set up around the gymnasium. You and a teammate will be required to visit each station, read the task card, perform the stated activity, and record your scores. Each pair of teammates will be assigned a station number, which is where you will begin. When you arrive at any station, read the task card carefully to determine what you are required to do. Pay attention to the floor diagram, picture, and cues to help you to perform the activities correctly. Once you have completed the activity, you will need to record all required information. This information is to be recorded on the **Fitness and Skills Combine Recording Sheet** in the "Postscore" row. Record carefully and use the row showing the example to ensure accurate scoring. After you and a teammate complete a station, you are free to rotate to a new station of your choice. Please look for open stations to rotate to, remembering that your goal is to complete every station today. Note the time criterion at each station and pace yourselves accordingly.

- Complete teacher demonstrations for at least one station and have students practice recording a mock score.
- Check for student understanding using questions, student demonstrations, or both.
    - Q1: "What are the purposes of the post-skills and fitness combine?"
    - Q2: "What is the first thing that each pair should do when arriving at a new station?"
    - Q3: "After reading the task card and performing the activity, what should you do?"
    - Q4: "Describe what happens after you record the required information at a station."
- Assign teammate pairs to a station and begin post-skills and fitness combine.

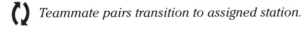 *Teammate pairs transition to assigned station.*

Lesson Body

- Complete post-skills and fitness combine.
- See station task cards for organizational and content information.
- Teacher manages and monitors learning environment.

Fitness Component Stations

1. PACER
2. BMI
3. Sit and reach
4. Shoulder stretch
5. Push-up
6. Curl-up
7. Modified pull-up
8. Trunk lift
9. Vertical jump
10. T-run
11. Shuttle run
12. Line jumps

Basketball Skill Stations

13. Low control dribble
14. Speed dribble
15. Layup
16. Set shot
17. Jump shot (midrange)
18. Jump shot (long range)
19. Rebounding
20. Pass: chest and bounce

Teammate pairs transition to common area for daily closure.

Suggested Floor Plan

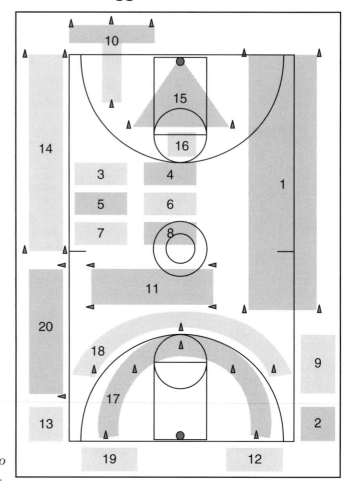

Closure

- Teacher reviews lesson purpose.
- Check for student understanding using questions and demonstrations (can refer back to questions and demonstrations from the introduction).
- Teacher discusses individuals' and pairs' daily performance.
- Allow for student questions and preview **lesson 22** (postseason tournament).
- Distribute the **PASE Outside-of-Class Physical Activity Participation Log** (each person).

Teammate pairs organize materials and exit class.

PASE BASKETBALL LESSON PLAN 22-24

Resources: Lesson Focus

- Numbered colored pinnies—six per team (also used during application contest)
- Basketballs—three to six per team (also used during application contest)
- Hula hoops—one per team (used to organize team materials)
- Stopwatches—one per team
- Pencils

Resources: Application Contest

- PASE Application Contest 22-24
- PASE Application Contest Scorecard 22-24
- PASE Official's Pocket Reference
- Two to four cones
- Boundary markers
- One clipboard
- Pencils
- Whistles
- Officials' pinnies

Instructional Materials

- PASE Attendance Recording Sheet (appendix B)
- PASE Roles and Responsibilities Assignments and Recording Sheet (appendix B)
- PASE Game Preparation Task Card 22-24
- PASE Fitness Activities Sheets (appendix B)
- PASE Personal or Team Fitness Recording Sheet (appendix B)
- PASE Individual or Team Activity Task Card Recording Sheet (appendix B)
- PASE Basketball Lesson Plan 25
- Postseason Tournament Rules (appendix D)
- Season Voting Ballots—lesson 24 (appendix E)
- PASE Acceptance Speech Criteria (appendix E)
- PASE Healthy Refreshments Sign-Up Sheet (appendix E)

Instructional Focus

Skills

- Review all

Tactics

- Review all

Objectives

- Further develop basketball skills and tactics by engaging in a postseason tournament game play
- Demonstrate personal and social responsibility

Team Role Check

- Students enter gymnasium and immediately report to home court area.
- Check daily roles and associated duties from materials provided.

() *Begin team warm-up.*

Team Warm-Up

- Fitness trainer leads team through warm-up using the PASE Fitness Activities Sheets.
- Fitness trainer or individuals record performance on team warm-up using either the **Personal** or **Team Fitness Recording Sheet.**

↻ *Teams transition to daily review.*

Coaches' Meeting

- All team coaches report to designated meeting area.
- Teacher informs coaches of postseason tournament schedule and provides coaches with **PASE Game Preparation Task Card 22-24** (postseason tournament).
- Teacher outlines the day's events.

↻ *Coaches transition to home court area and join warm-up.*

Team Review

- Review progress of team goals from **lessons 3-20.** This would be found in the student/team recording sheet which the students have every lesson.
- Identify areas of need from **lessons 3-20.**
- Prepare to practice in identified areas during team practice.

↻ *Teams transition to designated instructional area for teacher instructions.*

Teacher Instruction

- Introduce daily lesson focus.
- Provide anticipatory set:

💬 Today you will be involved in the postseason tournament. The purpose of today's lesson is to give your team an opportunity to apply the skills and tactics we have practiced during the preseason phase of our basketball season. Your team will have the opportunity to engage in a basketball warm-up and determine the officials and scorekeepers prior to each game. It is important that you keep in mind that each person has to fulfill the role of either scorekeeper or official at least once during the postseason tournament. You are not allowed to perform the role of scorekeeper or official during two consecutive games (you must alternate player roles with that of scorekeeper or official).

- Advise students that after completing the **PASE Game Preparation Task Card** they should be able to answer the following questions:
  - Q1: "What will your team do to be more successful during the postseason tournament than during the in-season round robin tournament?"
  - Q2: "What type of defense will you use?"
  - Q3: "Who are your official and scorekeeper for the day's game(s)?"
- Advise student officials that they will be responsible for all official's signals during the scrimmage.

↻ *Teams transition to home court area for daily team practice.*

Team Practice

- Team-directed practice begins (refer to **PASE Game Preparation Task Card 22-24**—postseason tournament and **Individual** or **Team Activity Task Card Recording Sheet**).
- Teacher moves through home court area to facilitate team practice.

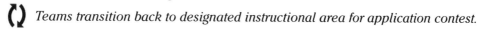

- ◆ Manage learning environment.
- ◆ Observe and assess individual and team performance.
- ◆ Provide encouragement and instructional feedback.

↻ *Teams transition back to designated instructional area for application contest.*

Application Contest

- ◆ Teacher explains and demonstrates daily contest (refer to **Application Contest 22-24** and **Postseason Tournament Roles**).
    - ◆ Identify tactical focus and related skills (refer to **Application Contest Scorecard 22-24**).
    - ◆ Identify contest goals.
    - ◆ Discuss procedures for scoring and refereeing.
- ◆ **Scoring:** Use nonshaded areas on **Application Contest Scorecard 22-24.**
- ◆ **Refereeing:** Refer to and use designated referee signals located on the Official's Pocket Reference.

↻ *Teams transition to designated contest areas to perform assigned duties.*

- ◆ Teacher actively monitors individual and team performance.

↻ *Teams transition to designated instructional area for closure.*

Closure

- ◆ Teacher reviews lesson focus.
- ◆ Teacher discusses assessment of individual and team performance.
- ◆ Check for student understanding using questions and demonstrations (refer back to questions and demonstrations from the introduction).
- ◆ Allow for student questions and preview **lessons 23-25.**

↻ *Teams transition to home court areas for individual and team assessment.*

Individual and Team Assessment

- ◆ Assessment summary
    - ◆ Summarize/Complete **Application Contest Scorecard 22-24** (scorekeeper).
    - ◆ Complete **PASE Attendance Recording Sheet** (coach).
    - ◆ Complete **PASE Roles and Responsibilities Recording Sheet** (each person)
    - ◆ Supervise assessment completion (coach).
- ◆ Distribute the following instructional materials:
    - ◆ **PASE Healthy Refreshments Sign-Up Sheet**
    - ◆ **PASE Season Voting Ballots** (each person)—collect in lesson 24
    - ◆ **PASE Acceptance Speech Criteria**—have ready for use in lesson 25
- ◆ All students should develop an acceptance speech for possible awards they may win. Use the **Awards Day Acceptance Speech Criteria** from appendix E.
- ◆ Collect the following in lesson 24:
    - ◆ **PASE Reflective Journal** (each person)

↻ *Teams organize materials and exit class from home court areas.*

PASE Basketball Game Preparation Task Card 22-24

Skills

- Passing
- Dribbling
- Shooting
- Offensive and defensive footwork
- Offensive and defensive tactics

Learning tasks	Self	Peer	Coach
1. During the postseason tournament, each team member will be required to perform the roles of official and scorekeeper at least once. Refer to the **Tournament Role Assignments** to determine your role responsibility line-up. This will help determine who will be the official and scorekeeper for today's games. Once roles are identified, get the scorecards, whistles, and so on and prepare to score or officiate your assigned game.	☐		
2. In partners, a dribbler should move from the baseline to the midcourt line while a partner plays defense on the ball. Rotate roles and repeat.		☐	
3. In team lines, perform V- and L-cuts while receiving chest, bounce, overhead, and sidearm passes. Players rotate from passer to receiver/cutter following each trial. Repeat until each player has attempted each type of pass once.			☐
4. In team lines, with one line shooting and one line rebounding, perform three right-handed and three left-handed layups.			☐
5. In team lines, with one line shooting and one line rebounding, perform three jump shots from the right side of the key and three jump shots from the left side of the key.			☐
6. Determine defensive assignments according to the following tournament schedule. If your team will use player-to-player defense, determine matchups. If your team will play zone, then determine player area (zone) assignments.			☐
7. Practice game scenarios of your choice. Base your choice on what you think your team needs the most practice on or what you think your upcoming opponent's game plan will be.			☐
8. In a team huddle, on the count of three, shout out your team cheer loud enough to show your team's spirit.			☐

From *Sport Education Seasons* by Sean M. Bulger et al., 2007, Champaign, IL: Human Kinetics.

Day 22	Visitors		Home
Game 1	5th seed	vs.	4th seed
Game 2	3rd seed	vs.	6th seed
Game 3	1st seed	vs.	Winner G1

Day 23	Visitors		Home
Game 4	Loser G2	vs.	Loser G3
Game 5	2nd seed	vs.	Winner G2
Game 6	Loser G1	vs.	Loser G5

DAY 24

Consolation finals

Game 7	Winner G6	vs.	Winner G4

Championship finals

Game 8	Winner G3	vs.	Winner G5

From *Sport Education Seasons* by Sean M. Bulger et al., 2007, Champaign, IL: Human Kinetics.

Equipment

- Two cones
- Pencils
- Boundary markers
- Whistles
- Lesson 22-24 Scorecard
- Officials' pinnies
- One clipboard
- Colored pinnies (teams)

Objectives

Demonstrate skills and tactics learned to date

Goals

Achieve the maximum number of successful jump shots or layups (or both) in two 5-minute trials

Application Description

This is a 4 vs. 4 competition, with four offensive players and four defensive players. The offense must begin play from the cone located at the top of the key via either passing the ball to a teammate or dribbling into the playing area. The same player cannot inbound the ball on two consecutive restarts. After the ball is in play, the offense must attempt to move the ball via dribbling, passing, and screening in an attempt to create successful jump shots and layups. Play is continuous even after missed shots. On every change of possession the ball must be cleared beyond the 3-point line. Play is restarted at the cone for one of the following reasons only: (1) a successful shot attempt, (2) ball knocked out of bounds, (3) a defensive foul, or (4) an offensive violation. The competition will last for four 5-minute trials, with possession of the ball changing on each new 5-minute trial. A 5-minute half-time will be instituted between the second and third periods. Substitutions enter the game at the beginning of each new 5-minute trial. Each team member must have participated during two of the four 5-minute trials. Repeat until each team has been on offense two times. The teacher should have multiple games going at the same time based on space and equipment and use a single game clock for all games.

Application Diagram

Start/restart play here

S

Key

X = Offensive players

D = Defender

O = Official

S = Scorekeeper

▲ = Cones

Scorekeeper's Guidelines

- 2 points per jump shot or layup that is successful.
- 1 point per defensive foul (point awarded to offense).
- Record scores for the offensive team after the official's signal indicating a successful shot or defensive foul.
- Combine all team points for a total team score.

Referee's Guidelines

- No points awarded if a jump shot is performed from the 3-point area.
- No points if same player shoots two consecutive times.
- Demonstrate appropriate signals for violations and fouls.
- Demonstrate appropriate signals related to scoring.
- Demonstrate appropriate clock-related signals.

From *Sport Education Seasons* by Sean M. Bulger et al., 2007, Champaign, IL: Human Kinetics.

PASE Basketball Application Contest Scorecard 22-24

Instructions: Nonshaded areas must be filled in by scorekeeper.

Team			Coach		Site		☐ Home		☐ Away
								FINAL SCORE	
Timer			Scorekeeper		Date				

TEAM SCORING BY PERIODS

	1st	2nd	3rd	4th	OT
Home					

SCORING

Player	1st trial	2nd trial	3rd trial	4th trial	OT
Practice row to be filled in by student.					

Fouls (each player row): 1 2 3 4 5

SUMMARY

	2 FG		3 FG		FT		Steals	Reb.	Pts.
	A	M	A	M	A	M			

Totals

Team fouls										
1	2	3	4	5	6	7	8	9	10	

Alternating jump ball possessions

TEAM TIME-OUTS

	1	2	3	4	5
	Away	Home	Away	Home	

Away	Home	Away	Home	Away	Home	Away	Home	Away	Home	Home

Running Score	1	2	3	4	5	6	7	8	9	10	11	12	13	14	15	16	17	18	19	20	21	22	23	24	25
	26	27	28	29	30	31	32	33	34	35	36	37	38	39	40	41	42	43	44	45	46	47	48	49	50
	51	52	53	54	55	56	57	58	59	60	61	62	63	64	65	66	67	68	69	70	71	72	73	74	75
	76	77	78	79	80	81	82	83	84	85	86	87	88	89	90	91	92	93	94	95	96	97	98	99	100

Coach's Signature _____

Scorekeeper's Signature _____

From *Sport Education Seasons* by Sean M. Bulger et al., 2007, Champaign, IL: Human Kinetics.

PASE BASKETBALL LESSON PLAN 25

Instructional Materials (Appendix E)

- Season Individual Awards
- Acceptance Speech Criteria
- Team Season Place Finish Awards
- Awards Day Itinerary
- Door prizes (optional)

Instructional Focus

To acknowledge and reward students for becoming more competent, literate, and enthusiastic basketball persons.

Objectives

- Establish a festive classroom environment based on mutual respect
- Bring the season to a festive conclusion
- Highlight personal and team accomplishments

Lesson Introduction

- Introduce lesson focus.
- Provide anticipatory set:

The purpose of today's lesson is to bring our basketball season to a festive close. Each of you will be recognized today for your contribution to the successful completion of this exciting basketball season. It is important that we maintain a classroom environment based on respect for opponents, as well as teammates.

- Provide itinerary for the awards day festival (refer to **PASE Basketball Awards Day Itinerary**).

I would like to welcome you to the awards day festival. This is lesson 25, our last lesson of the basketball season. As you can see from the itinerary that has been passed to you, we have a full day of festive activities planned. Following these announcements you will be allowed to get healthy refreshments. Once you have returned to your seat with your refreshments I will describe the awards that will be presented today. Afterward, each team will be presented with their individual and tournament place finish awards and provided time to deliver an acceptance speech. Next on our agenda will be presentation of the Season Championship Award and drawing for the door prizes. Lastly, I will wrap things up with closing remarks as we prepare for our next PASE season. Let's go ahead and get refreshments.

Lesson Body

- Describe **Season Individual Awards** and **Team Season Place Finish Awards** to be presented (refer to **PASE Basketball Season Voting Ballot**).
- Present awards to each team.
- Each team delivers acceptance speeches according to criteria provided after receiving awards. This should be set by the teacher ahead of time (discuss when passed out in lessons 22-24). (Refer to **PASE Acceptance Speech Criteria.**)
- Present Season Championship Award.

Remember, this award is based on the cumulative team point total across the season. This award recognizes the team that demonstrated the most consistent performance across the entire season related to the three major goals of a PASE season: to become competent, literate, and enthusiastic basketball players.

• Draw for door prizes and present the prizes to the winners.

Closure

I would like to thank each and every one of you for a fantastic basketball season. Every one of you has grown mentally, physically, and emotionally during this basketball season. It has been a pleasure to watch each of you accept more and more responsibility and respond to that increased responsibility is such a positive way. Truly, you have become more competent, literate, and enthusiastic basketball players and I look forward to our next PASE season with great anticipation. Have a great day and I will see you all in the next class.

• Collect the following:

  • **PASE Outside-of-Class Physical Activity Participation Log** (each person)
  • **PASE Independent Learning Activity** (each person)

Teams organize materials and exit class from home court areas.

Lessons 1 and 21 Instructional Materials

CONTENTS

PACER

Instructions: Run from end line to end line (20 meters) and reverse direction on each beep.

Rules: On each beep, reverse direction and continue to run. Exit when you fail to reach an end line before a beep for a second time. From end line to end line equals one lap.

Scoring: Record number of laps completed. Record HFZ results.

Time: Zero to 21 minutes.

CUES

1. Begin on first beep
2. Steady pace
3. Wait or reverse direction on each beep
4. Exit on second missed beep
5. Determine HFZ

PICTURE

HEALTHY FITNESS ZONE (HFZ)

Male		Female	
HFZ	Age		HFZ
23 – 61	10	–	7 – 41
23 – 72	11		15 – 41
32 – 72	12		15 – 41
41 – 83	13		23 – 51
41 – 83	14		23 – 51
51 – 94	15		32 – 51
61 – 94	16		32 – 61
61 – 106	17		41 – 61
72 – 106	17 +		41 – 72

Healthy Fitness Zone reprinted with permission from Cooper Institute, 2005, *FITNESSGRAM/ACTIVITYGRAM Test Administration Manual,* updated 3rd ed. (Champaign, IL: Human Kinetics), 61-62. From *Sport Education Seasons* by Sean M. Bulger et al., 2007, Champaign, IL: Human Kinetics.

Body Mass Index (BMI)

Instructions: Measure height in inches (in.); measure weight in pounds (lb).

Rules: Complete all measurements two times to ensure accuracy. Determine BMI two times using BMI chart to ensure accuracy.

Scoring: Record BMI and HFZ results.

Time: 2 minutes to complete test.

CUES

1. Measure height (in.)
2. Measure weight (lb)
3. Use BMI chart
4. Determine HFZ

PICTURE

HEALTHY FITNESS ZONE (HFZ)

Male		Age	Female	
HFZ	–	Age	–	HFZ
21.0 – 14.0		10		23.8 – 13.5
21.0 – 14.3		11		24.1 – 13.7
22.0 – 14.6		12		24.5 – 14.0
23.0 – 15.1		13		24.5 – 14.5
24.5 – 15.6		14		25.0 – 15.4
25.0 – 13.2		15		25.0 – 16.0
26.5 – 16.6		16		25.0 – 16.4
27.0 – 17.3		17		26.5 – 16.8
27.8 – 17.8		17 +		27.3 – 17.2

PASE Body Mass Index (BMI) Conversion Chart

Weight (lb)	48	49	50	51	52	53	54	55	56	57	58	59	60	61	62	63	Weight (lb)
80	24.4	23.4	22.5	21.6	20.8	20.0	19.3	18.6	17.9	17.3	16.7	16.2	15.6	15.1	14.6	14.2	80
85	25.9	24.9	23.9	23.0	22.1	21.3	20.5	19.8	19.1	18.4	17.8	17.2	16.6	16.1	15.5	15.1	85
90	27.5	26.4	25.3	24.3	23.4	22.5	21.7	20.9	20.2	19.5	18.8	18.2	17.6	17.0	16.5	15.9	90
95	29.0	27.8	26.7	25.7	24.7	23.8	22.9	22.1	21.3	20.6	19.9	19.2	18.6	17.9	17.4	16.8	95
100	30.6	29.3	28.2	27.1	26.1	25.1	24.2	23.3	22.5	21.7	21.0	20.2	19.6	18.9	18.3	17.8	100
105	32.1	30.8	29.6	28.4	27.4	26.3	25.4	24.5	23.6	22.8	22.0	21.3	20.5	19.9	19.2	18.6	105
110	33.6	32.3	31.0	29.8	28.7	27.6	26.6	25.6	24.7	23.9	23.0	22.3	21.5	20.8	20.2	19.5	110
115	35.2	33.7	32.4	31.2	30.0	28.8	27.8	26.8	25.8	24.9	24.1	23.3	22.5	21.8	21.1	20.4	115
120	36.7	35.2	33.8	32.5	31.3	30.1	29.0	27.9	26.8	26.0	25.1	24.3	23.5	22.7	22.0	21.3	120
125	38.2	36.7	35.2	33.9	32.6	31.4	30.2	29.1	28.1	27.1	26.2	25.3	24.5	23.7	22.9	22.2	125
130	39.8	38.1	36.6	35.2	33.9	32.6	31.4	30.3	29.2	28.2	27.2	26.3	25.4	24.6	23.8	23.1	130
135	41.3	39.6	38.0	36.6	35.2	33.9	32.6	31.4	30.3	29.3	28.3	27.3	26.4	25.5	24.7	24.0	135
140	42.8	41.1	39.5	37.9	36.5	35.1	33.8	32.6	31.4	30.4	29.3	28.3	27.3	26.5	25.6	24.8	140
145	44.3	42.5	40.9	39.3	37.8	36.4	35.0	33.8	32.6	31.4	30.4	29.3	28.4	27.5	26.6	25.7	145
150	45.9	44.0	42.3	40.6	39.1	37.6	36.2	34.9	33.7	32.5	31.4	30.4	29.4	28.4	27.5	26.6	150
155	47.4	45.5	43.7	42.0	40.4	38.9	37.5	36.1	34.8	33.7	32.5	31.4	30.3	29.3	28.4	27.5	155
160	48.9	47.0	45.1	43.4	41.7	40.1	38.7	37.3	35.9	34.7	33.5	32.4	31.3	30.3	29.3	28.4	160
165	50.5	48.4	46.5	44.7	43.0	41.4	39.9	38.4	37.1	35.8	34.6	33.4	32.3	31.2	30.2	29.3	165
170	52.0	49.9	47.9	46.0	44.3	42.6	41.1	39.6	38.2	36.9	35.6	34.4	33.3	32.2	31.2	30.2	170
175	53.5	51.4	49.3	47.4	45.6	43.9	42.3	40.8	39.3	37.9	36.7	35.4	34.2	33.1	32.1	31.1	175
180	55.0	52.8	50.7	48.8	46.9	45.1	43.5	41.9	40.4	39.0	37.7	36.4	35.2	34.1	33.0	32.0	180
185	56.5	54.3	52.1	50.1	48.2	46.4	44.7	43.1	41.5	40.1	38.7	37.4	36.1	35.0	33.9	32.8	185
190	58.1	55.8	53.5	51.5	49.5	47.7	45.9	44.3	42.7	41.2	39.8	38.5	37.2	36.0	34.8	33.7	190
195	59.6	57.2	55.0	52.8	50.8	48.9	47.1	45.4	43.8	42.3	40.8	39.5	38.2	36.9	35.7	34.6	195
200	61.2	58.7	56.4	54.2	52.1	50.2	48.3	46.6	44.9	43.4	41.9	40.5	39.1	37.9	36.7	35.5	200
205	62.7	60.2	57.8	55.5	53.4	51.4	49.5	47.7	46.1	44.5	42.9	41.5	40.1	38.8	37.6	36.4	205
210	64.2	61.6	59.2	56.9	54.7	52.7	50.7	48.9	47.2	45.5	44.0	42.5	41.1	39.7	38.5	37.3	210
215	65.7	63.1	60.6	58.2	56.0	53.9	51.9	50.1	48.3	46.6	45.0	43.5	42.1	40.7	39.4	38.2	215
220	67.3	64.6	62.0	59.6	57.3	55.2	53.2	51.2	49.4	47.7	46.1	44.5	43.1	41.7	40.3	39.1	220
225	68.8	66.0	63.4	60.9	58.6	56.4	54.4	52.4	50.5	48.8	47.1	45.5	44.0	42.6	41.2	39.9	225
230	70.3	67.5	64.8	62.3	59.9	57.7	55.6	53.6	51.6	49.9	48.2	46.6	45.0	43.5	42.2	40.8	230
235	71.9	69.0	66.2	63.7	61.2	58.9	56.8	54.7	52.8	51.0	49.2	47.6	46.0	44.5	43.1	41.7	235
240	73.4	70.4	67.6	65.0	62.5	60.2	58.0	55.9	53.9	52.0	50.3	48.6	47.0	45.4	44.0	42.6	240
245	74.9	71.9	69.0	66.4	63.8	61.5	59.2	57.1	55.0	53.1	51.3	49.6	47.9	46.4	44.9	43.5	245
250	76.4	73.4	70.5	67.7	65.1	62.7	60.4	58.2	56.2	54.2	52.4	50.6	48.9	47.3	45.8	44.5	250
255	77.8	74.7	71.7	69.0	66.4	63.8	61.5	59.3	57.2	55.2	53.3	51.5	49.8	48.2	46.6	45.2	255
260	79.3	76.1	73.1	70.3	67.6	65.1	62.7	60.4	58.3	56.3	54.3	52.5	50.8	49.1	47.5	46.1	260
265	80.9	77.6	74.5	71.6	68.9	66.3	63.9	61.6	59.4	57.3	55.4	53.5	51.7	50.1	48.5	46.9	265
270	82.4	79.1	75.9	73.0	70.2	67.6	65.1	62.7	60.5	58.4	56.4	54.5	52.7	51.0	49.4	47.8	270
275	83.9	80.5	77.3	74.3	71.5	68.8	66.3	63.9	61.6	59.5	57.5	55.5	53.7	52.0	50.3	48.7	275
280	85.4	82.0	78.7	75.7	72.8	70.1	67.5	65.1	62.8	60.6	58.5	56.5	54.7	52.9	51.2	49.6	280
285	87.0	83.4	80.1	77.0	74.1	71.3	68.7	66.2	63.9	61.7	59.6	57.6	55.7	53.8	52.1	50.5	285
290	88.5	84.9	81.5	78.4	75.4	72.6	69.9	67.4	65.0	62.7	60.6	58.6	56.6	54.8	53.0	51.4	290
Height (in.)	48	49	50	51	52	53	54	55	56	57	58	59	60	61	62	63	Height (in.)

Healthy Fitness Zone reprinted with permission from Cooper Institute, 2005, *FITNESSGRAM/ACTIVITYGRAM Test Administration Manual*, updated 3rd ed. (Champaign, IL: Human Kinetics), 61-62. From *Sport Education Seasons* by Sean M. Bulger et al., 2007, Champaign, IL: Human Kinetics.

PASE Body Mass Index (BMI) Conversion Chart

Weight (lb)	Height (in.) 48	49	50	51	52	53	54	55	56	57	58	59	60	61	62	63	Weight (lb)
80	24.4	23.4	22.5	21.6	20.8	20	19.3	18.6	17.9	17.3	16.7	16.2	15.6	15.1	14.6	14.2	80
85	25.9	24.9	23.9	23.0	22.1	21.3	20.5	19.8	19.1	18.4	17.8	17.2	16.6	16.1	15.5	15.1	85
90	27.5	26.4	25.3	24.3	23.4	22.5	21.7	20.9	20.2	19.5	18.8	18.2	17.6	17.0	16.5	15.9	90
95	29.0	27.8	26.7	25.7	24.7	23.8	22.9	22.1	21.3	20.6	19.9	19.2	18.6	17.9	17.4	16.8	95
100	30.6	29.3	28.2	27.1	26.1	25.1	24.2	23.3	22.5	21.7	20.0	20.2	19.6	18.9	18.3	17.8	100
105	32.1	30.8	29.6	28.4	27.4	26.3	25.4	24.5	23.6	22.8	22.0	21.3	20.5	19.9	19.2	18.6	105
110	33.6	32.3	31.0	29.8	28.7	27.6	26.6	25.6	24.7	23.9	23.0	22.3	21.5	20.8	20.2	19.5	110
115	35.2	33.7	32.4	31.2	30.0	28.8	27.8	26.8	25.8	24.9	24.1	23.3	22.5	21.8	21.1	20.4	115
120	36.7	35.2	33.8	32.5	31.3	30.1	29.0	27.9	27.0	26.0	25.1	24.3	23.5	22.7	22.0	21.3	120
125	38.2	36.7	35.2	33.9	32.6	31.4	30.2	29.1	28.1	27.1	26.2	25.3	24.5	23.7	22.9	22.2	125
130	39.8	38.1	36.6	35.2	33.9	32.6	31.4	30.3	29.2	28.2	27.2	26.3	25.4	24.6	23.8	23.1	130
135	41.3	39.6	38.0	36.6	35.2	33.9	32.6	31.4	30.3	29.3	28.3	27.3	26.4	25.6	24.7	24.0	135
140	42.8	41.1	39.5	37.9	36.5	35.1	33.8	32.6	31.5	30.4	29.3	28.3	27.4	26.5	25.7	24.9	140
145	44.3	42.5	40.9	39.3	37.8	36.4	35.0	33.8	32.6	31.4	30.4	29.3	28.4	27.5	26.6	25.7	145
150	45.9	44.0	42.3	40.6	39.1	37.6	36.2	34.9	33.7	32.5	31.4	30.4	29.4	28.4	27.5	26.6	150
155	47.4	45.5	43.7	42.0	40.4	38.9	37.5	36.1	34.8	33.6	32.5	31.4	30.3	29.3	28.4	27.5	155
160	48.9	47.0	45.1	43.3	41.7	40.1	38.7	37.3	35.9	34.7	33.5	32.4	31.3	30.3	29.3	28.4	160
165	50.5	48.4	46.5	44.7	43.0	41.4	39.9	38.4	37.1	35.8	34.6	33.4	32.3	31.2	30.2	29.3	165
170	52.0	49.9	47.9	46.6	44.3	42.6	41.1	39.6	38.2	36.9	35.6	34.4	33.3	32.2	31.2	30.2	170
175	53.5	51.4	49.3	47.4	45.6	43.9	42.3	40.8	39.3	37.9	36.7	35.4	34.2	33.1	32.1	31.1	175
180	55.0	52.8	50.7	48.8	46.9	45.1	43.5	41.9	40.4	39.0	37.7	36.4	35.2	34.1	33.0	32.0	180
185	56.6	57.3	52.1	50.1	48.2	46.4	44.7	43.1	41.6	40.1	38.7	37.4	36.2	35.0	33.9	32.8	185
190	58.1	55.8	53.5	51.5	49.5	47.7	45.9	44.3	42.7	41.2	39.8	38.5	37.2	36.0	34.8	33.7	190
195	59.6	57.2	55.0	52.8	50.8	48.9	47.1	45.4	43.8	42.3	40.8	39.5	38.2	36.9	35.7	34.6	195
200	61.2	58.7	56.4	54.2	52.1	50.2	48.3	46.6	44.9	43.4	41.9	40.5	39.1	37.9	36.7	35.5	200
205	62.7	60.2	57.8	55.5	53.4	51.4	49.5	47.7	46.1	44.5	42.9	41.5	40.1	38.8	37.6	36.4	205
210	64.2	61.6	59.2	56.9	54.7	52.7	50.7	48.9	47.2	45.5	44.0	42.5	41.1	39.8	38.5	37.3	210
215	65.7	63.1	60.6	58.2	56.0	53.9	51.9	50.1	48.3	46.6	45.0	43.5	42.1	40.7	39.4	38.2	215
220	67.3	64.6	62.0	59.6	57.3	55.2	53.2	51.2	49.4	47.7	46.1	44.5	43.1	41.7	40.3	39.1	220
225	68.8	66.0	63.4	60.9	58.6	56.4	54.4	52.4	50.5	48.8	47.1	45.5	44.0	42.6	41.2	39.9	225
230	70.3	67.5	64.8	62.3	59.9	57.7	55.6	53.6	51.7	49.9	48.2	46.6	45.0	43.5	42.2	40.8	230
235	71.9	69.0	66.2	63.7	61.2	58.9	56.8	54.7	52.8	51.0	49.2	47.6	46.0	44.5	43.1	41.7	235
240	73.4	70.4	67.6	65.0	62.5	60.2	58.0	55.9	53.9	52.0	50.3	48.6	47.0	45.4	44.0	42.6	240
245	74.9	71.9	69.0	66.4	63.8	61.5	59.2	57.1	55.0	53.1	51.3	49.6	47.9	46.4	44.9	43.5	245
250	76.4	73.4	70.5	67.7	65.1	62.7	60.4	58.2	56.2	54.2	52.4	50.6	48.9	47.3	45.8	44.5	250
255	77.8	74.7	71.7	68.9	66.3	63.8	61.5	59.3	57.2	55.2	53.3	51.5	49.8	48.2	46.6	45.2	255
260	79.3	76.1	73.1	70.3	67.6	65.1	62.7	60.4	58.3	56.3	54.3	52.5	50.8	49.1	47.5	46.1	260
265	80.9	77.6	74.5	71.6	68.9	66.3	63.9	61.6	59.4	57.3	55.4	53.5	51.7	50.1	48.5	46.9	265
270	82.4	79.1	75.9	73.0	70.2	67.6	65.1	62.7	60.5	58.4	56.4	54.5	52.7	51.0	49.4	47.8	270
275	83.9	80.5	77.3	74.3	71.5	68.8	66.3	63.9	61.6	59.5	57.5	55.5	53.7	52.0	50.3	48.7	275
280	85.4	82.0	78.7	75.7	72.8	70.1	67.5	65.1	62.8	60.6	58.5	56.5	54.7	52.9	49.6	48.1	280
285	87.0	83.4	80.1	77.0	74.1	71.3	68.7	66.2	63.9	61.7	59.6	57.6	55.7	53.8	52.1	50.5	285
290	88.5	84.9	81.5	78.4	75.4	72.6	69.9	67.4	65.0	62.7	60.6	58.6	56.6	54.8	53.0	51.4	290
	48	49	50	51	52	53	54	55	56	57	58	59	60	61	62	63	
	Height (in.)																

From *Sport Education Seasons* by Sean M. Bulger et al., 2007, Champaign, IL: Human Kinetics.

Weight (lb)	Height (in.)																Weight (lb)
	64	65	66	67	68	69	70	71	72	73	74	75	76	77	78	79	
80	13.7	13.3	12.9	12.5	12.2	11.8	11.5	11.2	10.8	10.6	10.3	10.0	9.7	9.5	9.2	9.0	80
85	14.6	14.1	13.7	13.3	12.9	12.6	12.2	11.9	11.5	11.2	10.9	10.6	10.3	10.1	9.8	9.6	85
90	15.4	15.0	14.5	14.1	13.7	13.3	12.9	12.6	12.2	11.9	11.6	11.2	11.0	10.7	10.4	10.1	90
95	16.3	15.8	15.3	14.9	14.4	14.0	13.6	13.2	12.9	12.5	12.2	11.9	11.6	11.3	11.0	10.7	95
100	17.2	16.7	16.2	15.7	15.2	14.8	14.4	14.0	13.6	13.2	12.9	12.5	12.2	11.9	11.6	11.3	100
105	18.1	17.5	17.0	16.5	16.0	15.5	15.1	14.7	14.3	13.9	13.5	13.2	12.8	12.5	12.2	11.8	105
110	18.9	18.3	17.8	17.3	16.8	16.3	15.8	15.4	14.9	14.5	14.2	13.8	13.4	13.1	12.7	12.4	110
115	19.8	19.2	18.6	18.0	17.5	17.0	16.5	16.1	15.6	15.2	14.8	14.4	14.0	13.7	13.3	13.0	115
120	20.6	20.0	19.4	18.8	18.3	17.8	17.3	16.8	16.3	15.9	15.4	15.0	14.6	14.3	13.9	13.5	120
125	21.5	20.8	20.2	19.6	19.0	18.5	18.0	17.5	17.0	16.5	16.1	15.7	15.2	14.9	14.5	14.1	125
130	22.4	21.7	21.0	20.4	19.8	19.2	18.7	18.2	17.7	17.2	16.7	16.3	15.9	15.4	15.1	14.6	130
135	23.2	22.5	21.8	21.2	20.6	20.0	19.4	18.9	18.3	17.8	17.4	16.9	16.5	16.0	15.6	15.2	135
140	24.1	23.3	22.6	22.0	21.3	20.7	20.1	19.6	19.0	18.5	18.0	17.5	17.1	16.6	16.2	15.8	140
145	24.9	24.2	23.5	22.8	22.1	21.5	20.8	20.3	19.7	19.2	18.7	18.2	17.7	17.2	16.8	16.3	145
150	25.8	25.0	24.3	23.5	22.9	22.2	21.6	21.0	20.4	19.8	19.3	18.8	18.3	17.8	17.4	16.9	150
155	26.7	25.8	25.1	24.3	23.6	22.9	22.3	21.7	21.1	20.5	19.9	19.4	18.9	18.4	17.9	17.5	155
160	27.5	26.7	25.9	25.1	24.4	23.7	23.0	22.4	21.7	21.2	20.6	20.0	19.5	19.0	18.5	18.0	160
165	28.4	27.5	26.7	25.9	25.1	24.4	23.7	23.1	22.4	21.8	21.2	20.7	20.1	19.6	19.1	18.6	165
170	29.2	28.3	27.5	26.7	25.9	25.2	24.4	23.8	23.1	22.5	21.9	21.3	20.7	20.2	19.7	19.1	170
175	30.1	29.2	28.3	27.5	26.7	25.9	25.2	24.5	23.8	23.1	22.5	21.9	21.3	20.8	20.3	19.7	175
180	31.0	30.0	29.1	28.3	27.4	26.6	25.9	25.2	24.5	23.8	23.2	22.5	22.0	21.4	20.8	20.3	180
185	31.8	30.8	29.9	29.0	28.2	27.4	26.6	25.9	25.1	24.5	23.8	23.2	22.6	22.0	21.4	20.8	185
190	32.7	31.7	30.7	29.8	28.9	28.1	27.3	26.6	25.8	25.1	24.4	23.8	23.2	22.6	22.0	21.4	190
195	33.5	32.5	31.5	30.6	29.7	28.9	28.0	27.3	26.5	25.8	25.1	24.4	23.8	23.2	22.6	22.0	195
200	34.4	33.4	32.3	31.4	30.5	29.6	28.8	28.0	27.2	26.4	25.7	25.1	24.4	23.8	23.2	22.5	200
205	35.3	34.2	33.2	32.2	31.2	30.3	29.5	28.7	27.9	27.1	26.4	25.7	25.0	24.4	23.7	23.1	205
210	36.1	35.0	34.0	33.0	32.0	31.1	30.2	29.4	28.5	27.8	27.0	26.3	25.6	25.0	24.3	23.7	210
215	37.0	35.9	34.8	33.7	32.8	31.8	30.9	30.0	29.2	28.4	27.7	26.9	26.2	25.5	24.9	24.2	215
220	37.8	36.7	35.6	34.5	33.5	32.6	31.6	30.7	29.9	29.1	28.3	27.6	26.8	26.1	25.5	24.8	220
225	38.7	37.5	36.4	35.3	34.3	33.3	32.4	31.4	30.6	29.7	28.9	28.2	27.4	26.7	26.1	25.3	225
230	39.6	38.4	37.2	36.1	35.0	34.0	33.1	32.1	31.3	30.4	29.6	28.8	28.1	27.3	26.6	25.9	230
235	40.4	39.2	38.0	36.9	35.8	34.8	33.8	32.8	31.9	31.1	30.2	29.4	28.7	27.9	27.2	26.5	235
240	41.3	40.0	38.8	37.7	36.6	35.5	34.5	33.5	32.6	31.7	30.9	30.1	29.3	28.5	27.8	27.0	240
245	42.1	40.9	39.6	38.5	37.3	36.3	35.2	34.2	33.3	32.4	31.5	30.7	29.9	29.1	28.4	27.6	245
250	43.0	41.7	40.4	39.2	38.1	37.0	35.9	34.9	34.0	33.1	32.2	31.3	30.5	29.7	29.0	28.2	250
255	43.8	42.4	41.2	39.9	38.8	37.7	36.6	35.6	34.6	33.6	32.7	31.9	31.0	30.2	29.5	28.7	255
260	44.6	43.3	42.0	40.7	39.5	38.4	37.3	36.3	35.3	34.3	33.4	32.5	31.6	30.8	30.0	29.3	260
265	45.5	44.1	42.8	41.5	40.3	39.1	38.0	37.0	35.9	35.0	34.0	33.1	32.3	31.4	30.6	29.9	265
270	46.3	44.9	43.6	42.3	41.0	39.9	38.7	37.7	36.6	35.6	34.7	33.7	32.9	32.0	31.2	30.4	270
275	47.2	45.8	44.4	43.1	41.8	40.6	39.5	38.4	37.3	36.3	35.3	34.4	33.5	32.6	31.8	31.0	275
280	48.1	46.6	45.2	43.8	42.6	41.3	40.2	39.0	38.0	36.9	35.9	35.0	34.1	33.2	32.4	31.5	280
285	48.9	47.4	46.0	44.6	43.3	42.1	40.9	39.7	38.6	37.6	36.6	35.6	34.7	33.8	32.9	32.1	285
290	49.8	48.3	46.8	45.4	44.1	42.8	41.6	40.4	39.3	38.3	37.2	36.2	35.3	34.4	33.5	32.7	290
	64	65	66	67	68	69	70	71	72	73	74	75	76	77	78	79	
	Height (in.)																

From *Sport Education Seasons* by Sean M. Bulger et al., 2007, Champaign, IL: Human Kinetics.

Back-Saver Sit and Reach

Instructions: Assume back-saver sit and reach position. Slowly reach forward as far as you can. Complete one trial with right leg fully extended and repeat with left leg fully extended.

Rules: Remove shoes. Hands must be placed atop one another with palms down and must remain even throughout forward motion. Bottom leg should remain straight throughout stretch. Hold stretch until measured.

Scoring: Record number of inches reached to the nearest 1/2 inch (1 centimeter). Maximum score = 12 inches (30 centimeters). Record HFZ results.

Time: 2 minutes to complete test.

PICTURE	CUES
	1. One leg bent, other leg straight
	2. Even hands
	3. Stretch slowly, no bounce, and hold
	4. Hips and shoulders square to box
	5. Determine HFZ

HEALTHY FITNESS ZONE (HFZ)

Male			Female		
HFZ	–	Age	–	HFZ	
8-12		10		9-12	
8-12		11		10-12	
8-12		12		10-12	
8-12		13		10-12	
8-12		14		10-12	
8-12		15		12	
8-12		16		12	
8-12		17		12	
8-12		17 +		12	

Healthy Fitness Zone reprinted with permission from Cooper Institute, 2005, *FITNESSGRAM/ACTIVITYGRAM Test Administration Manual*, updated 3rd ed. (Champaign, IL: Human Kinetics), 61-62. From *Sport Education Seasons* by Sean M. Bulger et al., 2007, Champaign, IL: Human Kinetics.

Shoulder Stretch

Instructions: Touch fingertips together behind your back. Complete one right shoulder stretch and one left shoulder stretch.

Rules: No physical assistance is allowed during the stretch.

Scoring: Record HFZ for right shoulder stretch and left shoulder stretch (HFZ = touching fingertips).

Time: 1 minute to complete test.

PICTURE

CUES

1. Over top, pat back with one hand

2. Reach up with other hand

3. Stretch slowly, no bounce, and hold

4. Reverse hands

5. Determine HFZ

HEALTHY FITNESS ZONE (HFZ)

Male		Female	
HFZ	–	Age	–	HFZ
		10	
		11	
		12	
		13	
		14	
		15	
		16	
		17	
		17 +	

Passing = touching fingertips together behind the back on both the right and left sides

Passing = touching fingertips together behind the back on both the right and left sides

Healthy Fitness Zone reprinted with permission from Cooper Institute, 2005, *FITNESSGRAM/ACTIVITYGRAM Test Administration Manual*, updated 3rd ed. (Champaign, IL: Human Kinetics), 61-62. From *Sport Education Seasons* by Sean M. Bulger et al., 2007, Champaign, IL: Human Kinetics.

Push-Up

Instructions: Complete as many push-ups as possible at a rhythmic pace.

Rules: Performer is finished when he or she (1) stops or fails to maintain rhythmic pace or (2) performs two incorrect push-ups. **Incorrect push-ups:** Elbows do not achieve a 90-degree angle in the down position during each repetition; arms do not achieve full extension in the up position during each repetition; or back, hips, or legs bend.

Scoring: Record number of correctly performed push-ups. Record HFZ results.

Rhythm: One push-up every 3 seconds, that is, 20 per minute.

CUES

1. Body like a board

2. Lower body and bend elbows to 90 degrees

3. Extend arms straight

4. Rhythm: one rep every 3 seconds

5. Determine HFZ

PICTURE

HEALTHY FITNESS ZONE (HFZ)

Male		Female	
HFZ	Age		HFZ
7-20	10	–	7-15
8-20	11		7-15
10-20	12		7-15
12-25	13		7-15
14-30	14		7-15
16-35	15		7-15
18-35	16		7-15
18-35	17		7-15
18-35	17 +		7-15

Healthy Fitness Zone reprinted with permission from Cooper Institute, 2005, *FITNESSGRAM/ACTIVITYGRAM Test Administration Manual*, updated 3rd ed. (Champaign, IL: Human Kinetics), 61-62. From *Sport Education Seasons* by Sean M. Bulger et al., 2007, Champaign, IL: Human Kinetics.

Curl-Up

Instructions: Complete as many curl-ups (75 maximum) as possible at a rhythmic pace.

Rules: Performer is finished when he or she (1) stops or fails to maintain a rhythmic pace or (2) performs two incorrect curl-ups. **Incorrect curl-up:** Heels lose contact with floor, head does not return to mat on each repetition, fingertips fail to touch far side of measuring strip.

Scoring: Record number of correctly performed curl-ups. Maximum is 75 curl-ups. Record HFZ results.

Rhythm: One curl-up every 3 seconds, that is, 20 per minute.

PICTURE

CUES

1. Feet flat, back flat
2. Slide fingers across strip
3. Head returns to mat
4. Rhythm: one rep every 3 seconds
5. Determine HFZ

HEALTHY FITNESS ZONE (HFZ)

Male		Female	
HFZ	–	Age –	HFZ
12-24		10	12-26
15-28		11	15-29
18-36		12	18-32
21-40		13	18-32
24-45		14	18-32
24-47		15	18-35
24-47		16	18-35
24-47		17	18-35
24-47		17 +	18-35

Healthy Fitness Zone reprinted with permission from Cooper Institute, 2005, *FITNESSGRAM/ACTIVITYGRAM Test Administration Manual*, updated 3rd ed. (Champaign, IL: Human Kinetics), 61-62. From *Sport Education Seasons* by Sean M. Bulger et al., 2007, Champaign, IL: Human Kinetics.

Modified Pull-Up

Instructions: Complete as many modified pull-ups as possible at a rhythmic pace.

Rules: Performer is finished when he or she (1) stops or fails to maintain rhythmic pace or (2) performs two incorrect pull-ups. **Incorrect pull-up:** Arms do not achieve full extension in the down position during each repetition; elbows do not achieve a 90-degree angle in the up position during each repetition; or back, hips, or legs bend.

Scoring: Record number of correctly performed pull-ups. Record HFZ results.

Rhythm: Approximately one pull-up every 5 seconds, that is, 12 per minute.

CUES

1. Body like a board
2. Pull and bend elbows to 90 degrees
3. Extend arms straight
4. Rhythm: one rep every 5 seconds
5. Determine HFZ

PICTURE

HEALTHY FITNESS ZONE (HFZ)

Male		Female	
HFZ	–	Age	–	HFZ
5-15		10		4-13
6-17		11		4-13
7-20		12		4-13
8-22		13		4-13
9-25		14		4-13
10-27		15		4-13
12-30		16		4-13
14-30		17		4-13
14-30		17 +		4-13

Healthy Fitness Zone reprinted with permission from Cooper Institute, 2005, *FITNESSGRAM/ACTIVITYGRAM Test Administration Manual*, updated 3rd ed. (Champaign, IL: Human Kinetics), 61-62. From *Sport Education Seasons* by Sean M. Bulger et al., 2007, Champaign, IL: Human Kinetics.

Trunk Lift

Instructions: Lying facedown and in a controlled motion, lift upper body off of the floor as high as possible (12 inches [30 centimeters] maximum) and hold for measurement.

Rules: Toes must remain pointed and in contact with ground throughout movement. Hands must remain positioned palms up and under thighs throughout movement. Do not bounce or use quick movements. Do not lift upper body higher than 12 inches from floor.

Scoring: Record number of inches reached to the nearest inch. Maximum height is 12 inches. Record HFZ results.

Time: 1 minute to complete test.

CUES

1. Lie facedown
2. Palms to thighs
3. Toes pointed
4. Lift slowly, no bounce, and hold
5. Determine HFZ

PICTURE

HEALTHY FITNESS ZONE (HFZ)

Male		Female	
HFZ	–	Age	–	HFZ
9-12		10		9-12
9-12		11		9-12
9-12		12		9-12
9-12		13		9-12
9-12		14		9-12
9-12		15		9-12
9-12		16		9-12
9-12		17		9-12
9-12		17 +		9-12

Healthy Fitness Zone reprinted with permission from Cooper Institute, 2005, *FITNESSGRAM/ACTIVITYGRAM Test Administration Manual*, updated 3rd ed. (Champaign, IL: Human Kinetics), 61-62. From *Sport Education Seasons* by Sean M. Bulger et al., 2007, Champaign, IL: Human Kinetics.

Vertical Jump

Instructions: Jump as high as possible. During each jump, reach for the sky as if you were rebounding a basketball.

Rules: Performer must take off and land on same spot. Feet must remain together during takeoff and landing.

Scoring: Complete three jumps and record the highest score.

Time: 1 minute to complete test.

FLOOR DIAGRAM	PICTURE	CUES
	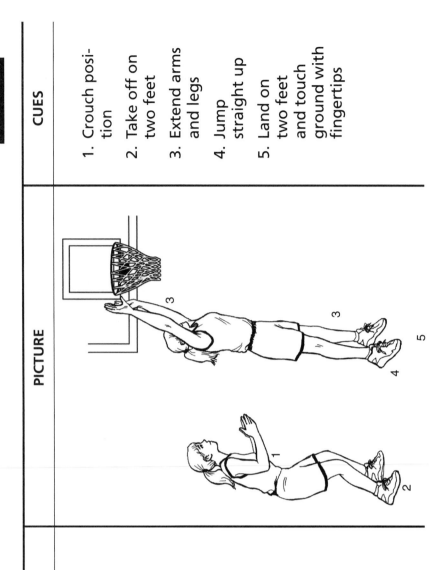	1. Crouch position
		2. Take off on two feet
Jump straight up in space provided		3. Extend arms and legs
		4. Jump straight up
		5. Land on two feet and touch ground with fingertips

T-Run

Instructions: Complete as many T-run repetitions as possible in time permitted. The runner should slide to the right on the first repetition and to the left on the next repetition and then repeat the T-run.

Rules: The runner must start from and return to the beginning cone during each repetition. The center and end cones must be touched on each sprint-slide-sprint sequence. Runner should always face the same direction during the slide portion of the T-run.

Scoring: Record the number of completed T-runs. One sprint-slide-sprint sequence equals one repetition.

Time: 30 seconds.

CUES

1. Sprint
2. Touch center cone
3. Side slide left, touch end cone, repeat to right
4. Side slide left, touch center cone
5. Backpedal to starting cone

PICTURE

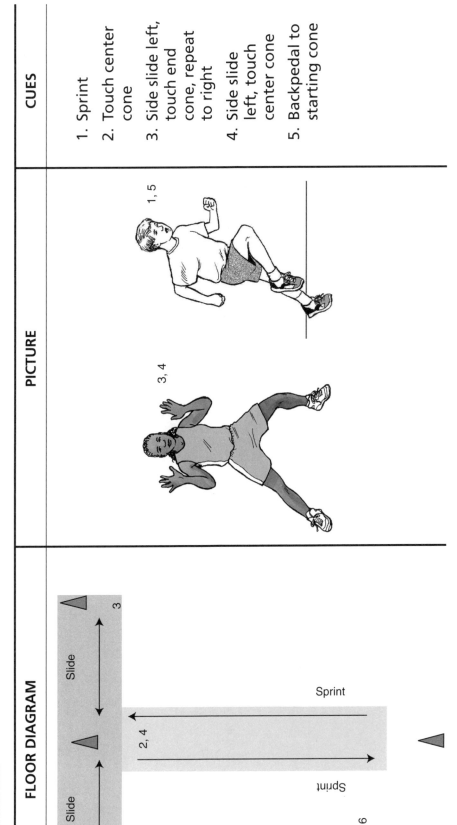

FLOOR DIAGRAM

From *Sport Education Seasons* by Sean M. Bulger et al., 2007, Champaign, IL: Human Kinetics.

Shuttle Run

Instructions: Complete as many sprints to and from the starting point as possible during time permitted.

Rules: The runner must touch each end line before changing directions. If the runner does not touch an end line before changing directions, the repetition does not count.

Scoring: Record the number of times the runner touches each end line. Each end line touched equals one repetition.

Time: 30 seconds.

FLOOR DIAGRAM	PICTURE	CUES
		1. Sprint
		2. Lean back and lower body to stop
		3. Touch end line
		4. Sprint back
		5. Repeat

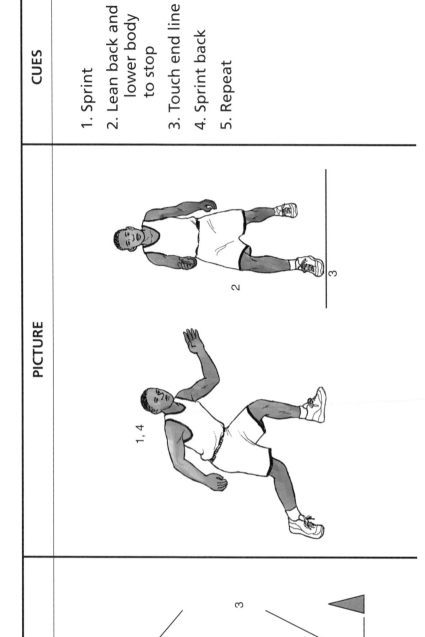

End line B

1, 5

End line A

A to B = 1 repetition

1, 4

2

3

3

Line Jump

Instructions: Perform as many line jumps as possible during the time permitted. Jumps may be in random order.

Rules: Performer must cross each line completely for the repetition to count. Feet must remain together during takeoff and landing.

Scoring: Record the number of lines jumped. Each line jumped equals one repetition.

Time: 30 seconds.

PICTURE

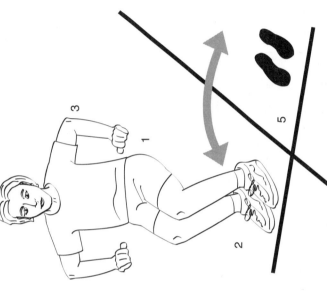

CUES

1. Slight crouched position

2. Take off and land on two feet

3. Use arms for balance

4. Jump randomly front-to-back, side-to-side, or diagonally

5. Quick feet

FLOOR DIAGRAM

From *Sport Education Seasons* by Sean M. Bulger et al., 2007, Champaign, IL: Human Kinetics.

Low Control Dribble

Instructions: Dribble ball while remaining stationary. Complete one trial with right hand and repeat with left hand.

Rules: Reset count at "0" if dribbler loses control during the timed trial. Ball must bounce to a height between the top of cone and the waist. Dribbler cannot move.

Scoring: Record number of consecutive dribbles. Each dribble equals 1 point. If dribbler loses control and resets count, record the highest score.

Time: 30 seconds for each hand.

FLOOR DIAGRAM	PICTURE	CUES
Stationary dribble here	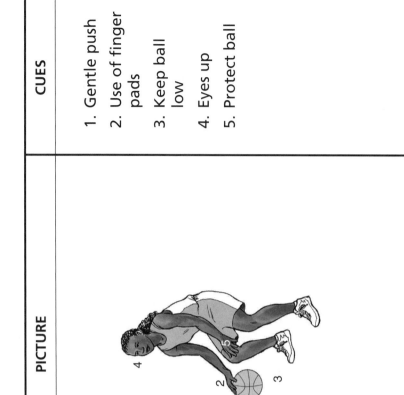	1. Gentle push 2. Use of finger pads 3. Keep ball low 4. Eyes up 5. Protect ball

From *Sport Education Seasons* by Sean M. Bulger et al., 2007, Champaign, IL: Human Kinetics.

Speed Dribble

Instructions: Dribble ball from end line A to end line B and back again. Continue sequence until time is up. Complete one timed trial with right hand and a second timed trial with left hand.

Rules: If dribbler loses control of ball, do not count that lap. Dribbler must cross each end line for a lap to count.

Scoring: Record number of laps completed. End lines A to B or end lines B to A equals one lap.

Time: 45 seconds for each hand.

FLOOR DIAGRAM	PICTURE	CUES
		1. Gentle push
		2. Use of finger pads
End line B		3. Ball under control
		4. Eyes up
A to B = 1 repetition		5. Push and chase
End line A		

From *Sport Education Seasons* by Sean M. Bulger et al., 2007, Champaign, IL: Human Kinetics.

Layup

Instructions: Complete as many layups as possible during time permitted. Complete one timed trial from right side and a second timed trial from left side.

Rules: Each layup attempt must begin from the designated starting spot. Layups not originating from designated starting spot do not count. Must use right hand on right-side layup, and left hand on left-side layup.

Scoring: Record number of layups made. Each layup made equals 1 point.

Time: 45 seconds from each side.

FLOOR DIAGRAM	PICTURE	CUES
Starting point left side Starting point right side		1. Power drive 2. Up with two hands 3. Left hand–right foot, right hand–left foot 4. One-hand gentle release 5. Bank ball

From *Sport Education Seasons* by Sean M. Bulger et al., 2007, Champaign, IL: Human Kinetics.

Set Shot

Instructions: Complete 10 set shots from the foul line.

Rules: Both feet must stay in contact with ground and remain behind the foul line.

Scoring: Record number of set shots made. Each set shot made equals 1 point.

Criteria: Number of set shots made out of 10 attempts.

FLOOR DIAGRAM	PICTURE	CUES
Set shot from foul line		1. Balanced position 2. Take up with two hands 3. Feet to floor 4. Straighten arm, wave good-bye to ball

From *Sport Education Seasons* by Sean M. Bulger et al., 2007, Champaign, IL: Human Kinetics.

Jump Shot (Midrange)

Instructions: Complete as many midrange jump shots as possible during the time permitted. Move to a different designated spot following each attempt. (Rebounding options: shooter or partner must be consistent on pre- and posttests.)

Rules: Player must shoot from one of the five designated spots. Player cannot shoot two consecutive shots from the same spot. Both feet must leave ground for a made shot to be counted.

Scoring: Record number of midrange jump shots made. Each midrange jump shot made equals 1 point.

Time: 45 seconds.

FLOOR DIAGRAM	PICTURE	CUES
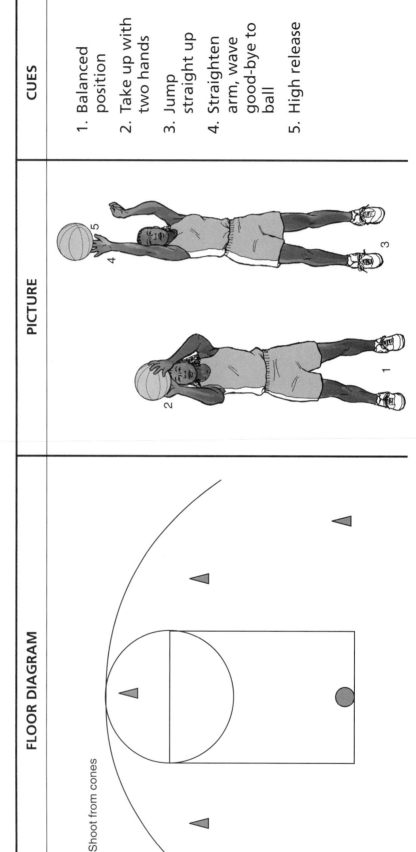 Shoot from cones		1. Balanced position 2. Take up with two hands 3. Jump straight up 4. Straighten arm, wave good-bye to ball 5. High release

From *Sport Education Seasons* by Sean M. Bulger et al., 2007, Champaign, IL: Human Kinetics.

Jump Shot (Long Range)

STATION
18

Instructions: Complete as many long-range jump shots as possible during the time permitted. Move to a different designated spot following each attempt. (Rebounding options: shooter or partner must be consistent on pre- and posttests.)

Rules: Player must shoot from one of the three designated spots. Player cannot shoot two consecutive shots from the same spot. Both feet must leave ground for a made shot to be counted.

Scoring: Record number of long-range jump shots made. Each long-range jump shot made equals 1 point.

FLOOR DIAGRAM	PICTURE	CUES
Shoot from cones		1. Balanced position
		2. Take up with two hands
		3. Jump straight up
		4. Straighten arm, wave good-bye to ball
		5. High release

From *Sport Education Seasons* by Sean M. Bulger et al., 2007, Champaign, IL: Human Kinetics.

Rebounding

Instructions: Secure as many consecutive rebounds as possible during the time permitted. Rebounder must begin at spot 1 by throwing ball at target area. Then rebounder must move to spot 2 to secure the rebound. Next, the rebounder repeats same sequence from spot 2. Repeat until time is up.

Rules: Ball must rebound off of designated target area (top-center of backboard). Rebounder cannot secure two consecutive rebounds from same spot. If rebounder loses control of ball, then that rebound does not count.

Scoring: Record number of secured rebounds. Each secured rebound equals 1 point.

Time: 30 seconds.

FLOOR DIAGRAM	PICTURE	CUES
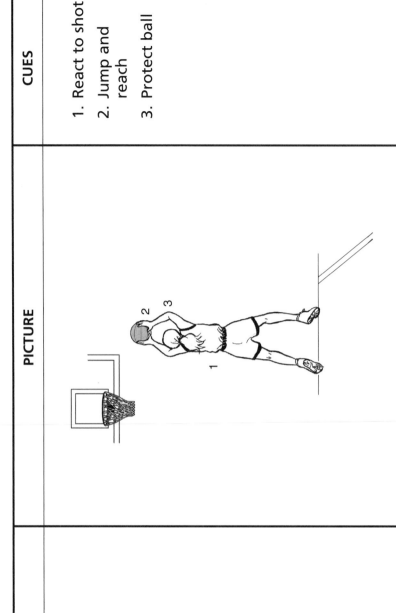	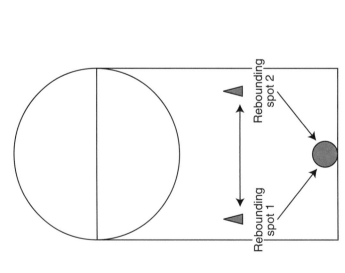	1. React to shot 2. Jump and reach 3. Protect ball

From *Sport Education Seasons* by Sean M. Bulger et al., 2007, Champaign, IL: Human Kinetics.

Passing: Chest and Bounce

Instructions: Start passing sequence from point A with a chest pass. Alternate chest and bounce passes while moving sideways. Make a pass only when directly in line with the target. Use chest passes to lower targets, bounce passes to higher targets. Continue from point A to B and back again until time is up. Make sure you use the same distance in lessons 1 and 21.

Rules: Chest passes count only if pass hits appropriate target area. Bounce passes count only if pass hits appropriate target area. Passer must remain behind passing line while attempting passes.

Scoring: Record number of accurate chest passes and number of accurate bounce passes separately. Each accurate pass equals 1 point.

Time: 45 seconds.

FLOOR DIAGRAM	PICTURE	CUES
		1. Use two hands
		2. Step
		3. Chest pass—push out; bounce pass—push down and out
		4. Chest pass—pass to chest level; bounce pass—bounce close to target

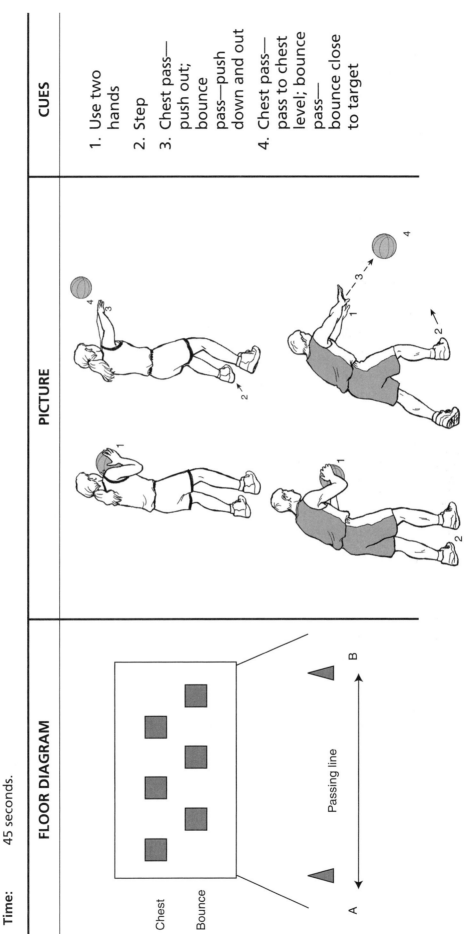

From *Sport Education Seasons* by Sean M. Bulger et al., 2007, Champaign, IL: Human Kinetics.

PASE Basketball Fitness Combine Recording Sheet

Name: _____ Age: _____ Gender: ☐ Male ☐ Female

INSTRUCTIONS

To record your fitness, combine information for each station:

1. Read the fitness combine activity task card.
2. Perform the activity according to the criteria on the task card.
3. Locate appropriate scoring box for the activity that you completed.
4. Record appropriate measure in the scoring box.
5. Refer to the row showing the example to help you record accurately.

Fitness Components

HEALTH-RELATED

Activity	Aerobic fitness (AF)	Body composition (BC)	Flexibility (Flx)		Muscular fitness (MF)			
	PACER	Body mass index	Sit and reach	Shoulder stretch	Push-up	Curl-up	Modified pull-up	Trunk lift
Station	1	2	3	4	5	6	7	8
Example	Laps # 19 ✓HFZ	BMI 19.6 ✓HFZ	Inches: 11.5 ✓HFZ	R:☐HFZ L:☐HFZ	Reps: 15 ✓HFZ	Reps: 29 ✓HFZ	Reps: 7 ✓HFZ	Inches: 10 ✓HFZ
Prescore	Laps # ☐HFZ	BMI ☐HFZ	Inches: ☐HFZ	R:☐HFZ L:☐HFZ	Reps: ☐HFZ	Reps: ☐HFZ	Reps: ☐HFZ	Inches: ☐HFZ
Goals	Laps #	BMI	Inches:	R:☐HFZ L:☐HFZ	Reps:	Reps:	Reps:	Inches:
Postscore	Laps # ☐HFZ	BMI ☐HFZ	Inches: ☐HFZ	R:☐HFZ L:☐HFZ	Reps: ☐HFZ	Reps: ☐HFZ	Reps: ☐HFZ	Inches: ☐HFZ

SKILL-RELATED

	Power	Agility	Speed	Balance
	Vertical jump	T-run	Shuttle run	Line jump
Station	9	10	11	12
Example	Inches: 18	Reps: 3	Reps: 7	Reps: 21
Prescore	Inches:	Reps:	Reps:	Reps:
Goals	Inches:	Reps:	Reps:	Reps:
Postscore	Inches:	Reps:	Reps:	Reps:

From *Sport Education Seasons* by Sean M. Bulger et al., 2007, Champaign, IL: Human Kinetics.

PASE Basketball Skills Combine Recording Sheet

Name: _____ Age: _____ Gender: ☐ Male ☐ Female

INSTRUCTIONS

To record your skills, combine information for each station:

1. Read the skills combine activity task card.
2. Perform the activity according to the criteria on the task card.
3. Locate appropriate scoring box for the activity that you completed.
4. Record appropriate measure in the scoring box.
5. Refer to the row showing the example to help you record accurately.

Basketball Skills

Activity	Ball handling			Scoring			Obtaining/Maintaining ball possession		
	Low control dribble	Speed dribble	Layup	Set shot	Jump shot (midrange)	Jump shot (long range)	Rebounding	Passing: chest	Passing: bounce
Station	13	14	15	16	17	18	19	20	
Example	R: 32 L: 17	R: laps 4 L: laps 2	R: 8 L: 5	4 /10	5	2	18	Ticks: IIII IIII IIII III Total #: 18	Ticks: IIII IIII IIII Total #: 14
Prescore	R: ___ L: ___	R: ___ laps L: ___ laps	R: ___ L: ___	___/10	___	___	___	Ticks: Total #:	Ticks: Total #:
Goals	R: ___ L: ___	R: ___ laps L: ___ laps	R: ___ L: ___	___/10	___	___	___	Ticks: Total #:	Ticks: Total #:
Postscore	R: ___ L: ___	R: ___ laps L: ___ laps	R: ___ L: ___	___/10	___	___	___	Ticks: Total #:	Ticks: Total #:

From *Sport Education Seasons* by Sean M. Bulger et al., 2007, Champaign, IL: Human Kinetics.

PASE Basketball Skills and Fitness Combine Draft Composite

Instructions: Place each student's name in the name column prior to the combine. Coaches should observe students' performance during the combine and determine a draft order for each student in the class. In addition, coaches should take notes to assist in making decisions during the team selection process.

Note: Coaches must keep all student performance and draft selection information confidential.

Name	Draft order	Notes

From *Sport Education Seasons* by Sean M. Bulger et al., 2007, Champaign, IL: Human Kinetics.

Instructions: The purpose of this draft is to use the information collected during the skills and fitness combine to create a successful basketball team. Each person will have the opportunity to select first in one of the selection rounds. As a player is selected from the combine sheet, simply draw a line through his or her name. This will aid in avoiding the duplication of selections in later rounds. After the draft is complete, teams will be placed into a pool. Each coach will then randomly select a team from the pool. It is important that you select the most fair and competent team possible during the draft because you may not end up coaching the team you drafted. It will be important to keep players' drafting order confidential in order to preserve the integrity of the process. Good luck.

Team: _____

Coach: _____

Round	Player's name
1	
2	
3	
4	
5	
6	
7	
8	

Lessons 2-24 Instructional Materials

CONTENTS

Basketball Team Roster

Team ___ Members

Jersey #	

From *Sport Education Seasons* by Sean M. Bulger et al., 2007, Champaign, IL: Human Kinetics.

PASE Basketball Roles and Responsibilities Assignments

Instructions: To determine your daily role, locate your name with the left index finger and the daily lesson number with the right index finger. Move the finger on your name from left to right and the finger on the daily lesson number from top to bottom. At the point where your fingers intersect, you have located a box with a letter in it. This letter corresponds to a particular role. Use the following key to identify your daily role. Next, pinpoint the responsibilities associated with your role using the "Role Responsibilities" table at the bottom of the page.

KEY

A = fitness trainer   B = sports information director   C = official   D = manager   E = scorekeeper

											LESSON										
Name	3	4	5	6	7	8	9	10	11	12	13	14	15	16	17	18	19	20	22	23	24
(COACH)	A	E	D	C	B	A	E	D	C	B	A	E	D	C	B	A	E	D	C	B	A
	B	A	E	D	C	B	A	E	D	C	B	A	E	D	C	B	A	E	D	C	B
	C	B	A	E	D	C	B	A	E	D	C	B	A	E	D	C	B	A	E	D	C
	D	C	B	A	E	D	C	B	A	E	D	C	B	A	E	D	C	B	A	E	D
	E	D	C	B	A	E	D	C	B	A	E	D	C	B	A	E	D	C	B	A	E

ROLE RESPONSIBILITIES

Coach
- Leads skill and strategy practice
- Assists teacher when needed
- Makes decisions about team lineup
- Provides leadership for team

A: Fitness Trainer
- Selects and leads team warm-up activities
- Records team warm-up information
- Reports injuries to teacher
- Aids teacher to administer first aid

B: Sports Information Director
- Acquires compiled records from scorekeeper
- Publicizes records via school newsletter and in other ways
- Reports daily progress to teammates
- Assumes role responsibilities for absent teammates

C: Official
- Manages the contests
- Interprets rules during contests
- Mediates conflicts
- Maintains contest pacing

D: Manager
- Inspects and cares for equipment
- Distributes and collects equipment
- Monitors teammates' role performance
- Organizes home court space
- Monitors time of lesson components
- Records daily attendance information
- Assumes administrative duties as assigned by teacher

E: Scorekeeper
- Records scores during contests
- Maintains ongoing team records
- Summarizes contest scores
- Provides final records to appropriate person

From *Sport Education Seasons* by Sean M. Bulger et al., 2007, Champaign, IL: Human Kinetics.

PASE Basketball Roles and Responsibilities Recording Sheet

Name: _____

Instructions: Determine your role and corresponding responsibilities for the day's lesson. At the end of the lesson you will be asked to determine the responsibilities that you successfully completed. For each responsibility successfully completed, place a check [✓] in the box. For each responsibility that you did not successfully complete, place a zero [0] in the box. If an opportunity to complete a responsibility did not occur, place "n/a" (not applicable) in the appropriate box.

Roles and responsibilities	Lesson																					
	3	4	5	6	7	8	9	10	11	12	13	14	15	16	17	18	19	20	21	22	23	24
Coach																						
• Leads skill and strategy practice																						
• Assists teacher when needed																						
• Makes decisions about team lineups																						
• Provides leadership for team																						
A. Fitness trainer																						
• Selects and leads team warm-up activities																						
• Records team warm-up information																						
• Reports injuries to teacher																						
• Aids teacher in administering first aid																						
B. Sports information director																						
• Acquires compiled records from scorekeeper																						
• Publicizes records via school newsletter and other means																						
• Reports progress daily to teammates																						
• Assumes role responsibilities of absent teammates																						
C. Official																						
• Manages contests																						
• Interprets rules during contests																						
• Mediates conflicts																						
• Maintains contest pacing																						
D. Manager																						
• Inspects and cares for equipment																						
• Distributes and collects equipment																						
• Monitors teammates' role performance																						
• Organizes home court space																						
• Monitors time of lesson components																						
• Assumes administrative duties assigned by teacher																						
E. Scorekeeper																						
• Records scores during contests																						
• Maintains ongoing team records																						
• Summarizes contest scores																						
• Provides final records to appropriate person																						

From *Sport Education Seasons* by Sean M. Bulger et al., 2007, Champaign, IL: Human Kinetics.

Basketball Tribune

Author: _____   Team: _____

Date: _____

Article title: _____

_____

_____

_____

_____

_____

_____

_____

_____

_____

_____

_____

_____

_____

_____

_____

_____

_____

_____

_____

_____

_____

Caption:

--(cut here)--

- Get scores (team and individual) for the day's game from your scorekeeper so that you can include this information in your article (don't take the stats sheet out of class—you may want to jot this info down on the back of the sports page).
- Publicize the day's events and records via a sports page article:
  - Must be neatly written.
  - Give your sports page article a title. Align article title with your team's color, mascot, name, and so on.
  - Article should cover each team member's contribution to the day's warm-up, review, practice, contest, and so on.
  - Include your name (author), your team's name, the date, location (i.e., home field nickname), and any other information that you deem important.
- This sports page article is due at the beginning of the next class. It must be returned and must meet the listed criteria in order for you to successfully complete your role.
- You will have the opportunity to share your article with your team and post it in your home field area.

From *Sport Education Seasons* by Sean M. Bulger et al., 2007, Champaign, IL: Human Kinetics.

PASE Basketball Personal Fitness Recording Sheet

Name: _____ Age: _____ Gender: ☐ Male ☐ Female

Instructions: To record your personal fitness information for each lesson:

1. Circle the number of the workout that you completed for each fitness component.
2. If a cell has the symbol "☐," check it off when the workout is correctly completed.
3. If a cell is empty, record a number (e.g., "14") when the workout is successfully completed.

KEY
HFZ = healthy fitness zone

FITNESS COMPONENTS

Prescore	Aerobic fitness (AF) and body composition (BC)	Flexibility (Flx)		Muscular fitness (MF)	Skill related (S-R)
	PACER:_____laps ☐ HFZ	Sit and reach	R:_____in. ☐ HFZ	Push-up: ☐ HFZ	1.
	BMI: ☐ HFZ		L:_____in. ☐ HFZ	Curl-up: ☐ HFZ	2.
	Height:_____in.	Shoulder stretch	R ☐ HFZ	Mod. pull-up: ☐ HFZ	3.
	Weight:_____lb		L ☐ HFZ	Trunk lift: ☐ HFZ	4.

Lesson	AF workout no.	Ending heart rate?	Red face?	Sweating?	Breathing heavy?	Flx workout no.	Stretch slowly?	Muscle tension?	No bounce?	Hold 10-30 sec.	MF workout no.	Activity repetitions A.	B.	C.	S-R workout no.	Repetitions
Example	1 2 3 4	152	☑	☑	☑	1 2 3 4	☑	☑	☑	☑	1 2 3 4	12	17	13	1 2 3 4	6
Practice	1 ②3 4		☐	☐	☐	1 ②3 4	☐	☐	☐	☐	1 ②3 4				1 ②3 4	
3.	1 2 3 4		☐	☐	☐	1 2 3 4	☐	☐	☐	☐	1 2 3 4				1 2 3 4	
4.	1 2 3 4		☐	☐	☐	1 2 3 4	☐	☐	☐	☐	1 2 3 4				1 2 3 4	
5.	1 2 3 4		☐	☐	☐	1 2 3 4	☐	☐	☐	☐	1 2 3 4				1 2 3 4	
6.	1 2 3 4		☐	☐	☐	1 2 3 4	☐	☐	☐	☐	1 2 3 4				1 2 3 4	
7.	1 2 3 4		☐	☐	☐	1 2 3 4	☐	☐	☐	☐	1 2 3 4				1 2 3 4	
8.	1 2 3 4		☐	☐	☐	1 2 3 4	☐	☐	☐	☐	1 2 3 4				1 2 3 4	
9.	1 2 3 4		☐	☐	☐	1 2 3 4	☐	☐	☐	☐	1 2 3 4				1 2 3 4	
10.	1 2 3 4		☐	☐	☐	1 2 3 4	☐	☐	☐	☐	1 2 3 4				1 2 3 4	
11.	1 2 3 4		☐	☐	☐	1 2 3 4	☐	☐	☐	☐	1 2 3 4				1 2 3 4	

From *Sport Education Seasons* by Sean M. Bulger et al., 2007, Champaign, IL: Human Kinetics.

Lesson	AF workout no.	Ending heart rate?	Red face?	Sweating?	Breathing heavy?	Flx workout no.	Stretch slowly?	Muscle tension?	No bounce?	Hold 10-30 sec.	MF workout no.	Activity repetitions A.	B.	C.	S-R workout no.	Repetitions
12.	1 2 3 4		☐	☐	☐	1 2 3 4	☐	☐	☐	☐	1 2 3 4				1 2 3 4	
13.	1 2 3 4		☐	☐	☐	1 2 3 4	☐	☐	☐	☐	1 2 3 4				1 2 3 4	
14.	1 2 3 4		☐	☐	☐	1 2 3 4	☐	☐	☐	☐	1 2 3 4				1 2 3 4	
15.	1 2 3 4		☐	☐	☐	1 2 3 4	☐	☐	☐	☐	1 2 3 4				1 2 3 4	
16.	1 2 3 4		☐	☐	☐	1 2 3 4	☐	☐	☐	☐	1 2 3 4				1 2 3 4	
17.	1 2 3 4		☐	☐	☐	1 2 3 4	☐	☐	☐	☐	1 2 3 4				1 2 3 4	
18.	1 2 3 4		☐	☐	☐	1 2 3 4	☐	☐	☐	☐	1 2 3 4				1 2 3 4	
19.	1 2 3 4		☐	☐	☐	1 2 3 4	☐	☐	☐	☐	1 2 3 4				1 2 3 4	
20.	1 2 3 4		☐	☐	☐	1 2 3 4	☐	☐	☐	☐	1 2 3 4				1 2 3 4	
22.	1 2 3 4		☐	☐	☐	1 2 3 4	☐	☐	☐	☐	1 2 3 4				1 2 3 4	
23.	1 2 3 4		☐	☐	☐	1 2 3 4	☐	☐	☐	☐	1 2 3 4				1 2 3 4	

Goals	PACER:_____laps ☐ HFZ	Sit and reach	R:_____in. ☐ HFZ	Push-up: ☐ HFZ	1.
	BMI/%: ☐ HFZ		L:_____in. ☐ HFZ	Curl-up: ☐ HFZ	2.
	Height:_____in.	Shoulder stretch	R ☐ HFZ	Mod. pull-up: ☐ HFZ	3.
	Weight:_____lb		L ☐ HFZ	Trunk lift: ☐ HFZ	4.
Postscore	PACER:_____laps ☐ HFZ	Sit and reach	R:_____in. ☐ HFZ	Push-up: ☐ HFZ	1.
	BMI/%: ☐ HFZ		L:_____in. ☐ HFZ	Curl-up: ☐ HFZ	2.
	Height:_____in.	Shoulder stretch	R ☐ HFZ	Mod. pull-up: ☐ HFZ	3.
	Weight:_____lb		L ☐ HFZ	Trunk lift: ☐ HFZ	4.

From *Sport Education Seasons* by Sean M. Bulger et al., 2007, Champaign, IL: Human Kinetics.

Team: _____

Instructions: To begin each lesson, select a warm-up (1, 2, 3, or 4) and circle your team's choice. Remember that your team cannot repeat a workout that they have previously done until your team has completed all four workouts. Check off each activity as your team completes it. After finishing the warm-up, record the names of your teammates who are absent or late on the Attendance Recording Sheet. Beside each name, use an "A" to indicate absent or an "L" to indicate late. Lastly, sign your name to indicate that the information is correct.

LESSONS

Warm-up activities	3				4				5				6				7			
	1	2	3	4	1	2	3	4	1	2	3	4	1	2	3	4	1	2	3	4
Aerobic fitness (AF)	☐				☐				☐				☐				☐			
Flexibility (Flx)	☐				☐				☐				☐				☐			
Muscular fitness (MF)	☐				☐				☐				☐				☐			
Skill-related fitness (S-R)	☐				☐				☐				☐				☐			
Fitness trainer signature																				

Warm-up activities	8				9				10				11				12			
	1	2	3	4	1	2	3	4	1	2	3	4	1	2	3	4	1	2	3	4
Aerobic fitness (AF)	☐				☐				☐				☐				☐			
Flexibility (Flx)	☐				☐				☐				☐				☐			
Muscular fitness (MF)	☐				☐				☐				☐				☐			
Skill-related fitness (S-R)	☐				☐				☐				☐				☐			
Fitness trainer signature																				

Warm-up activities	13				14				15				16				17			
	1	2	3	4	1	2	3	4	1	2	3	4	1	2	3	4	1	2	3	4
Aerobic fitness (AF)	☐				☐				☐				☐				☐			
Flexibility (Flx)	☐				☐				☐				☐				☐			
Muscular fitness (MF)	☐				☐				☐				☐				☐			
Skill-related fitness (S-R)	☐				☐				☐				☐				☐			
Fitness trainer signature																				

Warm-up activities	18				19				20				22				23			
	1	2	3	4	1	2	3	4	1	2	3	4	1	2	3	4	1	2	3	4
Aerobic fitness (AF)	☐				☐				☐				☐				☐			
Flexibility (Flx)	☐				☐				☐				☐				☐			
Muscular fitness (MF)	☐				☐				☐				☐				☐			
Skill-related fitness (S-R)	☐				☐				☐				☐				☐			
Fitness trainer signature																				

From *Sport Education Seasons* by Sean M. Bulger et al., 2007, Champaign, IL: Human Kinetics.

Instructions: Select one workout number (1, 2, 3, or 4) for each fitness component. Complete the workout to criteria and record the required information on your Team or Personal Fitness Recording Sheet. Remember to select a different workout number each day and to complete all four workouts before repeating any previously completed workout.

Aerobic Fitness

Criteria:
- Move continuously for 3 minutes
- Elevate heart rate
- Break a sweat
- Increase breathing rate
- Check heart rate when finished with AF activity

AF 1

JUMP ROPE

Options:
- One or two feet
- Alternating feet
- Swing rope to front or back

AF 2

JOGGING LAPS

Options:
- Power walk
- Vary pace
- Alone or with a partner
- Dribbling a ball

AF 3

DEFENSIVE SLIDE

Options:
- Vary pace
- Vary direction (slide left and right)
- Dribbling a ball

AF 4

PACER SPRINTS

Options:
- Power walk
- Vary pace
- Alone or with a partner
- Dribbling a ball

From Sport Education Seasons by Sean M. Bulger et al., 2007, Champaign, IL: Human Kinetics.

Flexibility

Criteria:
- Stretch slowly
- Stretch until muscle tension is felt
- Do not bounce

	FLX 1	FLX 2	FLX 3	FLX 4
Upper body	Latissimus dorsi	Triceps	Deltoids	Trapezius
Lower leg	Calves	Calves	Calves	Calves
Upper leg	Quadriceps	Gluteus	Hamstrings	Adductors
Torso	Obliques	Obliques	Abdominals	Obliques

From *Sport Education Seasons* by Sean M. Bulger et al., 2007, Champaign, IL: Human Kinetics.

Muscular Fitness

Criteria:
- Complete as many repetitions in one set as possible
- Maintain controlled rhythm
- Isolate performing muscles

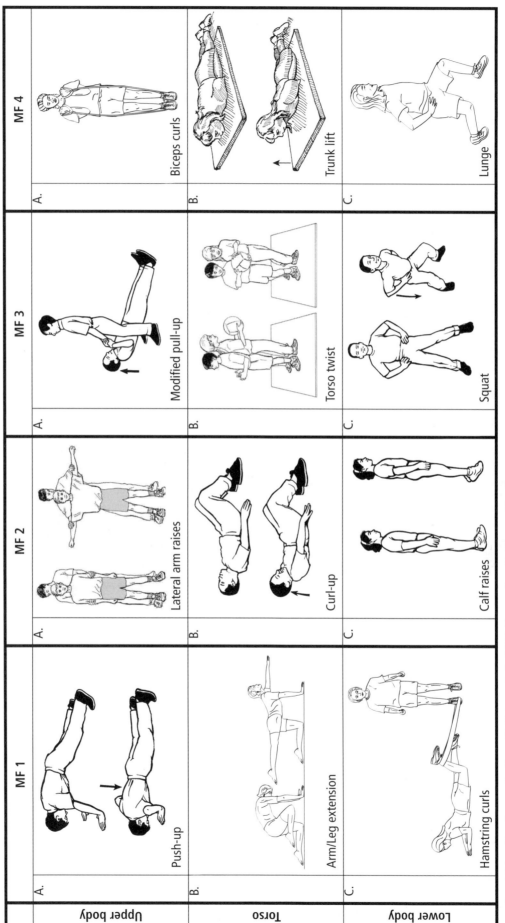

	MF 1	MF 2	MF 3	MF 4
Upper body	A. Push-up	A. Lateral arm raises	A. Modified pull-up	A. Biceps curls
Torso	B. Arm/Leg extension	B. Curl-up	B. Torso twist	B. Trunk lift
Lower body	C. Hamstring curls	C. Calf raises	C. Squat	C. Lunge

From *Sport Education Seasons* by Sean M. Bulger et al., 2007, Champaign, IL: Human Kinetics.

Skill-Related Fitness

Criteria:
- Complete as many repetitions as possible in 30 seconds
- Model picture during performance
- Be quick but under control

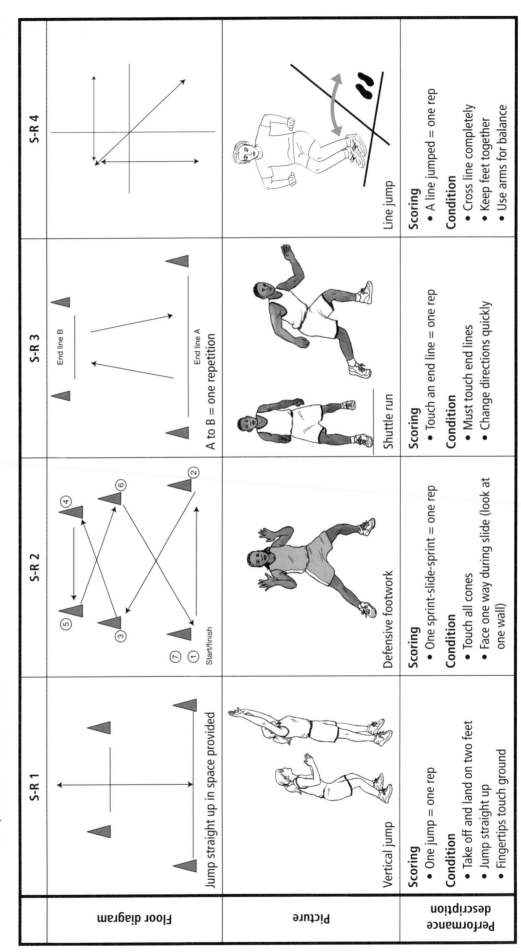

	S-R 1	S-R 2	S-R 3	S-R 4
Floor diagram	Jump straight up in space provided		End line B / End line A / A to B = one repetition	
Picture	Vertical jump	Defensive footwork	Shuttle run	Line jump
Performance description	**Scoring** • One jump = one rep **Condition** • Take off and land on two feet • Jump straight up • Fingertips touch ground	**Scoring** • One sprint-slide-sprint = one rep **Condition** • Touch all cones • Face one way during slide (look at one wall)	**Scoring** • Touch an end line = one rep **Condition** • Must touch end lines • Change directions quickly	**Scoring** • A line jumped = one rep **Condition** • Cross line completely • Keep feet together • Use arms for balance

From *Sport Education Seasons* by Sean M. Bulger et al., 2007, Champaign, IL: Human Kinetics.

PASE Basketball Individual Activity Task Card Recording Sheet

Name: _____   Team: _____

Instructions: Mark tasks off as you complete them. If a cell has the symbol "□," check it off (like this: "☑") when the task is completed. If a cell has the symbol "#," record a number (e.g., 14) when the task is completed. Leave empty cells blank.

KEY: 👤 = Self-evaluation   👥 = Peer evaluation   📋 = Coach evaluation

Task	Lesson 3 – Dribble to reposition (self)	(peer)	(coach)	Lesson 4 – Speed dribble and chest pass (self)	(peer)	(coach)	Lesson 5 – Dribble review and pass (self)	(peer)	(coach)	Lesson 7 – Shooting and def. mov't. (self)	(peer)	(coach)	Lesson 8 – Layup and give and go (self)	(peer)	(coach)
1.			□			□			□			□			□
2.			□			□			□			□			□
3.	□			□				□		□			□		
4.	□			□				□		□			#__		□
5.	□			□				□		□			□		
6.	□			□			#__		□		□			□	
7.		□			□			□		#__			□		
8.	#__		□	□			□			□			□		
9.	□			#__	□		□			□				□	
10.	□				□		#__		□	□			□		
11.	□			□			□				□		□		
12.	#__		□	□			□				□		□		
13.	□			#__	□			□		□			□		
14.	□				□		#__		□	□			#__		□
15.		□		□			#__		□	#__		□	#__		□
16.	#__		□	□			#__		□		□		#__		□
17.	□			#__	□						□				
18.	□			#__	□						□				
19.	□										□				
20.			□									□			
21.	#__		□							#__		□			
Coach's initials															

(continued)

From *Sport Education Seasons* by Sean M. Bulger et al., 2007, Champaign, IL: Human Kinetics.

PASE Basketball Individual Activity Task Card Recording Sheet *(continued)*

KEY: ♟ = Self-evaluation   ♟♟ = Peer evaluation   📋 = Coach evaluation

Task	Lesson 9 Shooting, layups, screening ♟	♟♟	📋	Lesson 11 Rebounding ♟	♟♟	📋	Lesson 12 Post play ♟	♟♟	📋	Lesson 13 Player-to-player defense ♟	♟♟	📋	Lesson 14 Team zone defense ♟	♟♟	📋
1.			☐			☐			☐			☐			☐
2.			☐			☐			☐			☐			☐
3.	☐				☐		☐					☐			☐
4.	☐				☐		☐				☐				☐
5.			☐		☐		☐				☐		☐		
6.		☐			☐		☐			#__	☐		☐		
7.		☐			☐		☐			#__	☐				☐
8.		☐			☐		☐						#__		☐
9.	#__		☐	#__		☐	#__		☐				#__		☐
10.	#__		☐	#__		☐	#__		☐				#__		☐
11.	#__		☐												☐
12.															
13.															
14.															
15.															
16.															
17.															
18.															
19.															
20.															
21.															
Coach's initials															

From *Sport Education Seasons* by Sean M. Bulger et al., 2007, Champaign, IL: Human Kinetics.

Team: _____

Instructions:

- Write each team member's name on the top of the following chart.
- At the end of team practice, record the last task completed.
- During the daily review portion of the lesson or on review days, resume incomplete task cards where you left off. For example, if during lesson 3 team practice you got to task 10, then during lesson 4 review time you can work to complete the lesson 3 task card by resuming practice with task 11.
- Once you have completed all tasks to criteria for a particular lesson, check "Yes."
- If you are unable to complete all tasks for a particular lesson by the end of the season, check "No."
- At the end of the season, certify your record by signing your initials at the bottom of your column.

Names														
Lesson (task card #)	Task number	Completed card by end of season?	Task number	Completed card by end of season?	Task number	Completed card by end of season?	Task number	Completed card by end of season?	Task number	Completed card by end of season?	Task number	Completed card by end of season?	Task number	Completed card by end of season?
Practice	—	☐ Yes ☐ No	—	☐ Yes ☐ No	—	☐ Yes ☐ No	—	☐ Yes ☐ No	—	☐ Yes ☐ No	—	☐ Yes ☐ No	—	☐ Yes ☐ No
3		☐ Yes ☐ No		☐ Yes ☐ No		☐ Yes ☐ No		☐ Yes ☐ No		☐ Yes ☐ No		☐ Yes ☐ No		☐ Yes ☐ No
4		☐ Yes ☐ No		☐ Yes ☐ No		☐ Yes ☐ No		☐ Yes ☐ No		☐ Yes ☐ No		☐ Yes ☐ No		☐ Yes ☐ No
5		☐ Yes ☐ No		☐ Yes ☐ No		☐ Yes ☐ No		☐ Yes ☐ No		☐ Yes ☐ No		☐ Yes ☐ No		☐ Yes ☐ No
7		☐ Yes ☐ No		☐ Yes ☐ No		☐ Yes ☐ No		☐ Yes ☐ No		☐ Yes ☐ No		☐ Yes ☐ No		☐ Yes ☐ No
8		☐ Yes ☐ No		☐ Yes ☐ No		☐ Yes ☐ No		☐ Yes ☐ No		☐ Yes ☐ No		☐ Yes ☐ No		☐ Yes ☐ No
9		☐ Yes ☐ No		☐ Yes ☐ No		☐ Yes ☐ No		☐ Yes ☐ No		☐ Yes ☐ No		☐ Yes ☐ No		☐ Yes ☐ No
11		☐ Yes ☐ No		☐ Yes ☐ No		☐ Yes ☐ No		☐ Yes ☐ No		☐ Yes ☐ No		☐ Yes ☐ No		☐ Yes ☐ No
12		☐ Yes ☐ No		☐ Yes ☐ No		☐ Yes ☐ No		☐ Yes ☐ No		☐ Yes ☐ No		☐ Yes ☐ No		☐ Yes ☐ No
13		☐ Yes ☐ No		☐ Yes ☐ No		☐ Yes ☐ No		☐ Yes ☐ No		☐ Yes ☐ No		☐ Yes ☐ No		☐ Yes ☐ No
14		☐ Yes ☐ No		☐ Yes ☐ No		☐ Yes ☐ No		☐ Yes ☐ No		☐ Yes ☐ No		☐ Yes ☐ No		☐ Yes ☐ No
Team's signatures														

From *Sport Education Seasons* by Sean M. Bulger et al., 2007, Champaign, IL: Human Kinetics.

Instructions: These cards are designed to be used as a quick reference to support officials as they learn to officiate soccer contests. Cut along the dotted lines and paste the Pocket Ref front to back on a 3- by 5-inch index card. Laminate the Pocket Ref to ensure extended use season after season.

✂ cut along dotted line

From *Sport Education Seasons* by Sean M. Bulger et al., 2007, Champaign, IL: Human Kinetics.

PASE Basketball Individual Responsibility Level (IRL) Rubric

Instructions: Use the following rubric to determine your individual level of responsibility for each lesson. Record your individual responsibility level on the Individual Responsibility Level Recording Sheet.

4		EXEMPLARY
	Preparedness	You were on time for class and prepared with appropriate clothes, shoes, and materials.
	Transition	You always stopped, cleaned up, and moved to the next lesson segment as efficiently as possible.
	On task	You were always engaged at a high level during practice and game times and you tried your best.
	Sportspersonship	You maintained a positive attitude throughout all daily activities and displayed good sportspersonship.
	Assessments	You completed all of the team and individual assessments during the lesson fully and honestly.
3		**ACCEPTABLE**
	Preparedness	You were late for class but came prepared with appropriate clothes, shoes, and materials.
	Transition	You stopped, cleaned up, and moved to the next lesson segment as efficiently as possible for most of the lesson.
	On task	You engaged at a high level during practice and game times for most of the lesson, but there were times when you did not try your best.
	Sportspersonship	You maintained a positive attitude throughout most daily activities and displayed good sportspersonship.
	Assessments	You completed most of the team and individual assessments during the lesson fully and honestly.
2		**NEEDS IMPROVEMENT**
	Preparedness	You were on time for class but did not come prepared with appropriate clothes, shoes, and materials.
	Transition	You rarely stopped, cleaned up, and moved to the next lesson segment as efficiently as possible.
	On task	You rarely engaged at a high level during practice and game times and there were times when you did not try your best.
	Sportspersonship	You maintained a negative attitude throughout most daily activities or displayed poor sportspersonship.
	Assessments	You completed most of the team and individual assessments during the lesson, but the information was not complete or honest.
1		**UNACCEPTABLE**
	Preparedness	You were late for class and did not come prepared with appropriate clothes, shoes, and materials.
	Transition	You never stopped, cleaned up, and moved to the next lesson segment as efficiently as possible.
	On task	You were never engaged at a high level during practice and game times and you did not try your best.
	Sportspersonship	You maintained a negative attitude throughout all daily activities and displayed poor sportspersonship.
	Assessments	You did not complete any of the team and individual assessments during the lesson.

From *Sport Education Seasons* by Sean M. Bulger et al., 2007, Champaign, IL: Human Kinetics.

Name: _____   Team: _____

Instructions: Determine your individual responsibility level (IRL) for each lesson using the individual responsibility rubric on page 307. Record your score in the "IRL" column and provide a rationale for why you were at that level. Set an IRL goal for the next lesson, and develop a strategy for meeting that goal.

Lesson	IRL	Reason?	IRL goal	Strategy for improvement
Example	1	I forgot my shoes. I got mad and yelled at Sue because she wouldn't pass me the ball.	2	I will leave a pair of shoes in my locker and I'll ask Sue to pass to me.
2				
3				
4				
5				
6				
10				
15				
20				

Team: _____

Instructions: During the individual and team progress report portion of the lesson, record information about your team's attendance behavior. You will record whether each of your teammates was present, late, dismissed early, or absent. "Present" indicates that a teammate was on time and in class for the entire period. "Late" indicates that a teammate was in class but arrived after the team warm-up had begun. "Early dismissal" indicates that a teammate was unable to complete the entire lesson because he or she left class before the period ended. "Absent" indicates that a teammate was not in class at all.

ATTENDANCE INFORMATION KEY

P = present　　　L = late　　　E = early dismissal　　　A = absent

Lessons	NAMES					
2.						
3.						
4.						
5.						
6.						
7.						
8.						
9.						
10.						
11.						
12.						
13.						
14.						
15.						
16.						
17.						
18.						
19.						
20.						
21.						
22.						
23.						
24.						
25.						

From *Sport Education Seasons* by Sean M. Bulger et al., 2007, Champaign, IL: Human Kinetics.

Name: _____   Team: _____

Instructions: Select at least four days this week on which you will participate in physical activity outside of class. Plan to do activities that will help increase your skill and fitness levels for the current sport season. Be realistic in setting your goals and planning these activities. Choose activities that you enjoy and can do with a friend or family member. Try to participate in a total of 30 to 60 minutes of physical activity on most, if not all, days of the week.

SCORING CRITERIA

☐ Planned for at least four days of activity by filling in the "Planned" columns for each day.

☐ Performed and completed required information in the "Actual" columns for each day planned.

☐ The activity engaged in aided in increasing levels of fitness or skill related to the season being taught.

☐ Signed by parent or guardian and student.

In order to improve my sport skills and health, this week I plan to do the following:

Day and date	Physical activity		How long?		With whom?		RPE	
	Planned	Actual	Planned	Actual	Planned	Actual	Planned	Actual
☐ Monday 05/05/06	In-line skating	In-line skating	1/2 hour	45 min	Alone	With brother	3	4
☐ ___/___/___								
☐ ___/___/___								
☐ ___/___/___								
☐ ___/___/___								
☐ ___/___/___								
☐ ___/___/___								
☐ ___/___/___								

RATING OF PERCEIVED ENJOYMENT SCALE

The activity I engage(d) in will be/was:

4—extremely enjoyable   2—somewhat enjoyable

3—mostly enjoyable   1—not enjoyable at all

Student signature _____

Parent/Guardian signature _____

Teacher signature _____

From *Sport Education Seasons* by Sean M. Bulger et al., 2007, Champaign, IL: Human Kinetics.

PASE Basketball Team Membership Inventory and Fair Play Agreement

Name: _____   Color: _____

Cheer: _____   Mascot: _____

Home court nickname: _____

PASE FAIR PLAY AGREEMENT

We, _____ agree to

- always follow the rules,
- work to achieve our personal and team goals,
- never argue with the officials,
- encourage all of our classmates,

- be gracious in victory and defeat,
- assist teammates at any time,
- show self-control at all times, and
- play hard and fair.

Pledge phrase: As part of this team, I promise to always follow the criteria outlined in the PASE Fair Play Agreement. Should I choose not to follow the agreement, I understand that there are consequences that my team and I must deal with in a responsible fashion.

Signature: _____   Date: _____

Signature: _____   Date: _____

Signature: _____   Date: _____

Signature: _____   Date: _____

Signature: _____   Date: _____

Signature: _____   Date: _____

Signature: _____   Date: _____

Signature: _____   Date: _____

From *Sport Education Seasons* by Sean M. Bulger et al., 2007, Champaign, IL: Human Kinetics.

Lessons 6 and 10 Instructional Materials

CONTENTS

PASE Basketball Team Goal-Setting Sheet

Team: _____

Instructions: To record team goals for each lesson, collaborate with your teammates to do the following:

1. Determine your team's overall performance for the day. Rate the level of performance on a scale from 1 to 4. 1 = unacceptable, 2 = needs improvement, 3 = acceptable, 4 = exemplary.

2. Identify one major strength and one major weakness for the day. Denote strengths with an "S" and weaknesses with a "W."

3. Develop goals (the *what*) to be accomplished in future lessons. Base goals on strengths and weaknesses.

4. Generate plans (the *how*) for goal attainment in future lessons.

5. Confirm goal attainment by checking the "Yes" box and indicating when the goal was met.

6. Revise goals and plans for improvement as assigned throughout the season.

Lesson	Team performance rating	Strengths and weaknesses	Goals	Plans for improvement	Goals met?
Example	3	S: Enthusiastic performance W: Team practice	Cooperate to complete all tasks during team practice	Listen to all teammates' suggestions and go through team practice as a team	☑ Yes Date 9/30/06
Practice					☐ Yes Date ___/___/___
6					☐ Yes Date ___/___/___
10					☐ Yes Date ___/___/___
15					☐ Yes Date ___/___/___

From *Sport Education Seasons* by Sean M. Bulger et al., 2007, Champaign, IL: Human Kinetics.

Instructions: Answer the following questions completely. Your responses should be related specifically to the lessons that have occurred since your last journal entry. To receive full credit for your journal entry, be sure to address each area of the scoring criteria. Journal writings will be due at the beginning of lessons 13 and 24. For lesson 13, answer questions 1 and 2; for lesson 24, answer questions 3, 4, and 5.

SCORING CRITERIA

☐ Answered assigned questions completely and honestly

☐ Provided specific, personal examples from physical education class to support answers

☐ Used proper grammar and punctuation

Questions

1. During the past lessons you have participated in a variety of different roles. You were required to plan for and organize certain aspects of the PASE basketball season.
   - Describe the parts of the season you planned for and organized. In what ways did your plans work or not work?
   - With what level of responsibility do you feel you completed your planning and organizational duties? Why?
   - How would you plan differently in the future?
   - What role did you enjoy most? Why?

2. In the various roles that you have engaged in as part of the PASE basketball season, you have provided leadership.
   - Describe one way in which you have displayed leadership to your team, to another team, or to the whole class.
   - How did this experience make you feel?
   - What can you do to become a better leader?

3. Throughout the PASE basketball season, your team has developed many goals.
   - List one goal that your team has set and achieved.
   - Provide an explanation as to how you and your teammates accomplished this goal.
   - Describe how meeting this goal made you feel.
   - List a goal that your team has set and has not yet achieved.
   - Provide an explanation of what is preventing your team from meeting that goal.
   - Describe how not yet meeting this goal has made you feel.

4. Your team has developed many rituals during this PASE basketball season.
   - Describe a unique ritual that you and your teammates have created during this PASE basketball season.
   - Why is this an appropriate ritual for this particular sport season?
   - Compare and contrast the ritual your team created with those of other teams.

5. Think back to a situation during the PASE basketball season when you feel you may have been treated unfairly.
   - List who was involved in the situation and describe why you believe the incident occurred.
   - How did you handle this incident?
   - How did this incident make you feel?
   - How could this issue have been handled to create a more positive outcome?

From *Sport Education Seasons* by Sean M. Bulger et al., 2007, Champaign, IL: Human Kinetics.

Instructions: Select one of the following roles that you would like to perform within the local community (e.g., the recreation center, the YMCA, for an afternoon). As you determine your choice, note that the criteria for each role are similar to responsibilities that you performed for these roles in physical education class. As you complete the optional role, check off each criterion. Once you have completed the optional role, summarize your experiences. This assignment is due at the beginning of lesson 25.

OPTIONAL ROLE CHOICES AND CRITERIA

Basketball Manager

- ☐ Inspected and cared for equipment
- ☐ Assumed administrative duties assigned
- ☐ Distributed and collected equipment
- ☐ Monitored time of activities
- ☐ Monitored participants' performance
- ☐ Organized practice/game space

Basketball Trainer

- ☐ Selected appropriate warm-up activities
- ☐ Reported injuries to appropriate personnel
- ☐ Led/monitored warm-up activities
- ☐ Aided in administering first aid if needed

Basketball Reporter

- ☐ Selected one player from each team to interview following the sporting event
- ☐ Selected one coach to interview following the sporting event
- ☐ Acquired statistics
- ☐ Wrote a 1/2-page sports column

SUMMARY OF EXPERIENCE

Instructions: Write a summary of your optional role experience. Use the following scoring rubric to help you write the summary. Provide an explanation of how you chose your role, how you prepared to complete your role to criteria, and how you met each criterion associated with your role.

SCORING RUBRIC

4 = exemplary
- Fully explained role choice and plan for completing role
- Completed all responsibilities associated with the selected role
- Explained each role responsibility, provided specific examples

3 = acceptable
- Mostly explained role choice and plan for completing role
- Completed most of the responsibilities associated with the selected role
- Explained most of the responsibilities, provided examples

2 = needs improvement
- Vaguely explained role choice and plan for completing role
- Completed few of the responsibilities associated with the selected role
- Explained a few of the responsibilities, used few examples

1 = unacceptable
- Did not explain role choice or plan for completing role
- Did not complete any of the responsibilities associated with the selected role
- Did not explain any of the responsibilities or provide any examples

Lessons 15-20 and 22-24 Instructional Materials

CONTENTS

Team: _____

Instructions: Determine individual roles for your team for each of the in-season round robin and championship tournament games. Every team member should perform each of the following roles at least once throughout lessons 16-24: scorekeeper, official, player. No team member is allowed to repeat the scorekeeper's or official's role until everyone else on the team has been either the scorekeeper or official. Once a team member has completed the role of scorekeeper or official, he or she must fulfill the role of player in the next game. If your team cannot decide on a role rotation, scratch out the role column and enter a teammate's name across a singe row, thus you will be using the predetermined rotation system denoted by the letters A through F.

TOURNAMENT GAMES

Role	Round robin game 1		Round robin game 2		Round robin game 3		Round robin game 4		Round robin game 5		Tourney game 1		Tourney game 2	
Official	A		B		C		D		E		F		A	
Player	B		C		D		E		F		A		B	
Player	C		D		E		F		A		B		C	
Player	D		E		F		A		B		C		D	
Scorekeeper	E		F		A		B		C		D		E	
Player	F		A		B		C		D		E		F	

ROLE RESPONSIBILITIES

Official (A)
- Manages the contests
- Interprets rules during contests
- Mediates conflicts
- Maintains contest pacing

Players (B, C, D, F)
- Participate in contests
- Maintain appropriate sportspersonship
- Utilize the skills learned
- Support teammates during contests

Scorekeeper (E)
- Records scores during contests
- Maintains ongoing team records
- Summarizes contest scores
- Provides final records to appropriate person

From *Sport Education Seasons* by Sean M. Bulger et al., 2007, Champaign, IL: Human Kinetics.

PASE Basketball Tournament Statistics Summary Sheet

Team: _____

Instructions: Transfer your teammates' data from the PASE Application Contest Scorecard individual scoring section.

Name: _____

Lessons		16	17	18	19	20	22	23	24	Total
2 FG	A									
	M									
	%									
3 FG	A									
	M									
	%									
Assists	#									
Steals	#									
Reb.	#									
Pts.	#									

Name: _____

Lessons		16	17	18	19	20	22	23	24	Total
2 FG	A									
	M									
	%									
3 FG	A									
	M									
	%									
Assists	#									
Steals	#									
Reb.	#									
Pts.	#									

From Sport Education Seasons by Sean M. Bulger et al., 2007, Champaign, IL: Human Kinetics.

Team: _____

Instructions: During the team review and practice, fill out the information on this sheet. This information will be used to introduce each individual from your team during the postseason championship tournament. These introductions will serve to heighten the festivity surrounding the event as well as provide the scorekeeper with a record of each team member. This sheet will be collected following your team warm-ups and game preparation. Prior to the consolation and championship games, players will be introduced one at a time.

Introduction example: Coming in at **[height]** with an impressive **[statistic category]** of **[statistic]**, hailing from **[hometown]**, the **[team name]**'s own **[player name]**.

Height	Statistics showcase: assists, rebounds, steals, points per game	Hometown or city, state	Player (first name, nickname, last name)
Example: 5 ft 3 in.	Assists per game: 2.3	Baltimore, Maryland	Sophia "Da Dish" Smith

TEAM SEASON DEMOGRAPHICS

Team round robin season record	Wins		Losses
Team final tournament seeding	Tournament seeding		
Record against today's opponent	Wins		Losses

From *Sport Education Seasons* by Sean M. Bulger et al., 2007, Champaign, IL: Human Kinetics.

- 3-on-3, half-court
- Four 3-minute quarters with a 3-minute half-time
- Subs at the beginning of each new quarter
- Each person can sub out only once per game
- All baskets made = 2 points
- All fouls = –1 point
- All plays restart at midcourt cone
- After each change of possession, ball must be cleared beyond 3-point arc
- Defense: person-to-person or zone
- Wins = 3 team points
- Fair play = 5 team points
  - Follows rules, never argues
  - Obeys official's calls, never influences officials
  - Cooperative, encouraging
  - Caring, under control
  - Gracious in victory or defeat

From *Sport Education Seasons* by Sean M. Bulger et al., 2007, Champaign, IL: Human Kinetics.

- 4-on-4, half-court
- Four 5-minute quarters with a 5-minute half-time
- Subs at the beginning of each new quarter
- Each person can sub out only once per game
- All baskets made = 2 points
- All fouls = –1 point
- All plays restart at midcourt cone
- After each change of possession, ball must be cleared beyond 3-point arc
- Defense: person-to-person or zone
- Wins = 2 team points
- Fair play = 10 team points
  - Follows rules, never argues
  - Obeys official's calls, never influences officials
  - Cooperative, encouraging
  - Caring, under control
  - Gracious in victory or defeat

From *Sport Education Seasons* by Sean M. Bulger et al., 2007, Champaign, IL: Human Kinetics.

Lessons 22-25 Instructional Materials

CONTENTS

PASE Basketball Voting Ballot

Instructions: For each award, vote for one person from your team. You cannot vote for a person more than once, and be sure to vote for yourself.

Award	Description	Name
MVP	Recognizes distinguished, consistent, and highly skilled performance across the season	
Hustle	Recognizes persistent energy and a vivacious spirit in the face of victory and defeat	
Most Improved	Recognizes an awareness of one's self and an enduring ability to monitor personal progress and obtain personal goals in any situation	
Fair Play	Recognizes an individual's sincere concern for others' rights during all facets of game play	
Best Official	Recognizes outstanding ability to interpret rules and regulate game play without bias	
Leadership	Recognizes unparalleled and potent aptitude to provide direction, overcome obstacles, and model appropriate behaviors in the face of adversity	

Instructions: Use the space below to create your own awards. For each award, vote for one person from your team. You cannot vote for a person more than once, and be sure to vote for yourself.

Award	Description	Name

Basketball Awards Day Itinerary

❖ ITINERARY ❖

Welcome & Announcements

❖

Healthy Refreshments

❖

Awards Descriptions

❖

Awards Presentation
and Acceptance Speeches

- Team 1
- Team 2
- Team 3
- Team 4
- Team 5
- Team 6

Season Championship Awards
Presentation

❖

Door Prize Drawing

❖

Closing Remarks

Basketball Awards Day Itinerary

❖ ITINERARY ❖

Welcome & Announcements

❖

Healthy Refreshments

❖

Awards Descriptions

❖

Awards Presentation
and Acceptance Speeches

- Team 1
- Team 2
- Team 3
- Team 4
- Team 5
- Team 6

Season Championship Awards
Presentation

❖

Door Prize Drawing

❖

Closing Remarks

Basketball Awards Day Itinerary

❖ ITINERARY ❖

Welcome & Announcements

❖

Healthy Refreshments

❖

Awards Descriptions

❖

Awards Presentation
and Acceptance Speeches

- Team 1
- Team 2
- Team 3
- Team 4
- Team 5
- Team 6

Season Championship Awards
Presentation

❖

Door Prize Drawing

❖

Closing Remarks

From *Sport Education Seasons* by Sean M. Bulger et al., 2007, Champaign, IL: Human Kinetics.

Instructions:

- Following the presentation of individual awards, your team will have the opportunity to deliver an acceptance speech.
- You may elect one or more spokespersons, or each individual can speak.
- Your team will have no longer than 3 minutes to deliver the acceptance speech, regardless of how many people choose to speak.
- Possible topics to discuss during acceptance speech:
  - Team cohesion or "gelling"
  - Spectacular efforts or contributions of individual team members
  - Team's development as it relates to the goals of the season
  - Obstacles that the team faced and overcame during the season
  - Any other important and relevant season highlights

OUR SPEECH OUTLINE

From *Sport Education Seasons* by Sean M. Bulger et al., 2007, Champaign, IL: Human Kinetics.

Physical Education

PASE BASKETBALL SEASON

Individual Awards

 Most Valuable Player

This award recognizes distinguished, consistent, and highly skilled performance across the basketball season.

_____
Name

_____
Teacher

_____
Date

Physical Education

PASE BASKETBALL SEASON

Individual Awards

Hustle

This award recognizes persistent energy and a vivacious spirit in the face of victory and defeat.

_____
Name

_____
Teacher

_____
Date

Physical Education

PASE BASKETBALL SEASON

Individual Awards

  *Most Improved*

This award recognizes an awareness of one's self and an enduring ability to monitor personal progress and obtain personal goals in any situation.

_____
Name

_____
Teacher

_____
Date

From *Sport Education Seasons* by Sean M. Bulger et al., 2007, Champaign, IL: Human Kinetics.

Physical Education

PASE BASKETBALL SEASON

Individual Awards

Fair Play

This award recognizes an individual's sincere concern for others' rights during all facets of game play.

Name _____

Date _____

Teacher _____

Physical Education

PASE BASKETBALL SEASON

Individual Awards

 Best Official

This award recognizes outstanding ability to interpret rules and regulate game play without bias.

_____
Name

_____
Teacher

_____
Date

Physical Education

PASE BASKETBALL SEASON

Individual Awards

Leadership

This award recognizes an unparalleled and potent aptitude to provide direction, overcome obstacles, and model appropriate behaviors.

Name _____

Date _____

Teacher _____

From *Sport Education Seasons* by Sean M. Bulger et al., 2007, Champaign, IL: Human Kinetics.

Physical Education

PASE BASKETBALL SEASON

Place Finish Awards

 Champions

This award documents the consistent development and execution of excellent performance across the basketball season.

Team

Teacher

Date

From *Sport Education Seasons* by Sean M. Bulger et al., 2007, Champaign, IL: Human Kinetics.

Physical Education
PASE BASKETBALL SEASON
Place Finish Awards

 First runner-up

This award documents the consistent development and execution of excellent performance across the basketball season.

Team _____

Teacher _____

Date _____

From *Sport Education Seasons* by Sean M. Bulger et al., 2007, Champaign, IL: Human Kinetics.

Physical Education
PASE BASKETBALL SEASON
Place Finish Awards

Second runner-up

This award documents the consistent development and execution of excellent performance across the basketball season.

_____
Team

_____
Date

_____
Teacher

Physical Education

PASE BASKETBALL SEASON

Place Finish Awards

Third runner-up

This award documents the consistent development and execution of excellent performance across the basketball season.

Team _____

Teacher _____

Date _____

PASE Basketball Healthy Refreshments Sign-Up Sheet

Instructions: Sign up once for an item you will bring in for the festival. Sign up by placing your name in the "Responsibility" column next to the item you will bring. Once finished, the team coach should pass this sheet to the next team until all have had an opportunity to sign up. Remember to bring enough of your item based on the number of students in the class.

FRUITS AND VEGETABLES

Quantity	Item/Description	Responsibility
	Apples (Granny Smith, Washington)	
	Oranges (navel)	
	Pears	
	Melons (watermelon, cantaloupe, honeydew)	
	Other:	

PAPER PRODUCTS

Quantity	Item/Description	Responsibility
	Plates	
	Napkins	
	Utensils (knives, forks, spoons)	
	Drinking cups	
	Other:	

BEVERAGES

Quantity	Item/Description	Responsibility
	Spring water	
	Sport drinks	
	Fruit juices (apple, orange, grape)	
	Milk (reduced fat)	
	Other:	

From *Sport Education Seasons* by Sean M. Bulger et al., 2007, Champaign, IL: Human Kinetics.

338

Soccer Season Overview

The sport of soccer maintains legions of players and fans across the globe. It remains an extremely popular choice for children's sport because it is demanding from a physiological perspective (e.g., aerobic fitness, speed, coordination, flexibility), yet highly enjoyable. Soccer can also be easily modified to accommodate a wide range of individual differences in the areas of facility and equipment access, skill level, participant interest, and physical fitness. For these primary reasons, this chapter includes an overview of a PASE Soccer Season. The chapter includes a soccer season syllabus, 25-lesson block plan, daily team points summary, and official's signals index.

SOCCER EDUCATION SEASON OVERVIEW CONTENTS

Instructor(s): _____

Class: _____

Time: _____

SOCCER SEASON DESCRIPTION

The soccer season consists of 25 lessons and is divided into three segments: preseason, an in-season round robin tournament, and a postseason championship tournament. Throughout the season, each student will be responsible for performing various tasks related to playing and managing a soccer season. Good luck!

SOCCER SEASON GOALS

To become . . .

- a **competent** soccer player: one who is a knowledgeable player and can successfully perform skills and strategies during a game of soccer.
- a **literate** soccer player: one who knows the rules and traditions of the sport and can identify appropriate and inappropriate soccer behaviors.
- an **enthusiastic** soccer player: one who is involved and behaves in ways that protect, preserve, and enhance the soccer culture.
- an **independent learner:** one who demonstrates responsibility for his or her own progress through appropriate goal-setting and goal-monitoring behaviors.

SEASON CONTENTS

Skills
- Dribbling
- Passing
- Trapping
- Shooting
- Goalkeeping
- Throw-ins
- Corner kicks
- Free kicks

Tactics
- Marking, covering, and balance
- Preventing the turn
- Delaying the attack
- Defending the goal
- Zone defense
- Distribution
- Timing runs
- Attacking the goal

From *Sport Education Seasons* by Sean M. Bulger et al., 2007, Champaign, IL: Human Kinetics.

SEASON REQUIREMENTS, POINTS, AND GRADING SCALE

Requirement		Point Value				
	Activity task cards	10	@	2	=	20
	Personal fitness assessments	20	@	1	=	20
	Pre- and post-fitness and skills combine	2	@	3	=	6
	Team goal setting	3	@	2	=	6
	Role performance	20	@	1	=	20
	Individual responsibility level (IRL)	8	@	1	=	8
	Written quizzes	2	@	2	=	4
	End-of-season awards voting	1	@	1	=	1
	Reflective journal	2	@	3	=	6
	Event task	1	@	4	=	4
	Outside-of-class participation log	5	@	1	=	5
				Total	=	100

Grading Scale		
A	95 – 100	Excellent
A-	93 – 94	
B+	91 – 92	Above average
B	87 – 90	
B-	85 – 86	
C+	83 – 84	Average
C	79 – 82	
C-	77 – 78	
D+	75 – 76	Below average
D	72 – 74	
D-	70 – 71	
F	Below 70	Failing

	Season bonus points	1st place	=	3.0 points	4th place	=	1.5 points

From *Sport Education Seasons* by Sean M. Bulger et al., 2007, Champaign, IL: Human Kinetics.

Instructions: Record your personal progress each day. As you complete a requirement, check it off like this "☑".

SEASON CALENDAR AND DAILY ASSESSMENTS

Lesson	1	2	3	4	5	6	7	8	9	10	11	12	13	14	15	16	17	18	19	20	21	22	23	24	25
Season	PRESEASON															IN-SEASON ROUND ROBIN						POSTSEASON			
Content	Pre-combine	Management	Dribble and marking	Preventing the turn	Passing and trapping	Review I	Covering and balance	Shooting	Timing runs	Review II	Goalkeeping	Distribution	Restarting play	Zones	Review III	RR tourney	RR tourney	RR tourney	RR tourney	RR tourney	Post-combine	Tourney	Tourney	Tourney	Festival
Date																									

Season Requirement Icons

Icon	1	2	3	4	5	6	7	8	9	10	11	12	13	14	15	16	17	18	19	20	21	22	23	24	25
(fire extinguisher)			☐	☐	☐		☐	☐	☐		☐	☐	☐	☐											
(wrench)			☐	☐	☐	☐	☐	☐	☐	☐	☐	☐	☐	☐	☐	☐	☐	☐	☐	☐		☐	☐		
(net/grid)	☐																				☐				
(people)						☐				☐					☐										
(cleat)		☐	☐	☐	☐	☐	☐	☐	☐	☐	☐	☐	☐	☐	☐	☐	☐	☐	☐	☐		☐	☐		
(glove)			☐	☐	☐	☐				☐					☐					☐					
(book)										☐					☐										
(whistle)													☐												
(smiley face)																								☐	☐
(frowning face)																								☐	☐
(bicycle)					☐					☐					☐					☐					
(plus)																									

From *Sport Education Seasons* by Sean M. Bulger et al., 2007, Champaign, IL: Human Kinetics.

	Activity task cards	A series of skill and strategy development activities that must be completed by individual team members during team practice in lessons 3-5, 7-9, and 11-14.
	Personal fitness assessment	A set of fitness development activities that are completed and whose results are recorded during the team warm-up portion of lessons 3-20, 22, and 23.
	Pre- and post-fitness and skills combine	A variety of stations designed to provide pre- and postseason information for goal setting and monitoring of personal progress between lessons 1 and 21.
	Team goal setting	A reflective activity used to identify team strengths and areas needing improvement. To be completed at the end of lessons 6, 10, and 15.
	Role performance	A performance of roles designed to help manage the soccer season. Daily roles and responsibilities are identified at the beginning of lessons 3-20, 22, and 23.
	Individual responsibility level (IRL)	A reflective activity used for identifying and monitoring one's personal behaviors throughout the soccer season. To be completed at the end of lessons 2-6, 10, 15, and 20.
	Written quizzes	A series of written activities used to determine one's knowledge of soccer. In-class or take-home quizzes will be given at lessons 10 and 15.
	End-of-season awards voting	A voting activity used to identify individuals for awards related to successful soccer performance during the season. Voting to be completed in lesson 24.
	Reflective journal	An activity used to promote critical thinking by exploring issues related to participation in the soccer season. Completed in lessons 13 and 24.
	Event task	A problem-solving scenario used to promote critical thinking, teamwork, and social responsibility. To be completed by lesson 25.
	Outside-of-class participation log	An activity designed to provide additional opportunities for students to engage in meaningful physical activity outside of the physical education class throughout the soccer season. To be completed and turned in at lessons 5, 10, 15, 20, and 25.
	Season bonus points	Throughout the season individuals will earn points for their team. Team points will be acquired from role performance, enthusiastic performance, and application contest scores.

Requirement Descriptions

From *Sport Education Seasons* by Sean M. Bulger et al., 2007, Champaign, IL: Human Kinetics.

| Day(s) | INSTRUCTIONAL FOCUS | | APPLICATION CONTEST | OFFICIAL'S SIGNALS | |
	Skills	Tactics		Signal	Index #
1	SKILLS AND FITNESS PRE-COMBINE				
2	Management day		Team cognitive challenge		
3	Dribble: control Offensive footwork	Dribble to reposition Marking	<u>1 vs. 1</u> Two 20 sec dribble challenges	Pushing	1
4	Dribble: speed	Preventing the turn Block and poke tackle	<u>1 vs. 1</u> Two 15 sec dribble challenges	Pushing Holding	1 2
5	Passing Trapping: foot/thigh/ chest	Distribution	<u>3 vs. 1</u> Two 40 sec pass/trap challenges	Handling the ball Misconduct	3 8
6	Review I: all skills	Review I: all tactics	<u>3 vs. 1</u> Two 60 sec pass/trap challenges	All previous	1-3, 8
7	Review: skills Team and self-assessment	Group defense: covering and balance	<u>3 vs. 3</u> Two 60 sec pass/trap challenges	Pushing Misconduct Charging	1 8 4
8	Shooting I	Position on goal	<u>3 vs. 2</u> Two 60 sec shooting challenges	Pushing Tripping Kicking	1 5 6
9	Shooting II	Timing runs: overlap and give and go	<u>3 vs. 2</u> Two 60 sec shooting/timing run challenges	Holding Misconduct Offside	2 8 7
10	Review II: all skills	Review II: all tactics	<u>3 vs. 2</u> Two 60 sec shooting/timing challenges	All previous	1-8
11	Goalkeeping I	Preventing scoring	<u>3 vs. 3</u> Two 60 sec goalkeeping run challenges	Handling the ball Misconduct	3 8
12	Goalkeeping II: rolling, sidearm throwing, and punting	Distribution	<u>3 vs. 4</u> Two 90 sec goalkeeping challenges	Handling the ball Misconduct	3 8
13	Restarting play: throw-in, corner kick, free kick	Attacking the goal	<u>3 vs. 4</u> Two 90 sec restarting play challenges	Corner kick Penalty kick Indirect goal kick	9 10 11
14	Review: skills team and self-assessment	Delaying the attack and zones	<u>3 vs. 5</u> Two 90 sec zone play challenges	Corner kick Penalty kick Indirect goal kick	9 10 11
15	Review III: all skills	Review III: all tactics	<u>5 vs. 5</u> Two 4 min halves: double-goal challenges	All	1-11

The left margin label reads "PRESEASON" spanning rows 8–14.

From *Sport Education Seasons* by Sean M. Bulger et al., 2007, Champaign, IL: Human Kinetics.

Day(s)		INSTRUCTIONAL FOCUS		APPLICATION CONTEST	OFFICIAL'S SIGNALS	
		Skills	Tactics		Signal	Index #
IN-SEASON ROUND ROBIN TOURNAMENT	16	Review: skills Team and self-assessment	Review: tactics Team and self-assessment	G1 = 1 vs. 6 G2 = 2 vs. 5 G3 = 3 vs. 4	All	1-11
	17	Review: skills Team and self-assessment	Review: tactics Team and self-assessment	G1 = 6 vs. 4 G2 = 5 vs. 1 G3 = 2 vs. 3	All	1-11
	18	Review: skills Team and self-assessment	Review: tactics Team and self-assessment	G1 = 6 vs. 2 G2 = 5 vs. 3 G3 = 1 vs. 4	All	1-11
	19	Review: skills Team and self-assessment	Review: tactics Team and self-assessment	G1 = 3 vs. 1 G2 = 4 vs. 2 G3 = 5 vs. 6	All	1-11
	20	Review: skills Team and self-assessment	Review: tactics Team and self-assessment	G1 = 3 vs. 6 G2 = 1 vs. 2 G3 = 4 vs. 5	All	1-11
	21	**SKILLS AND FITNESS POST-COMBINE**				
POSTSEASON TOURNAMENT	22	Review: skills Team and self-assessment	Review: tactics Team and self-assessment	G1 = 5th seed vs. 4th seed G2 = 3rd seed vs. 6th seed G3 = 1st seed vs. winner G1	All	1-11
	23	Review: skills Team and self-assessment	Review: tactics Team and self-assessment	G4 = loser G2 vs. loser G3 G5 = 2nd seed vs. winner G2 G6 = loser G1 vs. loser G5	All	1-11
FINALS	24	Review: skills Team and self-assessment	Review: tactics Team and self-assessment	Consolation G7 = winner G6 vs. winner G4 Championship G8 = winner G3 vs. winner G5	All	1-11
	25	Awards and festival day				

From *Sport Education Seasons* by Sean M. Bulger et al., 2007, Champaign, IL: Human Kinetics.

PASE Soccer Daily Team Points Summary

Teams / Lesson	Role performance	Fair play	Application contest	Team point deductions	Totals	Role performance	Fair play	Application contest	Team point deductions	Totals	Role performance	Fair play	Application contest	Team point deductions	Totals
2	n/a					n/a					n/a				
3															
4															
5															
6															
7															
8															
9															
10															
11															
12															
13															
14															
15															
16															
17															
18															
19															
20															
21	n/a	n/a				n/a	n/a				n/a	n/a			
22															
23															
24															

Role performance		Fair play		Application contest		Team point deductions	
Points	Description	Points	Description	Points	Place	Points	Infraction #
+7	All roles fulfilled	+7	All demonstrated fair play	+6	1st place	−1	1st offense
+6	6 roles fulfilled	+6	All but 1 demonstrated fair play	+5	2nd place	−3	2nd offense
+5	5 roles fulfilled	+5	All but 2 demonstrated fair play	+4	3rd place	−5	3rd offense
+4	4 roles fulfilled	+4	All but 3 demonstrated fair play	+3	4th place	−7	4th offense
+3	3 roles fulfilled	+3	All but 4 demonstrated fair play	+2	5th place	−10	5th offense
+2	2 roles fulfilled	+2	All but 5 demonstrated fair play	+1	6th place	−15	6th offense
+1	1 role fulfilled	+1	All but 6 demonstrated fair play			−25	7th offense
+0	No roles fulfilled	+0	No one demonstrated fair play				

From *Sport Education Seasons* by Sean M. Bulger et al., 2007, Champaign, IL: Human Kinetics.

DIRECT KICK FOULS

1 Pushing

2 Holding

3 Handling the ball

4 Charging

5 Tripping

6 Kicking

INDIRECT KICK FOULS

7 Offside (near, middle, and far)

UNSPORTING PLAY

8 Misconduct

TYPES OF KICKS

9 Point to corner area — Corner kick (direct)

10 Point to penalty area — Penalty kick (direct)

11 Indirect goal kick

From *Sport Education Seasons* by Sean M. Bulger et al., 2007, Champaign, IL: Human Kinetics.

References

Cooper Institute for Aerobics Research. 2004. *FITNESSGRAM/ACTIVITYGRAM test administration manual,* 3rd ed. Champaign, IL: Human Kinetics.

Griffin, L., Mitchell, S., and Oslin, J. 1997. *Teaching sport concepts and skills: A tactical games approach.* Champaign, IL: Human Kinetics.

Mohr, D.J., Townsend, J.S., and Bulger, S.M. 2001. A pedagogical approach to sport education season planning. *Journal of Physical Education, Recreation and Dance* 72(9):37-46.

Mohr, D.J., Townsend, J.S., and Bulger, S.M. 2002. Maintaining the PASE: A day in the life of sport education. *Journal of Physical Education, Recreation and Dance* 73(1):36-44.

Siedentop, D. 1994. *Quality PE through positive sport experiences: Sport education.* Champaign, IL: Human Kinetics.

Siedentop, D. 1998. What is sport education and how does it work? *Journal of Physical Education, Recreation and Dance* 69(4):18-20.

Siedentop, D. 2002. Sport education: A retrospective. *Journal of Teaching in Physical Education* 21:409-418.

Siedentop, D., and Tannehill, D. 2000. *Developing teaching skills in physical education,* 4th ed. Mountain View, CA: Mayfield.

Tannehill, D. 1998. Sport education introduction. *Journal of Physical Education, Recreation and Dance* 69(4):16-17.

Townsend, J.S., Mohr, D.J., Rairigh, R.M., and Bulger, S.M. 2003. *Assessing student outcomes in sport education: A pedagogical approach.* Reston, VA: NASPE.

About the Authors

Sean M. Bulger, EdD, is an assistant professor in the School of Physical Education at West Virginia University in Morgantown. Dr. Bulger earned his doctorate in physical education teacher education from West Virginia University in 2004. A member of American Alliance for Health, Physical Education, Recreation and Dance (AAHPERD), the National Association for Sport and Physical Education (NASPE), and the National Strength and Conditioning Association (NSCA), Dr. Bulger has been a health and physical education teacher and an exercise specialist in community and corporate health fitness facilities. He is a certified strength and conditioning specialist, having earned that certificate from the NSCA in 1992. He has authored many peer-reviewed papers and made numerous presentations in the areas of physical education teacher education and sport education. In his spare time, Dr. Bulger enjoys fitness activities, traveling, and reading.

Sean M. Bulger

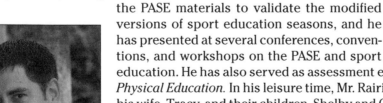

Derek J. Mohr, EdD, is an associate professor in the department of health, leisure, and exercise science at Appalachian State University in Boone, North Carolina. Dr. Mohr has more than a decade of experience in teaching and researching sport education and is a codeveloper of the Pedagogical Approach to Sport Education (PASE) curriculum and instructional model, which is foundational to this book and CD-ROM package. Dr. Mohr has conducted, presented, and published research on the PASE and has implemented the PASE in upper-elementary, middle and high school, and college levels. Dr. Mohr is an outdoor enthusiast whose leisure pursuits include farming Christmas trees, golfing, and camping. Dr. Mohr's greatest pleasure, however, is spending time with his daughter, Sophia, and wife, Maria.

Derek J. Mohr

Richard M. Rairigh, MS, is an instructor in the department of health, exercise, and sports science at Meredith College in Raleigh, North Carolina. He taught elementary physical education for four years, and has worked with the South Carolina Physical Education Assessment Programs at the elementary, middle, and high school levels. He has conducted research using the PASE materials to validate the modified versions of sport education seasons, and he has presented at several conferences, conventions, and workshops on the PASE and sport education. He has also served as assessment editor for *Teaching Elementary Physical Education*. In his leisure time, Mr. Rairigh enjoys spending time with his wife, Tracy, and their children, Shelby and Cole, playing golf, and working in his yard or on his house.

Richard M. Rairigh

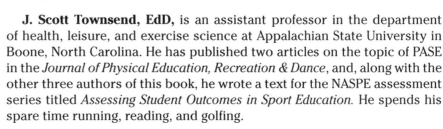

J. Scott Townsend, EdD, is an assistant professor in the department of health, leisure, and exercise science at Appalachian State University in Boone, North Carolina. He has published two articles on the topic of PASE in the *Journal of Physical Education, Recreation & Dance*, and, along with the other three authors of this book, he wrote a text for the NASPE assessment series titled *Assessing Student Outcomes in Sport Education*. He spends his spare time running, reading, and golfing.

J. Scott Townsend

*You'll find
other outstanding
sport education resources at*

www.HumanKinetics.com

In the U.S. call

1-800-747-4457

Australia	08 8372 0999
Canada	1-800-465-7301
Europe	+44 (0) 113 255 5665
New Zealand	0064 9 448 1207

HUMAN KINETICS
The Information Leader in Physical Activity
P.O. Box 5076 • Champaign, IL 61825-5076 USA

CD-ROM User Instructions

This CD-ROM expands the wealth of materials found in the book by providing PDF files of the complete soccer and fitness education seasons as well as a repeat of the basketball season from the book with more than 400 reproducibles.

If the CD-ROM does not start automatically when you place it in the CD-ROM drive, use the instructions listed under "User Instructions" to start up the CD-ROM. Once the CD-ROM is running, you will be greeted with a launch page that will include an introduction to the CD-ROM and a link to the CD-ROM Contents page. Click on the link to the CD-ROM Contents page, and you will see a list of the files found on the CD-ROM, including the complete fitness education, basketball, and soccer seasons and the appendixes for each season. Use these links to navigate to a detailed Contents page that appears at the beginning of each file in each season. This detailed Contents page will contain links to each separate document that appears in each season. Just print out the document you want, and it's ready to use.

MINIMUM SYSTEM REQUIREMENTS

The *Sport Education Seasons CD-ROM* can be used on either a Windows®-based PC or a Macintosh computer.

Windows

- IBM PC compatible with Pentium® processor
- Windows® 98/NT 4.0/2000/ME/XP
- Adobe Acrobat Reader®
- At least 16 MB RAM with 32 MB recommended
- 4x CD-ROM drive
- Inkjet or laser printer (optional)
- 256 colors
- Mouse

Macintosh

- Power Mac® recommended
- System 9.x or higher
- Adobe Acrobat Reader®
- At least 16 MB RAM with 32 MB recommended
- 4x CD-ROM drive
- Inkjet or laser printer (optional)
- 256 colors
- Mouse

USER INSTRUCTIONS

Windows

1. Insert the *Sport Education Seasons CD-ROM*. (*Note:* The CD-ROM must be present in the drive at all times.) The CD-ROM should launch automatically. If not, proceed to step 2.
2. Select the "My Computer" icon from the desktop.
3. Select the CD-ROM drive.
4. Open the "Launch.htm" file.
5. Follow the instructions on the screen.

Macintosh

1. Insert the *Sport Education Seasons CD-ROM*. (*Note:* The CD-ROM must be present in the drive at all times.)
2. Double-click the CD icon located on the desktop.
3. Open the "Start" file.
4. Follow the instructions on the screen.

Note: OSX users, you must first open Acrobat Reader®, then select the file you wish to view from your CD-ROM drive and open the file from within Acrobat Reader®. For MacOS 10.1 and 10.2, you may need to be in Classic mode for the links on the table of contents to work correctly.

For product information or customer support:

E-mail: support@hkusa.com
Phone: 217-351-5076 (ext. 2970)
Fax: 217-351-2674
Web site: **www.HumanKinetics.com**